Bucks County, Pennsylvania

Church Records of the 17th and 18th Centuries

Volume 3

Anna Miller Watring

Colonial Roots
Millsboro, DE
2016

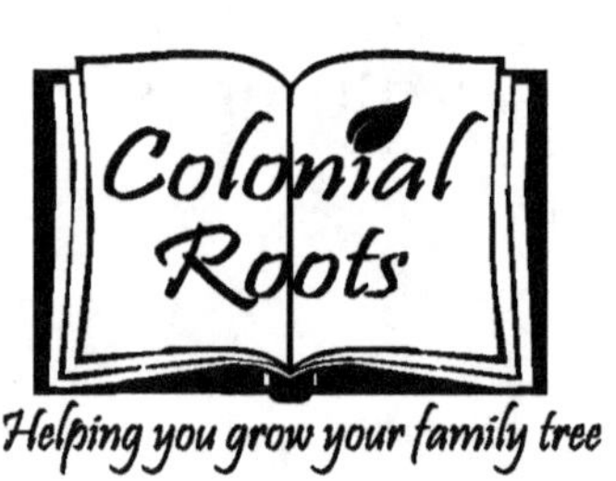

ISBN 978-1-68034-348-9

Printed in the United States of America

CONTENTS

Preface v

Introduction vii

Wrightstown Monthly Meeting
Births and Deaths 1
Monthly Meeting Certificates of Removal 23
Marriage Records 30
Men's Minutes 38

Richland Monthly Meeting
Births and Deaths 74
Men's Minutes 96

Buckingham Monthly Meeting
Births and Deaths 141

Makefield Monthly Meeting
Births and Deaths 192

Solebury Monthly Meeting
Births and Deaths 195

Index 197

PREFACE

It is our intent to complete these volumes as a collection of church registers and pastoral records of births, marriages and deaths in Bucks County of the 17th and 18th Century.

Our goal in gathering material for this project was to aid the genealogist by providing a single source of records. We find that many do not know the religious affiliation of their ancestors or the specific church; they do not know if records exist or where to find the records, if they do exist. Hopefully we have made the quest much easier. In looking for the records of a church one is burdened by the variations in church names and townships used by the various repositories. We hope that our approach eliminates all of these stumbling blocks.

Of enormous help in preparing the German church records has been the extensive research performed by Dr. Charles Glatfelter in his published work, *Pastors and People, Volume 1, Pastors and Congregations*. We have referred to it in locating and identifying the German congregations.

Other societies and repositories whose records we researched include the Evangelical and Reformed Historical Society; the Friends Historical Society, Swarthmore; the Historical Society of Pennsylvania, Philadelphia; and Bucks County Historical Society.

INTRODUCTION

The settlers who first came to Bucks County after the granting of Penn's charter were, with few exceptions, Quakers. Their settlements were concentrated in the southeastern part of the county. By May of 1682 William Penn had sold 565,000 acres to about 500 persons. Of these purchasers, about 50 acquired acreage in Bucks County.[1] These persons (one was a woman, Sarah Woolman) were mostly Quakers from Great Britain, especially England. The first settlers selected land along the Delaware as far up as the falls. By 1712 the general boundary of settlers had advanced to Plumstead. The Welsh Friends reached Richland in 1710. Welsh Baptists soon followed into Hilltown and New Britain. Early Dutch settlers, purchased land in Bensalem Township in 1689, namely, Nicholas, Leonard, Johannes and Frederick Vandygrift. Although less dominant in Bucks County than in other counties of Pennsylvania their immigration into Bucks County was becoming significant in the 1720s. By the time the Germans arrived most of the southern and central part of the county was already claimed by the Quakers and others. They settled in the northern part of the county and in those parts of Bucks County which became Northampton and Lehigh counties.

SOCIETY OF FRIENDS (QUAKERS)

FALLS

The first monthly meeting was held at the home of William Biles on May 13, 1683 in Falls Township. For a few years prior to this date they met at private homes and went to Burlington for business meetings. The minutes of the men's meeting state that there was a,

"Meeting held at William Biles house 2d day of the 3d month 1683. then held to wait upon the Lord for his wisdome to hear what should be offered in order to inspect into the affairs of the Church that all things might be kept therein sweet and Savory to the Lord and by our care over the Church helpfull in the Work of God and we whose names are as follow being then present thought it fit and necessary that a Monthly Meeting should be set up both of men and woemen for that purpose and that this meeting to be the first of the mens meetings after our arivall into these parts. The ffriends present William Yardley, James Harrison, Phineas Pemberton, William Biles, William Dark, Lyonell Brittanie, William Beaks."

MIDDLETOWN

In 1684 the monthly meeting was split into two monthly meetings, Falls and Neshaminy (later Middletown). Buckingham was set off as a monthly meeting in 1720. By 1800 a total of eight meetings had been established in Bucks County, Falls, Middletown, Wrightstown, Buckingham, Bristol, Plumstead, Richland and

Makefield.

BUCKINGHAM
Buckingham Meeting was established in 1701 for "the new settlers above Wrightstown to have a meeting for worship weekly among themselves and others that might think fit to visit them..." It became a monthly meeting in 1720.

WRIGHTSTOWN
A meeting was established there in 1686 to accommodate the families of James Radcliff and John Chapman. A meeting house was built in 1721. In 1724 Wrightstown Preparative meeting joined with Buckingham Monthly Meeting and the monthly meetings were then held alternately between the two locations until Wrightstown was set off as a monthly meeting in 1734. After that time the Buckingham Monthly Meeting was held alternately between Buckingham and Plumstead.

BRISTOL
Bristol Preparative Meeting was founded around 1704 and belonged to Falls Monthly Meeting until transferred to Middletown Monthly Meeting in 1788.

PLUMSTEAD
Friends first held meetings in Plumstead in 1727. It was a part of the Buckingham Monthly Meeting.

MAKEFIELD
This was a Preparative Meeting under Falls Monthly Meeting. The Friends of Makefield were allowed to hold a separate meeting during the winter months beginning in 1750. That year they were given permission to meet at Benjamin Taylor's and Benjamin Gilbert's. The Makefield Monthly Meeting was established in 1820, composed of Makefield and Newtown meetings and held alternately at the two locations.

RICHLAND
The first Quakers settled at Richland around 1710; it was known then as the Great Swamp. They established a preparative meeting as part of Gwynedd Monthly Meeting. It remained a part of the Gwynedd Monthly Meeting until 1742 when it was established as a monthly meeting under the Quarterly Meeting held at Philadelphia.

Quaker Records: Many of the Quaker records in this book were based on the copies made by William J. Buck. Mr. Buck was assigned to transcribe the Quaker records of Bucks County by the Library Committee of the Historical Society of Pennsylvania in 1870. This he completed by December 10, 1870; he also included in his copying, Quakertown, New Jersey and Gwynedd Monthly Meeting of Montgomery County, Pennsylvania. The Falls records prior to 1700 were previously thought to be lost but were supplied to him by a copy held in a Quarterly Meeting book of records, covering the period, 1683 through 1715 with births as early as 1662. He later commented that he found the records singularly perfect, so far as births, marriages and deaths were concerned, with but two exceptions, "that of Falls meeting which was so fortunately supplied, and the marriage book of Richland Monthly Meeting, from 1742 to 1804, the existence of which could not be discovered."

In our series of church records we have abstracted selected items from the minutes. Certain subjects (e.g., the selection of the burying ground, building the meeting house, etc.) were not included in this effort. The wording has been changed for brevity and clarity. For example, the phrase, "having this day declared their intentions of takeing each other in marriage," has been abbreviated to "intend to marry."

Quaker Marriages

In the case of marriages, the minutes sometimes contained no additional genealogical information. Other times the fact that the bride was a widow or the membership of the groom in another meeting was evident only in the minutes. And still other times information on the marriage was entirely missing from the register and from the record of the marriage certificates. That the clerk failed to record marriages was a concern to the monthly meeting and specific instructions were given to appointed members to oversee that "the marriage was orderly accomplished," AND that it was recorded in the records. The typical steps in marrying began at the monthly meeting when the couple announced their intentions. At a subsequent meeting, usually the next meeting, the couple announced their continued intention and at a subsequent meeting the committee appointed to oversee the marriage reported the marriage had been orderly accomplished. If the bride had children by a previous marriage a committee was assigned to ensure that the children's rights were protected. The marriage usually took place within the jurisdiction of the bride's monthly meeting. If the groom were a member of another monthly meeting he was required to produce a certificate recommending him as a worthy member and verifying that he was clear of any marriage engagements. After the marriage the bride might request a certificate (of removal) to be sent to the groom's monthly meeting indicating that the couple was planning to live "within the compass" of his monthly meeting.

Disorderly marriages

The Friends used several different phrases to indicate that a member had married contrary to their Rules of Discipline. The terms, "disorderly marriages," "out going in marriage," "married out of the unity of Friends," and "married by a hireling minister" - are virtually synonymous.[2]

Comparison to Hinshaw

William Wade Hinshaw is well-know for his monumental efforts in compiling many of the Quaker records. Volume 2 of his series,

Encyclopedia of American Quaker Genealogy included two Pennsylvania monthly meetings, Philadelphia and Falls.[3] In the preparation of this volume he was aided by Thomas W. Marshall and Walter C. Woodward. Marshall in his introduction, states that only those subjects having genealogical interest were incorporated. In comparing our compilations of the Falls Monthly Meeting contained in this book one will easily see that they omitted references to military service, fornication (usually alluding to pre-marital sex), marrying cousins, indebtedness, disagreements between two parties, and other situations. We have included the latter types of information.

WELSH BAPTISTS
Rev. Thomas Dungan led an small colony from Rhode Island to Bristol in Bucks County in 1682/84 and formed the Cold Spring Baptist Church. It disbanded in 1702. Prior to the disbandment of the Cold Spring group the Southampton Baptist Church was formed as a part of the Church at Pennepack. The Church at Pennepack agreed to the separation in 1746. Abstracts of baptisms and other data of genealogical interest are recorded in this series. Many of the Southampton group were other than Welsh; the Welsh were especially well established in New Britain and Hilltown. Records of the Hilltown Church from its beginning in 1782 have also survived and are included in this series.

GERMAN LUTHERAN AND REFORMED
A considerable number of Lutherans migrated from New York in 1723 into the Tulpehocken area. Shortly thereafter migrations began coming directly from Germany including many of the German Reformed. These German immigrants moved into the unsettled parts of the county to the north. Tohickon Church in Bedminster Township was probably the first.

LOWER MILFORD (Trumbauer's, Swamp Reformed)
The congregations begin in the 1760s. An acre of the land of Andrew Trumbauer was conveyed to the church in 1766.
Lutheran pastors: Philip Rapp, ca. 1766-1771; Peter Niemeyer, 1771-ca.1783; Christian Espich, 1792-1793; and Frederick Geissenhainer, 1793-1797.
Reformed pastors: John Christopher Gobrecht, 1769 - 1770; John Theobald Faber, Sr., 1772-1774; John William Pythan, 1774-1775; Casper Wack, 1776-1781; John Theobald Faber, Sr., 1782-1786; Frederick William Van der Sloot, 1786 (August - October); John Michael Kern, 1787-1788; John William Ingold, 1788-1790; and Nicholas Pomp, 1790-1797.
Present day address: Christ Church, 101 North Main St., Trumbauersville.
Records: The Reformed registers, found among the books of Rev. B. F. Luckenbill, begin in 1769. The first page has been lost while the second page shows that there were nine sets of sponsors, indicating that the records of at least nine baptisms

have been lost. The earliest births shown begin in 1772. These records were copied by Rev. A. S. Leiby and checked for accuracy by William J. Hinke. Leiby's original submission and Hinke's corrections are available at the Philip Schaff Library.

NESHAMINY
On June 18, three Dutch Lutherans, Abraham, Barnet and Christian Van Horn, purchased an acre of land, as a society of "People Distinguished by the name of Lutherans ..." In his will, dated November 12, 1750, Bernard van Dieren described himself as minister of the Lutheran congregations of Neshaminy. [Glatfelter] The relatively small group met in houses and barns, never building a church on the acre of ground which became the Feaster burying ground at Rockville, two miles south of Richboro.

NOCKAMIXON
The Lutheran congregation register was begun in 1766. The Reformed are mentioned in 1773 in the minutes of the coetus. By 1814 there was a union church here.
Lutheran pastors: Michael Enderlein, 1766-1770; possibly Philip Rapp, Frederick Miller, 1773-1774; Peter Ahl, 1789-1791; and Anthony Hecht, 1792-1794. Glatfelter states that Peter Niemeyer might have served the Lutheran congregation between 1774-1783.
Reformed pastors: Casper Wack, 1773-1786, possibly followed by Frederick Von der Sloot and John Mann.
Present day address: St. Luke's Lutheran Church, 1/2 mile west of Ferndale and St. Luke's United Church of Christ, Ferndale. [The union was dissolved in 1976/1977.]
Records: The Reformed records begin in 1773 and have been translated by C. W. Unger in June 1940. These are available at Philip Schaff Library. Charles R. Roberts performed an earlier translation in 1923. Some of his variations are shown in brackets in this book.
Lutheran Records: These records begin in 1766 and have been translated by William J. Hinke.

RIDGE VALLEY
Land was sold for the location of a Union church in 1792.
Location: St. John's Lutheran Church, 1207 Allentown Road, Sellersville; Ridge Valley United Church of Christ, Sellersville.

SCHEUTZ'S (Great Swamp)
Milford Township
It was begun in the 1730s. It continued as the Great Swamp Union church in Lower Milford Township, Lehigh County for about its first 30 years. In 1762 or 1763 the Lutherans left and built a church 1 to 2 miles across the county line on land owned by Elder Lewis Schuetz.
Pastors: Frederick Reiss, 1756-1764; Peter Niemeyer, 1764-1771; Conrad Roeller, 1772-1775; John Schwarbach, 1776-1786; Carl Danapfel, 1789-1790; Christian Espich, 1790-1793; and Frederick Geissenhainer, 1793-1808.

Location: St. John's Lutheran, Route 663, 1/2 mile west of Spinnerstown.
Records: The earliest existing register begins in the 1800s.

SPRINGFIELD (Trinity Union)
Springfield Township
The Reformed congregation was established in the 1740s and the Lutherans ca. 1751.
Lutheran pastors: Ludolph Schrenck, 1751-1754; Andrew Friderichs, 1754-1762; Otto Haase, 1763-1771; Christian Streit, 1772-1774; Peter Niemeyer, 1774-1783; Carl Friderick, 1784-1787; Peter Ahl, 1788-1790; and Anthony Hecht, 1791-1794.
Reformed pastors: John Conrad Wirtz, 1745-1749; Jacob Riess, 1760-1766; Egidius Hecker, 1766-1767; John Daniel Gros, 1770-1773; William Ingold, 1780-1781; Casper Wack, 1781-1786; Herman Wynckhaus, 1786-1790; John Mann, ca. 1792?; and Henry Hoffmeier, 1793.
Locations: Trinity Lutheran, 1/2 mile north of Pleasant Valley, on Route 212 and Trinity United Church of Christ, near Pleasant Valley.
Records: Lutheran records begin in 1751 (translated by William J. Hinke in 1927). The Reformed register begins in 1760 (translated by Hinke in 1921).

TINICUM
Bedminster Township
The Lutheran register begins ca. 1760. The Reformed congregation may have been established as early as 1789. The union began as early as 1808.
Glatfelter gives a tentative list of pastors: Lutheran - Wolfgang Leitzel, Frederick Miller, Peter Niemeyer, Peter Ahl and Anthony Hecht; and Reformed - Frederick Von der Sloot and John Mann.
Locations: Christ Lutheran Church, 2 miles east of Pipersville and United Church of Christ, Tinicum, Pipersville.

TOHICKON UNION
The congregations began in the late 1740s. The first church was built in Rockhill Township; a later church was built across the road in Bedminster Township.
Lutheran pastors: Martin Schaeffer, 1750-1753; Jacob Schertlin, 1754-1755; Joseph Roth, 1755-1758; Wolfgang Leitzel, 1760-1765; Philip Rapp, 1765-1773; and Conrad Roeller, 1774-1795.
Reformed pastors: Conrad Wirtz Gobrecht, 1766-1770; Casper Wack, 1771-1781; Theobald Faber, 1782-1786; Michael Kern, 1787-1788; William Ingold, 1788-1790; and Nicholas Pomp, 1790-1797.
Locations: Peace Lutheran Church, Hagersville, 3 miles north of Perkasie and St, Peter's United Church of Christ, Bethlehem Road, Perkasie.
Records: The Reformed register was begun in 1749 and the Lutheran register was begun in 1750.

TOHICKON LUTHERAN (Tohecka, Birkensee, Keller's)
Bedminster Township
This Lutheran congregation in Bedminster Township began in the 1740s. It is easily confused with the above union church located three and one-half miles to the southwest in the same township.
Pastors: Ludolph Schrenck, 1749-1751; Lucas Raus, 1751-1753; Frederick Schultz; Helfrich Schaum, 1754-1758; William Kurtz, 1758-1759; Conrad Walther, 1761; and Otto Haase, 1762-1764; Michael Enderlein, 1766-1770; Peter Niemeyer, 1774-1783; Anthony Hecht, 1784-1788, 1792-1794; and George Wichterman, 1791.
Location: St. Matthew's, Route 563, 8 miles northeast of Perkasie.
Records: Lucas Raus began a register in 1751. The earliest birth recorded is dated 1754.

DUTCH REFORMED
The Dutch Reformed preceded the German Reformed into Bucks County and settled along the Neshaminy Creek near what is now Churchville. In 1710 Paulus Van Vlecq, a Dutch Reformed pastor, organized a congregation in Neshaminy and Bensalem. He served for three years followed by a long period without a pastor.
Pastors: Paulus Van Vlecq, 1710-1713; Peter Dorsius, 1737-1748; Jonathan Du Bois, 1752-1772; William Schenck, 1777-1780; Matthew Leydt, 1780-1783; Peter Stryker, 1788-1790; John C. Brush, 1795-1796; Jacob Larzelere, 1797-1820.
Location: Churchville.
Records: The register begins in 1710.

NORTHAMPTON
A second congregation of Dutch Reformed was organized in the Neshaminy area and a church built in 1753.
Pastor: Jonathan Du Bois until his death in 1772 when the congregation joined the Dutch Reformed Church.
Location: Richboro, Northampton Township.

MENNONITES
The Mennonites established their first congregation in Bucks County in 1735 in the northwestern part of the county, known at the Swamp Church of Milford. Later a meeting house was built in Bedminster. In 1746 a church was given to the followers at the Deep Run settlement. In 1752 a log building was erected for worship in the northwestern part of New Britain. The Perkasie or Hilltown meeting house was built in 1753, Gehman's in Rockhill in 1773 and in Springfield ca. 1753/1765.
Records: There are no known records of birth, marriage or death.

ANGLICAN (Protestant Episcopal)
The Anglican Church came into existence at Burlington with Bristol included. St. James was established at Bristol in 1717. There are no known records prior to 1800.

METHODISTS

Captain Webb, of the British army, introduced Methodism into Bucks County when he preached at Bristol in 1771, enroute from New York to Philadelphia. Classes were formed after the Revolutionary War.

ROMAN CATHOLIC

There were German Catholics in Haycock and Nockamixon by the close of the Revolutionary War. Haycock (St. John the Baptist) is mentioned in St. Joseph's records as early as 1764 and in Goshenhoppen records at about the same time. The church was not fully organized until 1798. The parish included Bucks and Northampton Counties until 1833. For early references to Catholics in Bucks County, see records of St. Joseph's (Philadelphia) and Goshenhoppen (Berks).

PRESBYTERIANS

Records for the Presbyterian churches of Tinicum (Red Hill) and Neshaminy (Hartsville) in Warwick Township have survived and are included in this series. These records have been published in *Pennsylvania Archives*, Vol. IX, Second Series. In the Tinicum records baptisms begin in 1760. In the Neshaminy records marriages begin in 1788 and baptisms in 1788.
Ministers at Tinicum include Johann Wolff Lezel and Frederick Miller.
Ministers at Neshaminy Presbyterian Church include William Tennent, Charles Beatty, Samuel Blair and others.

Notes

1. J. H. Battle, Ed. *History of Bucks County*. The Reprint Company, 1985. Originally published: 1887, Philadelphia, PA. Names and acreages are given of those person who locate the whole or a part of their lands in Bucks County.

2. The term priest was also used to indicate a minister of another denomination, not necessarily Roman Catholic.

3. William Wade Hinshaw, Thomas Worth Marshall, compiler. *Encyclopedia Of American Quaker Genealogy*. Genealogical Publishing Company, 1969. Originally published: 1938, Ann Arbor.

BIBLIOGRAPHY

Battle, J. H. Ed. *History of Bucks County*. The Reprint Company, 1985. Originally published: 1887, Philadelphia, PA.

Bieber, Edmund Ellis. *History of Trinity Evangelical Lutheran Church of Springfield Twp. Bucks County, 1751-1953*. 1953.

Davis, William W. H. Edited by Warren S. Ely and John W. Jordan. *A Genealogical and Personal History of Bucks County, Pennsylvania*. Originally pub. as Vol. III of *History of Bucks County Pennsylvania*. 1905. Repr. by Genealogical Publishing Co., 1975.

Fisher, Allen S. *Lutheranism in Bucks County, 1734-1934*. Tinicum, PA, 1935.

Furey, Francis T. *The Goshenhoppen Registers, 1741-1819*. Originally pub. in Records of the American Catholic Historical Society of Philadelphia, in a series, beginning in 1886. Repr. Baltimore: Genealogical Publishing Co. (1984).

Glatfelter, Charles H. *Pastors and People*, Volume 1, Pastors and Congregations. Breinigsville, PA: The Pennsylvania German Society, 1980.

Green, Doron. *History of Bristol Borough*. 1911.

Hinke, William John, Ph.d., D.D. *A History Of The Tohickon Union Church, Bedminster Township, Bucks County Pennsylvania. With Copy of Church Records Reformed Congregation 1745-1869. Lutheran Congregation 1749-1840*. Meadville, PA: The Pennsylvania German Society.

Hinke, William J., Ph,. D., D.D. "Early History of Keller's Lutheran Church, Bedminster Township, Bucks County," *Collection of Papers read before Bucks County Historical Society*, Vol., pp. 363-378.

Hinshaw, William Wade and Thomas Worth Marshall, compiler. *Encyclopedia Of American Quaker Genealogy*. Genealogical Publishing Company, 1969. Originally published: 1938, Ann Arbor.

Humphry, John T. *Pennsylvania Births, Bucks County, 1682-1800*. Washington, D.C. Humphry Publications, 1993.

Myers, Albert Cook. *Irish Quakers into Pennsylvania*. 1902.

Pennsylvania Archives, Vol. IX, Second Series. 1895.

Reed, Dr. W. H. *Great Swamp Reformed Church Records, 1736-1822.* Translated from the original transcript by Dr. W. H. Reed, Norristown, Pa. 1906. Copied by J. Christie from a copy typewritten by William Summers. Conshohocken, Pa. 1907.

Roberts, Charles R. *St. Luke's Zion Church, Ferndale, Nockamixon Township, 1773-1897.* Allentown, PA. 1923

Roberts, Clarence V. Assisted by Warren S. Ely. *Early Friends Families of Upper Bucks. With Some Account of Their Descendants.* Originally published 1925. Repr. by Genealogical Publishing Co., 1975.

Roberts, Ellwood. *Old Richland Families.* 1898.

Streng, Samuel. *The History of North and Southampton Reformed Church, Churchville, Pa.* 1885.

Turner, D. K. *Neshaminy Presbyterian Church.* 1876.

CHURCHES FOR WHICH 17TH AND 18TH CENTURY REGISTERS EXIST

Map
Number

1. Falls Monthly Meeting (Falls Twp.)
2. Middletown Monthly Meeting (Middletown Twp.)
3. Buckingham Monthly Meeting (Buckingham Twp.)
4. Wrightstown Monthly Meeting (Wrightstown Twp.)
5. Bristol Meeting (Bristol Twp.)
6. Richland Meeting (Richland Twp.)
7. Southampton Baptist
8. Hilltown Baptist (Hilltown Twp.)
9. Lower Milford (Trumbauersville)
10. Neshaminy (Rockville)
11. Nockamixon (Ferndale)
12. Scheutz's (Milford Twp.)
13. Springfield (Springfield Twp.)
14. Tinicum (Bedminster Twp.)
15. Tohickon Union (First built in Rockhill Twp., later across the road in Bedminster Twp.)
16. Tohickon Lutheran (Bedminster Twp., 3 1/2 miles to the northeast of above Tohickon Union).
17. Northampton and Southampton Dutch Reformed (Churchville)
18. Bensalem Dutch Reformed (Bensalem)
19. Tinicum Presbyterian Church (Red Hill)
20. Neshaminy Presbyterian Church (Hartsville)

WRIGHTSTOWN MONTHLY MEETING

BIRTHS AND DEATHS
1716-1800

Stephen Twining d. 28th day of 6th month, 1772, in his 88th year. Margaret Twining, wife of Stephen, d. 9th day of 7th month, 1784, in her 99th year.

Children of Abraham and Susannah Chapman: John Chapman b. 23rd day of 6th month, 1716; Abraham Chapman b. 4th day of 4th month, 1718; William Chapman b. 24th day of 12th month, 1719/20 and d. 3rd day of 8th month, 1810; A daughter, b. & d. 26th day of 2nd month, 1722; Jane Chapman, who m. John Lacey, b. 2nd day of 3rd month, 1723; Thomas Chapman b. 8th day of 4th month, 1725; Benjamin Chapman b. 10th day of 9th month, 1727; Elizabeth Chapman b. 20th day of 3rd month, 1730; Joseph Chapman b. 28th day of 8th month, 1732 and d. 8th month, 1790.

Children of John and Rachell Lacey: Rachell Lacey b. 2nd day of 3rd month, 1718; Mary Lacey b. 5th day of 8th month, 1720; John Lacey b. 23rd day of 7th month, 1723; Joseph Lacey b. 9th day of 8th month, 1725; Jemima Lacey b. 23rd day of 6th month, 1727 and d. 20th day of 7th month, 1764; Isaac Lacey b. 5th day of 4th month, 1731 and was bur. the 28th day of 5th month, 1740; Martha Lacey was b. 13th day of 3rd month, 1733 and was bur. the 19th day of 5th month, 1740; Dorithy and Hannah Lacey (twins) were born 11th day of 4th month, 1735; Dorithy Lacey d. the 18th day of 1st month, 1738 and Hannah Lacey was bur. the 31st day of 5th month, 1740; William Lacey b. 25th day of 8th month, 1737; Sarah Lacey b. 20th day 5th month, 1743.

Rachel Lacey, wife of John Lacey, d. 13th day of 3rd month, 1761.

Children of Elijah and Katherine Doan: Ann Doan b. 24th day of 9th month, 1718; Mary Doan b. 24th day of 2nd month, 1721; Rebekah Doan b. 12th day of 6th month, 1723; Joannah Doan b. 8th day of 3rd month, 1725; Titus Doan b. 29th day of 3rd month, 1727; Katherine Doan b. 3rd day of 11th month, 1729.

Children of John and Mary Chapman: Mary Chapman b. 25th day of 5th month, o.s., 1740; Jos. Chapman b. 19th day of 11th month, o.s., 1742; James Chapman b. 13th day of 8th month, o.s., 1743 and d. 2nd day of 8th month, 1821; Elisa Chapman b. 23rd day of 2nd month, o.s., 1746; Robert Chapman b. 14th day of 4th month, o.s., 1748; Sarah Chapman b. 8th day of 1st month, o.s., 1750; Mira Chapman b. 24th day of 12th month, o.s., 1752; Charles Chapman b. 1st day of 1st month, n.s., 1754; Susanah Chapman b. 25th day of 12th month, n.s., 1755; Abraham Chapman b. 21st day of 11th month, n.s., 1757; Margaret Chapman b. 26th day of 1st month, n.s., 1760 and d. 19th day of 8th month, n.s., 1760.

Stephen Twining, son of Stephen Twining, b. 30th. Dec. 1684 and d. 28th. day of 6th. month, 1772. Eleazer Twining, son of Stephen

Twining, b. 26th Nov. 1686.
Nathaniel Twining, son of Stephen, b. 27th Mar. 1689.
Mercy Twining, dau. of Stephen Twining, b. 8th Sept. 1690.
John Twining, son of Stephen Twining, b. 5th Mar. 1693 and d. 21st day of 8th month, 1775.
Elizabeth Twining, wife of John Twining, b. 9th day of 3rd month, 1696 and d. 8th day of 11th month, 1774.

The above is a true copy taken out of the Book of Records in Eastham, in the county of Barnstable, in the Provence of the Massachusetts Bay, New England, May 31st, 1715 by John Paine, Town Clerk.

Entered here from the above mentioned copy by Joseph Chapman, Clerk to the Monthly Meeting of Friends at Wrightstown, 11th day of 1st month, 1776.

Children of Joseph and Agness (Croasdale), Warner: John Warner b. 16th day of 12th month, 1723/4; Mary Warner b. 28th day of 11th month, 1725/6; Joseph Warner b. 10th day of 11th month, 1727/8; Croasdale Warner b. 5th day of 12th month, 1729/30; Ruth Warner b. 8th day of 8th month, 1732; Abraham Warner b. 14th day of 7th month, 1735; Sarah Warner b. 7th day of 11th month, 1737/8; Isaac Warner b. 28th day of 9th month, 1741 and d. 28th day of 11th month, 1829; Thomas Warner b. 6th day of 10th month, 1746, and d. 19th day of 2nd month, 1821.

Children of Tho. and Phebe Lancaster: Phebe Lancaster b. 6th day of 6th month, 1726 and d. 24th day of 8th month, 1728; Tho. Lancaster b. 16th day of 12th month, 1727; John Lancaster b. 18th day of 11th month, 1730 and d. 28 day of 11th month, 1730; Benj. Lancaster b. last day of 12th month, 1731; John Lancaster b. 10th day of 12th month, 1733; Phebe Lancaster b. 4th day of 10th month, 1734; Job Lancaster b. 13th day of 8th month, 1736; Jos. Lancaster b. 21st day of 8th month, 1738; Jacob Lancaster b. 27th day of 3rd month, 1740; Isaac Lancaster b. 4th day of 12th month, 1742; Aaron Lancaster b. 24th day of 2nd month, 1744; Moses Lancaster b. 3rd day of 10th month, 1746; Elizabeth Lancaster b. 26th day of 6th month, 1748.

Children of William and Ann Reader: Margaret Reader b. 29th day of 4th month, 1747; Mary Reader b. 18th day of 12th month, 1749; William Reader b. 1st day of 4th month, 1751; Thomas Reader b. 31st day of 3rd month, 1754.

Children of William Smith and his (second) wife, Mercy: Jos. Smith b. 1st day of 11th month, 1721/2; John Smith b. 15th day of 11th month, 1723/4; Ralph Smith b. 28th day of 8th month, 1725; Esther Smith b. 11th day of 9th month, 1727; Elizabeth Smith b. 10th day of 7th month, 1730; Samuel Smith b. 23rd of 8th month, 1733; David Smith b. 25th day of 2nd month, 1736.

Children of John and Mary Butler: Thomas Butler b. 8th day of 12th month, 1740/1; Grace Butler b. 22nd day of 8th month, 1742 and d. the 9th day of 10th month, 1742. Mary Butler b. 19th day of 12th month, 1743/4; John Butler b. 3rd day of 6th month, 1747; Isaac Butler b. 8th day of 7th month, 1749.

Children of John and Sarah Twining: Joseph Twining b. 14th day of 8th month, 1748; Rachael Twining b. 15th day of 8th month, 1751.

Children of John and Elizabeth Warner: John Warner b. 3rd day of 12th month, 1750/1; Mary Warner b. 24th day of 8th month, 1752; Rachael Warner b. 27th day of 12th month, 1753; David Warner b. 29th day of 1st month, 1757 and d. 28th day of 1st month, 1849, age 93, wanting one day. Isaiah Warner b. 21st day of 8th month, 1760 and d. 16th day of 5th month, 1839, age 78-8-25; Jonathan Warner b. 29th day of 8th month, 1762 and d. 26th day of 12th month, 1826, aged 64-3-27; Simion Warner b. 3rd day of 7th month, 1765; Elizabeth Warner b. 27th day of 3rd month, 1768; Amos Warner b. 18th day of 3rd month, 1770 and d. 24th day of 4th month, 1869, aged 79-1-6.

Children of Robert Smith and Rachael, his wife, late Hibbs: Phebe Smith b. 16th day of 3rd month, 1754; John Smith b. 27th day of 7th month, 1756; Ann Smith b. 25th day of 12th month, 1758; Abra. Smith b. 13th day of 9th month, 1760; Hannah Smith b. 26th day of 11th month, 1762, married James Heston and d. the 11th day of 9th month, 1784, leaving one son, Jonathan, b. 2nd day of 9th month, 1784; Rachael Smith b. 3rd day of 6th month, 1765.

Robert Smith d. 8th day of 7th month, 1798.
Rachel Smith, wife of Robert Smith, d. 18th day of 9th month, 1767.

Children of Samuel and Jane Smith: William Smith b. 2nd day of 9th month, 1751; Tho. Smith b. 9th day of 4th month, 1753; Ann Smith b. 15th day of 11th month, 1754; Mahlon Smith b. 13th day of 8th month, 1756 and d. 30th day of same month; Eliz. Smith b. 1st day of 4th month, 1758; Phebe Smith b. 25th day of 2nd month, 1760; Hannah Smith b. 10th day of 4th month, 1761 and d. 14th day of 11th month, 1762; Jane Smith b. 14th day of 9th month, 1763; Samuel Smith b. 4th day of 10th month, 1765; Edith Smith b. 23rd day of 9th month, 1767.

Children of James and Rachael Spicer: Abra. Spicer b. 6th day of 8th month, o.s., 1751 and d. 31st day of 3rd month, 1754; Sarah Spicer b. 14th day of 2nd month, n.s., 1753; Amos Spicer b. 24th day of 11th month, 1754, n.s., and d. 2nd day of 12th month, 1756; James Spicer b. 2nd day of 11th month, n.s., 1756 and d. 30th day of 1st month, 1757; Eliz. Spicer b. 11th day of 8th month, n.s., 1758; James Spicer b. 30th day of 9th month, n.s., 1760; Ann Spicer b. 25th day of 5th month, n.s., 1762; Mary Spicer b. 1st day of 3rd month, n.s., 1764; Yeaman Spicer b. 16th day of 3rd month, n.s., 1766; Guly Elma Maria Spicer b. 22nd day of 11th month, n.s., 1767.

Mary Hamton, wife of Joseph Hamton and daughter of Thomas Canby,

b. 1697.

Children of Joseph and Mary Hamton: Sarah Hamton b. 30th day of 9th month, 1723 and m. Isaac Wilson; John Hamton b. 12th day of 1st month, 1725, and d. 10th day of 9th. month, 1775; Benja. Hamton b. 15th day of 7th month, 1728; Jane Hamton b. 26th. day of 1st month, 1731 and d. 31st day of 7th month, 1809, "an old maiden"; Joseph Hamton b. 29th day of 1st month, 1736 and d. 1740; David Hamton b. 22nd day of 8th month, 1737 and d. 3rd day of 1st month, n.s., 1751; Mary Hamton b. 12th day of 2nd month, 1739, m. James Stokes, and d. 15th day of 11th month, 1804.

Children of Joseph and Rachael Johnson: David Johnson b. 19th day of 2nd month, 1747; Mary Johnson b. 27th day of _ month, 1749; John Johnson b. 23rd day of 5th month, 1752; Sam. Johnson b. 22nd day of 1st month, 1755; Joseph Johnson b. 1st day of 5th month, 1759.

Rachel Johnson, wife of Joseph Johnson and daughter of Jacob Trego, b. 27th day of 7th month, 1719 in Chester, now Del. Co.

Children of John and Elizabeth Linton: Jacob Linton b. 29th day of 8th month, 1732 and d. 13th day of 12th month, 1774; Rebekah Linton b. 29th day of 7th month, 1734; David Linton b. 3rd day of 10th month, 1736 and d. 16th day of 4th month, 1739; Isaiah Linton b. 15th day of 11th month, 1739/40 and d. 26th day of 11th month, 1775; Wm. Linton b. 29th day of 1st month, 1742; Martha Linton b. 13th day of 5th month, 1744 and was bur. the 23rd day of 6th month, 1744; Elizabeth Linton b. 28th day of 8th month, 1751.

Children of Thomas and Elizabeth Stradling: Sarah Stradling b. 17th day of 8th month, 1746; Elizabeth Stradling b. 9th day of 2nd month, 1748; Lidya Stradling b. 6th day of 11th month, 1749; John Stradling b. 19th day of 11th month, 1751; Thomas Stradling b. 18th day of 1st month, 1753; Daniel Stradling b. 13th dau of 7th month, 175_; Katherine Stradling b. 25th day of 8th month, 1757.

Children of John Hamton and Ann, his wife, dau. of Jeremiah Croasdale: Asenath Hamton b. 18th day of 11th month, 1749; Sarah Hamton, who m. Isaac Smith, b. 3rd. day of 10th. month, 1751; Jos. Hamton b. 17th. day of 8th month, 1753; Hannah Hamton b. 6th day of 7th month, 1756 and d. 25th day of 12th month, 1756; David Hamton b. 24th day of 10th. month, 1757 and d. 8th day of 4th month, 1790; Jonathan Hamton b. 2nd day of 9th month, 1760; John Hamton b. 16th. day of 10th. month, 1763; Ann Hamton b. 6th. day of 4th. month, 1767.

Children of Benjamin Hamton and Ann, his wife, dau. of Jos. Wildman of Middletown: Mary Hamton b. 30th day of 10th month, 1752; Esther Hamton b. 19th day of 1st month, 1755 and was bur. 25th. day of 2nd month, 1755; Rachell Hamton b. 22nd day of 4th month, 1756 and was bur. 26th day of 12th month, 1756; Benjamin

Hamton b. 24th day of 10th month, 1758 and d. 2nd day of 8th month, 1828, age 69-9-8; Oliver Hamton b. 25th day of 7th month, 1761 and d. 14th day of 10th. month, 1826, age 65-2-19; James Hamton b. 24th day of 2nd month, 1764; Ann Hamton b. 11th day of 4th month, 1767; Sarah Hamton b. 13th day of 6th month, 1769; Elizabeth Hamton b. 22nd day of 5th month, 1772.

Children of Zebulon and Elizabeth (Buckman) Heston: Eliz. Heston b. 30th day of 4th month, 1727; Jemima Heston b. 27th. day of 8th month, 1728; Rebekah Heston b. 3rd day of 5th month, 1730; Rachell Heston b. 30th day of 11th month, 1731 and d. 12th day of 2nd month, 1826, age 94-2-12; Zebulon Heston b. 18th day of 11th month, 1733; Mary Heston b. 23rd. day of 4th. month, 1737; Wm. Heston b. 7th day of 5th month, 1739; John Heston b. 15th day of 5th month, 1742; Isaiah Heston b. 20th day of 8th month, 1744; David Heston b. 30th day of 9th month, 1748 and d. 16th day of 10th month, 1821, age 17-0-16.

Children of Jonathan and Jemimah Kinsey: Mary Kinsey b. 8th day of 10th month, 1752; Jonathan Kinsey b. 7th day of 4th month, 1754.

Children of John and Rachell Terry: Mary Terry b. 11th day of 3rd month, 1739 and d. the 20th day of 4th month, 1740; John Terry b. 24th day of 12th month, 1740.

Children of Thomas and Phebe Betts: Thomas Betts b. 3rd day of 8th month, 1745; Sarah Betts b. 14th day of 4th month, 1747; Ann Betts b. 1st day of 5th month. 1749; Rebekah Betts b. 18th day of 5th month, 1751; William Betts b. 3rd day of 12th month, 1752; John Betts b. 8th day of 5th month, 1755 and d. 27th day of 5th month, 1841, aged 86 years; Susannah Betts b. 20th day of 12th month, 1756; Stephen Betts b. 31st. day of 5th month, 1758; Mary Betts b. 2nd day of 10th month, 1760; Isaac Betts b. 2nd day of 1st month, 1763; Zachariah Betts b. 21st day of 10th month, 1764.

Thomas Betts b. 1st day of 9th month 1716 and d. 6th day of 6th month, 1783.
Phebe Betts, wife of Thomas Betts and daughter of William and Rebecca (Wilson) Smith, d. 25th day of 1st month, 1804?

Children of George and Mary Newborn: Hannah Newborn b. 10th day of 12th month, 1738/9; William Newborn b. 14th day of 1st month, 1740/1; Dorothy Newborn b. 1st day of 6th month, 1743; George Newborn b. 15th day of _ month, 1746; John Newborn b. 10th day of 12th month, 1748/9 and d. 27th day of 9th month, 1757; Mary Newborn b. 25th day of 11th month, 1751; David Newborn b. 20th day of 1st month, 1755.

Children of Thomas Atkinson and Mary, his wife, dau. of Joseph Wildman, of Middletown: Thomas Atkinson b. 9th day of 8th month, 1751 and d. 29th day of 1st month, 1815: Sarah Atkinson b. 12th day of 11th month, 1754 and d. 19th day of 1st month, 1759.

Children of John and Sarah Stockdale: Joseph Stockdale b. 11th day of the 12th.month, 1748 and d. 5th day of 8th month, 1777; John Stockdale b. 11th day of 7th month 1749.

Children of John Stockdale and Mary, his second wife: Mary Stockdale b. 26th day of 9th month, 1755 and d. 22nd day of 8th month, 1757; Elizabeth Stockdale b. 2nd day of 3rd month, 1757; Hannah Stockdale b. 17th day of 11th month, 1758; Sarah Stockdale b. 1st day of 12th month, 1753; Mary Stockdale b. 23rd day of 9th month, 1760; Rebeckah Stockdale b. 18th day of 10th month, 1762; Rachell Stockdale b. 29th day of 1st month, 1765; Susannah Stockdale b. 13th day of 2nd month, 1767 and d. 13th day of 8th month, 1777. Mercy Stockdale b. 9th day of 11th month, 1769.

Mary Stockdale d. 22nd day of 3rd month, 1789.

Children of Thomas Smith, son of Wm. Smith, and Sarah, his wife, late Townsend: William Smith b. _ day of 8th month, 1753; Sarah Smith b. 25th day of 10th month, 1755 and d. 1st day of 7th month, 1829, age 73-8-6; Mary Smith b. 3rd day of 1st month, 1758; Thomas Smith b. 6th day of 7th month, 1760 and d. 9th day of 9th month, 1813, age 52-4-3; Rebeckah Smith b. 31st day of 1st month, 1763 and d. 23rd day of 6th month, 1826, age 63-6-23; Stephen Smith b. 28th day of 10th month, 1765; Isaac Smith b. 22nd day of 4th month, 1767; Joseph Smith b. 31st day of 12th month, 1770; John Smith b. 11th day of 9th month, 1773.

Children of John and Elizabeth Gourley: John Gourley b. 23rd of 4th month, o.s., 1748; Joseph Gourley b. 6th day of 12th month, o.s., 1749; Samuell Gourley b. 30th day of 5th month, o.s., 1751; Mary Gourley b. 15th day of 3rd month, n.s., 1753; Sarah Gourley b. 16th day of 12th month, n.s., 1754 and d. 22nd day of 3rd month, 1759; Elizabeth Gourley b. 6th day of 8th month, n.s., 1756; Margaret Gourley b. 1st day of 2nd month, n.s., 1758.

Children of John and Rachel Penquite: Jane Penquite b. 25th day of 9th month, 1723; Abigaile Penquite b. 25th day of 1st month, 1726; Mercy Penquite b. 19th day of 6th month, 1730; Sarah Penquite b. 1st day of 10th month, 1732.

John Penquite d. 28th day of 6th month, 1750.
Rachael Penquite d. 28th day of 12th month, 1777

Children of Nathaniel Twining and Sarah, his wife, late Kirk: Nathaniel Twining b. 25th day of 2nd month, 1730; Samuell Twining b. 24th day of 2nd month, 1726; Benjamin Twining b. 3rd day of 6th month, 1728; Isaac Twining b. 25th day 5th month, 1724.

Children of John and Elizabeth Twining: John Twining b. 20th day of 8th month, 1719; Joseph Twining b. 1st day of 11th month, 1720; David Twining b. 17th day of 6th month, 1722; Elieazer Twining b. 8th day of 6th month, 1724; William Twining b. 25th day of 1st month, 1726; Thomas Twining b. 28th day of 6th month, 1728; Jacob Twining b. 25th day 10th month, 1730; Rachel Twining

b. 11th day of 11th month, 1732; Stephen Twining b. 5th day of 4th month, 1733.

Children of James Wood and Mary, his wife, dau. of William Smith: James Wood b. 11th day of 9th month, 1753; Matthew Wood b. 9th day of 7th month, 1755; John Wood b. 22nd day of 1st month, 1757; William Wood b. 7th day of 11th month, 1758; Aaron Wood b. 23rd day of 3rd month, 1760; Moses Wood b. 3rd day of 12th month, 1761 and d. 1st day of 6th month, 1764; Septimus Wood b. 3rd day of 10th month, 1763; Mary Wood b. 8th day of 4th month, 1765; Sarah Wood b. 18th day of 1st month, 1767; Rachell Wood b. 19 day of 12th month, 1768; Rebekah Wood b. 12th day of 5th month, 1771.

Children of John and Elizabeth Story: Mary Story b. 10th day of 8th month, 1748 and d. 3rd day of 9th month, 1821, age 73-0-23; Amos Story b. 18th day of 9th month, o.s., 1750 and was bur. 2nd day of 8th month, 17_ _; John Story b. 11th day of 3rd month, 1753; Thomas Story b. 19th day of 7th month, 1755 and d. 16th day of 12th month, 1818, age 63-4-27; Elizabeth Story b. 23rd day of 1st month, 1758 and was bur. 24th day of 6th month, 17_ _; David Story b. 20th day of 4th month, 1760 and d. 23rd day of 2nd month, 1832, age 72-9-27.

Children of Isaac Wilson and Sarah, his wife, dau. of Joseph Hamton: Sarah Wilson b. 31st day of 1st month, 1746/7 and was bur. 24th day of 11th month, 1746/7; Isaac Wilson b. 30th day of 9th month, 1747; Hamton Wilson b. 15th day of 8th month, 1750; Pleasant Wilson b. 30th day of 12th month, 1752 and was bur. 20th day of 9th month, 1767; Mary Wilson b. 21st day of 4th month, 1756; Stephen Wilson b. 4th day of 9th month, 1758; Mercy Wilson b. 21st day of 4th month, 1761.

Children of John Verily and Elizabeth, his wife, late Duckworth: Mary Verily b. 17th day of 5th month, 1721; John Verily b. 25th day of 7th month, 1724.

Children of William and Mary Atkinson: William Atkinson b. 14th day of 5th month, 1743 and d. 20th day of 2nd month, 1763; Mary Atkinson b. 8th day of 10th month, 1744 and d. 7th day of 11th month, 1831; John Atkinson b. 6th day of 9th month, 1746 and d. 9th day of 10th month, 1821; Sarah Atkinson b. 16th day of 7th month, 1748 and d. 20th day of 10th month, 1829; Eleanor Atkinson b. 13th day of 9th month, 1750, mar. Wm. Lee and d. 6th day of 7th month, 1786, in Maryland; Jos. Atkinson b. 28th day of 11th month, 1753 and d. 1st day of 3rd month, 1763; Phebe Atkinson b. 29th day of 11th month, 1756 and d. 14th day of 12th month, 1756; Thomas Atkinson b. 8th day of 10th month, 1757 and d. 15th day of 2nd month, 1763; Phebe Atkinson b. 6th day of 12th? month, 1760; Isaac Atkinson b. 12th day of 12th month, 1762; William Atkinson b. 12th day of 3rd month, 1765; Joseph Atkinson b. 10th day of 2nd month, 1768 and d. 16th day of 3rd month, 1841; Elizabeth Atkinson b. 3rd day of 8th month and d. 7th day of 8th month, 1770.

Children of John and Mary Hirst: John Hirst b. 5th day of 12th month, 1761; Rebeckah Hirst b. 6th day of 5th month, 1763; Sarah Hirst b. 27th day of 7th month, 1764; Jesse Hirst b. 18th day of 12th month, 1765.

Children of Zebulon and Dorothy Heston: Rachel Heston b. 29th day of 9th month, 1699, mar. John Lacey and d. 13th day of 3rd month, 17_ _; Hannah Heston b. 16th day of 10th month, 1701 and d. the following month; Zebulon Heston b. 4th day of 11th month, 1702 and d. _ day of 3rd month, _ _; John Heston b. 25th day of 5th month, 1705; Jemima Heston b. 24th day of 9th month, 1707 and d. 14th day of 2nd month, 1724; Stephen Heston b. 5th day of 11th month, 1710; Jacob Heston b. 20th day of 5th month, 1713; Isaac Heston b. 17th day of 5th month, 1716 and d. 19th day of 1st month, 1729; Thomas Heston b. 3rd day of 8th month, 1718.

Children of John and Hannah Balderston: John Balderston b. 26th day of 10th month, 1739 and d. 27th day of 4th month, 1821; Jonathan Balderston b. 26th day of 10th month, 1741 and d. 25th day of 8th month, 1825; Bartho. Balderston b. 4th day of 9th month, 1743; Timothy Balderston b. 10th day of 10th month, 1745 and d. 14th day of 5th month, 1827; Jacob Balderston b. 27th day of 12th month, 1748/9; Hannah Balderston b. 11th day of 1st month, 1751/2; Isaiah Balderston b. 24th? day of 9th month, 1753; Mordacai Balderston b. 31st day 1st month, 1755; Sarah Balderston b. 21st day of 2nd month, 1757; Lydia Balderston b. 1st day of 7th month, 1759; Mary Balderston b. 11th day of 6th month, 1762.

Jonathan Cooper, the elder, d. 12th day of 2nd month, 1769, being 98 years old.

Children of Stephen Twining, son of John Twining and Mary, his wife, dau. of John Wilkinson: John Twining b. 20th day of 4th month, 1767; Elias Twining b. 26th day of 3rd month, 1769; Rachel Twining b. 25th day of 8th month, 1771; Tamar Twining b. 10th day of 2nd month, 1774; Jacob Twining b. 28th day of 1st month, 1776.

Children of Elias Twining, who d. 20th day 8th month, 1832, and Mary, his wife, late Stokes: Ann Twining b. 28th day of 11th month, 1795; Sarah Twining b. 24th day 12th month, 1797 and d. 19th day 3rd month, 1826, age 28-2-25.

Children of Joseph and Ruth Warner: Cuthbert Warner b. 10th day of 3rd month, 1753; Joseph Warner b. 23rd day of 4th month, 1755; Aseph Warner b. 14th day of 8th month, 1757; Ezekiah Warner b. 2nd. day of 1st month, 1761; Mordeca Warner b. 24th day of 12th month, 1763; Silas Warner b. 15th day of 4th month, 1766.

Children of Thomas Smith, son of Thomas Smith, and Mary, his wife, dau. of Thomas Ross: Samuel Smith b. 20th day of 9th month, 1753; Joseph Smith b. 13th day of 5th month, 1757 and d. 11th day of 1st month, 1837, age 79-7-28; Kezia Smith b. 11th day of 8th month, 1759; John Smith b. 27th day of 11th month, 1761; Susanna

Smith b. 28th day of 8th month, 1764; Ezra Smith b. 15th day of 4th month, 1767 and d. 5th day of 3rd month, 1838; Thomas Smith b. 23rd day of 8th month, 1769; Margaret Smith b. 10th day of 4th month, 1772.

Mary Smith, wife of Thomas Smith, b. 1st day of 2nd month, 173_, d. 5th day of 9th month, 1777, and was bur. the 6th day of same month.

Children of Joseph Hamton, son of John Hampton, and Mary, his wife, dau. of John Blaker: Mary Hamton b. 26th day of 10th month, 1776; David Hamton b. 21st day of 7th month, 1778; John Hamton b. 12th day of 5th month, 1780; Joseph Hamton b. 17th day of 2nd month, 1782; Abner Hamton b. 5th day of 12th month, 1783; Samuel Hamton b. 1st day of 11th month, 1785; Hannah Hamton b. 19th day of 9th month, 1787; Amos Hamton b. 10th day of 12th month, 1789.

John Buckman b. 15th day of 5th month, 1721 and d. 27th day of 2nd month, 1790, in his 69th year

Children of John Buckman and Elinor, his wife, late Briggs: John Buckman b. 24th day of 7th month, 1748 and d. 2nd day of 11th month, 1837, age 89-36; David Buckman b. 14th day of 4th month, 1750 and d. 1st day of 9th month, 1810; Margaret Buckman b. 10th day of 4th month, 1753; Jonathan Buckman b. 29th day of 4th month, 1755 and d. 4th day of 10th month, 1826, age 71-5-5; Rachael Buckman b. 21st day of 5th month, 1757; Saml. Buckman b. 23rd day of 6th month, 1763 and d. 3rd day of 2nd month 1847, age 83-7-10; Ruth Buckman b. 3rd day of 2nd month, 1766; Abdon Buckman b. 20th day of 7th month, 1768 and d. 24th day of 8th month, 1856.

Children of Joseph Tomlinson, son of Joseph Tomlinson, and Margaret, his wife, dau. of _ _ Baker: Phebe Tomlinson b. 15th day of 11th month, 1752 and d. 8th day of 8th month, 1756, Sarah Tomlinson b. 25th day of 10th month, 1754; Joseph Tomlinson b. 24th day of 1st month, 1757; Rachael Tomlinson b. 20th day of 5th month, 1759; Mary Tomlinson b. 24th day of 4th month, 1761; Hannah Tomlinson b. 28th day of 11th month, 1763; Margaret Tomlinson b. 30th day of 3rd month, 1766; Samuel Tomlinson b. 2nd day of 4th month, 1769; Lydia Tomlinson b. 12th day of 2nd month, 1773.

Phebe Stokes, daughter of James and Hannah Stokes b. 20th day of 6th month, 1763.
Hannah Stokes d. 2nd day of 12th month, 1765.

Children of James Stokes and Mary, his wife, dau. of Joseph Hamton: Joseph Stokes b. 31st day of 8th month, 1769; Mary Stokes b. 9th day of 9th month, 1771; Susanna Stokes b. 6th day of 10th month, 1773; Hannah Stokes b. 15th day of 4th month, 1776 and d. 14th day of 8th month, 1777; Jane Stokes b. 4th day of 9th month, 1778; Sarah Stokes b. 13th day of 5th month, 1781.

Children of William Trego, who d. 1827, and Rebeckah, his wife, late Hibbs: Thomas Trego b. 15th day of 7th month, 1769 and d. _ day of 8th month, 1837; Mahlon Trego b. 25th day of 11th month, 1770 and d. 22nd day of 3rd month, 1849, age 78-3-28; Joseph Trego b. 10th day of 11th month, 1772; William Trego b. 29th day of 9th month, 1774 and d. 14th day of 7th month, 1850; John Trego b. 20th day of 12th month, 1776 and d. 16th day of 10th month, 1832; Mary Trego b. 8th day of 10th month, 1778 and d. 26th day of 10th month, 1784; Jacob Trego b. 8th day of 10th month, 1780 and d. 10th day of 3rd month, 1870, age 89-5-2; Jesse Trego b. 9th day of 8th month, 1782 and d. 10th day of 4th month, 1787; Hannah Trego b. 23rd day of 10th month, 1784, m. Isaac Beans and d. in Ohio; Rebecca Trego b. 21st day of 8th month, 1786, m. Thomas Biggs, who d. in 1861, and she d. 7th day of 8th month, 1875; Mary Trego b. 3rd day of 10th month, 1788.

Children of Robert Verree and Ann, his wife, late Chapman: Mary Verree b. 5th day of 3rd month, 1761; James Verree b. 19th day of 7th month, 1764.

Children of John Ballance, son of Thomas Ballance, and Dorithy, his wife, dau. of John Carr: Joseph Ballance b. 11th day of 9th month, 1755.

Children of John Warner, son of John Warner, and Phebe, his wife, dau. of Robert Smith: Rachael Warner b. 8th day of 8th month, 1774; John Warner b. 2nd day of 4th month, 1776; Mercy Warner b. 24th day of 9th month, 1777; Joseph Warner b. 10th day of 10th month, 1779; Seneca Warner b. 29th day of 7th month, 1781.

Children of Jacob Heston and Mary, his wife, late Warner, who mar. 11th day of 11th month, 1739: Mary Heston b. 13th day of 11th month, 1740; Jesse Heston b. 25th day of 6th month, 1743; Edward Warner Heston b. 16th day of 3rd month, 1745; Isaac Heston b. 30th day of 10th month, 1746; Jacob Warner b. 9th day of 11th month, 1749; Thomas Heston b. 22nd day of 4th month, 1753; Rachel Heston b. 10th day of 3rd month, 1758.

Children of Joseph Buckman and Martha, his wife, late Carr: Hester Buckman b. 22nd day of 8th month, o.s., 1747 and d. 28th day of 12th month, 1812; Mary Buckman b. 1st day of 10th month, o.s., 1748; Agnes Buckman b. 15th day of 12th month, o.s., 1748.; Letitia Buckman b. 5th day of 1st month, o.s., 1751 and d. 27th day of 9th month, 1833; Joseph Buckman b. 31st day of 8th month, o.s., 1752 and d. 17th day of 9th month, 1828, age 76-0-17; Sarah Buckman b. 22nd day of 11th month, o.s., 1753 and d. 10th day of 9th month, 1831; Elizabeth Buckman b. 12th day of 9th month, 1756; Asenath Buckman b., 2nd day of 4th month 1761, mar. David Warner, and d. 31st day of 12th month, 1837.

Children of Thomas and Mary Strickland: Mary Strickland b. 17th day of 6th month, 1737; Thomas Strickland b. 9th day of 2nd month, 1740; Miles Strickland b. 8th day of 2nd month, 1743; John Strickland b. 18th day of 6th month, 1745.

Children of Nicholas and Abigail Penquite: Hester Penquite b. 21st day of 12th month, 1727/8; Agnes Penquite b. 16th day of 5th month, 1730; Johannah Penquite b. 13th day of 9th month, 1732.

Children of Isaac and Elizabeth Kirk: Mary Kirk b. 1st day of 9th month, 1731; Isaac Kirk b. 15th day of 8th month, 1733.

Children of Jesse Heston and Mary, his wife, dau. of Isaac Stackhouse of Middletown: Mary Heston b. 17th day of 5th month, 1767; Jacob Heston b. 17th day of 5th month, 1769 and d. 1st day of 4th month, 1856; Isaac Heston b. 1st day of 5th month, 1771; Jonathan Heston b. 14th day of 11th month, 1773 and d. 22nd day of 5th month, 1833; John Heston b. 9th day of 2nd month, 1776 and d. 6th day of 6th month, 1853; Ann Heston b. 8th day of 12th month, 1778; Rachael Heston b. 4th day of 5th month, 1781.

Children of John Atkinson and Mary, his wife, dau. of William and Mary Smith: John Atkinson b. 18th day of 6th month, 1718; William Atkinson b. 17th day of 2nd month, 1721; Thomas Atkinson b. 5th day of 3rd month, 1722; Christopher Atkinson b. 18th day of 12th month, 1723/4; Mary Atkinson b. 20th day of 8th month, 1725, mar. 9th month, 1752, John Stockdale and d. 22nd day of 3rd month, 1789; Ezekiel Atkinson b. 10th day of 10th month, 1728; Cephus Atkinson b. 7th day of 5th month, 1730; Elizabeth Atkinson b. 12th day of 4th month, 1732.

Children of Joseph and Mary Doan: Joseph Doan b. 6th day of 8th month, and d. 7th day of 9th month, 1727; Mary Doan b. 6th day of 9th month, 1728 and d. 1st day of 3rd month, 1743; John Doan b. 30th day of 11th month, 1731; Ebenezer Doan b. 5th day of 7th month, 1733; Martha Doan b. 21st day of 9th month, 1735; Mahittable Doan b. 10th day of 11th month, 1738; Grace Doan b. 19th day of 1st month, 1740; James Doan b. _ day of _ month, _ _.

Children of John Lacey, son of John Lacey, and Jane, his wife, dau. of Abraham Chapman: Rachael Lacey b. 15th day of 9th month, 1747 and d. 16th day of 6th month, 1760; Susanna Lacey b. 19th day of 2nd month, 1750; John Lacey b. 4th day of 12th month, 1752; Abraham Lacey b. 4th day of 1st month, 1754 and d. 28th day of 10th month, 1764; James Lacey b. 19th day of 8th month, 1756; Benjamin Lacey b. 23rd day of 7th month, 1760; William Lacey b. 9th day of 2nd month, 1765.

Children of Joseph Chapman, son of Abraham Chapman, and Ann, his wife, dau. of John Fell: Jonathan Chapman b. 3rd day of 4th month, 1759 and d. 6th day of 5th month, 1778; Joseph Chapman b. 8th day of 9th month, 1760 and d. 12th day of 7th month, 1772; Edward Chapman b. 26th day of 12th month, 1761 and d. 9th day of the 10th month, 1853; Isaac Chapman b. 14th day of 12th month, 1763 and d. 8th day of 2nd month, 1837; Elizabeth Chapman b. 20th day of 11th month, 1765 and d. 23rd day of 7th month, 1774; Abraham Chapman b. 18th day of 8th month, 1767 and d. 24th day of 2nd month, 1856; Ann Chapman b. 8th day of 11th month, 1768; Thomas Chapman b. 7th day of 12th month, 1770 and d. 22nd day of

3rd month, 1849; Sarah and Joseph (twin) Chapman b. 21st day of 5th month, 1774; Benjamin Chapman b. 27th day of 9th month, 1775; John Chapman b. 29th day of 9th month, 1779 and d. 14th day of 9th month, 1850; Jonathan Chapman b. 19th day of 6th month, 1779; Samuel Chapman b. 22nd day of 5th month, 1781 and d. 21st day of 7th month, 1781.

Ann Chapman d. 9th day of 3rd month, 1828, aged 88 years

Children of John Watson, son of Joseph Watson, and Mary, his wife, daughter of Benjamin Hampton: Alice Watson b. 4th day of 12th month, 1772; John Watson b. 25th day of 8th month, 1774; Frances Watson b. 7th day of 6th month, 1777; Ann Watson b. 12th month of 9th day, 1778; Rachael Watson b. 15th day of 1st month, 1781.

Children of Charles Chapman, son of John Chapman, and Elizabeth, his wife, daughter of John Linton: Susannah Chapman b. 14th day of 9th month, 1777; Isaiah Chapman b. 1st day of 11th month, 1778; Rebeckah Chapman b. 11th day of 1st month, 1780; Stephen Chapman b. 16th day of 9th month, 1781; Elizabeth Chapman b. 26th day of 5th month, 1783; Mercy Chapman b. 23rd day of 9th month, 1784; Mary Chapman b. 12th day of 11th month, 1786; Charles Chapman b. 16th day of 4th month, 1788; Letitia Chapman b. 27th day of 1st month, 1790; Joseph Chapman b. 28th day of 5th month, 1791.

Children of Jacob Buckman, son of William Buckman, and Mary, his wife, daughter of Peter Tayler: Mary Buckman b. 15th day of 4th month, 1758 and d. 26th day of 8th month, 1771; Hester Buckman b. 7th day of 11th month, 1759 and d. 19th day of 11th month, 1809; Sarah Buckman b. 7th day of 10th month, 1761, m. William Smith and d. 8th day of 10th month, 1851.

Mary Buckman d. 24th day of 3rd month, 1777.

Children of William Buckman, son of William Buckman, and Jane, his wife, daughter of William Briggs: William b. 19th day of 7th month, 1745. O.S.; Sarah Buckman b. 2nd day of 9th month, 1747 O.S. and d. 29th day of 9th month, 1752; Elizabeth Buckman b. 2nd day of 1st month, 1750. O.S.; Abner Buckman b. 19th day of 10th month, 1752 O.S.; Sarah Buckman b. 7th day of 6th month, 1755 O.S., mar. William Chapman and d. 5th day of 9th month, 1787; James Buckman b. 6th day of 10th month, 1758 O.S. and d. 10th day of 12th month, 1840; Jane Buckman b. 17th day of 2nd month, 1761 O.S.; Ellin Buckman b. 14th day of 12th month, 1765 O.S. and d. 28th day of 2nd month, 1789; Phinias Buckman b. 14th day of 2nd month, 1767 O.S..

Jane Buckman d. 21st day of 2nd month, 1777.
William Buckman d. 6th day of 9th month, 1782.

Children of Benjamin Wiggins, son of Bozaleel Wiggins, and Sarah, his wife, dau. of Joseph Warner: Rachael Wiggins b. 3rd day of

6th month, 1761, mar. John Lacey and d. 28th day of 12th month, 1839; Joseph Wiggins b. 30th day of 9th month, 1762 and d. 25th day of 9th month, 1825; Agnes Wiggins b. 16th day of 4th month, 1767, mar. David Simpson and d. 25th day of 3rd month, 1831; Benjamin Wiggins b. 26th day of 3rd month, 1774 and d. 31st day of 8th month, 1863; Sarah Wiggins b. 3rd day of 6th month, 1782.

Children of John Wilkenson, son of John Wilkenson, and Jane, his wife, dau. of Abraham Chapman: John Wilkenson b. 12th day of 8th month, 1770; Abraham Wilkenson b. 12th day of 4th month, 1772 and d. 12th day of 3rd month, 1816; Elias Wilkenson b. 12th day of 1st month, 1774 and d. 9th month, 1774; Amos Wilkenson b. 3rd day of 10th month, 1776.

Children of William and Hannah Buckman: Amos Buckman b. 9th day of 3rd month, 1771 and d. 23rd day of 12th month, 1776; Abner Buckman b. 10th day of 11th month, 1772; Hannah Buckman b. 13th day of 4th month, 1776 and d. 3rd day of 1st month, 1777; Elizabeth Buckman b. 2nd day of 11th month, 1777; Dilworth Buckman b. 26th day of 3rd month, 1780; Lidia Buckman b. 11th day of 6th month, 1782; William Buckman b. 11th day of 8th month, 1785; Sarah Buckman b. 26th day of 12th month, 1787; Martha Buckman b. 14th day of 5th month, 1790.

Children of Isaiah Linton, son of John Linton, and Sarah, his wife, dau. of John Hirst: Laura Linton b. 22nd day of 3rd month, 1766 and d. 30th day of 9th month, 1828; Thomas Linton b. 3rd day of 1st month, 1768; James Linton b. 10th day of 12th month, 1769; William Linton b. 13th day of 1st month, 1772; Sarah Linton b. 23rd day of 2nd month, 1774.

Children of William Linton, son of John Linton, and Sarah, his wife, dau. of John Penquite: John Linton b. 1st day of 4th month, 1767; Elizabeth Linton b. 3rd day of 12th month, 1768.

Sarah Linton d. 3rd month, 1786.

Children of John Buckman, son of John Buckman, and Susannah, his wife, dau. of William Chapman: Margaret Buckman b. 29th day of 3rd month, 1774, mar. Benjamin Wiggins and d. 3rd day of 9th month, 1840; Susanna Buckman b. 17th day of 8th month, 1775 and d. 29th day of 5th month, 1859; George Buckman b. 13th day of 12th month, 1777 and d. 1st day of 9th month, 1883; Amos Buckman b. 31st day of 7th month, 1779 and d. 13th day of 8th month, 1883: Jane Buckman b. 8th day of 8th month, 1782 and d. 21st day of 8th month, 1783; Chapman Buckman b. 31st day of 7th month, 1784 and d. 19th day of 11th month, 1859; John Buckman b. 22nd day of 6th month, 1786 and d. 7th day of 8th month, 1844; Jacob Buckman b. 2nd day of 9th month, 1791 and d. 3rd day of 12th month, 1869; Ann Buckman b. 23rd day of 6th month, 1793 and d. 7th day of 9th month, 1863; Ezra Buckman b. 10th day of 9th month, 1795 and d. 28th day of 10th month, 1836.

Susanna Buckman d. 12th day of 10th month, 1817

Children of Thomas Wilborn, son of Samuel Wilborn, and Sarah, his wife, dau. of Bartlet Brundage: Anna Wilborn b. 10th day of 6th month, 1775; Hannah Wilborn b. 12th day of 1st month, 1777 and d. 6th day of 9th month, 1778; Amos Wilborn b. 9th day of 9th month, 1778; John Wilborn b. 20th day of 9th month, 1780; Rachael Wilborn b. 10th day of 2nd month, 1783; Stephen Wilborn b. 27th day of 2nd month, 1785; Joseph Wilborn b. 6th day of 3rd month, 1787; Phebe Wilborn b. 2nd day of 2nd month, 1789.

Children of Hamton Wilson, son of Isaac Wilson, and Anne, his wife, dau. of James Briggs: Sarah Wilson b. 6th day of 6th month, 1776 and d. 17th day of 8th month, 1776; Amos Wilson b. 23rd day of 9th month, 1777; Rachael Wilson b. 5th day of 10th month, 1779; Anne Wilson b. 12th day of 2nd month, 1782.

Children of John Smith, son of Robert Smith, and Sarah, his wife, dau. of Thomas Smith: Mary Smith b. 19th day of 8th month, 1778; Robert Smith b. 15th day of 6th month, 1780; David Smith b. 13th day of 4th month, 1782 and d. 10th day of 1st month, 1841; Sarah Smith b. 3rd day of 5th month, 1784; Hannah Smith b. 11th day of 11th month, 1787; James Smith b. 20th day of 2nd month, 1790; Abraham Smith b. 29th day of 1st month, 1793; Rachael Smith b. 1st day of 12th month, 1795.

Children of James Dillon, son of John Dillon, and Rebecca, his wife, dau. of Eleazer Doan: Moses Dillon b. 25th day of 2nd month, 1762.

Children of Stephen Twining and Sarah Twining: Stephen Twining b. 9th day of 8th month, 1776; Mary Twining b. 15th day of 9th month, 1774; Stephen Twining d. 3rd day of 8th month, 1777.

William Chapman was b. 1st day of 10th month, 1744.

Children of William Chapman, son of William Chapman and Sarah, his wife, dau. of William Buckman: Rachael Chapman b. 29th day of 11th month, 1775 and d. 9th day of 8th month, 1777; Aaron Chapman b. 25th day of 5th month 1777; Tamar Chapman b. 21st day of 2nd month, 1779 and d. 4th day of 8th month, 1783; Penquite Chapman b. 23rd day of 7th month, 1781 and d. 3rd day of 2nd month, 1785; David Chapman b. 25th day of 7th month, 1783; William Chapman b. 4th day of 9th month, 1787 and d. 11th day of 9th month, 1787.

Sarah Chapman d. 5th day of 9th month, 1787

Children of John Rose and Mary, his wife, dau. of William Atkinson: Mary Rose b. 11th day of 8th month, 1767; Deborah Rose b. 24th day of 5th month, 1769 and d. 4th day of 4th month, 1826; John Rose b. 19th day of 1st month, 1771 and d. 4th day of 5th month, 1806; Atkinson Rose b. 27th day of 8th month, 1773; Thomas Rose b. 1st day of 6th month, 1775; Phebe Rose b. 30th day of 1st month, 1777; Sarah Rose b. 7th day of 3rd month, 1778; Hannah Rose b. 3rd day of 3rd month, 1780; William Rose b. 20th day of 4th month, 1782 and d. 26th day of 7th month, 1798; James Rose b.

19th day of 3rd month, 1784 and d. 14th day of 1st month, 1788. Jonathan Rose b. 4th day of 9th month, 1785.

Children of John Hayhurst and Mary, his wife, widow of John Wiggins: Rachel Hayhurst b. 20th day of 7th month, 1763, mar. Joseph Smith and d. 9th day of 11th month, 1836; Bazaleel Hayhurst b. 2nd day of 2nd month, 1766; Margery Hayhurst b. 27th day of 3rd month, 1768, mar. Ezra Smith and d. 9th day of 4th month, 1858. Elizabeth Hayhurst b. 24th day of 5th month, 1771, mar. Banner Knoles and d. 25th day of 5th month, 1846; Benjamin Hayhurst b. 8th day of 6th month, 1773; John Hayhurst b. 8th day of 2nd month, 1776 and d. 15th day of 8th month, 1777; Ruth Hayhurst b. 23rd day of 6th month, 1778.

Mary Hayhurst d. 11th day of 7th month, 1808.

Children of Isaac and Susannah Wilson: Elizabeth Wilson b. 1st day of 4th month, 1774; Susannah Wilson b. 7th day of 7th month, 1775; Abraham Wilson b. 10th day of 4th month, 1777; Mary Wilson b. 31st of 10th month, 1779; Sarah Wilson b. 13th day of 9th month, 1883; Hannah Wilson b. 6th day of 12th month, 1785; Jane Wilson b. 20th day of 1st month, 1789 and d. 19th day of 11th month, 1789.

Children of James Briggs and Mary, his wife, dau. of John Story: Amos Briggs b. 13th day of 2nd month, 1766 and d. 19th day of 9th month, 1823; Elizabeth Briggs b. 29th day of 4th month, 1768 and d. 2nd month, 1830; Phineas Briggs b. 10th day of 11th month, 1771 and d. 22nd day of 11th month, 1823; Thomas Briggs b. 7th day of 11th month, 1773 and d. 7th day of 7th month, 1861; Ann Briggs b. 9th day of 6th month, 1776 and d. 13th day of 10th month, 1855; James Briggs b. 21st day of 7th month, 1779 and d. 7th day of 8th month, 1826; John Briggs b. 10th day of 12th month, 1781 and d. 5th day of 3rd month, 1787; David Briggs b. 6th day of 2nd month, 1784 and d. 18th day of 12th month, 1860; Mary Briggs b. 11th day of 8th month, 1786 and d. 14th day of 10th month, 1843; Rachael Briggs b. 21st day of 4th month, 1788 and d. 21st day of 8th month, 1821.

Children of Daniel and Margaret Lee: Sarah Lee b. 5th day of 4th month, 1775; Ellen Lee b. 21st day of 11th month, 1776; Rachael Lee b. 19th day of 11th month, 1778; John Lee b. 31st day of 1st month, 1781; Elizabeth Lee b. 20th day of 2nd month, 1783 and d. 20th day of 8th month, 1889; Deborah Lee b. 12th day of 6th month, 1785 and d. 12th day of 8th month, 1789; Ruth Lee b. 17th day of 9th month 1787; Mary Lee b. 10th day of 12th month, 1789 and d. 23rd day of 12th month, 1789; Margaret Lee b. 15th day of _ month, 1791.

Children of Eleazer and Mary Twining: Mahlon Twining b. 25th day of 3rd month, 1761 and d. 6th day of 12th month, 1786; Hannah Twining b. 21st day of 12th month, 1762; Silas Twining b. 13th day of 2nd month, 1765 and d. 26th day of 2nd month, 1827; Ann Twining b. 21st day of 2nd month, 1767; David Twining b. 10th day of 5th month, 1769 and d. 16th day of 4th month, 1823; Eleazer Twining b. 13th day of 11th month, 1771 and d. 21st day of 12th month, 1789; Mary Twining b. 20th day of 2nd month, 1774.

Mary Twining d. 17th day of 4th month, 1790.

Children of Isaac and Joyce (Fell) Buckman: David Buckman b. 15th day of 8th month, 1780 and d. 29th day of 11th month, 1804; Deborah Buckman b. 2nd day of 8th month, 1782 and d. 22nd day of 5th month, 1787; Mary Buckman b. 11th day of 3rd month, 1784 and d. 11th day of 12th month, 1806; Charles Buckman b. 15th day of 9th month, 1785 and d. 21st day of 5th month, 1787; Hannah Buckman b. 6th day of 10th month, 1787 and d. 8th day of 11th month, 183_; Elizabeth Buckman b. 10th day of 12th month, 1789 and d. 1st day of 4th month, 1830; Zenas Buckman b. 30th day of 12th month, 1791 and d. 22nd day of 9th month, 1836; Rachael Buckman b. 11th day of 3rd month, 1794; Isaac Buckman b. 17th day of 2nd month, 1796 and d. 13th day of 6th month, 1868.

Joyce Buckman d. 18th day of 9th month, 1823.

Children of David and Hester Buckman: Hannah Buckman b. 28th day of 7th month, 1780; Rachael Buckman b. 28th day of 9th month, 1781; John Buckman b. 12th day of 6th month, 1783; David Buckman b. 23rd day of 1st month, 1785; Edmund Buckman b. 4th day of 7th month, 1788; Deborah Buckman b. 16th day of 2nd month, 1790; Oliver Buckman b. 17th day of 10th month, 1791; Benjamin Buckman b. 10th day of 9th month, 1793; Esther Buckman b. 9th day of 1st month, 1796; Anna Buckman b. 18th day of 10th month, 1797; Cadwalader Buckman b. 11th day of 12th month, 1799.

Children of Thomas and Sarah Atkinson: Mary Atkinson b. 30th day of 1st month, 1780, mar. John Atkinson and d. 29th day of 3rd month, 1803; Jonathan Atkinson b. 19th day of 3rd month, 1782 and d. 7th day of 11th month, 1852; Timothy Atkinson b. 25th day of 5th month, 1784 and d. 20th day of 12th month, 1866; Thomas Atkinson b. 8th day of 10th month, 1786 and d. 6th day of 7th month, 1864; Mahlon Atkinson b. 11th day of 4th month, 1790; Sarah Atkinson b. 23rd day of 2nd month, 1793, mar. Jacob Heston, Jr. and d. 11th day of 3rd month, 1826; Joseph Atkinson b. 22nd day of 8th month, 1795 and d. 1st day of 2nd month, 1815.

Sarah Atkinson d. 19 day of 10th month, 1830, aged 75 years.

Children of Thomas Smith, son of Samuel Smith, and Ellen, his wife: Joseph Smith b. 12th day of 6th month, 1779 and d. 20th day of 9th month, 1785; Letitia Smith b. 29th day of 9th month, 1782, mar. Joseph Trego; Joseph Smith b. 5th day of 2nd month, 1786; Jane Smith b. 5th day of 10th month, 1789; Martha Smith b. 11th day of 8th month, 1792, mar. Charles B. Trego and d. 9th month, 1883.

Children of Isaac Smith, son of William and Rebeckah Smith, and Sarah, his wife, dau. of John Hamton: Eber Smith b. 4th day of

9th month, 1772; David Smith b. 10th day of 4th month, 1774; Hannah Smith b. 26th day of 4th month, 1776; Sarah Smith b. 9th day of 11th month, 1778; Isaac Smith b. 16th day of 6th month, 1781; Asenath Smith b. 14th day of 11th month, 1783 and d. 29th day of 12th month, 1785; Aseneth Smith b. 3rd day of 6th month, 1787; Jonathan Smith b. 10th day of 4th month, 1790; Rachael Smith b. 3rd day of 10th month, 1792.

Martha Terry, daughter of Jasper and Lucy Terry, b. 19th day of 5th month, 1778.

Children of Benjamin and Mary Smith: Esther b. 26th day of 6th month, 1786; Sarah b. 27th day of 12th month, 1788; Mary b. 21st day of 1st month, 1799.

Benjamin Smith, the Elder, son of Robert and Phebe Smith, d. about the 5th day of 9th month, 1771, about 36 years old. Sarah Smith, his wife, dau. of Samuel Eastburn, d. 3rd day of 11th month, 1803, about 67 years old.

Children of Thomas and Rachael Storey: Elizabeth Storey b. 18th day of 11th month, 1787; Mary Storey b. 17th day of 1st month, 1790 and d. 31st day of 1st month, 1793; Rebecca Storey b. 28th day of 3rd month, 1792; Thomas Storey b. 26th day of 12th month, 1796; Samuel Storey b. 1st day of 3rd month, 1804.

Children of Abraham and Esther Smith: Howard Smith b. 24th day of 5th month, 1799 and d. 9th day of 8th month, 1801; Sarah Williams Smith b. 26th day of 2nd month, 1801; Robert Smith b. 3rd day of 12th month, 1803 and d. 5th day of 12th month, 1803; Matilda Smith b. 6th day of 2nd month, 1805.

Children of Edward Chapman and Rachael, his wife, dau. of William Blackson of Wrightstown: Jesse Chapman b. 13th day of 2nd month, 1795 and d. 19th day of 6th month, 1814; Martha Chapman b. 5th day of 6th month, 1797; Charles Chapman b. 19th day of 7th month, 1798 and d. 21st day of 9th month, 1813; Amos Chapman b. 6th day of 10th month, 1800 and d. 7th day of 9th month, 1873; Ann Chapman (twin) b. 6th day of 10th month, 1800 and d. 9th day of 9th month, 1862.

Children of Abraham and Elizabeth Reeder: Hannah Reeder b. 11th day of 3rd month, 1780; Abraham Reeder b. 14th day of 8th month, 1782; Elenor Reeder b. 10th day of 5th month, 1784; William Reeder b. 8th day of 2nd month, 1788; Joseph Reeder b. 2nd day of 3rd month, 1790; Isaac Reeder b. 15th day of 1st month, 1792; Charles Reeder b. 18th day of 7th month, 1794; Elizabeth Reeder b. 15th day of 7th month, 1796; John Reeder b. 9th day of 9th month, 1799.

Children of John Chapman, and Rebecca, his wife, late Hutchinson: John Chapman b. 13th day of 7th month, 1800 and d. 2nd day of 3rd month, 1873; William Ross Chapman b. 4th day of 11th month, 1803.

Children of Jacob Heston, of Wrightstown, and Elizabeth, his wife, dau. of Benjamin Smith: Benjamin Heston b. 24th day of 3rd month, 1793; Elizabeth Heston b. 25th day of 2nd month, 1795; Jacob Heston b. 18th day of 6th month, 1796.

Children of Isachar and Hannah Morris, of Wrightstown: Lydia Morris b. 7th day of 2nd month, 1774; Elizabeth Morris b. 28th day of 2nd month, 1776; Isachar Morris b. 10th day of 8th month, 1778; Mary Morris b. 20th day of 5th month, 1781, mar. John Trego and d. 10th day of 1st month, 1830; Joseph Morris b. 15th day of 9th month, 1784; Sarah Morris b. 13th day of 7th month, 1788; Hannah Morris b. 30th day of 4th month, 1791.

Children of Samuel Davis and Lidia, his wife, dau. of Isacher and Hannah Morris: Seth Davis b. 14th day of 3rd month, 1796; Morris Davis b. 20th day of 9th month, 1798 and d. 29th day of 10th month, 1821; Samuel Davis b. 30th day of 7th month, 1801 and d. 6th day of 9th month, 1801; Lidia Davis (twin) b. 30th day of 7th month, 1801 and d. 8th day of 9th month, 1825.

Samuel Davis d. 6th day of 2nd month, 1825.
Lidia Davis d. 9th day of 9th month, 1801, aged 26-7-10

Children of Ezra Warton, of Upper Makefield, and Martha, his wife, dau. of Jasper Terry: Joel Warton b. 1st day of 1st month, 1798; Anna Warton b. 17th day of 7th month, 1800; Amos Warton b. 28th day of 2nd month, 1803; Linton Warton b. 27th day of 9th month, 1805; Hannah Warton b. 31st day of 3rd month, 1808; Daniel and Jasper (twin) Warton b. 7th day of 1st month, 1811; James Warton b. 1st day of 8th month, 1813; Silas Warton b. 16th day of 1st month, 1817.

Children of Thomas Smith, son of Thomas and Sarah Smith, and Letitia, his wife, dau. of Crispin and Martha Blackston: Thomas Smith b. 14th day of 11th month, 1785; Moses Smith b. 29th day of 9th month, 1787 and d. 15th day of 7th month, 1855, in Philadelphia; Aaron Smith b. 27th day of 5th month, 1789; Letitia Smith b. 25th day of 5th month, 1790; Edward Smith b. 30th day of 5th month, 1792 and d. 5th day of 10th month, 1828; Oliver Smith b. 23rd day of 10th month, 1794; Mary Smith b. 3rd day of 1st month, 1797; Job Smith b. 29th day of 4th month, 1799; Elijah Smith b. 2nd day of 5th month, 1801; Septimus Smith b. 4th day of 5th month, 1803.

Children of Benjamin and Margaret Hamton, of Wrightstown: Moses Hamton b. 25th day of 7th month, 1787; Benjamin Hamton b. 20th day of 9th month, 1790; Sarah Hamton b. 26th day of 10th month, 1792; Joseph Hamton b. 1st day of 9th month, 1794; Margaret Hamton b. 23rd day of 12th month, 1796; Hannah Hamton b. 17th day of 10th month, 1799, mar. Mahlon Hall and d. 30th day of 10th month, 1827; Mary and Ann (twin) Hamton b. 9th day of 9th month, 1800; Katherine Hamton b. 19th day of 6th month, 1805.

Children of John Eastburn, of Upper Makefield Tp., and Elizabeth, month, 1788 and d. 28th day of 4th month, 1863; Barzalleel Eastburn b. 14th day of 8th month, 1791 and d. 19th day of 12th month, 1845; Jane Eastburn b. 22nd day of 9th month, 1794, mar. James Worstall and d. 6th day of 11th month, 1825; John Eastburn b. 9th day of 4th month, 1801 and d. 29th day of 1st month, 1878.

Elizabeth Eastburn b. 21st day of 9th month, 1760 and d. 3rd day of 6th month, 1801.

Children of John and Rachael Lacey, of Wrightstown: Benjamin Lacey b. 18th day of 8th month, 1795; Esther Lacey b. 27th day of 10th month, 1797; Isaac Lacey b. 21st day of 6th month, 1800; Warner Lacey b. 18th day of 4th month, 1803.

Children of Abraham and Mary Clark: Sarah Clark b. 10th day of 1st month, 1777; Ann Clark b. 9th day of 2nd month, 1779; Joseph Clark b. 3rd day of 1st month, 1782 and d. 14th day 8th month, 1828; Mary Clark b. 28th day of 7th month, 1784; Elizabeth Clark b. 29th day of 6th month, 1787 and d. 27th day 9th month, 1852; Hannah Clark b. 6th day of 7th month, 1790; Benjamin Clark b. 7th day of 8th month, 1793; Solomon Clark b. 1st day of 4th month, 1796; Esther Clark b. 10th day of 10th month, 1799; Jane Clark b. 23rd day of 8th month, 1802.

Children of David Storey and Rachael, his wife, dau. of William Richardson: Rebeckah Storey b. 15th day of 1st month, 1793; Hannah Storey b. 23rd day of 3rd month, 1794; John Storey b. 15th day of 1st month, 1796; William Storey b. 10th day of 9th month, 1797 and d. 16th day of 9th month, 1822; Mary Storey b. 23rd day of 3rd month, 1800; Elizabeth Storey b. 6th day of 3rd month, 1807.

Children of David and Martha Twining, of Warwick Tp: Mahlon Twining b. 8th day of 3rd month, 1795; William Twining b. 13th day of 4th month, 1797; John Twining b. 23rd day of 3rd month, 1799; Eleazer Twining b. 3rd day of 11th month, 1800 and d. 9th day of 4th month, 1827; Isaac Twining b. 16th day of 8th month, 1802; Phebe Twining b. 23rd day of 12th month, 1804; Thomas Twining b. 16th day of 2nd month, 1808; Beulah Twining b. 15th day of 12th month, 1811.

Children of Joseph Wiggins, of Upper Makefield, and Mary, his wife, dau. of Jesse Heston: Barzaleel Wiggins b. 4th day of 11th month, 1789; Mary Wiggins b. 6th day of 9th month, 1791; Jesse Wiggins b. 23rd day of 4th month, 1794; Sarah Wiggins b. 25th day of 2nd month, 1798; Rachael Wiggins b. 31st day of 10th month, 1799; Ann Wiggins b. 4th day of 5th month, 1802.

Children of John and Alice Paist, of Wrightstown: John Paist b. 7th day of 12th month, 1774; Robert Paist b. 1st day of 1st month, 1777; Jolly Paist b. 8th day of 2nd month, 1779; Alice Paist b. 23rd day of 3rd month, 1781; George Paist b. 30th day of 3rd month, 1783; Jonathan Paist b. 17th day of 5th month, 1804; Yuclydus Paist b. 15th day of 8th month, 1785.

Yuclydus Paist b. 15th day of 8th month, 1785.

Children of John and Elizabeth Simpson, of Solebury Tp: Robert Simpson b. 28th day of 8th month, 1796; Hannah Simpson b. 17th day of 1st month, 1798, mar. Cyrus Betts and d. 2nd day of 3rd month, 1830, leaving 2 children; James Simpson b. 23rd day of 8th month, 1799 and d. 3rd day of 9th month, 1828; Elinor Simpson b. 18th day of 12th month, 1802, mar. Andrew Collins, Jr. and d. 3rd day of 2nd month, 1837, leaving 3 children; Elizabeth Simpson b. 30th day of 12th month, 1805, mar. Mark Wright and d. 23rd day of 1st month, 1844, leaving 5 children; Martha Simpson b. 18th day of 5th month, 1807, mar. Silas Twining and d. 24th day of 8th month, 1840, leaving 2 children; Ruth Simpson b. 26th day of 12th month, 1808, mar. Edmund L. Atkinson and d. 5th day of 3rd month, 1839, leaving 3 children; Isaac Simpson b. 8th day of 11th month, 1812.

Children of Ezra Smith, of Upper Makefield, and Margery, his wife, dau. of John Hayhurst: Mary Smith b. 6th day of 4th month, 1793; Margaret Smith b. 1st day of 7th month, 1795 and d. 17th day of 5th month, 1819; Ross Smith b. 5th day of 6th month, 1797; Ezra Smith b. 27th day of 7th month, 1799; Ann Smith b. 23rd day of 10th month, 1801; Margery Smith b. 20th day of 2nd month, 1804; Ralph Smith b. 26th day of 8th month, 1806; Watson Smith b. 15th day of 8th month, 1809; Jane Smith b. 15th day of 7th month, 1812.

Children of Benjamin Worthington, of Buckingham Tp., and Mary, his wife, dau. of Watson Welding: Watson Worthington b. 6th day of 8th month, 1796; Elizabeth Worthington b. 13th day of 10th month, 1797; Esther Worthington b. 15th day of 4th month, 1800; Amasa Worthington b. 11th day of 1st month, 1802; Ruth Worthington b. 19th day of 5th month, 1804; Benjamin Worthington b. 21st day of 4th month, 1806; Amos Worthington b. 18th day of 2nd month, 1810; Mary Ann Worthington b. 18th day of 6th month, 1815.

Children of William and Margaret Worthington, of Warwick Tp: Thomas Worthington b. 23rd day of 9th month, 1792; William Worthington b. 30th day of 10th month, 1793; Mary Worthington b. 23rd day of 3rd month, 1796; Jesse Worthington b. 8th day of 8th month, 1798; Spencer Worthington b. 21st day of 12th month, 1799; Esther Worthington b. 1st day of 1st month, 1802.

Children of William and Mary (?2nd wife) Worthington: Margaret Worthington b. 27th day of 11th month, 1806; Aseneth Worthington b. 25th day of 4th month, 1808; Mahlon Worthington b. 27th day of 9th month, 1809; Martha Worthington b. 4th day of 6th month, 1811; John Carver Worthington b. 20th day of 9th month, 1815.

Children of Joseph Smith, of Upper Makefield, and Rachael, his wife, dau. of John Hayhurst: Kezia Smith b. 2nd day of 2nd month, 1786; John Smith b. 16th day of 11th month, 1788; Eli Smith b. 27th day of 3rd month, 1791; Susanna Smith b. 3rd day of 9th

3rd month, 1801; Jesse Smith b. 3rd day of 7th month, 1804; Mary and Martha (twin) Smith b. 4th day of 3rd month, 1806.

Children of Samuel and Sarah Smith, of Wrightstown: John Smith b. 12th day of 12th month, 1794; Rebeccah Smith b. 20th day of 8th month, 1796; Phebe Smith b. 14th day of 6th month, 1798 and d. 6th day of 2nd month, 1801; Hannah Smith b. 27th day of 10th month, 1800; Benjamin Smith b. 9th day of 3rd month, 1803; Phebe Smith b. 5th day of 6th month, 1805; Samuel Smith b. 9th day of 7th month, 1808.

Children of Andrew Collins, of Buckingham Tp., and Martha, his wife, dau. of Joseph Lacey: Esther Collins, who m. William Wetherill, b. 24th day of 3rd month, 1783; Mary Collins b. 5th day of 3rd month, 1785; Andrew Collins b. 14th day of 2nd month, 1790 and d. 30th day of 8th month, 1847; Joseph Collins b. 15th day of 9th month, 1791; Rachael Collins b. 19th day of 2nd month, 1793; Martha Collins b. 11th day of 11th month, 1797.

Martha Collins d. 28th day of 2nd month, 1831.

Children of Silas Twining, of Northampton, and Elizabeth, his wife, dau. of Watson and Ruth Welding: Eleazer Twining b. 27th day of 5th month, 1794 and d. 1st day of 2nd month, 1797; Mary Twining b. 1st day of 2nd month, 1796 and d. 4th day of 2nd month, 1797; Ruth Twining b. 31st day of 11th month, 1797; Watson Twining b. 20th day of 11th month, 1799; Ann Twining b. 15th day of 7th month, 1801; Alice Twining b. 13th day of 8th month, 1803; Letitia Twining b. 25th day of 10th month, 1805; Silas Twining b. 27th day of 3rd month, 1807; Elizabeth Twining b. 10th day of 7th month, 1809; Samuel Twining b. 12th day of 12th month, 1810; Amos Twining b. 30th day of 4th month, 1813; Mary Twining b. 5th day of 11th month, 1817.

Children of Benjamin and Martha Hayhurst, of Upper Makefield (Removed to Solebury in 1822): Sarah Hayhurst b. 6th day of 3rd month, 1798; John Hayhurst b. 8th day of 9th month, 1799; Rachael Hayhurst b. 25th day of 4th month, 1801; Marmaduke Kinsey Hayhurst b. 5th day of 9th month, 1804 and d. 2nd day of 10th month, 1823; Ethelbert Hayhurst b. 3rd day of 12th month, 1806; Kezia Hayhurst b. 21st day of 8th month, 1810; Isaac Wiggins Hayhurst b. 26th day of 3rd month, 1813; Esther Kinsey Hayhurst b. 10th day of 2nd month, 1815; Margery Ann Hayhurst b. 10th day of 9th month, 1817; Lamar Wells Hayhurst b. 3rd day of 4th month, 1823.

Children of Mahlon and Rachael Trego, of Upper Makefield: Charles Trego b. 25th day of 11th month, 1794; Albert Trego b. 21st day of 4th month, 1796 and d. 10th day of 5th month, 1797; Phinehas Trego b. 12th day of 1st month, 1798; Elizabeth Trego b. 26th day of 11th month, 1799; Lewis Trego b. 1st day of 11th month, 1801; Robert Trego b. 24th day of 9th month, 1803; Mary Trego b. 14th day of 9th month, 1805; James Trego b. 1st day of 8th month, 1807; Joseph Briggs Trego b. 18th day of 5th month, 1809; Cyrus day of 9th month, 1805; James Trego b. 1st day of 8th month, 1807; Joseph Briggs Trego b. 18th day of 5th month, 1809; Cyrus Trego b. 15th day of 9th month, 1810; Edward Trego b. 3rd day of 11th month, 1812; Mahlon Trego b. 8th day of 9th month, 1815.

Children of David and Aseneth Warner, of Wrightstown: David Warner b. 9th day of 11th month, 1788; Joseph Warner b. 12th day of 4th month, 1793 and d. 25th day of 3rd month, 1867; Jonathan Warner (triplet) b. 27th day of 10th month, 1796 and d. 10th day of 11th month, 1796; Benjamin Warner (triplet) b. 27th day of 10th month, 1796 and d. 14th day of 11th month, 1796; Aseneth Warner (triplet) b. 27th day of 10th month, 1796; Elizabeth Warner b. 26th day of 7th month, 1798 and d. 14th day of 11th month, 1871.

Children of Jacob and Sarah Twining, of Wrightstown: Elizabeth Twining b. 21st day of 3rd month, 1782; John Twining b. 11th day of 8th month, 1783; Sarah Twining b. 5th day of 11th month, 1784; Jacob Twining b. 30th day of 6th month, 1786; Mahlon Twining b. 20th day of 11th month, 1787 and d. 11th day of 10th month, 1789; Susanna Twining b. 22nd day of 1st month, 1789; David Twining b. 5th day of 2nd month, 1791; William Twining b. 12th day of 2nd month, 1794 and d. 31st day of 3rd month, 1794; Rachael Twining b. 4th day of 3rd month, 1796; Henry M. Twining b. 17th day of 10th month, 1799

Children of William and Anna Smith, of Upper Makefield: Henry Smith b. 14th day of 2nd month, 1783; Mary Smith b. 23rd day of 11th month, 1784; Jane Smith b. 4th day of 11th month, 1786; Beaulah Smith b. 21st day of 3rd month, 1789; Nathan Smith b. 2nd day of 12th month, 1791; Aaron Smith b. 18th day of 2nd month, 1794; Samuel Smith b. 23rd day of 3rd month, 1796; Harvey Smith b. 27th day of 11th month, 1798; Anna Smith b. 17th day of 4th month, 1801.

Children of William Smith, of Solebury, son of Thomas and Sarah Smith, and Sarah, his wife, dau. of Jacob Buckman: William Smith b. 3rd day of 4th month, 1781; Sarah Smith b. 28th day of 6th month, 1783; Mary Smith b. 5th day of 6th month, 1785, mar. John Watts and d. 11th day of 10th month, 1809; Esther Smith b. 5th day of 4th month, 1787; Jacob B. Smith b. 28th day of 8th month, 1789; Amos Smith b. 10th day of 10th month, 1791; Rebeccah Smith b. 8th day of 7th month, 1794; Samuel Smith b. 4th day of 3rd month, 1797 and d. 18th day of 3rd month, 1797; Jane Smith b. 5th day of 8th month, 1798; John Smith b. 2nd day of 4th month, 1803.

Mary Smith Watts, dau. of above named Mary Smith, b. 19th day of 9th month, 1809.

Children of John Heston and Rachael, his wife, late Warner, of Wrightstown: Rebeckah Heston b. 7th day of 10th month, 1798; Esther Heston b. 3rd day of 6th month, 1800; Mercy Heston b. 25th day of 11th month, 1801; Hannah Heston b. 9th day of 9th month, 1805.

had lived most of their lives in Newtown Tp. but of late are of Buckingham Tp: Cyrus Buckman b. 27th day of 2nd month, 1796; Jane Buckman b. 10th day of 3rd month, 1806.

Children of James Dubre and Sarah, his wife, dau. of Joseph Lacey: Rachael Dubre b. 16th day of 10th month, 1779; Lemiramis Dubre b. 4th day of 12th month, 1780; Armella Dubre b. 16th day of 9th month, 1782; Esther Dubre b. 16th day of 7th month, 1784; Joseph Dubre b. 15th day of 8th month, 1786; Mary Dubre b. 16th day of 8th month, 1789; Martha Dubre b. 21st day of 3rd month, 1792.

Children of Isaiah Warner and Elizabeth, his wife: Hannah Warner b. 23rd day of 1st month, 1785 and d. 24th day of 1st month, 1827; John Warner b. 14th day of 1st month, 1787 and d. 1st day of 6th month, 1858; Amos Warner b. 21st day of 9th month, 1788 and d. 11th day of 3rd month, 1873; Elizabeth Warner b. 21st day of 2nd month, 1795 and d. 8th day of 11th month, 1865; Isaiah Warner b. 27th day of 7th month, 1798 and d. 10th day of 2nd month, 1848.

WRIGHTSTOWN MONTHLY MEETING CERTIFICATES OF REMOVAL

Mary Tomlinson, wife of William - certificate to Fairfax, Va. - 7th day of 2nd month, 1786.

John Merrick, wife Sarah, and children Elizabeth, Sarah, Amos, John and ___ - certificate to Buckingham - 7th day of 2nd month, 1786.

David Heston and children Tacey, David and Rachael - certificate to Northern District of Philadelphia - 2nd day of 5th month, 1786.

John Schoolfield, Jr. - certificate to Buckingham - 6th day of 6th month, 1786.

Mary Scott, wife of Benjamin - certificate to Buckingham - 5th day of 9th month, 1786.

Esther Penquite - certificate to Abington - 5th day of 9th month, 1786.

Oliver Hamton - certificate to Buckingham - 5th day of 9th month, 1786.

Rebeckah Gillam and husband - certificate to Sadsbury - 2nd day of 1st month, 1787.

Thomas Whilson, Jr. - certificate to Sadsbury - 3rd day of 4th month, 1787.

Thomas Buckman - certificate to the Falls - 5th day of 6th month, 1787.

Isaiah Quinby and wife, Mariam - certificate to Buckingham - 6th day of 2nd month, 1787.

Zebulon Heston, wife Rebecca, and children Hannah and Sarah - certificate to Gwynedd - 3rd day of 7th month, 1787.

Jesse Betts - certificate to Middletown - 4th day of 12th month, 1787.

Elizabeth Fell, wife of Thomas Fell - certificate to New Garden, in Chester Co. - 6th day of 5th month, 1788.

in Chester Co. - 6th day of 5th month, 1788.
Rebeckah Swiney, wife of James Swiney - certificate to Byberry - 3rd day of 6th month, 1788.
William Heston, wife Mercy and children Phineas, Marcy and Amos - certificate to Goose Creek, in Loudon Co., Va. - 8th day of 7th month, 1788.
William Heston - certificate to Goose Creek, Loudon Co., Va. - 8th day of 7th month, 1788.
Mark Watson - certificate to Abington - 5th day of 8th month, 1788.
Zacheriah Betts, wife Mary and children Marian, Esther, Samuel, Mercy, Thomas and Rachael - certificate to the Falls - 5th day of 8th month, 1788.
Jesse Leedom and wife Mary - certificate to Philadelphia - 2nd day of 9th month, 1788.
Benjamin Buckman - certificate to Middletown - 7th day of 10th month, 1788.
Rachael Scarborough - certificate to Buckingham - 4th day of 11th month, 1788.
Joseph Smith, wife Phebe and children Timothy, John, Rachael and Benjamin - certificate to Byberry - 4th day of 11th month, 1788.
Mary Lee - certificate to Gunpowder, Md. - 2nd day of 12th month, 1788.
Dorothy Balance - certificate to Northern District, Philadelphia 7th day of 4th month, 1789.
Sarah Scott, wife of John Scott - certificate to Little Falls of the Gunpowder - 5th day of 5th month, 1789.
William Briggs - certificate to Sadbury, Lancaster Co. - 2nd day of 6th month, 1789.
Joseph Johnson and wife Rachael - certificate to the Falls - 2nd day of 6th month, 1789.
Ann Doan - certificate to Middletown - 2nd day of 6th month, 1789.
Mahlon Heston and wife Jane - certificate to Horsham - 2nd day of 6th month, 1789.
James Hampton - certificate to Northern District, Philadelphia - 6th day of 10th month, 1789.
John ?Glulma, wife Elizabeth, and minor children Thomas and Benjamin - certificate to the Falls - 6th day of 10th month, 1789.
Hannah Watson - certificate to the Falls - 8th day of 12th month, 1789.
Samuel Smith - certificate to Indian Springs, Md. - 5th day of 1st month, 1790.
Seth Chapman, a minor, with consent of his father - certificate to Goshan, Chester Co. - 5th day of 1st month, 1790.
Susanna Stokes - certificate to Chesterfield - 2nd day of 2nd month, 1790.
John Heston - certificate to Goose Creek, Loudon Co., Va. - 2nd day of 3rd month, 1790.
David Davis - certificate to Horsham - 2nd day of 3rd month, 1790.
Mary Reeder - certificate to Goose Creek, Loudon Co., Va. - 17th

day of 3rd month, 1790.
Laura Linton - certificate to Buckingham - 8th day of 6th month, 1790.
Mary Whitson - certificate to the Falls - 8th day of 6th month, 1790.
Robert Thomas - certificate to Wilmington - 5th day of 10th month, 1790.
Rachael Fell, wife of Mahlon, and her children Ezra, Ann, Aaron, Moses, Elizabeth and Mahlon - certificate to Buckingham, then to Westland - 6th day of 4th month, 1790.
Ann Livezley - certificate to Haverford, Del. Co. - 6th day of 4th month, 1790.
John Stockdale - certificate to Gunpowder, in Md. - 3rd day of 5th month, 1791.
Joseph Knowles - certificate to the Falls - 4th day of 5th month, 1790.
Jason Merrick - certificate to Middletown - 8th day of 5th month, 1790.
Mary Jenks, late Hutchinson, wife of William Jenks - certificate to Middletown - 8th day of 3rd month, 1791
Elizabeth Taylor and husband - certificate to the Falls - 8th day of 3rd month, 1791.
Peter Blaker, his wife Sarah and minor children Abraham, Amos and David - certificate to Fairfax, Va. - 8th day of 3rd month, 1791.
John Blaker - certificate to Fairfax, Va. - 8th day of 3rd month, 1791.
Joseph Blaker - certificate to Fairfax, Va. - 8th day of 3rd month, 1791.
Susanna Newburn and children Susanna, William and John - certificate to Salem, N. J. - 5th day of 7th month, 1791.
Mary Curry and husband - certificate to Salem, N. J. - 5th day of 7th month, 1791.
Stephen Field, Jr. - certificate to Middletown - 5th day of 7th month, 1791.
Margaret Field - certificate to Middletown - 2nd day of 8th month, 1791.
Phebe and Abraham Hibbs, minor children of Abraham Hibbs, dec'd, to remove with their mother - certificate to the Falls - 6th day of 9th month, 1791.
Benjamin, Susanna and Hannah Hibbs, minor children of Abraham Hibbs, dec'd., to be placed as apprentices - certificate to Middletown - 6th day of 9th month, 1791.
Phebe Tomlinson - certificate to Byberry - 4th day of 10th month, 1791.
Phineas Buckman and children Susanna and Ruth - certificate to Buckingham - 4th day of 10th month, 1791.
Mary Hibbs - certificate to the Falls - 8th day of 11th month, 1791.
Deidamy Conrad, wife of Dennis - certificate to Horsham - 6th day of 12th month, 1791.
Isaac Wiggins and wife Phebe - certificate to Maidencreek - 3rd day of 4th month, 1792.
Ulyssies Wiggins and wife Sarah - certificate to Maidencreek -

3rd day of 4th month, 1792.

Elizabeth Wiggins - certificate to Maidencreek - 3rd day of 4th month, 1792.

Martha Wiggins - certificate to Maidencreek - 3rd day of 4th month, 1792.

Daniel Lee, wife Margaret and children Sarah, Eleanor, Rachael, John, Ruth and Margaret - certificate to Buckingham - 3rd day of 4th month, 1792.

Rebecca Hamton and daughter Mercy - certificate to Buckingham - 8th day of 6th month, 1792.

William Pennington, his wife Anna and children Martha, Thomas and Elizabeth - certificate to Horsham - 5th day of 6th month, 1792.

Jonathan Hampton and wife Elizabeth - certificate to Buckingham - 5th day of 6th month, 1792.

Ann Hampton, will go to reside with her daughter - certificate to Horsham - 4th day of 9th month, 1792.

Thomas Hilbourn, his wife and 6 minor children; Amos, John, Rachael, Stephen, Joseph and Phebe - certificate to Exeter - 4th day of 9th month, 1792.

Anna Hillbourn and her father - certificate to Exeter - 4th day of 9th month, 1792.

Joseph Chapman, as apprentice to Nathan Harper - certificate to Abington - 4th day of 9th month, 1792.

Thomas Smith - certificate to the Falls - 4th day of 9th month, 1792.

Elizabeth Hillbourn - certificate to Exeter - 2nd day of 10th month, 1792.

Randle Smith, a minor, to reside with his father Jacob Smith - certificate to Westland - 4th day of 12th month, 1792.

James Paxson and wife Mary - certificate to Exeter - 2nd day of 4th month, 1793.

Benjamin Chapman, a minor, to serve as apprentice to Joseph Budd certificate to Philadelphia - 5th day of 7th month, 1793.

James Simpson, to serve as apprentice to Hugh Davids - certificate to Rahway - 5th day of 7th month, 1793.

Rachael Beans - certificate to Buckingham - 8th day of 1st month, 1793.

Robert Faste, a minor, to serve as apprentice to Joseph Duer, Jun. - certificate to Buckingham - 11th day of 5th month, 1793.

John Ross, who settled in Easton, in Northampton Co. - certificate to Richland - 3rd day of 12th month, 1793.

Charles Chapman, his wife and children Susanna, Isaiah, Rebecca, Stephen, Elizabeth, Mercy, Mary, Charles, Letitia and Joseph - Certificate to Exeter - 4th day of 2nd month, 1794.

Isaac Smith - certificate to Gwined - 4th day of 2nd month, 1794.

Joseph Hampton, his wife Mary and children Mary, David, John, Joseph, Abner, Samuel, Hannah, Amos, Jonathan and Ann - certificate to Exeter - 2nd day of 4th month, 1794.

Precillia Reeder - certificate to Exeter - 8th day of 4th month, 1794.

Bezaleel Hayhurst, wife Susanna and children Thomas and William - certificate to Exeter - 8th day of 4th month, 1794.

Cephas Ross - certificate to New York - 6th day of 5th month, 1794.

David Tucker, wife Elizabeth and minor children James and Hannah - certificate tp Buckingham - 6th day of 5th month, 1794.

Mary Townall certificate to Buckingham - 8th day of 7th month, 1794.

Mercy Stockdale - certificate to the Falls - 7th day of 10th month, 1794.

Atkinson Ross - certificate to Philadelphia - 4th day of 11th month, 1794.

Joseph Scarborough - certificate to Buckingham - 3rd day of 3rd month, 1795.

Oliver Hampton - certificate to Buckingham - 7th day of 4th month, 1795.

Joseph Chapman, a minor, as apprentice to George ?Penock - certificate to Philadelphia - 6th day of 1st month, 1795.

Hannah Shinn, wife of Samuel Shinn - certificate to North Philadelphia - 6th day of 1st month, 1795.

Eber Smith - certificate to the Falls - 4th day of 8th month, 1795.

David Smith - certificate to the Falls - 4th day of 8th month, 1795.

Susannah Lownes - certificate to the Falls - 8th day of 9th month, 1795.

Hannah Smith - certificate to the Falls - 8th day of 9th month, 1795.

Amos Cooper - certificate to Horscham - 6th day of 10th month, 1795.

Catherine Wells, wife of John Wells - certificate to Newgarden - 5th day of 1st month, 1796.

Mary Rose, Jr. - certificate to High Street, Philadelphia - 5th day of 1st month, 1796.

John Past, Jr. - certificate to the Falls - 5th day of 4th month, 1796.

Jane Hamton - certificate to Catewisy - 7th day of 6th month, 1796.

Isaac Atkinson - certificate to Gunpowder, in Md. - 5th day of 7th month, 1796.

Margaret Smith - certificate to Cattawissy - 2nd day of 8th month, 1796.

Zebulon and Sarah Heston - certificate to Westland, Washington Co. - 6th day of 9th month, 1796.

Ebor Heston, wife Ann and children Abraham, Latitia, Ann, Mary and Sarah - certificate to Westland - 6th day of 9th month, 1796.

Daniel Linton - certificate to Westland - 6th day of 9th month, 1796.

Timothy Balderston, wife Rachael and minor children John, David, Mary, Lydia, Timothy and Isaiah - certificate to the Falls - 4th day of 10th month, 1796.

Sarah Balderston, to reside with her parents - certificate to the Falls - 4th day of 10th month, 1796.

Elizabeth Balderston, to reside with her parents - certificate to the Falls - 4th day of 10th month, 1796.

Rachael Balderston, to reside with her parents - certificate to the Falls - 4th day of 10th month, 1796.
Amos Briggs - certificate to the Falls - 4th day of 10th month, 1796.
Ruth Worstal, wife of John Worstal - certificate to the Falls - 4th day of 10th month, 1796.
Thomas Ross - certificate to High Street, Philadelphia - 8th day of 11th month, 1796.
James Buckman, wife Sarah and children Phineas, Rachael, Jane, Lydia, Julian, James, Amos and Sarah - certificate to the Falls - 3rd day of 1st month, 1797.
Sarah Ross, wife of William Ross - certificate to Philadelphia - 3rd day of 1st month, 1797
Rachael Watson - certificate to the Falls - 7th day of 3rd month, 1797.
Ann Schoolfield - certificate to Indian Spring, Md. - 7th day of 3rd month, 1797.
Deborah Rose - certificate to High Street, Philadelphia - 4th day of 4th month, 1797.
Strickland Martingill - certificate to the Falls - 4th day of 4th month, 1797.
John Paste, wife Alice and children Jolly, Alice, George, Jonathan and Eucloridas - certificate to the Falls - no date given.
Hannah Heston, Mercy Heston and Sarah Heston, minor children of Zebulon Heston, to reside with their mother Rebeckah - certificate to Calawisy - 2nd day of 5th month, 1797.
Sarah Shallcross, wife of Benjamin - certificate to Abington - 4th day of 7th month, 1797.
Tamar Palmer, wife of David - certificate to the Falls - 6th day of 2nd month, 1798.
Rachael Wisnar - certificate to Calawisy - 6th day of 2nd month, 1798.
Aldon Buckman - certificate to the Falls - 2nd day of 1st month, 1798.
Ann Lee - certificate to Buckingham - 6th day of 3rd month, 1798.
Isaiah Heston, who resides with Atkinson Rose - certificate to Philadelphia - 3rd day of 4th month, 1798.
Sarah Cooper - certificate to Horsham - 8th day of 5th month, 1798.
Amos Wilkinson - certificate to Philadelphia - 8th day of 5th month, 1798.
Samuel Ross - certificate to Philadelphia - 8th day of 5th month, 1798.
Thomas Chapman - certificate to Richland - 5th day of 6th month, 1798.
Elizabeth Warton, wife of William Warton - certificate to the Falls - 7th day of 8th month, 1798.
Mary Vanhorn - certificate to Middletown - 4th day of 9th month, 1798.
Ely Welding - certificate to North Philadelphia - 6th day of 11th month, 1798.
Elizabeth Heston - certificate to Westland - 8th day of 1st month, 1799.

Sarah Warner, wife of Benjamin Warner - certificate to Catterwisy - 5th day of 2nd month, 1799.
Margaret Chapman - certificate to New Garden - 2nd day of 4th month, 1799.
Jane Hilborn - certificate to Buckingham - 7th day of 5th month, 1799.
Amos Hilborn, wife Ruth, infant son John, and Amos Wilborn's brother John, a minor - certificate to Horsham - 7th day of 5th month, 1799.
Armella Dubre, a minor, who has removed with John Hampton - certificate to Middletown - 4th day of 6th month, 1799.
Mary Hillborn - certificate to Horsham - 4th day of 6th month, 1799.
David Buckman wife Esther, and 8 minor children John, David, Edmund, Deborah, Oliver, Benjamin, Esther and Anna - certificate to the Falls - 2nd day of 7th month, 1799.
Sarah Linton - certificate to Middletown - 2nd day of 7th month, 1799.
Elizabeth Price, wife of John Price - certificate to Buckingham - 6th day of 8th month, 1799.
William Cooper, wife Mary, and 7 minor children John, Mary, Henry, Rachael, Caroline, James and Elizabeth - certificate to Horsham -3rd day of 9th month, 1799.
Samuel Smith - certificate to Sudsbury - 3rd day of 9th month, 1799.
Bridgit Smith - certificate to Buckingham - 5th day of 11th month, 1799.
Joseph Wilson - certificate to Abington - 5th day of 11th month, 1799.
David Newburn - certificate to Redstone _ 3rd day of 12th month, 1799.
Mary Jewel - certificate to Baltimore - 7th day of 1st month, 1800.
Elizabeth Knowles, wife of Banner Knowles - certificate to the Falls - 4th day of 3rd month, 1800.
John Simpson and wife Ruth - certificate to Horsham - 8th day of 4th month, 1800.
Rachael Buckman - certificate to the Falls - 4th day of 6th month, 1799.
Joseph Ballance, wife Anna and children John, Rachael, Mary, Simeon, Catherine, Susanna and Joseph - certificate to the Falls - 6th day of 5th month, 1800.
David Heston, wife Phebe and minor children Elizabeth Heston, Mary Heston, Jesse Heston, Phebe Smith, Marshall Smith and Cyrus Smith - certificate to Buckingham - 5th day of 8th month, 1800.
Tasey Heston - certificate to Buckingham - 5th day of 8th month, 1800.
Rachael Heston - certificate to Buckingham - 5th day of 8th month, 1800.
David Heston, Jr. - certificate to Buckingham - 5th day of 8th month, 1800.
Sarah Dubre - certificate to the Falls - 2nd day of 9th month, 1800.

Mercy Chapman, to reside with brother-in-law William Ross - certificate to Philadelphia - 7th day of 10th month, 1800.
Mahlon Cooper and children John, Ester and Levy - certificate to Buckingham - 5th day of 5th month, 1800.

WRIGHTSTOWN MONTHLY MEETING MARRIAGE RECORDS

Isaac Kirk, of Buckingham Tp., Bucks Co., son of John Kirk, of Darby Tp., co. aforesaid, m. 9th day of 10th month, 1730, Elizabeth Twining, dau. of Stephen Twining, of Newtown, co. aforesaid.
Thomas Lancaster, of Wrightstown, Bucks Co., m. 19th day of 8th month, 1725, Phebe Wardell, of same place.
Zebulon Heston, nr. Wrightstown, Bucks Co., m. 22nd day of 4th month, 1726, Elizabeth Buckman, of Newtown, co. aforesaid.
Jonathan Wilson, son of David Wilson, of Southampton Tp., Bucks Co., m. 25th day of 4th month, 1759, Sarah Mardon, dau. of Thomas Mardon, of Bybury, Philadelphia Co.
Thomas Atkinson, son of John Atkinson of Wrightstown, Bucks Co., m. 18th day of 8th month, 1744, Mary Wildman, of Middletown, co. aforesaid.
Daniel Pennington, of Newbritain, Bucks Co., m. 26th day of 3rd month, 1760, Martha Ball, of Wrightstown, co. aforesaid.
Benjamin Wiggins, son of Berzeleel Wiggins, of Bucks Co. m. 14th day of 5th month, 1760, Sarah Warner, dau. of Joseph Warner, late of Wrightstown, co. aforesaid, dec'd.
Benjamin Hamton, of Wrightstown, Bucks Co., m. 28th day of 9th month, 1750, Ann Wildman, of same place.
Mechack Mitchener, son of William Mitchener, of Plumstead, Bucks Co., m. 24th day of 11th month, 1761, Mary Trego, dau. of John Trego, of Upper Makefield Tp., co. aforesaid.
William Lacey, son of John Lacey, of Buckingham Tp., Bucks Co., m. 15th day of 4th month, 1760. Elizabeth Gourley, of Wrightstown, co. aforesaid.
John Hirst, son of John Hirst, late of Buckingham Tp., Bucks Co., dec'd, m. 30th day of 4th month, 1760, Mary Heston, dau. of Zebulon Heston, of Upper Makefield Tp., co. aforesaid.
Francis Good, of Plumstead Tp., Bucks Co., m. 11th day of 11th month. 1762, Sarah Roberts, of same place.
James Hibbs, son of William Hibbs, of Northampton Tp., Bucks Co., m. 21st day of 4th month, 1762, Sarah Blaker, dau. of John Blaker, of same.
Isaac Buckman, son of William Buckman, late of Newtown, Bucks Co., m. 28th day of 10th month, 1762, Sarah Cutter, dau. of Thomas Cutter, late of same place, dec'd.
Daniel Richardson, son of Daniel Richardson, of Buckingham Tp., Bucks Co., dec'd. m. 24th day of 11th month, 1762, Sarah Janney, dau. of Thomas Janney, of Newtown, co. aforesaid, dec'd.
Richard Mason, son of Benjamin Mason, of No. Liberties of City of Philadelphia, m. 16th day of 6th month, 1762, Elizabeth Chapman, dau. of Abraham Chapman, of Wrightstown, Bucks Co., dec'd.

18th day of 4th month, 1765, Mary Wilkinson, dau. of John Wilkinson, os Wrightstown, co. aforesaid.
John Hayhurst, son of Cuthbert Hayhurst, of Northampton, Bucks Co., m. 9th day of 6th month, 1762, Mary Wiggins, dau. of Berzaleel Wiggins, of Upper Makefield, co. aforesaid.
William Heston, son of Zebulon Heston, of Upper Makefield, Bucks Co., m. 14th day of 12th month, 1763, Mercy Cutter, dau. of Benjamin Cutter, of Middletown, co. aforesaid.
James Spicer, of Buckingham Tp. Bucks Co., m. 28th day of 9th month, 1750, Rachael Wildman, of Wrightstown, co. aforesaid.
William Atkinson, of Makefield Tp., Bucks Co., m. 1st of 7th month, 1742, Mary Tomlinson, of same.
Joseph Wiggins, joiner, son of Bazaleel Wiggins, of Upper Makefield, Bucks Co., m. 7th day of 9th month, 1768, Sarah Trego, dau. of John Trego, yeoman, of same.
Timothy Balderston, son of John Balderston, of Solebury, Bucks Co., m. 4th day of 4th month, 1770, Rachael Twining, dau. of John Twining, of Newtown, co. aforesaid.
David Hallowell, son of William Hallowell, of Cheltingham Tp., Philadelphia Co., yeoman, m. 13th day of 4th month, 1770, Abigale Comly, dau. of Joseph Comly, of Wrightstown, Bucks Co.
Jonathan Scholfield, son of John Scholfield, late of Solebury, Bucks Co., dec'd, m. 17th day of 5th month, 1769, Rebeckah Beaumont, dau. of John Beaumont, of Upper Makefield Tp., co. aforesaid.
Joseph Twining, of Newtown, Bucks Co., son of John Twining, the younger, m. 27th day of 12th month, 1769, Mary Lee, dau. of William Lee, of Upper Makefield, co. aforesaid.
John Carver, son of John Carver, yeoman, of Byberry Tp., Philadelphia Co., m. 22nd day of 5th month, 1771, Mary Buckman, dau. of Joseph Buckman, of Newtown, Bucks Co.
Anthony Hartly, son of Thomas Hartly, of Solebury Tp., Bucks Co., m. 17th day of 4th month, 1771, Sarah Betts, dau. of Thomas Betts, of Buckingham, co. aforesaid.
John Watson, son of Joseph Watson, Esq., of Buckingham Tp., Bucks Co., Practitioner in Physickn. 1st day of 1st month, 1772, Mary Hampton, dau. of Benjamin Hampton, of Wrightstown, co. aforesaid.
Joseph Smith, son of Timothy Smith, of Buckingham Tp., Bucks Co., Blacksmith, m. 9th day of 11th month, 1774, Ann Smith, dau. of Samuel Smith, of Upper Makefield, co. aforesaid.
Joseph Hillborn, son of Samuel Hillborn, of Lower Smithfield, Co. of Northampton, yeoman, m. 10th day of 5th month, 1775, Ann Wilkinson, dau. of Ichabod Wilkinson, of Solebury Tp., Bucks Co.
Joseph Hamton, son of John Hamton, late of Wrightstown, Bucks Co., yeoman, dec'd, m. 20th day of 12th month, 1775, Mary Blaker, dau. of John Blaker, of Northampton Tp., co. aforesaid.
William Trego, cordwainer, son of John Trego, yeoman, of Upper Makefield Tp., Bucks Co., m. 14th day of 9th month, 1768, Rebeckah Hibbs, dau. of William Hibbs, of Biberry, Co. of Philadelphia, cordwainer.
George Mitchell, son of William Mitchell, dec'd, of Buckingham

George Mitchell, son of William Mitchell, dec'd, of Buckingham Tp., Bucks Co., m. 9th day of 10th month, 1776 Susanna Betts, dau. of Thomas Betts, of Wrightstown, co. aforesaid.
Robert Ware, of Wrightstown, Bucks Co., m. 21st day of 10th month, 1778, Elizabeth Paxson, of Upper Makefield Tp., co. aforesaid.
William Buckman, Jr., of Newtown, Bucks Co., m. 3rd day of 11th month, 1744, Jane Biggs, of same.
James Dubre, of Solebury, Bucks Co., m. 17th day of 2nd month, 1779, Sarah Lacey, of Buckingham Tp., co. aforesaid.
Zachariah Betts, of Solebury, Bucks Co., son of Thomas Betts, dec'd, m. 20th day of 4th month, 1779, Mary Lacey, dau. of Joseph Lacey, late of Buckingham Tp., co. aforesaid, dec'd.
Isaiah Linton, of Wrightstown, Bucks Co., m. 24th day of 10th month, 1764, Sarah Hirst, of same place.
William Linton, son of John Linton, late of Wrightstown, Bucks Co., dec'd, m. 30th day of 4th month, 1766, Sarah Penquite, dau. of John Penquite, late of Wrightstown, co. aforesaid, dec'd.
Joseph Heston, son of Zebulon Heston, of Upper Makefield, Bucks Co., m. 12th day of 4th month, 1780, Phebe Smith, dau. of Samuel Smith, of same place.
Joel Carver, son of Joseph Carver, of Buckingham Tp., Bucks Co., m. 26th day of 11th month, 1776, Ann Smith, dau. of Robert Smith, of Wrightstown, co. aforesaid.
Charles Chapman, son of James Chapman, late of Wrightstown, Bucks Co., dec'd, m. 15th day of 11th month, 1775, Elizabeth Linton, Jr., dau. of John Linton, late of same place, dec'd.
Edward Blackfan, son of Crispin Blackfan, of Solebury Tp., Bucks Co., yeoman, m. 12th day of 12th month, 1781, Mary Smith, dau. of Thomas Smith, of same place, shopkeeper.
Daniel Carlile, son of John Carlile, of Plumstead Tp., Bucks Co., m. 19th day of 12th month, 1781, Elizabeth Smith, dau. of Samuel Smith, of Upper Makefield, co. aforesaid.
Joshua Vansant, son of Joshua Vansant, of Lower Makefield Tp., Bucks Co., yeoman, m. 21st day of 2nd month, 1769, Elizabeth Buckman, dau. of William Buckman, of Newtown, co. aforesaid, yeoman.
John Wilkinson, Jr. son of John Wilkinson, Esq., of Wrightstown, Bucks Co., m. 26th day of 4th month, 1769, Jane Chapman, dau. of Abraham Chapman, of same place, yeoman.
John Terry, son of John Terry, of Wrightstown, Bucks Co., m. 22nd day of 11th month, 1769, Sarah Davis, dau. of Griffith Davis, of Solebury, co. aforesaid.
John Chapman, of Wrightstown, Bucks Co., son of John Chapman, surveyor, and Ruth, his wife, of same place, m. 25th day of 6th month, 1767, Mercy Beaumont, dau. of John and Sarah Beaumont, of Upper Makefield Tp., co. aforesaid.
Thomas Wilson, son of Samuel Wilson, of Buckingham, Bucks Co., m. 20th day of 3rd month, 1765, Macre Crosdale, of Newtown, co. aforesaid.
Joseph Lees, of Blockly , Co. of Philadelphia, m. 4th day of 12th month, 1759, Elizabeth Strandling, of Newtown, Bucks Co.
John Butler, of Newtown, Bucks Co., m. 17th day of 1st month,

1740, Mary Fisher, of same place.
Joseph Paxon, of Solebury, m. 28th day of 6th month, 1758, Mary Heston, Jr., of Upper Makefield, Bucks co.
James Wood, of Wrightstown, Bucks Co., m. 23rd day of 11th month, 1752, Mary Smith, of same place.
Abraham Chapman, of Wrightstown, Bucks Co., m. 2nd day of 2nd month, 1740, Elizabeth Briggs, of Newtown, co. aforesaid.
Daniel White, of Buckingham, Bucks Co., m. 12th day of 9th month, 1751, Mary Laycock, Jr., of Wrightstown, co. aforesaid.
John Titus, of Hemstead, in Queens Co., on Long Island, m. 4th day of 5th month, 1757, Phebe Thomas, of Upper Makefield Tp., Bucks Co.
Robert Smith, of Wrightstown, Bucks Co., m. 11th day of 4th month, 1750, Rachael Hibbs, of Buckingham Tp., co. aforesaid.
Thomas Betts, of Middletown, m. 21st day of 9th month, 1744, Sarah Smith, of Makefield Tp., Bucks Co.
Isaac Wilson, of Makefield, Bucks Co., m. 19th day of 10th month, 1744, Sarah Hamton, of Wrightstown, co. aforesaid.
John Lacey, of Buckingham, Bucks Co., m. 14th day of 3rd month, 1746, Jane Chapman, of Wrightstown, co. aforesaid.
Jacob Neulings, of Eveshane, Co. of Burlington, in New Jersey, m. 27th day of 9th month, 1750, Agnes Buckman of Newtown, Bucks Co.
James Moore, son of Andrew Moore, dec'd, of Sadsbury Tp., Lancaster Co., m. 3rd day of 10th month, 1764, Mary Atkinson, widow of Thomas Atkinson, late of Wrightstown, Bucks Co
Thomas Wilson, of Bristol Tp., Bucks Co., son of Samuel Wilson, of Buckingham Tp., co. aforesaid, m. 14th day of 4th month, 1779, Sarah Fell, dau. of John Fell, late of Warwick Tp., co. aforesaid, dec'd.
James Burson, of Springfield, Bucks Co., son of Joseph Burson, m. 6th day of 2nd month, 1782, Sarah Twining, of Wrightstown, co. aforesaid, dau. of William Worth, of Windsor, Co. of Middlesex, in E. New Jersey.
Levi Pownall, of Solebury Tp., Bucks Co., son of Simeon Pownall, late of same place, dec'd, m. 12th day of 6th month, 1782, Elizabeth Buckman, dau. of Joseph Buckman, of Newtown Tp., co. aforesaid
John Warner, Jr., son of John Warner, of Wrightstown, Bucks Co., yeoman, m. 18th day of 11th month, 1772, Phebe Smith, dau. of Robert Smith, of same place, yeoman.
Joseph Ely, son of George Ely, of Solebury, m. 12th day of 3rd month, 1783, Mary Whilson, dau. of Thomas Whilson, of same.
Hamton Wilson, son of Isaac Wilson, late of Upper Makefield, Bucks Co., dec'd, m. 15th day of 11th month, 1774, Ann Briggs, dau. of James Briggs, of Newtown, co. aforesaid.
Mahlon Worthington, son of Richard Worthington, of Buckingham Tp., Bucks Co., m. 10th day of 11th month, 1779, Mary Smith, of Wrightstown, co. aforesaid.
Andrew Collins, Jr., son of Andrew Collins, of Upper Makefield Tp., Bucks Co., m. 15th day of 5th month, 1782, Martha Lacey, dau. of Joseph Lacey, late of Buckingham Tp., co. aforesaid, dec'd.
Stephen Wilson, son of Isaac Wilson, of Upper Makefield, Bucks

Co., m. 10th day of 9th month, 1783, Mercy Doan, dau. of Benjamin Doan, of same place.

John Buckman, son of John Buckman, of Lower Makefield, Bucks Co., yeoman, m. 21st day of 4th month, 1773, Susannah Chapman, dau. of William Chapman, of Wrightstown, co. aforesaid.

Eber Heston, son of Zebulon Heston, of Upper Makefield Tp., Bucks Co., m. 12th day of 11th month, 1783, Ann Spicer, dau. of James Spicer, of Baltimore Co., in State of Md.

William Hopkins, son of Samuel Hopkins, late of Baltimore Co., State of Md., dec'd, m. 12th day of 11th month, 1783, Elizabeth Twining, dau. of David Twining, of Newtown, Bucks Co.

John Smith, son of Robert Smith, of Wrightstown, Bucks Co., m. 19th day of 11th month, 1777, Sarah Smith, dau. of Thomas Smith, of Upper Makefield, co. aforesaid.

Joseph Kinsey, of Buckingham Tp., Bucks Co., son of Joseph Kinsey, dec'd, m. 19th day of 11th month, 1783, Ann Plunkitt, dau. of John Plunkitt, of Wrightstown, co. aforesaid.

Isaiah Warner, of Wrightstown, Bucks Co., son of John Warner, dec'd, m. 14th day of 4th month, 1784, Elizabeth Closon, dau. of John Closon, of Plumstead, co. aforesaid.

Isaiah Quinby, of Amwell Tp., Hunterdon Co., New Jersey, m. 20th day of 9th month, 1786, Mariam Betts, of Solebury Tp., Bucks Co.

William Chapman, son of William Chapman, of Wrightstown, Bucks Co., miller, m. 21st day of 12th month, 1774, Sarah Buckman, dau. of William Buckman, of Newtown, co. aforesaid, yeoman.

Jesse Leedom, son of Richard Leedom, of Northampton Tp., Bucks Co., m. 23rd day of 4th month, 1788, Mary Twining, dau. of David Twining, of Newtown, co. aforesaid, yeoman.

William Linton, son of John Linton, of Wrightstown, Bucks Co., dec'd, m. 19th day of 3rd month, 1788, Mary Janney, dau. of Thomas Janney, of Newtown, co. aforesaid.

Joseph Wiggins, son of Benjamin Wiggins, of Upper Makefield Tp, Bucks Co, m. 12th day of 11th month, 1788, Mary Heston, dau. of Jesse Heston, of same place.

Mahlon Heston, son of Zebulon Heston, of Upper Makefield Tp., Bucks Co., m. 19th day of 11th month, 1788, Jane Smith, dau. of Samuel Smith, of same place.

John Rose, son of James Rose, of Wrightstown, Bucks Co., weaver, m. 29th day of 10th month, 1766, Mary Atkinson, dau. of William Atkinson, of Upper Makefield, co. aforesaid, yeoman.

William Jenks, son of Joseph Jenks, of Middletown, Bucks Co., m. 20th day of 10th month, 1790, Mary Hutchinson, dau. of Michael Hutchinson, late of Lower Makefield, co. aforesaid, dec'd.

Jesse Lacey, son of Joseph Lacey, late of Buckingham Tp., Bucks Co., dec'd, m. 7th day of 11th month, 1790, Tamer Worthington, dau. of Richard Worthington, of same place.

Dennis Conrod, of Horsham Tp., in Co. of Montgomery, m. 7th day of 10th month, 1791, Dudamia Briggs, dau. of Edmund Biggs, late of Bucks Co., dec'd.

Isaac Wiggins, son of Bezeleel Wiggins, of Upper Makefield, Bucks Co., m. 12th day of 12th month, 1764, Phebe Blaker, dau. of John Blaker, of Northampton, co. aforesaid.

John Lacey, son of John Lacey, late of Buckingham Tp., Bucks Co., dec'd, m. 21st day of 3rd month, 1792, Rachael Wiggins, dau. of Benjamin Wiggins, of Upper Makefield Tp., co. aforesaid.
Mahlon Beans, son of Jacob Beans, of Solebury Tp., Bucks Co., m. 17th day of 10th month, 1792, Rachel Hillborn, dau. of Robert Hilborn, of Newtown, co. aforesaid.
David Simpson, son of John Simpson, of Solebury Tp., Bucks Co., m. 14th day of 5th month, 1794, Agnes Wiggins, dau. of Benjamin Wiggins, of Upper Makefield Tp., co. aforesaid
Samuel Shinn, of co. of Philadelphia, m. 18th day of 3rd month, 1795, Hannah Simpson, dau. of John Simpson, of Solebury, Bucks Co.
Silas Twining, son of Eleazer Twining, of Warwick Tp., Bucks Co., m. 13th day of 11th month, 1793, Elizabeth Wilding, dau. of Watson Wilding, of Wrightstown, co. aforesaid.
Jacob Heston, Jr., son of Jesse Heston, of Upper Makefield, Bucks Co., m. 22nd day of 4th month, 1795, Rachael Terry, dau. of John Terry, of Wrightstown, co. aforesaid.
Samuel Davis, son of Samuel Davis, of Solebury Tp., Bucks Co., m. 20th day of 5th month, 1795, Lydia Morris, dau. of Issachar Morris, of Wrightstown, co. aforesaid.
William Lownes, Jr., son of William Lownes, of Upper Makefield, Bucks Co., m. 10th day of 6th month, 1795, Susanna Stokes, dau. of James Stokes, of same place.
John Fell, son of Joseph Fell, late of Upper Makefield Tp., Bucks Co., dec'd, and Rachael, his wife, m. 14th day of 10th month, 1795, Edith Smith, dau. of Samuel and Jane Smith, of same.
Abraham Wilkinson, son of John Wilkinson, dec'd, of Warwick, m. 18th day of 11th month, 1795, Mary Twining, dau. of Eleazer Twining, of same place.
Benjamin Worthington, son of William Worthington, of Buckingham Tp., Bucks Co., m. 21st day of 10th month, 1795, Mary Wilding, dau. of Watson Wilding, of Wrightstown, co. aforesaid.
John Worstall, of the Falls Tp., Bucks Co., son of James and Esther (she being dec'd) Worstall, of co. aforesaid, m. 18th day of 5th month, 1796, Ruth Hilbourn, dau. of Samuel Hilbourn, dec'd, and Ruth, his wife, of Newtown, co. aforesaid.
William Ross, merchant, of City of Philadelphia, son of Thomas Ross, of City and State of New York, and Ann, his wife, dec'd, m. 19th day of 10th month, 1796, Sarah Chapman, dau. of John Chapman, of Upper Makefield, Bucks Co., and Mercy, his wife., dec'd.
Charles Reeder, son of David Reeder, of Upper Makefield, Bucks Co., m. 19th day of 10th month, 1796, Jane Atkinson, dau. of John Atkinson, of same place.
David Watson, son of Joseph and Rachael Watson, of Lower Makefield, Bucks Co., m. 16th day of 11th month, 1796, Rachael Twining, dau. of Stephen and Mary Twining, of Newtown Tp., co. aforesaid.
Isaac Wilson, son of Isaac Wilson, of Upper Makefield Tp., Bucks Co., dec'd, m. 14th day of 12th month, 1796, Rachael Smith, dau. of Joseph Smith, of Wrightstown, co. aforesaid.
Ezra Wharton, son of Daniel Wharton, of Lower Makefield Tp.,

Bucks Co., m. 19th day of 4th month, 1797, Martha Terry, dau. of Jasper Terry, of Upper Makefield Tp., co. aforesaid.

Benjamin Shallcross, son of Leonard Shallcross, of Co. of Philadelphia, m. 10th day of 5th month, 1797, Sarah Chapman, dau. of Joseph Chapman, dec'd, of Bucks Co.

[John Balderston, of Falls Tp., Bucks Co., son of John and Deborah Balderston, of Solebury Tp., said co., m. 19th day of 11th month, Elizabeth Buckman, daughter of William Buckman, of Newtown Tp., co aforesaid.]

John Betts, of Buckingham, Bucks Co., son of Thomas Betts, dec'd, and Sarah, his wife, m. 10th day of 5th month, 1797, Hannah Kirk, dau. of Stephen and Phebe Kirk, both dec'd, of Springfield, co. aforesaid.

David Palmer, son of Jonathan and Ann Palmer, of Lower Makefield, Bucks Co., m. 15th day of 11th month, 1797, Tamar Twining, dau. of Stephen and Mary Twining, of Newtown Tp, co. aforesaid.

John Heston, son of Jesse Heston, of Upper Makefield Tp., Bucks Co., m. 2nd day of 11th month, 1797, Rachael Warner, dau. of John Warner, of Goshen Tp., Co. of Chester.

Amos Hilbourn, son of Robert Hilbourn, late of Newtown Tp., Bucks Co., dec'd, m. 13th day of 12th month, 1797, Ruth Simpson, dau. of John Simpson, of Solebury, co. aforesaid.

Benajah Hayhurst, of Upper Makefield, Bucks Co., son of John and Mary Hayhurst, of same place, m. 10th day of 5th month, 1797, Martha Kinsey, dau. of Benjamin Kinsey, late of Plumstead, co. aforesaid, dec'd, and Martha, his wife.

William Wharton, son of William and Mary Wharton, of Lower Makefield, Bucks Co., , m. 16th day of 5th month, 1798, Elizabeth Morris, dau. of Isachar and Hannah Morris, of Wrightstown, co. aforesaid.

John Chapman, Jr., of Upper Makefield, Bucks Co., son of John Chapman, and Mercy, his wife, dec'd, of same place, m. 13th day of 6th month, 1798, Rebekah Hutchinson, dau. of John Hutchinson, of Bristol Tp., co. aforesaid.

Edmund Smith, of Upper Makefield, Bucks Co., son of Thomas Smith, of Buckingham Tp., co. aforesaid, and Elizabeth, his wife, m. 11th day of 4th month, 1798, Mary Briggs, dau. of John Storey and Elizabeth, his wife.

Jacob Thomas, son of Mordecai Thomas and Elizabeth, his wife, of Moreland Tp., Co. of Montgomery, m. 14th day of 11th month, 1798, Rachael Leedom, dau. of Richard Leedom, and Sarah, his wife, of Northampton Tp., Bucks Co.

Benjamin Warner, of Muncy, in Co. of Lycoming m. 5th day of 12th month, 1798, Sarah Terry, of Wrightstown, Bucks Co.

Amos Warner, of Wrightstown, Bucks Co., son of Crosdale Warner, of Co. of Harford, State of Md., m. 24th day of 4th month, 1799, Susannah Buckman, dau. of John Buckman, of Newtown, co.

Banner Knowles, son of John and Mary Knowles, of Upper Makefield, Bucks Co., m. 11th day of 12th month, 1799, Elizabeth Hayhurst, dau. of John and Mary Hayhurst, of same place.

David Heston, son of Zebulon Heston, late of Upper Makefield, Bucks Co., yeoman, dec'd, m. 21st day of 5th month, 1800, Phebe Smith, dau. of Thomas Marshall, late of Concord, Co. of

Chester, yeoman, dec'd.

Benjamin Wiggins, Jr., son of Benjamin and Sarah Wiggins, of Upper Makefield, Bucks Co., m. 12th day of 11th month, 1800, Mary Buckman, dau. of John and Susannah Buckman, of Newtown, co. aforesaid.

John Balderston, of the Falls Tp., son of John and Deborah Balderston, of Solebury, m. 19th day of 11th month, 1800, Elizabeth Buckman, dau. of William Buckman, of Newtown.

John Buckman, son of John Buckman, of Lower Makefield Tp., Bucks Co., yeoman, m. 21st day of 4th month, 1773, _ _ _ ?, dau. of William, of Wrightstown, blacksmith.

Samuel Swain, of Bristol Tp., Bucks Co., son of Abraham and Sarah Swain, m. 14th day of 1st month, 1800, Sarah Briggs, dau, of John and Letitia Briggs, of Wrightstown, co. aforesaid.

Elias Twining, son of Stephen Twining, of Newtown Tp., Bucks Co., m. 16th day of 4th month, 1794, Mary Stokes, dau. of James Stokes, of Upper Makefield Tp., co. aforesaid.

Jacob Heston, son of Jacob Heston, of Upper Makefield Tp., Bucks Co., m. 13th day of 11th month, 1791, Elisabeth Smith, dau. of Benjamin Smith, of Buckingham Tp., co. aforesaid.

EXTRACTS FROM MEN'S MINUTES OF WRIGHTSTOWN MONTHLY MEETING

Only those items pertaining to marriages and removal have been extracted [occasionally other breaches of discipline have been included here]. The reader may wish to examine copies of the complete minutes regarding other aspects of individual discipline [failure to pay just debts, drinking to excess, fighting, serving in the militia, attending shooting matches, etc.], and items of business of the Meeting [building repairs, appointments of overseers, committees, etc.] all of which have not been transcribed here. References to unspecified breaches of discipline were not included.

These minutes (1734-1790) were transcribed by C. Arthur Smith, Wycombe, Pa. in 1934. Information in brackets was obtained in a later minute.

3/7/1734 - At a Quarterly Meeting held at Middletown in Bucks Co. 29th of 6th month 1734 [was established the monthly meetings of Wrightstown, Buckingham and Plumstead.]
5/8/1754 - Jacob Jones requests certificate to Monthly Meeting at Phila.
4/1/1734 - Bezeliell Wiggins and Rachel Hayhurst, a member of Middletown Monthly Meeting, to marry.
1/2/1735 - John Cooper condemns his outgoing, his wife being with child before marriage. Cephas Child requests certificate for his family to Buckingham Monthly Meeting.
3/4/1735 - Marriage of Thomas Furnis and Rachel Hillborne accomplished. [Thomas belongs to another mm.]
3/5/1735 - John Blaker and Catherine Williams, dau. of Isaac Williams of Middletown Monthly Meeting, to marry.
3/6/1735 - Marriage of Henry Tyson and Ann Harker accomplished on 16/5/1735. [Henry produces certificate from Abington Monthly Meeting.]
3/12/1735 - Thomas Strickland requests certificate to Monthly Meeting at Phila.
2/1/1736 - Samuel Hilborn and Abigail Twining to marry. Nicholas Penquite requests certificate for himself and wife and family to Monthly Meeting at Buckingham.
6/2/1736 - By his father, John Strickland requests certificate to Monthly Meeting of Phila for himself and family. Informed that Samuel Hillborn and Abigail Twining have taken another way to consummate their marriage.
4/3/1736 - Amos Strickland produces certificate from Abington Monthly Meeting. Thomas Butler requests certificate for himself and family to Buckingham Monthly Meeting.
6/5/1736 - Marriage of Adrian Daws and Susannah Wilkinson accomplished [Adrian has produces certificate from Gwynedd Monthly Meeting.]
7/7/1736 - James Rose produces certificate from Buckingham Monthly Meeting. George Newburn produces certificate from Gwynedd Monthly Meeting. Marriage of John Trego and Hannah Lester accomplished 25th of last month.
2/9/1736 - Marriage of Amos Strickland and Agnes Buckman

accomplished [Agnes is a widow with children.] John Terry produces certificate from Monthly Meeting at the falls.

7/10/1736 - John Schofield has sustained a great loss by fire.

1/12/1736 - James Dean produces certificate from Monthly Meeting at Belanacre in the county north of Ireland. [*probably means in the northern part of Ireland. Ed.*]

1/1/1737 - Reported the Isaac Ashton has proceeded in marriage with Dorathy Carr contrary to the rules of our Society.

5/5/1737 - Marriage of James Rose and Deborah Stuchbury accomplished.

6/7/1737 - Thomas Robinson produces a certificate from Buckingham Monthly Meeting.

1/9/1737 - Certificate requested for Benjamin Fereby and family to Buckingham Monthly Meeting.

6/10/1737 - William Lee requests to be joined as a member of our Society.

7/12/1737 - Marriage of Thomas Robinson and Katherine Dean accomplished. Katherine is a widow with children. James Arbuckle requests certificate for himself and wife to Middletown Monthly Meeting.

4/2/1738 - Marriage of George Newborn and Mary Stockdale accomplished on 15th of last month.

2/3/1738 - Marriage of Peter Ball and Plain Wilkinson accomplished 11th of last month. [Peter produces certificate from Gwynedd.]

6/4/1738 - Marriage of John Terry and Rachel Lacey accomplished on 31st of last month.

1/6/1738 - Henry Tyson produces certificate for himself and wife from Abington Monthly Meeting. Informed that Isaac Penington has removed himself to within the compass of the Falls Monthly Meeting and requests certificate for himself and wife.

5/7/1738 - Samuel Dean requests certificate to Abington Monthly Meeting. James Dean intends to remove himself and most of his family from this province to Ireland and requests certificate.

5/4/1739 - Thomas Strickland produces certificate from Monthly Meeting at Phila. John Hilborn requests certificate for himself and family to Monthly Meeting at Phila. John Simpson produces certificate from Monthly Meeting at Abington for himself and wife.

3/5/1739 - William Briggs produces certificate from Monthly Meeting at Gwynedd for himself and wife.

4/10/1739 - Marriage of John Chapman Jr. and Mary Twining accomplished 8th of last month. Joseph Hampton requests certificate on account of his intended marriage with Mary Warner, a member of Harford meeting.

1/11/1739 - Marriage of John Chapman and Ruth Wilkinson accomplished on 6/10/1739.

4/1/1740 - Marriage of John Doan and Hannah Wilson accomplished on 13/12/1739.

3/4/1740 - Marriage of John Wilkinson Jr. and Mary Lacey accomplished on 27th day of last month.

1/5/1740 - Marriage of John Smith and Mary Stradling accomplished on 19th of last month. John produces certificate from Falls Monthly Meeting. John Thomas requests certificate for himself and wife to Buckingham Monthly Meeting.

4/9/1740 - Timothy Price having some months ago requested to join as a member of our Society and is now received.

2/2/1741 - Jeremiah Cooper requests certificate to Middletown Monthly Meeting in order to proceed in marriage with Rebecca Wildman, a member of that meeting.

1/7/1741 - Samuell Blaker requests certificate for himself and such of his family as resided with him to the Monthly Meeting at Buckingham.

5/11/1741/2 - Marriage of Benjamin Taylor Jun. and Sarah Buckman acc. on 2nd day of last month. [Benjamin produces certificate from Falls Monthly Meeting.] Alexander Dean produces certificate from the Grange in the north of Ireland. Timothy Price and his wife condemn their marrying another way, she being with child before marriage.

2/12/1741/2 - Alexander Dean to transport himself to Ireland and requests certificate. Thomas Lancaster requests certificate for himself and family to Gwynedd Monthly Meeting.

6/2/1742 - John Smith requests certificate to Buckingham Monthly Meeting.

4/3/1742 - David Dawes produces certificate for himself and family from Buckingham Monthly Meeting. Joseph Tomblinson produces certificate from Abington Monthly Meeting for himself and wife.

1/4/1742 - John Wilson produces certificate from himself and wife from Monthly Meeting at the falls.

7/7/1742 - James Briggs requests certificate to Middletown Monthly Meeting in order to proceed in marriage with Ann Croasdale, a member of that meeting.

2/9/1742 - Alexander Dean and James Dean Jun. produces certificate from the six weeks meeting at Antrim in Ireland.

4/11/1742 - Samuell Dean produces certificate from six weeks meeting at Antrim in Ireland.

1/12/1742 - Ichobed Wilkinson produces certificate from Monthly Meeting at Smithfield in Rhode Island.

7/4/1743 - Marriage of John Twining Jr. and Sarah Dawes accomplished on 17th of last month.

2/6/1743 - Petter Cloak requests certificate for himself and wife [to where?. Subsequent meeting is informed that since Petter left this meeting and went to live in Phila Co. he hath been often overtaken with strong drink and may attempt to leave the province in a clandestant manner to avoid creditors.]

4/8/1743 - Joseph Smith requests certificate [to Middletown Monthly Meeting] in order to proceed in marriage with Rachell Wildman. Marriage of Ichabod Wilkinson and Sarah Chapman accomplished on 7th day of last month.

1/9/1743 - John Simson requests certificate for himself, wife and family to Buckingham Monthly Meeting.

6/10/1743 - Stephen Comfort requests certificate to Middletown Monthly Meeting.

7/12/1743 - William Reader requests to be joined as a member of this Society.

6/1/1743/4 - Informed that Petter Cloak is now released from his confinement.

4/7/1744 - David Buckman requests certificate to Abington Monthly Meeting in order to proceed in marriage with Mary Knite. Thomas Atkinson requests certificate to Middletown Monthly Meeting in order to proceed in marriage with Mary Wildman.

6/9/1744 - Thomas Stradling requests certificate to Buckingham Monthly Meeting in order to proceed in marriage with Elizabeth Fisher. Joseph Dean requests certificate for himself and family to Buckingham Monthly Meeting.

1/11/1744/5 - Marriage of William Chapman and Jane Penquite accomplished on 20th of last month.

5/1/1744/5 - William Baldwin requests certificate to Monthly meeting at Opecan in Virginia. Reported that James Dean has married a woman not of our society.

2/2/1745 - William Briggs Jun. by his father requests certificate to Middletown Monthly Meeting in order to proceed in marriage with Mary Crosdale. Reported that Jonathan Coop Jun. has married a woman not of our Society, she having another husband.

7/3/1745 - Joseph Buckman produces certificate from falls Monthly Meeting where he served his apprenticeship.

4/4/1745 - Marriage of Joseph Watson and Alice Mitchell accomplished on 28th of last month. Joseph belongs to another mm. John Beaumont produces certificate from falls Monthly Meeting.

2/5/1745 - Alexander Dean requests certificate to Antrim in Ireland.

3/7/1745 - Reported that James Dean has accompanied his brother Samuell in his disorderly marriage.

5/9/1745 - Thomas Furnis requests certificate to Phila Monthly Meeting and produces a few lines from Plumstead concerning his conduct while he lived with them. John Penquite Jun. produces certificate to Monthly Meeting at Gwynedd.

3/10/1745 - Judah Williams produces certificate for himself and family.

4/1/1745/6 - Thomas Robinson requests certificate for himself and family to Bethlehem Monthly Meeting. Daniel Stradling requests certificate in order to proceed in marriage with Sarah Scarbrough, a member of Buckingham Monthly Meeting.

1/2/1746 - Joseph Yeats continues his request to come under the care of Friends.

_/3/1746 - Marriage of John Martindale and Mary Strickland accomplished on 9th of last month. [John belongs to another mm.] Juday Williams requests certificate for himself and family to Woodbridge Monthly Meeting. Joseph Yeats requests certificate to Monthly Meeting at Opecton in Virginia. Ralph Smith requests certificate to Woodbridge Monthly Meeting.

1/5/1746 - Thomas Betts produces certificate from Middletown Monthly Meeting for himself and wife. William Briggs, Jun. condemns his misconduct with his wife who was with child before marriage. William Reader requests certificate to Buckingham Monthly Meeting in order to proceed in marriage with Ann Burgess of that meeting.

5/6/1746 - Reported that John Buckman hath been guilty of committing fornication with Rebeckah Welsh.

7/8/1746 - Marriage of John Stockdale and Sarah Tomblinson accomplished on 4th of last month. Isaac Kirk requests certificate to Buckingham Monthly Meeting in order to proceed in marriage with Rachell Kinsey. Joseph Buckman requests certificate to fall Monthly Meeting in order to proceed in marriage with Martha Carr.

6/11/1746/7 - John Dean produces certificate from the 6 weeks meeting at the grange in Ireland.

3/12/1746/7 - Eldad Roberts and Elizabeth Mitchell to marry. [Eldad produces certificate from Monthly Meeting of Gwynedd. No record of this marriage being accomplished.]

7/2/1747 - John Gourley produces certificate for himself and wife from Buckingham Monthly Meeting.

5/11/1747/8 - Marriage of Titus Fell and Elizabeth Heston Junior accomplished 15th of last month. [Titus produces certificate from Buckingham Monthly Meeting.]

2/12/1747/8 - John Penquite Junior requests certificate to Buckingham Monthly Meeting.

5/2/1748 - James Briggs requests certificate for himself and family to the falls Monthly Meeting.

3/3/1748 - Marriage of William Lee Jun. and Hannah Sanders accomplished on 13th of last month. Robert Comforte produces certificate from Middletown Monthly Meeting. Thomas Lewes produces certificate from Smithfield, Rhode Island.

7/4/1748 - Marriage of John Buckman and Elennor Briggs accomplished on 18th of last month. John Story condemns his having married contrary to the good order amongst Friends.

2/6/1748 - Joseph Smith requests certificate to Middletown Monthly Meeting.

6/7/1748 - Thomas Chapman condemns his misconduct in taking another way to consummate his marriage.

4/8/1748 - Ralf Smith produces certificate from Woodbridge in East Jersey. Joseph Lacey requests certificate in order to proceed in marriage with Esther Warner, member of Harford Monthly Meeting. John Hamton requests certificate in order to proceed in marriage with Ann Croasdale, dau. of Jeremiah Croasdale, a member of Middletown Monthly Meeting.

1/9/1748 - Marriage of Joseph Wilkinson and Barbary Lacey accomplished on 13th of last month. Richard Betts requests certificate to Abington Monthly Meeting.

6/10/1748 - Marriage of Thomas Lacey and Esther Smith accomplished on 22nd of last month.

7/1/1748/9 - John Lee requests certificate to falls Monthly Meeting in order to proceed in marriage with Sarah Carr.

3/8/1749 - John Dean requests certificate to Ireland. Joseph Hibbs requests certificate to Buckingham Monthly Meeting in order to proceed in marriage with Catharine Love.

5/10/1749 - Marriage of Richard Mitchell and Agnis Warner, widow, accomplished on 15th of last month.

6/1/1749/50 - Reported that Jacob Cooper hath misconducted himself in his marriage. James Wood requests to be taken under the care of Friends.

1/3/1750 - Marriage of John Warner and Eliza: Dawes accomplished on 25th of last month. Marriage of Thomas Fell and Jane Kirk accomplished on 24th of last month. [He produces certificate from Buckingham Monthly Meeting.]

5/4/1750 - William Briggs Jur. requests certificate to Middletown Monthly Meeting. Christopher Atkinson requests certificate to Buckingham Monthly Meeting.

4/7/1750 - Thomas Smith requests certificate to Buckingham Monthly Meeting in order to proceed in marriage with Mary Ross. Samuell Smith requests certificate to Buckingham Monthly Meeting in order to proceed in marriage with Jane Scolfield. Jacob Cooper requests certificate to Monthly Meeting of Nottingham.

4/10/1750 - Marriage of James Wildman and Mary Warner accomplished 21st of last month. [James produces certificate from Middletown Monthly Meeting.]

1/11/1750 - Marriage of Ralph Smith and Mercy Penquite accomplished on 20th of last month.

2/2/1751 - Ichobod Wilkinson requests certificate for himself and wife to Buckingham Monthly Meeting.

4/4/1751 - Marriage of George Fell and Sarah Kirk accomplished 21st of last month. [George produces certificate from Buckingham Monthly Meeting.]

6/6/1751 - Marriage of Eleazer Doan and Rebeckah Dawes [widow with children] accomplished 23rd of last month. Joseph Tomblinson Jur. requests certificate to the Falls Monthly Meeting in order to proceed in marriage with Margret Baker.

5/9/1751 - Samuell Mirick produces certificate from the Falls Monthly Meeting.

8/10/1751 - Marriage of Christopher Atkinson and Elizabeth Wilson accomplished on 20th of last month. [Christopher produces certificate from Buckingham Monthly Meeting.] John Smith requests certificate to Buckingham Monthly Meeting in order to proceed in marriage with Martha Burgess.

7/1/1752 - Marriage of Jonathan Kinsey and Jemima Heston accomplished on 11th of last month. [Jonathan produces certificate from another mm.] Marriage of John Dillon and Hannah Richardson accomplished on 18th of last month.

4/2/1752 - Marriage of Samuel Mirick and Rachel Heston accomplished on 29th of last month. Thomas Smith requests certificate to Buckingham Monthly Meeting in order to proceed in marriage with Sarah Townsend.

3/3/1752 - Cephas Atkinson requests certificate to Gwynedd Monthly Meeting in order to proceed in marriage with Hannah Nailer. James Neal has incurred a great loss by fire. Petter Ball produces certificate from Buckingham Monthly Meeting.

7/4/1752 - Joseph Warner and Ruth Hayhurst to marry. [No record of marriage.] Benjamin Briggs condemns his outgoing in marriage. Daniell Stradling requests certificate to Buckingham Monthly Meeting.

2/6/1752 - Stephen Wilson requests certificate for himself, wife and three youngest children, Frances, Joseph and William, to Middletown Monthly Meeting. Reported that Joseph Hibbs misconducted himself with his wife so that she was with child before marriage.

7/7/1752 - Joseph Smith produces certificate for himself and wife from Middletown Monthly Meeting.

1/9/1752 - Samuel Twining requests certificate to Middletown in order to proceed in marriage with Mary Jenks.

3/10/1752 - Marriage of John Stockdale and Mary Atkinson accomplished 20th of last month.

5/12/1752 - Marriage of William Preston and Elizabeth Smith, widow, accomplished on 15th of last month. [William produces cert. William's request to consummate his marriage at Buckingham Monthly Meeting was granted.] Marriage of Thomas Lancaster and Sarah Taylor, widow, accomplished on 28th of last month. [Thomas produces cert.]

2/1/1753 - Reported that Robert Comforte misconducted himself with his wife so that she was with child before marriage. William Dillon desires to be taken under the care of Friends.

6/3/1753 - Samuel Twining requests certificate to Middletown Monthly Meeting. James Spicer produces certificate from Buckingham Monthly Meeting.

3/4/1753 - James Thackry Jur. requests certificate from Falls Monthly Meeting. Reported that Benjamin Twining misconducted himself with his wife so that she was with child before marriage. Reported that Isaac Buckman was outgoing in marriage with his wife and his misconduct with her is that she was with child before marriage.

1/5/1753 - Marriage of Robert Smith and Rachell Hibbs accomplished 11th of last month. [Robert produces certificate from Buckingham Monthly Meeting.] Ezekiell Atkinson requests certificate to Falls Monthly Meeting in order to proceed in marriage with Rachel Gilbird.

3/7/1753 - Marriage of John Preston and Sarah Richardson, widow, accomplished on 27th of last month. [John produces certificate from Buckingham Monthly Meeting.] Thomas Ross produces certificate for himself, wife and son Thomas and Deborah Jones. Thomas Lacey requests certificate to Buckingham Monthly Meeting.

7/8/1753 - Paul Penington produces certificate from Abington Monthly Meeting.

2/10/1753 - Samuel Lee condemns his unchaste conversation before marriage with his present wife which caused them to take another way to consummate marriage.

4/12/1753 - Marriage of Joseph Briggs and Margret Yeats accomplished 28th of last month. Eleaser Dean Jur. condemns his unchaste conversation with his cousin which occasioned his marrying her contrary to the good order amongst Friends.

5/3/1754 - Marriage of William Mitchiner Jur. and Martha Doan accomplished 13th of last month. [He produces a cert.] Isaac Chapman requests certificate to Phila Monthly Meeting in order to proceed in marriage with Mary Mason. Thomas Lee requests certificate to Buckingham Monthly Meeting in order to proceed in marriage with Mary Burgess. Thomas Lewes requests certificate to Buckingham Monthly Meeting in order to proceed in marriage with Sarah Watson.

7/5/1754 - Marriage of Judadiah Adams and Rebeckah Sanders accomplished on 1st of last month. [*They announced their intentions to marry for the second time on 1/4/1754. Did they marry that day or was the intended date of marriage actually 1/5/1754? Ed.*] - Henry Simons produces certificate from the Falls Monthly Meeting. Joseph Heaton Jur. condemns his marrying with one not of our Society.

2/7/1754 - Stephen Comforte produces certificate for himself, wife and children. William Stockdale produces certificate for himself, wife and children.

3/9/1754 - William Smith Jur. requests certificate to Buckingham Monthly Meeting in order to proceed in marriage with Ann Williams.

7/1/1755 - Marriage of Petter Fipps and Mary Chapman accomplished on 18th of last month. [He produces a cert.] Benjamin Briggs requests certificate for himself, wife and children, to Buckingham Monthly Meeting.

4/2/1755 - Thomas Lacey produces certificate for himself and wife from Buckingham Monthly Meeting.

1/4/1755 - John Lee requests certificate for himself and wife to Radnor Monthly Meeting. William Heaton requests certificate to Buckingham Monthly Meeting.

6/5/1755 - Stephen Comfort requests certificate for himself, wife and children to Middletown Monthly Meeting. Daniel Knight acquainted Friends that he had two of his young children, Ann and Thomas Knight, with David Buckman, a member of this meeting, and that they might be looked upon as under the care of this meeting. Recorded are the extracts of the last will of Adam Harker. [He mentions his brother James Harker and his wife Amy.] James being deceased his wife Amy was placed at John Lintons 1st of last 2nd month at the rate of 12 pounds for the ensuing year.

3/6/1755 - Marriage of Thomas Wilson and Rachel Strickland accomplished 14th of last month. [He prod. a cert.] Marriage of Henry Carver and Rachell Smith accomplished on 21st of last month. [He produces a cert.] Stephen Wilson requests certificate to Buckingham Monthly Meeting. Reported that John Dillon, having been joined to Friends and was permitted to marry amongst us, she being with child by him at the same time.

1/7/1755 - William Cooper condemns his proceeding in marriage contrary to the good order amongst Friends. William Reeder requests certificate to Buckingham Monthly Meeting.

5/8/1755 - Marriage of William Dillon and Rachel Yeates Junr. accomplished on 30th of last month.

2/9/1755 - Henry Tyson has departed from amongst us without requesting a certificate.

4/11/1755 - Marriage of Anthony Hartly and Elizabeth Smith. [He produces cert.] Paul Penington requests certificate to Abington Monthly Meeting. Jonathan Willet produces certificate for himself and his wife from Flushing Monthly Meeting. Joseph Heaton requests certificate for himself, his wife and family to Buckingham Monthly Meeting.

2/12/1755 - Marriage of John Wilson and Mary Simmons accomplished on 19th of last month.

6/1/1756 - Marriage of William Carver Jur. and Sarah Strickland accomplished on 31st of last month. [He produces cert.]

William Smith Jur. requests certificate to Buckingham Monthly Meeting. Overseers have spoken with Thomas Buckman concerning his taking another way to consummate his marriage.

4/5/1756 - Marriage of Croasdale Warner and Mary Briggs accomplished on 14th of last month.

3/8/1756 - Zebulon Heston Junr. requests certificate to Buckingham Monthly Meeting in order to proceed in marriage with Sarah Burgess. Overseers have spoken to Nathaniel Twining concerning his going out with his marriage and his having a child by another woman.

2/11/1756 - Samuel Smith (blacksmith) condemns his proceeding with marriage contrary to the rules of our Society.

7/12/1756 - John Blaker requests certificate to Middletown Monthly Meeting in order to proceed in marriage with Mary Briggs. Jacob Buckman requests certificate to Falls Monthly Meeting in order to proceed in marriage with Mary Taylor. Samuel Briggs requests certificate to Falls Monthly Meeting.

4/1/1757 - Overseers have spoken to Joseph Hibbs Junr. concerning his conduct with his wife who was with child before marriage.

5/4/1757 - John Hayhurst produces certificate from Middletown Monthly Meeting.

3/5/1757 - Henry Simmons requests certificate to Middletown Monthly Meeting.

2/8/1757 - James Briggs produces certificate from Middletown Monthly Meeting for himself, wife and children.

6/9/1757 - Joseph Paxson requests certificate to Buckingham Monthly Meeting. George Newburn accused by his sister in law Sarah Stockdale of unlawful conversation with her. Certificate for Phebe Titus and her dau. Elizabeth Lancaster to Monthly Meeting at Westbury on Long Island.

4/10/1757 - Memorials: John Routledge d. 21/5/1725. Ann Parsons sister of Abraham Chapman; she d. 9/10/1732, age 57 years. David Daws d. 24/12/1748/9. John Laycock d. about middle of 8th month 1750. Joseph Chapman d. 26/2/1752, age 67 years. Abraham Chapman, brother of Joseph, d. 23/2/1755, age 70 years. Benjamin Twining requests certificate to Monthly Meeting at Abington.

6/12/1757 - Thomas Lewis requests certificate for himself and wife to Buckingham Monthly Meeting. John Beaumont returned a certificate to this meeting which he had with him to Europe. Accounts to be settled concerning David Buckman's clothing and boarding of Jeremiah Bowman.

7/2/1758 - Benjamin Warner requests certificate to Buckingham Monthly Meeting in order to proceed in marriage with Sarah Ely. Reported that Jonathan Willet and his family have sometime since removed back to Long Island.

7/3/1758 - Joseph Chapman requests certificate to Buckingham Monthly Meeting in order to proceed in marriage with Ann Fell.

4/4/1758 - Joseph Briggs requests certificate for himself and wife to Falls Monthly Meeting. Robert Comfort requests certificate for himself, wife and children to Middletown Monthly Meeting.

2/5/1758 - Daniel Doan produces certificate from the Falls Monthly Meeting.

6/6/1758 - Miriam Doan produces certificate from Kingwood Monthly Meeting. Certificate for Rebekah Adams to Falls Monthly Meeting. Letter from Ruth Dean condemning her misconduct in her last marriage.
4/7/1758 - Women Friends produces certificate recommending Mary Blaker to this meeting.
1/8/1758 - Rachel Carter produces certificate from East Nottingham.
5/9/1758 - Ann Chapman produces certificate from Buckingham Monthly Meeting.
3/10/1758 - Ichabod Wilkinson produces certificate from Buckingham Monthly Meeting for himself, wife and children. Humphrey Parker produces certificate from Falls Monthly Meeting for himself and wife. Susannah Betts produces certificate from Abington Monthly Meeting.
5/12/1758 - Marriage of Benjamin Doan and Jemima Kinsey, widow, accomplished on 22nd of last month. Marriage of Thomas Kinsey and Margaret Smith accomplished on 28th of last month. [Thomas produces certificate from Buckingham Monthly Meeting.] Overseers have spoken to James Paxson concerning his unchaste conversation with a woman which he has afterwards married. Isaac Hollingsworth produces certificate Monthly Meeting at Fairfax in Virginia.
2/1/1759 - One of the overseers has spoken to John Parsons concerning his proceeding in marriage contrary to the rules of our Society.
6/3/1759 - Daniel Richardson request to come under the Care of Friends.
3/4/1759 - John Roberts requests certificate to Monthly Meeting of Mirion.
1/5/1759 - Agnis Vance produces certificate from Buckingham Monthly Meeting. Thomas Lacey requests certificate for himself and family to Buckingham Monthly Meeting.
5/6/1759 - Sarah Warner produces certificate from Buckingham Monthly Meeting.
3/7/1759 - The Women Friends produces certificates for Sarah Carver to Buckingham Monthly Meeting, one for Sarah Wilson to Middletown Monthly Meeting and one for Mary Kirk to Abington Monthly Meeting. Certificate produced for Joseph and Isaac Lancaster from Richland Monthly Meeting.
7/8/1759 - Certificate produced for David Stockdale from Middletown Monthly Meeting. Meeting is uneasy with David Newborn's being so long removed and not having requested a certificate.
4/9/1759 - Memorial for Agness Penquite who d. 20/11/1758, age upwards of 100 years old. She brought a certificate from Urope (Europe) dated 6/2/1686. William Hoge produces certificate from Richland Monthly Meeting.
1/1/1760 - William Hoge requests certificate to Burlington Monthly Meeting.
5/2/1760 - Marriage of John Winder Jur. and Margret Briggs Jur. accomplished on 23rd of last month. Stephen Kirk requests certificate to Buckingham Monthly Meeting.
13/2/1760 - Joseph Hamton produces certificate for Zebulon

Heston.

1/4/1760 - Certificate produced for Hannah Dillon to this meeting. John Butler requests certificate for himself, wife and children to Monthly Meeting of Merion. An overseer has spoken to Samuel Smith (blacksmith) concerning his going to Virginia without a cert.

6/5/1760 - Marriage of Robert Verree and Ann Chapman accomplished on 16th of last month. [He produces certificate from Abbington Monthly Meeting.] James Dillon requests to come under the care of Friends. Sarah Dungan produces certificate from Middletown Monthly Meeting. Reported that Samuel Smith (of Newtown), being too familiar with his late housekeeper and that she is with child by him. Charges appear to be true based on what Julian Price herself says and circumstances related by others. Joseph Lancaster requests certificate to Philadelphia Monthly Meeting. Daniel Knigh informed this meeting that as he had placed his son Thomas Knigh with a Friend of this meeting, he has now bound his son with a member of another mm.

3/6/1760 - Marriage of Joseph Palmer and Hannah Pancoast accomplished on 27th of last month. [Joseph produces certificate from Falls Monthly Meeting.] Marriage of John Scarbrough and Margaret Kirk accomplished 8th of last month. [John produces cert.] Certificate for Martha Penington to Buckingham Monthly Meeting. Thomas Lee requests certificate to Abbington Monthly Meeting. Spoke to Joseph Lacey concerning his proceeding in marriage contrary to the rules of our Society.

1/7/1760 - Certificate for Ann Knight to Abington Monthly Meeting.

5/8/1760 - John Chapman requests certificate to Richland Monthly Meeting for himself, wife and children.

2/9/1760 - Thomas Ross Jur. requests certificate to Monthly Meeting in Newport, Rhode Island or elsewhere in the said colony.

7/10/1760 - Marriage of James Dillon and Rebekah Doan Jur. accomplished on 10th of last month. James Paxson requests certificate to Buckingham Monthly Meeting.

4/11/1760 - Mary Forster condemns her outgoing in marriage. Peter Ball requests certificate for himself, wife and children he has at home, to Gunpowder Monthly Meeting, Maryland. David Newborn requests certificate for himself, wife and children to Buckingham Monthly Meeting.

2/12/1760 - Marriage of Richard Tomlinson and Hannah Hillborn accomplished 26th of last month. Samuel Hillborn condemns his misconduct with his wife so that she was with child before marriage.

6/1/1761 - Emanuel Walker produces certificate from Middletown Monthly Meeting for himself and wife.

3/2/1761 - Spoke to William Lacy for having a child too soon after marriage.

3/3/1761 - Certificate produced for David Parry from Abbington Monthly Meeting who is an apprentice to Robert Verree.

7/4/1761 - Certificate for Elizabeth Lees and her dau. Sarah

Stradling to Derby Monthly Meeting. Determined that David Newborn is a member of this meeting and a certificate produced for him, his wife and children: Isaac, David, George, Ann, Solomon, Ashton, Hannah and John.

5/5/1761 - Reported that the twin children of William Lacey and his wife were born 7 months after their marriage; the twins were weakley and behaved with moderation.

1/9/1761 - Certificate from Falls Monthly Meeting for Abegale Doan. Spoke to Ralph Smith concerning his being the father of his late housekeeper, Mary Smith's child.

6/10/1761 - Thomas Ross Jur. produces certificate from Friends in Providence, Rhode Island. Certificate for Mary Briggs, wife of Samuel Briggs from Falls Monthly Meeting. Spoke to Richard Tomlinson concerning his familiarity with his wife before marriage so that she was with child. Spoke with Eleazer Twining concerning his familiarity with his wife before marriage so that she was with child, and his outgoing in marriage.

1/12/1761 - Certificate from Richland Monthly Meeting for John Chapman and Mary his wife and five of their children: Elizabeth, Mira, Charles, Susannah and Abraham.

5/1/1762 - Joseph Smith and Mary his wife produces certificate from Buckingham Monthly Meeting.

2/2/1762 - William Carter accepted into the Society.

2/3/1762 - Certificate from Middletown Monthly Meeting for Sarah Cawley. Joseph Wilkinson requests certificate for himself, wife and children, to Chester Monthly Meeting. Benjamin Paxson requests certificate to Buckingham Monthly Meeting. Spoke to Joseph Smith (wheelwright) concerning his going from among friends with his marriage.

6/4/1762 - David Lewis desires to be joined in membership. Spoke to Richard Parsons Jur. concerning his marriage out of unity of Friends. Reference to statement made by William Lacey late husband of Elizabeth Lacey concerning his misconduct before marriage. Statement was spoken by Elizabeth Lacey on 8/3/1762. Spoke to David Smith concerning his marriage out of the unity of Friends and for attending his brother's disorderly marriage. Thomas Ross Jur. requests certificate to Gunpowder in Maryland.

4/5/1762 - John Wilson Jun. requests certificate to Middletown Monthly Meeting. Samuel Briggs requests certificate to Monthly Meeting at Goshen in Chester Co.

1/6/1762 - Robert Hillborn condemns his disorderly method he took to consummate his marriage. Zachariah Betts produces certificate from Abington Monthly Meeting.

6/7/1762 - Daniel Doan requests certificate to Abington Monthly Meeting.

3/8/1762 - Marriage of David Stockdale and Joyce Trego accomplished 7th of last month.

7/9/1762 - Marriage of David Lewis and Elizabeth Doan, widow, accomplished on 11th of last month.

2/11/1762 - Marriage of William Newburn and Susannah Betts accomplished on 27th of last month. Marriage of James Stokes and Hannah Tomlinson accomplished on 20th of last month. Amos

Strickland requests certificate to Middletown Monthly Meeting in order to proceed in marriage with Margret Thornton Jur. Joseph Lacey requests certificate to Goshen Monthly Meeting.

7/12/1762 - John Chapman requests certificate to Phila Monthly Meeting. Stephen Kirk requests certificate to Richland Monthly Meeting.

1/3/1763 - Certificates produced for Mary Renolds to Goshen Monthly Meeting, Sarah Hibbs to Middletown Monthly Meeting and Margret Scarbrough to Buckingham Monthly Meeting. Testimony against Deborah Dillon, wife of Josiah Dillon. Reported that James Rose has gone out in marriage. William Carter requests certificate to Middletown Monthly Meeting.

5/4/1763 - Thomas Lee produces certificate for himself and wife from Abington Monthly Meeting. James Dillon requests certificate to Fairfax Monthly Meeting, Va. Isaac Lancaster requests certificate to Phila Monthly Meeting. Christopher Atkinson requests certificate to Buckingham Monthly Meeting in order to proceed in marriage with Lydia Canby.

3/5/1763 - Marriage of Peter Blaker and Sarah Hibbs accomplished on 28th of last month. [He produces certificate from Buckingham Monthly Meeting.] William Linton requests certificate to Phila. Emanuel Walker requests certificate to Abbington Monthly Meeting.

7/6/1763 - Benjamin Lacey requests certificate to Providence Monthly Meeting in Chester Co.

5/7/1763 - Phebe Garner requests to be taken under the care of Friends. William Cooper requests certificate to Friends at Kingwood in West Jersey.

4/10/1763 - Joseph Johnson requests certificate to Monthly Meeting at Warrington in York Co., PA for himself and family.

6/12/1763 - Thomas Whitson produces certificate for himself from Kingwood Monthly Meeting in West Jersey. Spoke with Amos Strickland concerning his having a child born about 4 months and 2 weeks after marriage. Jonathan Scholfield requests certificate to mm at Providence.

7/2/1764 - John Wilson requests certificate for himself and wife to Gwynedd Monthly Meeting.

6/3/1764 - John Sanders requests certificate to Gwynedd Monthly Meeting.

3/4/1764 - William Dillon requests certificate for himself, wife and children to Monthly Meeting at Fairfax, Virginia. Zachariah Betts requests certificate to Buckingham Monthly Meeting.

1/5/1764 - Reported that John Hibbs has gone out in marriage and removed to Virginia.

5/6/1764 - Benjamin Smith and wife Sarah produces certificate from Buckingham Monthly Meeting. Spoke to John Gibson concerning his proceeding in marriage contrary to the discipline of Friends and his driving a wagon with military stores to the Army.

3/7/1764 - Testimony against Mary Atkinson, wife of John Atkinson of Newtown. Certificate for Grace Doan to Monthly Meeting at Cane Creek in Orange Co., North Carolina. Certificate for Mare Croasdale from Middletown Monthly Meeting. Deborah

Dillon condemns her going out in her marriage.
4/9/1764 - Spoke to William Heston concerning his having a child born 8 months after his marriage. Spoke to Isaac Hibbs concerning his going out with his marriage and having a child born soon after. Spoke to Zachariah Betts concerning his having a child born in less that 3 months after marriage.
2/10/1764 - William Linton produces certificate from Phila Monthly Meeting.
6/11/1764 - Reported that Isaac Hibbs's wife's sister has charged him with being the father of her child which he denies.
4/12/1764 - Certificate for Mary Moor to Sadsbury Monthly Meeting.
5/2/1765 - John Chapman produces certificate from Phila Monthly Meeting.
5/3/1765 - Thomas Chapman requests certificate to Newgarden in Carolina.
2/4/1765 - Certificate from Falls Monthly Meeting for Ann Briggs wife of John Briggs. John Briggs requests certificate for himself, wife and children to Goshen Monthly Meeting, Chester Co.
7/5/1765 - John Winder requests certificate for himself and wife to Abington Monthly Meeting.
4/6/1765 - Samuel Wilson has suffered a loss by fire consuming most of his effects.
12/16/1765 - 2/7/1765 - Ann Clerk requests to come under the care of Friends.
6/8/1765 - Benjamin Lacey produces certificate from Monthly Meeting at Providence, Chester Co.
3/9/1765 - Robert Comfort produces certificate from Middletown for himself, wife and children. Certificate for Phebe Linton to Middletown. Certificate for Mary Ball to this meeting. Ann Clarke received into membership. John Rose produces certificate from Buckingham Monthly Meeting.
1/10/1765 - Jacob Heston requests certificate for himself, wife and such of his children as shall remove with him to Monthly Meeting of Haverford. Jesse Heston requests certificate to Middletown Monthly Meeting in order to proceed in marriage with a member of that meeting. John Balderston Jur. requests certificate to mm in Norwick in Northfolk Co. in Old England, he having a mind to visit relations in those parts.
5/11/1765 - Agness Carter condemns her misconduct in marriage. Spoke to Samuel Hillborn Jur. concerning his marrying contrary to the rules of the Society. Jacob Heston, minor, recommended to Phila Monthly Meeting, he being place out as an apprentice to Thomas Williams, a member of that meeting.
3/12/1765 - Spoke with William Parsons concerning his marrying contrary to the rules of Friends.
7/1/1766 - Marriage of John Wilkinson and Elizabeth Lacey, widow, accomplished on 11th of last month. [He produces certificate from Buckingham Monthly Meeting.] Mary Heston returned certificate that her husband Jacob Heston and she had obtained; as he had died after the date of the certificate it was directed that she might have one exclusive of his name and that three of her children's names be included: Edward, Thomas

and Rachel. Spoke with James Briggs Jur. [wife's name is Mary] concerning his outgoing in marriage.

4/2/1766 - Ephriam Smith and wife Rachel produces certificate from Buckingham Monthly Meeting.

4/3/1766 - David Newburn and his wife Hannah requests certificate from our mm dated 7/4/1761 to Buckingham. After they removed they buried one of their children at Plumstead and set up a stone at the grave and Friends were uneasy therewith and asked them to remove said stone which they refused; they made away with their certificate, not exchanging it for another as requested. Friends who visited the family state that David Newburn Jur. [son of David and Hannah] is guilty of taking the Lord's name in vain and George Newburn Jur. [son of David and Hannah] has married contrary to the rules of Friends; Ann dressed unbecoming of a Friend.

1/4/1766 - Thomas Ross produces certificate from Friends of Perquimons in North Carolina. Spoke to Benjamin Lacey concerning his marrying by a hireling priest.

6/5/1766 - Benjamin Warner requests certificate for himself and wife to Buckingham Monthly Meeting.

1/7/1766 - Spoke to Thomas Ross concerning his consummating his marriage contrary to the rules of Friends.

5/8/1766 - David Parry requests certificate to Abbington Monthly Meeting.

2/9/1766 - John Rose and Mary Atkinson to marry. [No record of marriage being accomplished.] Joseph Johnson and Rachel his wife produces certificate from Warrington Monthly Meeting. Determined that Thomas Ross Jur. married 4th of last 12th month and had a child 8 months after marriage.

7/10/1766 - John Balderston Jun. returned from Europe and produces certificate from Monthly Meeting in Norwick, County of Norfolk of Great Britain.

4/11/1766 - David Stockdale requests certificate to Falls Monthly Meeting in order to proceed in marriage with Jane Whiteacre.

2/12/1766 - Thomas Ross Jun. and his wife Ann acknowledge their unchastity which occasioned their marrying contrary to the rules of Friends.

3/2/1767 - Marriage of William Beans and Hannah Balderson Jur. accomplished 28th of last month. [He produces certificate from Buckingham Monthly Meeting.]

3/3/1767 - Certificate for Daniel, Deborah and Meribah Lee as Friends children, children being put under the care of David Buckman, Joseph Buckman and John Story. Spoke with William Blaker concerning his being charged with being the father of one child born before marriage and another soon after and going out with his marriage. Thomas Warner requests certificate to Middletown. John Hirst requests certificate for himself and family to Buckingham Monthly Meeting.

7/4/1767 - Henry Widdowfield produces certificate from Kingwood Monthly Meeting at Hardwick, West Jersey. John Balderson requests certificate for himself, wife and such of his children as are under age, Jacob, Isaiah, Mordicah, Sarah, Lydia and Mary, to Buckingham Monthly Meeting.

5/5/1767 - Spoke with John Cooper Jur., William Cooper Jur.,

Joseph Briggs and Peter Blaker son of John Blaker, concerning their pulling down a mill dam on the Meshiminy Creek. Isaiah Heston requests certificate to Middletown Monthly Meeting in order to proceed in marriage with Ann Lenard. Joseph Wiggins produces certificate from Buckingham Monthly Meeting.

7/7/1767 - John Wilkinson requests certificate from Buckingham Monthly Meeting.

4/8/1767 - James Hughes and Ursella his wife produces certificate for themselves and dau. Deborah from Chesterfield Monthly Meeting.

1/9/1767 - John Balderson Jur. requests certificate to Falls Monthly Meeting in order to proceed in marriage with Deborah Watson.

6/10/1767 - Thomas Strickland has returned from Carolina. William Lee Jun. requests to be taken under the care of Friends. Certificate from Middletown Monthly Meeting for Ann Heston, one from Shrewsbury Monthly Meeting for Rebekah Bills.

3/11/1767 - Certificate from Sadsbury Monthly Meeting for Sarah Dungan. Certificate for Margaret Field to Chesterfield Monthly Meeting. Joseph Hamton for many years a clerk of this meeting, being deceased, the meeting appoints Joseph Chapman. John Balderson Jun. requests certificate to Buckingham Monthly Meeting.

1/12/1767 - Marriage of George Ewers and Hannah Newburn accomplished on 19th of last month. George produces certificate from Abington Monthly Meeting. Marriage of Thomas Rose and Rebecca Betts accomplished on 24th of last month. [Thomas produces certificate from Buckingham Monthly Meeting.] Marriage of Joseph Jeans and Jane Chapman accomplished on 24th of last month. William Lee, carpenter, received as a member.

5/1/1768 - Certificate from Richland Monthly Meeting for Sarah Chapman. Reported that Samuel Kirk hath gone out with his marriage and hath a child by his wife between 6 and 7 months after marriage.

2/2/1768 - Thomas Chapman produces certificate from Cane Creek Monthly Meeting in North Carolina, for himself, wife and children, to wit: Alice, Anne, Thomas and Miles.

5/4/1768 - Certificate for Jane Hamton from Buckingham Monthly Meeting. Certificate for Rachel Bills from Shrewsbury Monthly Meeting. Humphrey Parker requests certificate to Hardwick Monthly Meeting in West Jersey for himself, wife and children.

3/5/1768 - Certificate for Hannah Dillon to Fairfax Monthly Meeting, Virginia. Joseph Jeans requests certificate to Gwynedd Monthly Meeting. Thomas Parker requests certificate to Hardwick Monthly Meeting in New Jersey.

7/6/1768 - Rebecca Hibbs requests to be joined in membership. Conrod Shriver requests to be joined in membership.

5/7/1768 - Certificate for Rebecca Rose to Falls Monthly Meeting.

6/9/1768 - Testimony against Ann Smally (formerly Ann Newburn). Elizabeth Twining wife of David Twining accepted as a member. Thomas Cooper produces certificate from Middletown Monthly Meeting for himself, Phebe his wife and children, Phebe, Thomas and Mary. Certificate from Kingwood Monthly Meeting for Ebenezer Lunday, an apprentice lad to the care of this meeting. Samuel Smith requests certificate for his son William to Concord Monthly Meeting, he being put an apprentice to Nathan Yarnal, a Friend belonging to that meeting.

1/11/1768 - Marriage of James Stokes and Mary Hampton Jr. accomplished on 12th of last month. David Smith requests certificate for himself, wife and children [Margaret, Mercy and Hannah], to Bush River Monthly Meeting in South Carolina. Judith Hirst received into membership.

6/12/1768 - Abraham Warner requests certificate to Falls Monthly Meeting in order to proceed in marriage with Ann Yardley.

3/1/1769 - Spoke with Ebenezer Large on account of his going out with his marriage.

7/2/1769 - Marriage of John Dawes and Alice Janney accomplished on 25th of last month. [John produces certificate from Buckingham Monthly Meeting.] Thomas Buckman produces certificate from Falls Monthly Meeting. Certificate from Middletown Monthly Meeting for Susannah Stokes. Spoke to Joseph Wiggins for having a child about 4 months after his marriage. Henry Widowfield requests certificate to Kingwood Monthly Meeting at Hardwick in the Jerseys. Jane Hilborn requests to join in membership.

7/3/1769 - Certificate from Buckingham Monthly Meeting recommending Arnold Mitchener, placed an apprentice with William Trego prod. Certificate for Mary Headley to Monthly Meeting at Salem.

4/4/1769 - Elizabeth Manning received into membership. Thomas Whitson intends to move to Salem. Marriage of John Briggs and Letitia Buckman accomplished on 22nd of last month.

6/6/1769 - Certificate for Rebecca Bills and Rachel Bills to Buckingham Monthly Meeting. Certificate requested to Deer Creek Monthly Meeting, Maryland, in order to place John Smith as an apprentice to his Uncle Samuel Smith. David Buckman to replace Joseph Hamton sometime since deceased, as Elder.

4/7/1769 - Spoke with John Cooper Junr., accused by Sarah Atkinson of his being father of her child; and of going out with his marriage with her that is now his wife.

1/8/1769 - Marriage of John Hair and Elizabeth Manning accomplished on 5th of last month. [He produces certificate from Falls Monthly Meeting.] Certificate for Ebenezer Lundy to Middletown Monthly Meeting.

5/9/1769 - Zachariah Betts requests certificate to Middletown Monthly Meeting in order to proceed in marriage with Barthula Cary.

3/10/1769 - Certificate for Mary Cutler to Falls Monthly Meeting. Certificate for Rachel Smith an orphan child, from Sadsbury Monthly Meeting who was placed as an apprentice to William Linton. Certificate for Enoch Mitchel for time he was an apprentice in the verge of Abington Monthly Meeting.

7/11/1769 - John Wilkinson requests certificate to Buckingham Monthly Meeting. Marriage of William Lee, carpenter, and Eleanor Atkinson accomplished on 1st of this month. Marriage of John Atkinson and Hannah Lee accomplished on 18th of last month. Thomas Atkinson produces certificate from New Garden.

Certificate for Mary Derborah to Phila Monthly Meeting. Thomas Whitson to move himself and family to Virginia.

6/2/1770 - Certificate from Middletown Monthly Meeting for Barthula Betts. Marriage of John Terry and Sarah Richardson accomplished on 31st of last month.

6/3/1770 - James Spicer requests certificate to Gunpowder Monthly Meeting, Maryland. Ephraim Smith and Richard Parsons to move their families to Virginia and Maryland, respectively. John Heston requests certificate in order to proceed in marriage with Hannah Jarret, a member of Abington Monthly Meeting. William Buckman Jr. requests certificate in order to proceed in marriage with Hannah Dilworth, member of Abington Monthly Meeting. George Newburn Jun. requests certificate in order to proceed in marriage with Amy Wilson, member of Buckingham Monthly Meeting.

3/4/1770 - Certificate for Hannah Beans to Buckingham Monthly Meeting. James Hughes requests certificate for himself, wife [Ursula] and three children [Deborah, Abraham and Sarah] to Chesterfield Monthly Meeting, New Jersey. Croasdel Warner requests certificate for himself, wife [Mary] and children [Hannah, Mary, Aaron, Amos, Croasdell and Sarah - all minors] to Gunpowder Monthly Meeting. Certificate requested for Samuel Gourly [minor] to Abington Monthly Meeting.

1/5/1770 - James Worstal requests certificate to Merion Monthly Meeting. Certificate for Rachel Atkinson and five children, Benjamin, Thomas, Watson, Rachel and Ezekiel, to Abington Monthly Meeting. Certificate for Alice Dawes to Buckingham Monthly Meeting. Certificate for Hannah Tomkins to Abington Monthly Meeting. Certificate from Buckingham Monthly Meeting for Mary White and children, John, Ann and Mary.

5/6/1770 - Certificate from Buckingham Monthly Meeting for Hannah Wilkinson.

7/8/1770 - Jeremiah Cooper, one of whose parents was a member, requests to be joined in membership. [Rejected because of his disorderly conduct.] Jane Smith to succeed Sarah Beaumont deceased as Elder. Certificates for Amy Newburn and Elizabeth Comly from Buckingham Monthly Meeting. Certificate for Abigail Hollowell to Abington Monthly Meeting.

4/9/1770 - Sarah Siddal desires assistance of Friends, she being in low circumstances.

2/10/1770 - Certificate for Hannah Heston from Abington Monthly Meeting. Mary Scott condemns her going out in marriage. Rebecca Collins received into membership.

6/11/1770 - Marriage of William Cooper Jr. and Mary Briggs accomplished on 17th of last month. Certificate for Hannah Buckman from Abington Monthly Meeting. Certificate for Alice Rose to Evesham Monthly Meeting. Spoke to Eleazer Doan on account of his going out in marriage and having a child born in about 3 months after marriage. Jonathan Balderson requests certificate to Buckingham Monthly Meeting.

4/12/1770 - Jonathan Scholfield produces certificate from Buckingham Monthly Meeting. Certificate for Rachel Martindale from Middletown Monthly Meeting.

1/1/1771 - Joshua Vansant produces certificate from Falls Monthly

Meeting. Joseph Stockdale requests certificate to Buckingham Monthly Meeting in order to proceed in marriage with Elizabeth Smith.

5/2/1771 - Abraham Warner requests certificate to Falls Monthly Meeting.

5/3/1771 - Mary Ashton received into membership. Spoke to Joseph Briggs on account of his going out in his marriage and having a child by his wife 7-8 months after marriage. Joseph Warner requests certificate for himself, wife and children [Cuthbert, Joseph, Asaph, Hezekiah, Mordica and Silas] to Deer Creek Monthly Meeting, Maryland.

2/4/1771 - Richard Leedom produces certificate from Abington for himself and 4 sons, William, Jesse, Benjamin and Joseph. William Worthington produces certificate from Abington Monthly Meeting for himself and children: Mary, William, Jesse and John. Joseph Wiggins requests certificate for himself and family [Sarah his wife and two children, Tracey and Bezaleel] to Deer Creek Monthly Meeting, Maryland. Isaiah Linton requests certificate for himself and family [wife Sarah, children, Laura, Thomas and James] to Gunpowder Monthly Meeting, Maryland. Edward Cunnard requests certificate to Gunpowder Monthly Meeting, Maryland.

7/5/1771 - Marriage of Isaac Comley and Asceneth Hamton accomplished on 10th of last month. [He produces certificate from Abington Monthly Meeting.] Marriage of David Heston and Rachel Briggs accomplished on 24th of last month. Marriage of Paul Blaker and Agnes Buckman accomplished on 1st of this month.

4/6/1771 - Certificate for Sarah Hartley to Buckingham Monthly Meeting. Certificate for Judith Hirst to Gunpowder Monthly Meeting. Christopher Atkinson has placed his son Moses an apprentice to Thomas Ross of Buckingham Monthly Meeting. Jacob Linton requests certificate to Gunpowder Monthly Meeting.

2/7/1771 - Marriage of Abraham Hibbs and Hannah Buckman accomplished on 6th of last month. [He produces certificate from Middletown Monthly Meeting.] Certificate for Asceneth Comly to Abington Monthly Meeting. Certificate for Elizabeth Spicer to Gunpowder Monthly Meeting. Sobiah Ink condemns her unchaste conduct before marriage with him that is now her husband, and in going out in her marriage.

6/8/1771 - Marriage of Isaac Smith and Sarah Hamton accomplished on 10th of last month. Certificate from Buckingham for Elizabeth Stockdale. Certificate from Middletown Monthly Meeting for Ruth Warner. Abraham Scott produces certificate from Uwchland Monthly Meeting for himself, wife Elizabeth and children, Rachel, Amos, Jesse, Roscester, Esther and Thomas. Thomas Warner produces certificate from Middletown Monthly Meeting. Abraham Scott requests certificate to Gunpowder Monthly Meeting, Maryland. Thomas Cary requests certificate to South Carolina.

3/9/1771 - Certificate for Sarah Dungan to Middletown Monthly Meeting.

5/11/1771 - William Chapman Jr does not deny unchaste conduct with Rachel Ely but denies being the father of her child. Certificate from Middletown Monthly Meeting for Catharine Abbett. Spoke with William Lee, son of William Lee Junr., concerning his going out in marriage and having a child by his wife in about 3 months after marriage.

3/12/1771 - Timothy Balderson produces certificate from Buckingham Monthly Meeting. Cert for Mary Carver to Abington Monthly Meeting.

7/1/1772 - Reported that Jeremiah Boaman is in a weak and helpless condition.

4/2/1772 - David Johnston requests certificate to Falls Monthly Meeting. [Copy of will of Benjamin Hamton].

3/3/1772 - Since the last meeting Jeremiah Boaman has died. John Hirst produces certificate from Buckingham Monthly Meeting. Joseph Johnson requests certificate for himself and family [Rachel his wife and children, Samuel and Joseph] to Falls Monthly Meeting. James Wood requests certificate for himself and family [wife Mary and children, James, John, Aaron, Septimus, Mary, Sarah, Rachel and Rebecca] to Chester Monthly Meeting at Providence. Thomas Smith requests certificate for himself and family [Mary his wife, and children, Samuel, Joseph, Keziah, John, Susanna, Ezra and Thomas] to Buckingham Monthly Meeting.

7/4/1772 - Certificate for Mary Johnson to Falls Monthly Meeting. Mary McGray received into membership. Thomas Whitson requests that his children, Benjamin, Thomas, Mary, Ann, Elizabeth, Deborah and John be taken under the care of Friends.

5/5/1772 - Certificate for Sarah Paxson to Buckingham Monthly Meeting. Hannah Hibbs condemns her having a child between 6 and 7 months after marriage.

2/6/1772 - Certificate for Mary Chapman to Abington Monthly Meeting.

7/7/1772 - Certificate from Buckingham Monthly Meeting for James Dubre and Hannah his wife. John Watson produces certificate from Buckingham Monthly Meeting. John Hare produces certificate from Falls Monthly Meeting. John Parsons requests certificate, having removed out of the Province.

4/8/1772 - To treat with James Ross concerning his suing his brother Thomas. Nathan Hummer produces certificate from Abington Monthly Meeting. Informed that Jacob Verrity has gone out in his marriage.

1/9/1772 - Spoke to John Stockdale Junr. concerning his going out in marriage. Isacher Morris requests to be joined in membership with Friends.

6/10/1772 - Certificate for Elizabeth Smith to Buckingham Monthly Meeting. Certificate from Abington Monthly Meeting for Ann Gomery and Joseph Gomery, two minor children, placed at David Buckman's, a member. Sarah Scott condemns her going out in marriage. Moses Smith about to take a voyage to Charlestown, South Carolina. Spoke to Ebenezer Large concerning his going out in marriage and having a child born 3-4 months after marriage.

3/11/1772 - John Buckman requests certificate for himself, wife and such of his children as are under age, to Falls Monthly

Meeting. David Buckman Jur. requests certificate to Falls Monthly Meeting. Spoke to Ebenezer Wilson concerning his going out in his marriage.

5/1/1773 - Stephen Large requests certificate to Buckingham Monthly Meeting. Certificate for Margaret Buckman to Falls Monthly Meeting. Moses Smith returned certificate with indorsement from Friends in Charleston, South Carolina.

2/2/1773 - Testimony against Priscilla Reeder (late Rose). --- Pearson requests certificate to Middletown Monthly Meeting.

2/3/1773 - John Hair requests certificate for himself and family to Gunpowder Monthly Meeting. Arnold Mitchener requests certificate to Abington Monthly Meeting. Isacher Morris requests certificate to Buckingham Monthly Meeting. George Hulme requests certificate to Falls Monthly Meeting.

6/4/1773 - Marriage of Isaac Warner and Martha Janney accomplished on 31st of last month. Robert Verree requests certificate for Abington Monthly Meeting for himself, wife, two children and Thomas Stockdale. Richard Betts requests certificate for himself and daughter to Bush Creek Monthly Meeting in Frederick Co., Maryland. [Probable means Pipe Creek Monthly Meeting of which Bush Creek was a preparative meeting.] Thomas Cary requests certificate to Middletown Monthly Meeting. Spoke with John Blaker concerning his going out in marriage and having a child born about 5 months after marriage and charged by another woman that she was with child by him. William Smith produces certificate from preparative Monthly Meeting.

4/5/1773 - Marriage of Isaac Wilson and Susanna Chapman accomplished 27th of last month. Marriage of John Buckman and Susanna Chapman accomplished on 21st of last month. [Sic. There are two different Susanna Chapmans mentioned in this minute and the earlier ones.] Sarah Janney requests to be taken under the care of Friends with her children Ann and Jacob.

1/6/1773 - Certificate for Sarah Smith and her son Samuel Smith, in his minority, to Buckingham Monthly Meeting. Sarah Good condemns her unchastity with him that is now her husband and having a child born within 5 months after marriage. John Johnson requests certificate to Falls Monthly Meeting.

6/7/1773 - Certificate for Elizabeth Hulme wife of John Hulme from Middletown Monthly Meeting. Certificate for Lydia Heaton Jur. to Bush River, South Carolina [to go with her parents].

7/9/1773 - Certificate for Sarah Good to Buckingham Monthly Meeting. Samuel Hilborn has met with considerable loss by fire.

5/10/1773 - Certificate from Buckingham Monthly Meeting for Hannah Morris, wife of Isacher Morris.

2/11/1773 - Abraham Hibbs produces certificate from Middletown Monthly Meeting for himself and his children, Thomas and Mary. Samuel Lee requests certificate for himself and children [Thomas, Samuel, Hannah, John, William, Mary and Ann] to Gunpowder Monthly Meeting. [Cert prepared for Samuel, wife Mary and children.]

4/1/1774 - Jonathan Scholfield requests certificate for himself, wife and child to Buckingham Monthly Meeting. Marriage of Stephen Twining and Sarah Janney accomplished on 15th of last month.

1/3/1774 - Certificate for John Smith, Martha his wife and children, Mary, Martha, Ann, John and Esther, to Buckingham Monthly Meeting. Job Cooper requests to be joined in membership.

5/4/1774 - Certificate for Alice Blaker from Abington Monthly Meeting. John Heston requests certificate for himself, his wife and children [wife Hannah, children, Jarret and Levi], to Abington Monthly Meeting. John Hirst requests certificate for himself, wife and children [wife Mary, children, John, Rebecca, Sarah, Jesse, David, Ann and Thomas], to Fairfax Monthly Meeting, Virginia. Cornelius Shepherd requests certificate for himself, wife and children to Gwynedd Monthly Meeting. James Dubre requests certificate for himself, wife and child, to Buckingham Monthly Meeting. Daniel Lee requests certificate to Falls Monthly Meeting in order to proceed in marriage with Margaret Buckman.

3/5/1774 - Certificate for Mary McGray to Fairfax Monthly Meeting, Virginia. Benjamin Lacey requests certificate to Fairfax Monthly Meeting, Virginia. Job Cooper requests certificate to Fairfax Monthly Meeting, Virginia. Elizabeth Hibbs received into membership.

7/6/1774 - Marriage of Joseph Martindale and Hannah Buckman accomplished on 1st of this month. John Wildman produces certificate from Middletown Monthly Meeting for himself, Mary his wife and children, Sarah, Enos, Betsey, Rachel, John and Josepf. Certificate for Catharine Abbett to Richland Monthly Meeting.

6/9/1774 - Testimony against Elizabeth Doan for having two children in an unmarried state (by different men).

4/10/1774 - Certificate from Falls Monthly Meeting for Margaret Lee.

1/11/1774 - Cephas Atkinson requests certificate for himself and family to Warrington Monthly Meeting.

6/12/1774 - Certificate for Jane Atkinson for Warrington Monthly Meeting in York Co. Certificate for Margaret Atkinson, minor, to Gwynedd Monthly Meeting, being placed by her father with Joseph Ambler of that meeting. Certificate for Sarah Paxson from Buckingham Monthly Meeting. Testimony against Susannah Bender for going out in marriage with a man not of our Society. William Betts requests certificate to Buckingham Monthly Meeting.

3/1/1775 - Certificate for Mary Ashton to Evesham Monthly Meeting.

7/2/1775 - James Paxson whose father was a member, requests to join in membership.

4/4/1775 - Certificate for Hannah Ewers, wife of George Ewers, to Abington Monthly Meeting, Ann Smith, wife of Joseph Smith and Rachel Cooper, both to Buckingham Monthly Meeting. Isaac Warner requests certificate to Abington Monthly Meeting for himself, wife [Martha] and child [Mary]. William Briggs requests certificate to Gunpowder Monthly Meeting.

2/5/1775 - Certificate from Middletown Monthly Meeting for Deidamia Briggs. John Wilkinson requests certificate to Buckingham Monthly Meeting for himself, wife [Elizabeth] and five children [Hannah Lacey, her daughter by a former husband, and William, Anna, Jonathan and David].

4/7/1775 - Stephen Smith requests certificate to Buckingham Monthly Meeting. Reported that Samuel Smith moved away without paying his creditors. Informed that Isaac Heston hath gone out in his marriage. Certificate for Mira [female] Chapman to Richland Monthly Meeting. Testimony against Ann Sample (late Betts).

1/8/1775 - Certificate for Phebe Wey from Monthly Meeting in New York. Thomas West requests to join in membership.

3/10/1775 - Certificate for Phebe Smith, wife of Stephen Smith from Buckingham Monthly Meeting. Certificate for Elizabeth Smith, dau. of Benjamin Smith, dec'd., to Buckingham Monthly Meeting. Certificate from Middletown Monthly Meeting for Benjamin Stackhouse, minor, placed with Thomas Warner a member of this meeting. Thomas Chapman requests certificate to Monthly Meeting in Orange Co., North Carolina for himself, wife [Margaret] and son Miles.

11/10/1775 - Certificate for Alice Chapman and Ann Chapman, daus. of Thomas Chapman, to Monthly Meeting in Orange Co., North Carolina.

7/11/1775 - Marriage of John Wilkinson Jun. and Elizabeth Gourly [Gourley] accomplished on 11th of last month. [He produces certificate from Buckingham Monthly Meeting.]

5/12/1775 - Certificate for Abigail Doan to Middletown Monthly Meeting. Certificate for Rebecca Malmsbury to Chesterfield Monthly Meeting in New Jersey. Certificate for David Hamton, minor, placed an apprentice with John Merrick, a Friend at Falls Monthly Meeting. Elizabeth Tomlinson (late Comly) condemns her marriage before a priest with a man not of our Society.

2/1/1776 - Certificate for Margaret Gourly to Buckingham Monthly Meeting. Spoke to Abner Buckman concerning his going out in his marriage with a woman not of our Society and their having a child born in about 6 months after marriage.

6/2/1776 - Marriage of James Paxson and Mary Hilborn accomplished on 10th of last month. Certificate for Elizabeth Tomlinson to Abington Monthly Meeting.

2/4/1776 - Marriage of Thomas West and Elizabeth Hibbs accomplished on 20th of 1st month. Certificate from Gunpowder Mm for Sarah Linton, widow of Isaiah Linton with her children, Laura, Thomas, James, William and Sarah. Certificate from Abington for Phebe Tomlinson. Certificate for Elizabeth Wilkinson Jur. to Buckingham Monthly Meeting.

7/5/1776 - Joseph Johnson produces certificate from Fall Monthly Meeting for himself, Rachel his wife and their son Joseph.

4/6/1776 - Certificate from Buckingham Monthly Meeting for Sarah Fell. Mathias Harvey Jur. requests to be joined in membership.

2/7/1776 - Zebulon Heston being deceased.

6/8/1776 - John Wildman requests certificate to Middletown

Monthly Meeting for himself, wife [Mary] and children [Sarah, Enos, Betsy, Rachel, John and Joseph]. Memorial for Zebulon Heston, d. 12/3/1776 in his 74th year.

3/9/1776 - Certificate for Phebe Wey to Richland Monthly Meeting. Certificate from Monthly Meeting for Northern Dist. of Phila for Elizabeth Carr. Certificate from Monthly Meeting at Gun Powder for Ann Spicer, minor, placed at William Linton's. Richard Parsons Jun. requests to have his children: Mahlon, Joshua, Naomi, Rebecca, Jemima and Mary, taken under the care of Friends.

5/11/1776 - Robert Ware requests to be joined in membership.

6/12/1776 - Elizabeth Harvey (late Stockdale) condemns her misconduct in consummating her marriage contrary to the rules of Friends.

7/1/1777 - Thomas West requests certificate to Buckingham Monthly Meeting.

4/2/1777 - Certificate for Susanna Mitchel wife of George Mitchel to Buckingham Monthly Meeting. Jemima Parsons wife of Richard Parsons requests to be joined into membership.

3/6/1777 - Certificate for Elizabeth Smith from Buckingham Monthly Meeting. Reported that Thomas Buckman is father of a child by a single woman he keeps in his house. George Jewel requests that he and his three children be joined in membership. Elizabeth Paxson received into membership.

5/8/1777 - Stephen Field produces certificate from Chesterfield Monthly Meeting. He requests that his two children Margaret and Stephen, minors, also be taken under the care of Friends.

2/9/1777 - Rachel Cary (late Doan) condemns her going out in her marriage. John Merrick requests certificate to Buckingham Monthly Meeting in order to proceed in marriage with Sarah Armitage.

7/10/1777 - Mary Clark (late White) condemns her going out in her marriage.

4/11/1777 - Spoke to Achilles Blaker concerning his consummating his marriage before a hireling minister. [Wife's name is Sarah]

2/12/1777 - Certificate for Ann Hamton to Middletown Monthly Meeting. Also one recommending her dau. Ann, minor, to Abington Monthly Meeting, she being placed with Isaac Comley, member of that meeting. Marriage of Mathias Harvey and Esther Lee accomplished on 19th of last month.

3/2/1778 - Certificate for Sarah Merrick, wife of John Merrick, from Buckingham Monthly Meeting. Mary Curry (late Newburn) condemns her consummating her marriage before a hireling priest. Thomas Smith son of Samuel Smith requests certificate to Buckingham Monthly Meeting in order to proceed in marriage with Eleanor Smith.

3/3/1778 - Certificate for Elizabeth Stockdale and her children, Sarah, Elizabeth, John and Mary, to Buckingham Monthly Meeting. Certificate for Hannah Tomlinson to Abington Monthly Meeting, she being placed with Bartholomew Mathers, a member of that meeting.

7/4/1778 - Certificate for Mary Heston from Buckingham Monthly Meeting.

2/6/1778 - Thomas West produces certificate from Buckingham Monthly Meeting for himself, Elizabeth his wife and Enos their son. Thomas Hilborn Jun. condemns his marrying before a hireling minister.
7/7/1778 - Spoke to John Martindale Jr. on account of his having been unchaste before marriage with her that is now his wife and consummating marriage before an hireling minister.
23/9/1778 - Certificate for Sarah Wilson, wife of Samuel Wilson, taylor, and their children, Jane, Samuel, Stephen, Joseph, Rachel, Mary and Nancy, all minors, to Fairfax Monthly Meeting, Virginia. Certificate for John Smith, Martha his wife and their children, Mary, Martha, Ann, John and Esther, to Buckingham Monthly Meeting, which John has neglected to deliver to that meeting.
6/10/1778 - Certificate for Eleanor Smith, wife of Thomas Smith, from Buckingham Monthly Meeting. Eleazer Doan requests certificate to Buckingham Monthly Meeting for himself, Mary his wife and children, Susanna, Jonas, Rebecca and Jonathan.
3/11/1778 - Certificate for Sarah Linton to Buckingham Monthly Meeting. Certificate for Susanna Betts, dau. of Richard Betts to Pike Creek Monthly Meeting in Virginia. Jonathan Buckman produces certificate for himself and Sarah his wife, from Falls Monthly Meeting.
5/1/1779 - Certificate for Rachel Cary, wife of Samuel Cary, to Buckingham Monthly Meeting.
20/1/1779 - Thomas Atkinson requests certificate to Buckingham Monthly Meeting in order to proceed in marriage with Sarah Smith Junior.
2/2/1779 - Certificate from Kingwood Monthly Meeting in New Jersey for Prudence Philips.
2/3/1779 - Marriage of James Dubre and Sarah Lacey Jur. accomplished on 17th of last month. [He produces certificate from Buckingham Monthly Meeting.] William Wood requests certificate to Chester Monthly Meeting at Providence. David Newburn requests certificate to Buckingham Monthly Meeting in order to proceed in marriage with Tamar Bains.
6/4/1779 - William Taylor produces certificate from Falls Monthly Meeting. William Briggs produces certificate from Gunpowder Monthly Meeting, Maryland. Spoke with Thomas Lee on account of his having gone out from amongst Friends in his marriage within 7 months after the decease of his former wife.
4/5/1779 - Marriage of Matthew Wood and Mary Worthington Junior accomplished on 21st of last month. Phebe Harding condemns her going out in her marriage.
1/6/1779 - Marriage of William Martindale and Esther Buckman accomplished on 19th of last month. John Carlisle Junior requests certificate to Buckingham Monthly Meeting. Sarah Hilborn, wife of Thomas Hilborn, continues her requests for membership with Friends. Certificate for Susanna Stokes to Chesterfield Monthly Meeting, New Jersey. Certificate for Sarah Dubre wife of James Dubre to Buckingham Monthly Meeting.
6/7/1779 - Robert Thomas condemns his marrying with one not in membership before an hireling minister. Spoke to Abner Buckman on account of his consummating his marriage before a

hireling minister.

3/8/1779 - Certificate for Phebe Tomlinson, wife of Thomas Tomlinson to Monthly Meeting at Abington. Certificate for Sarah Wilson wife of Thomas Wilson to Middletown. Certificate for Sarah Smith, dau. of Benjamin Smith, dec'd., to Buckingham Monthly Meeting. Certificate for Sarah Smith from Buckingham. Certificate for Sarah Atkinson, wife of Thomas Atkinson. Certificate for Tamar Newburn from Buckingham Monthly Meeting. Mahlon Fell produces certificate from Buckingham Monthly Meeting for himself, wife Rachel and son Ezra. Marriage of David Whitson and Sarah Stockdale accomplished on 28th of last month. [He produces certificate from Buckingham Monthly Meeting.] Marriage of Benjamin Whitson and Mary Stockdale Jur. accomplished on 28th of last month. Mahlon Worthington requests to be joined in membership.

7/9/1779 - Certificate from Haverford Monthly Meeting for Dorothy Ballance. Abraham Reeder requests to be joined in membership. Isaac Buckman Jun. requests certificate to Buckingham Monthly Meeting in order to proceed in marriage with Joyce Fell. John Beaumont Jr. requests certificate to Buckingham Monthly Meeting in order to proceed in marriage with Jane Brown.

5/10/1779 - Robert Smith requests certificate to Buckingham Monthly Meeting in order to proceed in marriage with Bridget Dillon.

7/12/1779 - Marriage of Jacob Buckman and Rebecca Smith accomplished 17th of last month. Certificate from Pipe Creek Monthly Meeting for Susannah Betts.

4/1/1780 - Marriage of John Wetherel [Weatheral] and Sarah Worthington accomplished on 15th of last month. [He produces certificate from Falls Monthly Meeting.]

7/3/1780 - Testimony against Sarah Wilson (late Tomlinson). Sarah Varnow (late Doan) condemns her outgoings in consummating her marriage before an hireling minister with one not in membership with Friends.

4/4/1780 - Certificate from Middletown Monthly Meeting for Ann Hamton. Certificate from Buckingham Monthly Meeting for Bridget Smith. Certificate for Joice Buckman. Cert requested for Nathan Doan, son of John Doan, who is placed an apprentice with John Kinsey, member of Buckingham Monthly Meeting.

2/5/1780 - Certificate from Buckingham Mm for Jane Beaumont, wife of John Beaumont Jr.

6/6/1780 - Marriage of William Smith and Sarah Buckman accomplished on 31st of last month. Marriage of Abraham Reeder and Elizabeth Lee accomplished on 17th of last month. Asaph Warner produces certificate from Monthly Meeting of Deer Creek, Maryland. Certificate for Hester Penquite to Abington Monthly Meeting. Certificate for Phebe Harding to Buckingham Monthly Meeting. Joseph Speakman produces certificate from Monthly Meeting at Richland for himself, wife Catharine and three small children, Townsend, Mary and Keziah. Spoke to Joseph Tomlinson (John's son) concerning his being charged by Ann Hilborn with being the father of her illegitimate child. Spoke with Benjamin Whitson concerning his having a child within six months after his marriage.

1/8/1780 - James Buckman requests certificate to Falls Monthly Meeting in order to proceed in marriage with Sarah Burroughs. Stephen Field requests certificate to Abington Monthly Meeting.
3/10/1780 - Testimony against Jane Tomlinson, late Buckman. Testimony against Richard Tomlinson and Hannah his wife. George Jewell requests certificate to Monthly Meeting at the little Falls in Maryland for himself, wife [Mary] and children [Alice and Mary]. Thomas West requests certificate to Monthly Meeting at the little Falls in Maryland for himself, wife [Elizabeth] and children [Enos and Stacey]. The following men were spoken with concerning paying military (militia) fines: Richard Leedom, Zechariah Betts, Abraham Hibbs, William Heston, Isachar Morris, Thomas Story, William Martindale, Daniel Lee, John Buckman Jr., John Stockdale Jr., Paul Blaker, Benjamin Buckman and Miles Martindale.
7/11/1780 - Marriage of Joseph Walton and Deborah Lee accomplished on 1st of this month. [He produces certificate from Abington Monthly Meeting.] Certificate for Hester Allibone from Buckingham Monthly Meeting.
10/1/1781 - Certificate for John, Rachel, Isaac, Joseph and Charity Scarbrough.
6/2/1781 - Certificate for Deborah Walton to Abington Monthly Meeting. Certificate for Elizabeth Smith to Buckingham Monthly Meeting. Spoke to Daniel Richardson concerning his committing fornication with her that is his wife and consummating his marriage out of the Unit of Friends. Spoke with following men concerning paying military (militia) fines: John Rose, John Atkinson, Joseph Kirk and Thomas Kirk.
6/3/1781 - Spoke to Miles Martindale concerning his consummating his marriage by the assistance of a hireling minister. Certificate for Sarah Buckman wife of James Buckman. Richard Parsons Jr. requests certificate for himself and family [wife Jemima, children, Mahlon, Joshua, Naomi, Rebecca, Jemima, Mary and William] to Monthly Meeting of Chester at Providence.
3/4/1781 - Certificate for Susanna Betts to Buckingham Monthly Meeting. Certificate for Sarah Witherell to the Falls Monthly Meeting. Asaph Warner requests certificate to Buckingham Monthly Meeting in order to proceed in marriage with Ruth Ellicott.
1/5/1781 - Joseph Speakman requests certificate for himself, wife [Catharine] and children, Townsend, Kezia, Mary, Lydia and Esther, to the Falls Monthly Meeting. Following men spoken to concerning their paying military fines: Matthias Harvey, Jonathan Kinsey and Thomas Story.
3/7/1781 - Certificate from Indian Spring Monthly Meeting, Maryland, for Ann Scholfield. Matthew Wood requests certificate for himself, wife [Mary] and child [Jacob] to Chester Monthly Meeting at Providence.
7/8/1781 - Mary Allibone (late Ball) condemns her misconduct.
4/9/1781 - James Love condemns his outgoing in marriage.
19/9/1781 - Spoke to John Briggs for paying substitute and muster fines.
2/10/1781 - Joseph Ballance requests certificate to Buckingham

Monthly Meeting to proceed in marriage with Anna Pownal.

4/12/1781 - Certificate for Esther Allibone to Phila Monthly Meeting.

5/2/1782 - Certificate for Ann Doan to Middletown Monthly Meeting. Certificate for Sarah Dennis to Richland Monthly Meeting. Certificate for Dorothy Kinsey to Buckingham Monthly Meeting.

5/3/1782 - Certificate for Mary Blackfan to Buckingham Monthly Meeting. William Smith (tanner) requests certificate to the Falls Monthly Meeting. John Hamton requests certificate to Middletown Monthly Meeting.

2/4/1782 - Andrew Collins requests to be joined in membership. Mary Redder condemns her marrying her first cousin. Certificate for Anna Ballance to this meeting. Reported that John Tomlinson accomplished his marriage out of Unity of Friends.

7/5/1782 - Certificate for Sarah Burson and her children, Mary Twining and Stephen Twining to Monthly Meeting of Richland. Jonathan Buckman requests certificate for himself and family [Sarah his wife and children, Stacy and Mahlon] to Gwynedd Monthly Meeting. Certificate for Elizabeth Carlile to the Falls Monthly Meeting. Cert for William Lee for himself, Eleanor his wife and their children, Mary, Sebilla, David and Eleanor, to Gunpowder Monthly Meeting.

6/8/1782 - Spoke with Jacob Twining concerning his marriage by the assistance of a hireling minister with a woman not in membership. Richard Betts requests certificate to Buckingham Monthly Meeting. Reported that William and Joseph Hibbs had removed with their parents in their minority without certificate to Loudoun Co. Virginia. Reported that David Chapman, Amos Chapman and Abraham Chapman Jur. sometime ago removed to New York or Long Island without certificates.

3/9/1782 - Spoke with Jacob Twining concerning his accomplishing his marriage by the assistance of a hireling minister with a woman not in membership with Friends. Certificate for Sarah Varnal to Falls Monthly Meeting. Certificate for William and Joseph Hibbs and their three sisters, Sarah, Mary and Elizabeth to Fairfax Monthly Meeting. Reported that Amos Chapman and Abraham Chapman Jur. have entered into military service.

1/10/1782 - John Atkinson, son of Cephas, produces certificate from Warrington Monthly Meeting. Certificate for Elizabeth Pownall to Buckingham Monthly Meeting.

11/12/1782 - Isaac Buckman Jun. requests certificate for himself and family [Joyce his wife, children, David and Deborah] to Monthly Meeting at Buckingham. Spoke with William Lee the Younger concerning paying fines and Stephen Wilkinson for serving with the Militia. Spoke to John Betts concerning his accomplishing his marriage out of the Unity of Friends with a woman not in membership with Friends. Spoke with Zebulon Heston Jr. concerning his accomplishing his marriage by the assistance of a hireling minister.

4/2/1783 - Certificate for Sarah Linton to Buckingham Monthly Meeting. Jonathan Hamton requests certificate to Buckingham

Monthly Meeting. Thomas Smith for his son Stephen Smith requests certificate for his son to Buckingham Monthly Meeting who is placed an apprentice with Thomas Ellicott, and for his son Isaac to the Monthly Meeting at Phila who is placed an apprentice with Joseph Bacon. Spoke with John Beaumont and William Smith son of Thomas, concerning militia training.

4/3/1783 - Certificate for Elizabeth Whitson Jun., minor, to Buckingham Monthly Meeting. Thomas Whitson requests certificate for himself and minor children [Deborah, John, Henry, Margaret and Burt] to Sadsbury Monthly Meeting.

1/4/1783 - Certificate for Mary Whitson wife of Benjamin Whitson and their children, Joseph, John and Henry, to Sadsbury Monthly Meeting. Certificate for Anne Whitson to same meeting. Ephraim Smith requests certificate for himself and family [wife Rachel and children, Elizabeth, Ephraim, Rachel, Mary, Ann, Sarah, Samuel and Jane] to East Caln Monthly Meeting, Chester Co.

6/5/1783 - Certificate for Mary Clark to Little Falls in Harford Co., Maryland. John Watson requests certificate for himself and family to Buckingham Monthly Meeting. John Warner Jun. requests certificate for himself and family [wife Phebe, children, Rachel, John, Mercy, Joseph and Seneca] to Horsham Monthly Meeting.

3/6/1783 - Certificate to Buckingham Monthly Meeting for John Watson, his wife Mary, and children, Alice, John, Frances, Ann and Rachel. Certificate for Anna Smith wife of William Smith to this meeting. Certificate for Elizabeth Hilborn to Buckingham Monthly Meeting and Mary Ely to the same place.

1/7/1783 - Certificate for Sarah Linton to Falls Monthly Meeting. Spoke to Thomas Buckman concerning his committing fornication with her that is now his wife and accomplishing his marriage out of the Unity of Friends.

5/8/1783 - Certificate for Phebe Harding. Robert Thomas requests certificate to Providence Monthly Meeting in Chester Co.

2/9/783 - Ann Plunkett requests to be joined in membership. Elizabeth Twining Jun.requests to be joined in membership. Certificate for Jane Lacey and her two children, Elizabeth and William to Monthly Meeting at Indian Spring, Maryland.

7/10/1783 - Certificate for Maria Spicer from Little Falls Monthly Meeting in Maryland. Certificate for Hannah Tomlinson from Abington Monthly Meeting. Thomas Smith Junr. requests certificate to Buckingham Monthly Meeting in order to proceed in marriage with Latitia Blackfann.

4/11/1783 - Children of John Dillon (to wit), Ann, John, Sarah, Hannah and Josiah, who left these parts in their minority requests certificate to Monthly Meeting of Fairfax in Virginia. John Story requests certificate for his son Samuel to Monthly Meeting of Phila, who is placed apprentice with Arthur Howell.

2/12/1783 - Elizabeth Closon requests to be joined in membership. Stephen Wilson requests certificate for himself and wife [Mercy] to Monthly Meeting of Wilmington.

6/1/1784 - Rachel Weaber condemns her consummating marriage by the assistance of a hireling minister. James Love requests certificate to Monthly Meeting at Fairfax in Virginia. Jacob Verity hath resided some years within the verge of Richland Monthly Meeting without taking a cert. William Hibbs removed to Abington Monthly Meeting under similar circumstances.

3/2/1784 - Certificate for Ann Kinsey to Buckingham Monthly Meeting.

2/3/1784 - Certificate for Sarah Whitson wife of David Whitson and her children, William and Joseph to Monthly Meeting at the little Falls, Harford Co., Maryland.

6/4/1784 - Certificate for Elizabeth Harvey to Little Falls Monthly Meeting in Maryland.

4/5/1784 - Marriage of Edmund Plumley and Elizabeth Worthington accomplished on 28th of last month. [He produces certificate from Middletown Monthly Meeting.] William Hibbs condemns his entering into military service. Certificate for Elizabeth Hopkins to Monthly Meeting of the Northern Dist. of Phila. Mary Pownall condemns her consummating her marriage by the assistance of a hireling minister. Oliver Hamton requests certificate to Buckingham Monthly Meeting.

6/7/1784 - Edmund Smith produces certificate from Buckingham Monthly Meeting for himself, Deborah his wife, Jonathan, Samuel, Edmund, Benjamin, Joshua and Jesse their children.

3/8/1784 - David Buckman produces certificate from the Falls Monthly Meeting for himself, Esther his wife and children, Hannah, Rachel and John. Certificate for Ann Hamton to Middletown Monthly Meeting.

5/10/1784 - Certificate for Elizabeth Plumley wife of Edmund Plumley to Middletown Monthly Meeting. Spoke to Joseph Terry concerning his attending militia exercise. Jacob Verity requests certificate to Richland Monthly Meeting.

2/11/1784 - Thomas Ross son of Thomas Ross Jun. requests certificate to Phila Monthly Meeting, he being placed an apprentice to a member of that meeting.

7/12/1784 - Certificate from Middletown Monthly Meeting for Esther Penquite. Certificate from Gunpowder Monthly Meeting for Mary Lee. Thomas Prall produces certificate from Kingwood Monthly Meeting. Spoke with David Newburn concerning his associating with the militia. Spoke to Ralph Lee concerning his accomplishing his marriage out of the Unity of Friends with a woman not in membership with us, and associating with the militia at their training.

1/2/1785 - Benjamin Stackhouse requests certificate to Monthly Meeting at the Falls Spoke to John Atkinson (weaver) concerning his accomplishing his marriage out of the Unity of Friends.

1/3/1785 - Certificate from Buckingham Monthly Meeting for Elizabeth Hibron. Jacob Heston produces certificate from Phila Monthly Meeting. Asaph Warner requests certificate to Buckingham Monthly Meeting. Samuel Doan requests certificate to the Falls Monthly Meeting.

5/4/1785 - Sarah Dungan condemns her consummating her marriage by the assistance of a hireling minister. Certificate from Buckingham Monthly Meeting for Elizabeth Smith. Spoke to Robert Weaver concerning his attending militia. Jonathan

Warner requests certificate to Falls Monthly Meeting.

3/5/1785 - Rachel Harding condemns her marrying out of the Unity of Friends.

7/6/1785 - Marriage of Benjamin Smith and Mary Worthington accomplished 11th of last month. Marriage of Joseph Smith and Rachel Hayhurst accomplished on 11th of last month. [He produces certificate from Buckingham Monthly Meeting.] Certificate for Sarah Hamton, minor, to Buckingham Monthly Meeting. Abraham Chapman deceased was surviving trustee of the old grave Yard. Abraham Chapman his son is now his surviving executor.

5/7/1785 - Oliver Hamton produces certificate from Buckingham Monthly Meeting. Certificate for Gulielma Maria Spicer to Buckingham Monthly Meeting. Joseph Heston requests certificate for himself, wife and children, to Gwynedd Monthly Meeting.

6/9/1785 - Joseph Smith produces certificate from Buckingham Monthly Meeting. Certificate for Ann Buckman to Middletown Monthly Meeting.

4/10/1785 - Informed by one of his near neighbours that Jesse Comfort has accomplished his marriage out of the Unity of Friends. Cert for Elizabeth Fell from Buckingham Monthly Meeting.

8/11/1785 - Certificate for Sarah Linton from Falls Monthly Meeting.

3/1/1786 - Jacob Smith produces certificate from Woodberry Monthly Meeting for himself, Phebe his wife and children, Thomas, Jonathan, Randal, Elizabeth, Ann, Israel and William. Certificate for Rachel Weaber to Buckingham Monthly Meeting. Certificate produced from Falls Monthly Meeting for Joseph Smith, Phebe his wife and their children, Timothy, John, Rachel and Joseph. To prepare essay of notification to Kingwood Monthly Meeting respecting Prudence Force (late Philips). John Merrick requests certificate for himself, wife [Sarah] and children [Elizabeth, Sarah, Amos, John and ---], to Buckingham Monthly Meeting.

7/2/1786 - Certificate for Mary Tomlinson wife of William Tomlinson to Fairfax Monthly Meeting, Virginia. Spoke to Joseph Twining concerning his accomplishing his marriage out of the unity of Friends. Spoke to Ezekiel Atkinson concerning his accomplishing his marriage out of the Unity of Friends.

7/3/1786 - Benjamin Hamton Jun. requests certificate to Buckingham Monthly Meeting. Spoke to Jonathan Newburn concerning his accomplishing his marriage by assistance of a hireling minister with a woman not in membership with Friends. Reported that John Story Jr. has removed to Phila and not taken a cert.

4/4/1786 - James Hamton requests certificate to Gwynedd Monthly Meeting. David Heston requests certificate for himself and children to Monthly Meeting for the Northern Dist. of Phila.

2/5/1786 - David Davis produces certificate from Horsham Monthly Meeting. John Scholfield requests certificate to Buckingham Monthly Meeting.

6/6/1786 - Marriage of John Eastburn and Elizabeth Wiggins Jun.

accomplished on 10th of last month. [He produces certificate from Buckingham Monthly Meeting.] Cert from Buckingham Monthly Meeting for Rachel Heston.

4/7/1786 - Joseph Smith condemns his keeping a disorderly Public House. Certificate for Rebecca Heston from Falls Monthly Meeting.

8/8/1786 - Certificate for Pleasant Smith from Falls Monthly Meeting. Certificate from Buckingham for Margaret Hamton. Oliver Hamton requests certificate to Buckingham Monthly Meeting.

5/9/1786 - Certificate for Esther Penquite to Abington Monthly Meeting. Certificate for Mary Scott to Buckingham Monthly Meeting. Thomas Story requests certificate to Middletown Monthly Meeting in order to proceed in marriage with Rachel Jenks.

3/10/1786 - Certificate for Ann Hamton from Middletown Monthly Meeting. Zebulon Heston requests certificate for himself, wife [Rebecca] and children [Hannah and Sarah], to Gwynedd Monthly Meeting.

7/11/1786 - Abner Heston now resides in Virginia.

5/12/1786 - Certificate for Rachel Smith to Fairfax Monthly Meeting in Loudoun Co., Virginia. John Simpson produces certificate from Buckingham Monthly Meeting for himself, wife Ruth and children, David, Hannah, John, Ruth and James.

13/12/1786 - Joel Carver produces certificate from Buckingham Monthly Meeting for himself and children, Joseph, Rachel Martha, Robert and Ann. Spoke to Abraham Buckman concerning his accomplishing marriage out of the Unity of Friends. Spoke to Thomas Kinsey concerning his associating with the militia.

2/1/1787 - Certificate for Mary Whitson from Buckingham Monthly Meeting. Certificate for Rebecca Gillum to Sadsbury Monthly Meeting.

6/2/1787 - Certificate from Buckingham Monthly Meeting for Ann Hamton Jun. Spoke to Amos Martindale concerning his associating with the militia.

6/3/1787 - Certificate from Chesterfield Monthly Meeting in the Jerseys for Sarah Wetherell with children, William and Rebecca Wetherell. Mahlon Fell requests certificate for himself and family to Buckingham Monthly Meeting.

3/4/1787 - Certificate for Isaac Buckman from Buckingham Monthly Meeting, his wife Joyce, and children, David, Deborah, Mary and Charles. Certificate for Rachel Story from Middletown Monthly Meeting. Thomas Buckman requests certificate to the Falls Monthly Meeting.

8/5/1787 - John Cooper and Ester his wife requests to be admitted as members of the meeting. Reported that Mahlon Pursel has accomplished his marriage out of the Unity of Friends.

5/6/1787 - Children of John and Esther Cooper received as members: Mahlon, Sarah, John, Jacob, Henry, Esther, Martha, Margaret and Chilion. Certificate from Chester Monthly Meeting for Susanna Stokes. Certificate for Catharine Abbet to Gwynedd Monthly Meeting.

3/7/1787 - James Hamton produces certificate from Gwynedd Monthly Meeting. Jasper Terry produces certificate for himself, Lucy his wife and dau. Martha, from Middletown Monthly Meeting. Jesse Betts requests certificate to Buckingham Monthly Meeting in order to proceed in marriage with Hannah Paxson.

2/10/1787 - Spoke to Strickland Martindale concerning his marrying out of the Unity of Friends with a woman not in membership with Friends.

6/11/1787 - Certificate for Mary Whitson to Westbury Monthly Meeting on Long Island. Jesse Buckman requests certificate to the Falls Monthly Meeting in order to proceed in marriage with Hannah Taylor. Jesse Betts requests certificate to Middletown Monthly Meeting. Spoke with Benjamin Chapman Junior concerning his accomplishing his marriage out of Unity of Friends with a woman not in membership.

4/12/1787 - Joshua Vansant and Mary Wilkinson to marry. [The minutes which would have reported the marriage accomplished, are missing.] Ruth Hilborn requests for herself and three daus., Ruth, Hannah and Mary to be taken into membership.

8/1/1788 - Marriage of David Warner and Asceneth Buckman accomplished on 26th of last month. Recommendation for Mary Reeder, who sometime ago acknowledged her going out with her first cousin in marriage, desires to be united with Friends.

End of Book A.

Note: The first leaf (pages 1 and 2) in Book B is lost. It contains the minutes of the 5th of the 2nd month and part of the 4th of the 3rd month.

8/4/1788 - Joseph Martindell requests certificate to the Falls Monthly Meeting.

6/5/1788 - Marriage of Enos Merrick and Mercy Wilson accomplished on 30th of last month. Marriage of Bezaleel Hayhurst and Susanna Smith accomplished on 16th of last month. Certificate for Elizabeth Fell wife of Thomas Fell to Newgarden Monthly Meeting in Chester Co. Testimony against Mary Hamton for accomplishing her marriage without her father's consent and out of the unity of Friends. Testimony against Ann Osmond for accomplishing her marriage out of the unity of Friends with a men not of our Society. William Heston requests certificate for himself, wife [Mercy] and children [Phinehas, Mercy and Amos] to Goose Creek Monthly Meeting, Virginia. William Heston Jur. requests certificate to same place. Lydia Barcroft condemns her marrying before a Magistrate with a man not in membership with us.

3/6/1788 - Certificate for Rebekah Swinney to Byberry Monthly Meeting.

8/7/1788 - John Linton charged by a young woman with being the father of her illegitimate child and he declines marrying her. Zachariah Betts requests certificate for himself, wife [Mary] and children [Miriam, Samuel, Esther, Mercy, Thomas and Rachel, to Falls Monthly Meeting. Jesse Leedom requests certificate for himself and wife [Mary], to Monthly Meeting of Phila. Mark Watson requests certificate to Abington Monthly Meeting.

5/8/1788 - Coothbert Wiggins produces certificate from Deer Creek Monthly Meeting. Ann Doan produces certificate from Middletown Monthly Meeting.

2/9/1788 - Hannah Watson produces certificate from Falls Monthly Meeting. Benjn. Buckman requests certificate to Middletown Monthly Meeting.
7/10/1788 - Certificate for Mary Whitson from West Bury Monthly Meeting on Long Island. Spoke with Amos Doan concerning his accomplishing his marriage from amongst Friends, with a woman not in membership with us. Joseph Smith requests certificate for himself, wife [Phebe] and children [Timothy, John, Rachel and Benjamin] to Horsham Monthly Meeting.
4/11/1788 - Certificate for Rachel Scarborough to Buckingham Monthly Meeting. John Chapman requests certificate to the Falls Monthly Meeting.
2/12/1788 - Certificate for Mary Lee to Gunpowder Monthly Meeting, Maryland. Isaac Smith produces certificate from Monthly Meeting for Northern Dist. of Phila. Marriage of Thomas Hillborn and Margaret Tomlinson Jur. accomplished on 19th of last month.
6/1/1789 - Certificate for Ellenor Harvey from Falls Monthly Meeting. Certificate for Ann Hamton dau. of Benjamin Hamton to Buckingham Monthly Meeting. Certificate for Sarah Hamton from Buckingham Monthly Meeting.
3/2/1789 - Testimony against Ruth Hibbs (late Holmes) for consummating her marriage contrary to the rules of Friends. John Paste and Alice his wife requests certificate for themselves and children [John, Robert, Jolly, Alice, George, Jonathan and Euclideus] to be joined in membership.
3/3/1789 - Testimony against Rachel Heston (late Huff, Hough) for her consummating her marriage with her first cousin by marriage. Margery Chapman produces certificate for herself and one for her dau. Mary Hutchinson, from Falls Monthly Meeting. Thomas Worthington requests certificate to Buckingham Monthly Meeting in order to proceed in marriage with Emmy Paxson.
7/4/1789 - Certificate for Dorathy Ballance to Monthly Meeting of the Northern Dist. of Phila.
5/5/1789 - Daniel Lee condemns his paying militia fines. Rachel Harvey (late Vansant) for accomplishing her marriage contrary to the rules of our Discipline. Testimony concerning Thomas Ross who died at the House of our Friend Lindley Murray at Holgate near the City of York in old England, 13/2/1786 in his 78th year. He was born in Ireland, County Tyrone, descendant of Episcopal parents. He came to America about the 20th year of his age and settled within the limits of Buckingham Monthly Meeting and removed to Wrightstown in 1753 at a place near equally distant from either meeting. He embarked for Ireland in the 4th month 1784. Certificate from Falls Monthly Meeting for Hannah Buckman, wife of Jesse Buckman. Certificate for Sarah Scott wife of John Scott to Little Falls of Gunpowder, Maryland. Jos. Johnson requests certificate for himself and wife [Rachel] to Falls Monthly Meeting. John Holmes requests certificate for himself, wife [Elizabeth] and children [Thomas and Benjamin] to Falls Monthly Meeting. William Briggs requests certificate to Sadsbury Monthly Meeting. Mahlon Heston requests certificate for himself and wife [Jane] to

Horsham Monthly Meeting.

2/6/1789 - Testimony against Rachel Wisener for accomplishing marriage with a man not of our Society. Certificate for Lydia Barcraft, wife of John Barcraft to Buckingham Monthly Meeting. Certificate for Ann Doan to Middletown Monthly Meeting. Spoke to Jonathan Martindell concerning his paying militia fines.

7/7/1789 - Oliver Hamton produces certificate from Buckingham Monthly Meeting. Reported that Sarah Price, member of this meeting together with her husband and 6 small children, at the time of the late war, were driven from their habitation (over the Blue Mountain) for four years, and thereby reduced in their circumstances. Thomas Hillborn and family likewise driven from their habitation.

4/8/1789 - William Pennington produces certificate from Horsham Monthly Meeting for himself, Anna his wife and their children, Martha and Thomas.

8/9/1789 - James Hamton requests certificate to Monthly Meeting at Phila for the Northern Dist.

6/10/1789 - Certificate from Buckingham Monthly Meeting for Amy Worthington.

3/11/1789 - Certificate for Samuel Smith from Buckingham Monthly Meeting. Seth Chapman requests certificate to Goshen Monthly Meeting in Chester Co. Samuel Smith Jur. requests certificate to Indian Spring Monthly Meeting, Maryland.

8/12/1789 - Zebulon Heston Jur. produces certificate from Gwynedd Monthly Meeting for himself, wife Rebekah and children, Hannah and Sarah. Certificate for Hannah Watson to Falls Monthly Meeting. Spoke to Amos Martindell concerning his accomplishing his marriage out of the unity of Friends.

5/1/1790 - Testimony against Sarah Wilson for marrying a man not of our Society. Testimony against Joseph Stokes and his wife Rebekah for marrying out of the unity of Friends.

2/2/1790 - Marriage of John Livesey and Ann Hamton Jur. accomplished on 20th of last month. [He produces certificate from Haverford Monthly Meeting.] Certificate for Susannah Stokes to Monthly Meeting at Chesterfield New Jersey. Spoke to John Worthington [wife Hannah] concerning his accomplishing his marriage out of the unity of Friends. John Heston requests certificate to Goose Creek Monthly Meeting, Virginia. David Davis requests certificate to Horsham Monthly Meeting.

2/3/1790 - Spoke with Simeon Warner concerning his marriage out of the unity of Friends. Reported that Isaac Atkinson hath accomplished his marriage out of the unity of Friends with a woman not in membership with Friends. Spoke with William Atkinson Jur. concerning accomplishing his marriage with a woman not in membership with Friends. Phineas Buckman requests certificate to the Falls Monthly Meeting in order to proceed in marriage with Susannah Leedom.

17/3/1790 - Certificate for Mary Reeder to Goose Creek Monthly Meeting, Virginia.

6/4/1790 - Certificate for Rachel Fell wife of Mahlon Fell with her children, Ezra, Aaron, Ann, Elizabeth, Moses and Mahlon to Westland Monthly Meeting. Certificate for Ann Livezey to Haverford Monthly Meeting, Delaware Co. Margaret Smith produces certificate from Abington Monthly Meeting. Jane Tomlinson condemns her accomplishing her marriage out of the unity of Friends. William Ross, minor, requests certificate to New York Monthly Meeting.

4/5/1790 - Certificate for Tamer Newburn, wife of David Newburn and her children, John, Rachel, Sarah, Dorathy, Hannah and Jacob to Westland Monthly Meeting. Jason Merrick requests certificate to Middletown Monthly Meeting.

8/6/1790 - Certificate for Mary Whitson to Falls Monthly Meeting.

6/7/1790 - Abraham Chapman produces certificate from Goshen Monthly Meeting.

RICHLAND MONTHLY MEETING

BIRTHS AND DEATHS

Children of John and Ann Adamson: Thomas Adamson b. 23rd day of 12th month, 1717; Betty Adamson b. 9th day of 6th month, 1719; Hester Adamson b. 9th day of 10th month, 1721; John Adamson b. 1726; Ann Adamson b. 25th day of 9th month, 1728; Susanna Adamson b. 1st day of 9th month, 1730.

Children of Thomas and Mary Adamson: Rachel Adamson b. 4th day of 9th month, 1739; Ann Adamson b. 12th day of 9th month, 1742, m. Abraham Ball, and d. 8th day of 8th month, 1784; Joseph Adamson b. 17th day of 1st month, 1745; Mary Adamson b. 7th day of 12th month, 1747; Hannah Adamson b. 15th day of 5th month, 1749; Esther Adamson b. 2nd day of 4th month, 1751; John Adamson b. 1st day of 11th month, 1753; Deborah Adamson b. 8th day of 12th month, 1755; James Adamson b. 4th day of 1st month, 1757; Martha Adamson b. 2nd day of 11th month, 1760; Sarah Adamson b. 14th day of 1st month, 1763.

Robert Ashton, son of Peter and Mary Ashton (born in Ireland), b. 15th day of 10th month, 1725 and d. 22nd day of 10th month, 1816. Sarah, wife of Robert Ashton, and daughter of Samuel and Margaret Thomas, d. 25th day of 1st month, 1786.

Children of Robert and Sarah Ashton, of Springfield Tp: Peter Ashton b. 16th day of 8th month, 1760 and d. 30th day of 12th month, 1821; Mary Ashton b. 4th day of 8th month, 1761 and d. 15th day of 2nd month, 1786; Margaret Ashton b. 24th day of 3rd month, 1765; Samuel Ashton b. 17th day of 7th month, 1766; Robert Ashton b. 1st day of 4th month, 1768; Sarah Ashton b. 10th day of 5th month, 1770.

Children of Samuel and Jane Ashton, of Springfield Tp: Phebe Ashton b. 28th day of 3rd month, 1796; Eleanor Ashton b. 22nd day of 6th month, 1798; Thomas Ashton b. 22nd day of 9th month, 1799; Sarah Ashton b. 15th day of 7th month, 1801; Eliza Roberts Ashton b. 27th day of 8th month, 1803; Abigail Ashton b. 26th day of 7th month, 1807.

Children of Joseph and Sarah Ball: John Ball b. 18th day of 4th month, 1750; Jesse Ball b. 26th day of 5th month, 1756; Margaret Ball b. 28th day of 9th month, 1758; Elizabeth Ball b. 13th day of 1st month, 1763.

Joseph Ball, the father, d. 31st day of 10th month, 1792, aged 74 yrs, 2 mo.
Sarah Ball, the month, d. 21st day of 3rd month, 1796, aged 72 yrs.
Catherine Ball, wife of John Ball, d. 28th day of 3rd month, 1764, aged 73 yrs.
John Ball d. 22nd day of 9th month, 1767, upwards of 80 yrs.

Children of John and Ann Ball: Joel Ball b. 29th day of 9th month, 1779; Joseph Ball b. 29th day of 4th month, 1782; Margaret Ball b. 30th day of 6th month, 1784; Jesse Ball b. 20th day of 9th month, 1786; Sarah Ball b. 4th day of 3rd month, 1788; James Ball b. 5th day of 2nd month, 1790; Susanna Ball b. 5th day of 6th month, 1792; Iden Ball b. 25th day of 9th month, 1794.

Children of Aaron and Margaret Ball, of Richland Tp: Hannah Ball b. 4th day of 6th month, 1787 and d. 2nd day of 3rd month, 1847; Rebecca Ball b. 2nd day of 3rd month, 1789, m. Evan Penrose, and d. 5th day of 1st month, 1852; William H. Ball b. 9th day of 11th month, 1790 and d. 19th day of 2nd month, 1863; Aaron Ball b. 26th day of 10th month, 1792 and d. 22nd day of 11th month, 1856.

Hannah Ball, wife of John Ball, b. 16th day of 12th month, 1798 and d. 1st day of 7th month, 1865.

Children of Thomas and Elizabeth Blacklidge: William Blacklidge b. 16th day of 1st month, 17_ _; Elizabeth BLacklidge b. 11th day of 6th month, 1758; Rachel Blacklidge b. 13th day of 4th month, 1760.

Children of John and Sarah (Caldwalter) Bond: Benjamin Bond b. 11th day of 3rd month, 1726; John Bond, Jr. b. 7th day of 5th month, 1727 and d. 4th day of 10th month, 1731; Joshua Bond b. 12th day of 9th month, 1729; Abraham Bond b. 21st day of 5th month, 1731; Rebecca Bond b. 31st day of 3rd month, 1733; John Bond, the 2nd, b. 14th day of 2nd month, 1735; Hannah Bond b. 6th day of 9th month, 1736; Edward Bond b. 4th day of 9th month, 1738; Mary Bond b. 6th day of 7th month, 1741.

James Boon, of Exeter, d. 1st day of 7th month, 1785, aged 75 yrs.
John Boon d. 5th day of 8th month, 1785.

Children of William and Ann Burr: Martha Burr b. 6th day of 6th month, 1764 and d. 31st day of 3rd month, 1765; Reuben Burr b. 14th day of 3rd month, 1766; Jane Burr b. 1st day of 5th month, 1768; Timothy Burr b. 19th day of 4th month, 1770 and d. 17th day of 8th month, 1801, at Penns Neck, Salem Co; Samuel Burr b. 2nd day of 3rd month, 1772 and d. 26th day of 8th month, 1798, at Philadelphia; Martha Burr b. 25th day of 1st month, 1775; David Burr b. 10th day of 5th month, 1777; William Burr b. 13th day of 2nd month, 1779; Joseph Burr b. 31st day of 12th month, 1780; Henry Burr b. 27th day of 11th month, 1782.

Robert Burr d. 5th day of 2nd month, 1778.
Ann Burr d. 10th day of 10th month 1795.

John Chapman b. 30th day of 1st month, 1742 and d. 2nd day of 2nd month, 1771.
Hannah Chapman b. 3rd day of 2nd month, 1742 and d. 30th day of 10th month, 1778.

Jane Chapman, daughter of John and Hannah Chapman b. & d. 20th day of 10th month, 1770.

Children of James and Rebecca Chapman, of Richland Tp: Jacob Abbott Chapman b. 19th day of 2nd month, 1773; Elizabeth Chapman b. 8th day of 9th month, 1776 and m. Samuel Iden; Abigail Chapman b. 31st day of 12th month, 1779.

Children of Samuel and Mary Clark: William Clark b. 6th day of 2nd month, 1739; Sarah Clark b. 23rd day of 1st month, 1741; Elizabeth Clark b. 11th day of 9th month, 1743; Michael Clark b. 2nd day of 1st month, 1744; Mary Clark b. 24th day of 9th month, 1746; Abigail Clark b. 21st day of 4th month 1747; Walter Clark b. 3rd day of 6th month, 1749 and d. 22nd day of 11th month, 1785; Samuel J. Clark b. 7th day of 12th month, 1751.

Children of William and Hannah Clark: Thomas Clark b. 13th day of 12th month, 1766; Gabriel Clark b. 13th day of 3rd month, 1769; Thomas Clark, 2nd, b. 25th day of 4th month, 1770; William Clark b. 17th day of 8th month, 1771; Eleazer Clark b. 18th day of 1st month, 1773; Martha Clark b. 11th day of 11th month, 1776/7.

Joseph Custard (Surname is frequently spelled Custer), son of George and Mary Custard, b. 1st day of 5th month, 1751 and d. 12th day of 1st month, 1801.
Amelia Custard, daughter of Samuel and Ann Faulke, b. 3rd day of 7th month, 1753 and d. 7th day of 8th month, 1811, aged 58 years, 1 mo.

Children of Joseph and Amelia Custard: Ann Custard b. 14th day of 8th month, 1787; George Custard b. 30th day of 11th month, 1789 and d. "suddenly", 1st day of 10th month, 1854; Mary Custard b. 19th day of 11th month, 1792.

Mary Davies, wife of John, d. 6th day of 2nd month, 1755.
John Davies d. 16th day of 2nd month, 1756.
Susanna Davies d. 28th day of 12th month, 1785, ages 70 years.

Children of John and Kezia Dennis: Joseph Dennis b. 14th day of 12th month, 1741; Ezekiel Dennis b. 17th day of 12th month, 1742; Catherine Dennis b. 1st day of 11th month, 1744; John Dennis, Jr., b. 26th day of 1st month, 1746; Sarah Dennis b. 21st day of 12th month, 1749; Kezia Dennis b. 22nd day of 2nd month, 1753; Tamar Dennis b. 10th day of 8th month, 1755.

Children of Joseph and Hannah Dennis: Ezekiel Dennis b. 12th day of 6th month, 1753; Jesse Dennis b. 30th day of 1st month, 1755; Sarah Dennis b. 11th day of 4th month, 1757; Anne Dennis b. 11th day of 10th month, 1758; Lewis Dennis b. 22nd day of 4th month, 1761; Joseph Dennis b. 18th day of 7th month, 1763; Hannah Dennis b. 22nd day of 5th month, 1765.

Children of William and Martha Edwards, of Milford Tp: Mary Edwards b. 14th day of 7th month, 1739 and d. 17th day of 12th month, 1755; Thomas Edwards b. 6th day of 1st month, 1742 and d. 13th day of 5th month, 1745; Ann Edwards b. 26th day of 12th month, 1743/4; William Edwards, Jr., b. 13th day of 5th month, 1746; Thomas Edwards b. 28th day of 2nd month, 1749; Martha Edwards b. 7th day of 6th month, 1751; Hugh Edwards b. 13th day of 2nd month, 1754 and d. 30th day of 8th month, 1760; Mary Edwards b. 15th day of 6th month, 1756 and d. 19th day of 1st month, 1770; Hannah Edwards b. 10th day of 7th month, 1758; Hugh Edwards b. 16th day of 3rd month, 1761 and d. 4th day of 10th month, 1764.

William Edwards, the father, d. 13th day of 8th month, 1764, in his 52nd year.
Martha Edwards, widow of William, d. 17th day of 4th month, 1781, aged 65.

Children of John and Mary Edwards: Margaret Edwards b. 13th day of 8th month, 1753; William Edwards b. 5th day of 6th month, 1755 and d. 1st day of 8th month, 1760; Mary Edwards b. 13th day of 8th month, 1756; John Edwards b. 3rd day of 8th month, 1759.

John Edwards, Sr., the father, d. 29th day of 3rd month, 1756?
Mary Edwards, widow of John, d. 10th day of 5th month, 1759.
Mary Edwards, wife of John Edwards, Jr., b. 1st day of 8th month, 1760.

Children of William and Meribah Edwards, of Milford Tp: Margaret Edwards b. 28th day of 2nd month, 1768; Samuel Edwards b. 4th day of 3rd month, 1770; Nathan Edwards b. 20th day of 2nd month, 1772 and d. 17th day of 10th month, 1855; William Edwards b. 18th day of 4th month, 1774; Martha Edwards b. 6th day of 7th month, 1776, m. Enoch Penrose, and d. 8th day of 5th month, 1804; Mary Edwards b. 10th day of 9th month, 1778 and d. 15th day of 9th month, 1779; Joel Edwards b. 3rd day of 7th month, 1780; Caleb Edwards b. 23rd day of 10th month, 1782 and d. 5th day of 10th month, 1862; Thomas Edwards b. 28th day of 9th month, 1784; Amos Edwards b. 4th day of 10th month, 1786; Hannah Edwards b. 3rd day of 7th month, 1788 and d. 26th day of 9th month, 1801; Ann Edwards b. 11th day of 2nd month, 1790, m. Samuel M. Foulke, and d. 28th day of 12th month, 1816.

Meribah Edwards, wife of William, d. 8th day of 9th month, 1794.
Sarah Edwards, wife of Caleb, b. 21st day of 11th month, 1788 and d. 1860.
Lydia R. Edwards, widow of William Edwards and daughter of Israel and Ann Roberts, b. 14th day of 4th month, 1783 and d. 5th day of 1st month, 1866.
Susanna Edwards, of Richland Tp., daughter of Abel Roberts, b. 13th day of 12th month, 1748 and d. 26th day of 2nd month, 1818.

Morris Fell, son of Sarah Fell, d. 24th day of 11th month, 1785.

Zachariah Flagler, son of John L. Flagler, b. 26th day of 1st month, 1795.

Hugh Foulke, son of Edward Foulke, formerly of Wales, great Britain, b. 6th day of 7th month, 1685 and d. 21st day of 5th month, 1760.
Anne, wife of Hugh Foulke, b. 6th day of 11th month, 1693 and d. 10th day of 9th, 1763.

Children of Hugh and Anne Foulke: Mary Foulke b. 24th day of 9th month, 1714, m. _ _ _ Boon, and d. 20th day of 2nd month, 1756; Martha Foulke b. 2nd day of 5th month, 1716; Samuel Foulke b. 4th day of 12th month, 1718, m. Ann Greasley, and d. 21st day of 1st month, 1797; Elinor Foulke b. 19th day of 1st month, 1720 and m. Isaac Lester; John Foulke b. 21st day of 12th month, 1722, m. Mary Roberts, and d. 25th day of 5th month, 1787; Thomas Foulke b. 14th day of 1st month, 1724, m. Jane Roberts, and d. 31st day of 3rd month, 1786; Theophilus Foulke, b. 21st day of 12th month, 1726, m. Margaret Thomas, and d. 4th day of 11th month, 1785; William Foulke b. 10th day of 12th month, 1728, m. Priscilla Lester, and d. 11th day of 4th month, 1796; Edward Foulke b. 10th day of 10th month, 1729 and d. 8th day of 1st month, 1747; Ann Foulke b. 1st day of 1st month, 1732 and m. William Thomas; Jane Foulke b. 3rd day of 1st month, 1734, m. John Greasley, and d. 8th month, 1771.

Children of Samuel and Ann Foulke: Eleanor Foulke b. 5th day of 11th month, 1744, m. Randal Iden, and d. 6th day of 7th month, 1833; Thomas Foulke b. 11th day of 4th month, 1746 and d. 7th day of 10th month, 1784; Israel Foulke b. 13th day of 9th month, 1749 and d. 19th day of 9th month, 1754; Judah Foulke b. 20th day of 4th month, 1752 N.S. and d. 16th day of 6th month, 1752; Amelia Foulke b. 3rd day of 7th month, 1753, m. Joseph Custer, and d. 7th day of 8th month, 1811; Hannah Foulke b. 15th day of 9th month, 1756; Israel Foulke b. 4th day of 2nd month, 1760 and d. 27th day of 9th month, 1824; Judah Foulke b. 18th day of 1st month, 1763; Cadwallader Foulke b. 14th day of 7th month, 1765; John Foulke b. 6th day of 12th month, 1767 and d. 5th day of 4th month, 1840.

Ann Foulke d. 5th month, 1797.

Children of John and Mary Foulke: Martha Foulke b. 16th day of 7th month, 1758; Anne Foulke b. 27th day of 10th month, 1760; Jane Foulke b. 2nd day of 8th month, 1763 and d. 18th day of 3rd month, 1780; Aquila Foulke b. 2nd day of 3rd month, 1766; Margaret Foulke b. 17th day of 10th month, 1768; Evan Foulke b. 6th day of 5th month, 1771; Lydia Foulke b. 2nd day of 10th month, 1775.

Mary Foulke, wife of John Foulke, b. 16th day of 4th month, 1730 and d. 2nd day of 10th month, 1787, "much lamented."

Children of Thomas and Jane Foulke: Everard Foulke b. 8th day of 9th month, 1755 and d. 5th day of 9th month, 1827; Edward Foulke b. 17th day of 12th month, 1756 and d. 17th day of 1st month, 1757; Samuel Foulke b. 3rd day of 1st month, 1761 and d. 5th month, 1763; Abigail Foulke b. 4th day of 10th month, 1763; Susanna Foulke b. 5th day of 11th month, 1766; Samuel Foulke b. 19th day of 11th month, 1769 and d. 25th day of 12th month, 1787.

Jane Foulke, widow of Thomas, b. 3rd day of 11th month, 1732 and d. 25th day of 7th month, 1822.

Children of Theophilus and Margaret Foulke: Hugh Foulke b. 29th day of 8th month, 1758; Jane Foulke b. 22nd day of 8th month, 1759.

Margaret Foulke, wife of Theophilus, b. 3rd day of 4th month, 1734 O.S.

Children of William and Priscilla Foulke: Asher Foulke b. 15th day of 2nd month, 1758; Isacher Foulke b. 31st day of 1st month, 1760; Jesse Foulke b. 28th day of 4th month, 1762; John Foulke b. 18th day of 10th month, 1764 and d. 28th day of 12th month, 1765; Mary Foulke b. 24th day of 10th month, 1766; Phebe Foulke b. 10th month, 1769 and d. 13th day of 11th month, 1773.

Priscilla Foulke, wife of William, b. 18th day of 1st month, 1736 and d. 17th day of 3rd month,1795.
Sarah Foulke d. 19th day of 12th month, 1800.

Children of Israel and Elizabeth Foulke, of Richland Tp: William Foulke b. 18th day of 8th month, 1783 and d. 2nd day of 9th month, 1784; Thomas Foulke b. 31st day of 12th month, 1784 and d. 4th day of 6th month, 1832; David Foulke b. 21st day of 12th month, 1786; Cadwallader Foulke b. 22nd day of 5th month, 1789 and d. 22nd day of 8th month, 1794; Jane Foulke b. 26th day of 3rd month, 1791 and d. 24th day of 6th month, 1794; Hugh Foulke b. 8th day of 9th month, 1793 and d. 24th day of 6th month, 1794; Phebe Foulke b. 27th day of 12th month, 1795; Amos Foulke b. 10th day of 8th month, 1798; Deborah Foulke b. 13th day of 8th month, 1800 and d. 29th day of 12th month, 1806.

Edward Foulke b. 16th day of 7th month, 1758.
Elizabeth Foulke, daughter of Thomas J. and Latitia Roberts, b. 7th day of 8th month, 1759 and d. 25th day of 7th month, 1793.

Children of Edward and Elizabeth Foulke, of Richland Tp: Jane Foulke b. 20th day of 8th month, 1782; Rowland Foulke b. 29th day of 12th month, 1783; Agnes Foulke b. 27th day of 8th month, 1785; Mary R. Foulke b. 29th day of 9th month, 1787 and d. 19th day of 9th month, 1847; John Foulke b. 28th day of 10th month, 1789; Edward Foulke b. 26th day of 5th month, 1792 and d. 16th day of 2nd month, 1859.

Children of Judah and Sarah Foulke: Samuel Foulke b. 12th day of 8th month, 1787; Eleanor Foulke b. 25th day of 2nd month, 1789; Mary Foulke b. 8th day of 3rd month, 1791; Ann Foulke b. 9th day of 12th month, 1792; Thomas Foulke b. 7th day of 5th month, 1795; Elizabeth Foulke b. 19th day of 5th month, 1797; Jane Foulke b.

19th day of 6th month, 1799; Amelia Foulke b. 20th day of 6th month, 1801; Cadwallader Foulke b. 25th day of 5th month, 1803; Jesse Foulke 18th day of 9th month, 1805; Mercy Foulke b. 6th day of 5th month, 1808; Grace Foulke b. 29th day of 1st month, 1810; Silas Foulke b. 18th day of 3rd month, 1812.

Children of John and Latitia Foulke, of Richland Tp: James Foulke b. 2nd day of 8th month, 1790 and d. 8th day of 4th month, 1866; Sidney Foulke b. 30th day of 12th month, 1791, m. Samuel Shaw, and d. 12th month, 1862; Abigail Foulke b. 5th day of 1st month, 1794 and m. Thomas Wright; Elizabeth Foulke b. 13th day of 10th month, 1795; Ann Foulke b. 23rd day of 11th month, 1797; Hannah Foulke b. 4th day of 7th month, 1799 and m. Bartholomew Mather; Kezia Foulke b. 4th day of 4th month, 1804; Mary Foulke b. 5th day of 12th month, 1806 and m. Joseph Paul.

Latitia Foulke, widow of John Foulke, and daughter of Thomas and Latitia Roberts, b. 10th day of 9th month, 1767 and d. 18th day of 10th month, 1854.

Children of Everard and Ann Foulke: Abigail Foulke b. 18th day of 5th month, 1779 and m. Abel Penrose; Eleanor Foulke b. 18th day of 7th month, 1781 and d. 28th day of 4th month, 1815; Caleb Foulke b. 29th day of 8th month, 1783 and d. 22nd day of 2nd month, 1852; Samuel Foulke b. 28th day of 3rd month, 1786; Thomas Foulke b. 13th day of 4th month, 1789; Susanna Foulke b. 18th day of 9th month, 1791; Anna Foulke b. 3rd day of 5th month, 1794 and d. 16th day of 9th month, 1820; Margaret Foulke b. 24th day of 12th month, 1796 and m. Peter Lester; Everard Foulke b. 21st day of 7th month, 1800.

Children of Asher and Alice Foulke: Phebe Foulke b. 27th day of 10th month, 1781; Anthony Foulke b. 19th day of 6th month, 1784; William Foulke b. 15th day of 5th month, 1786 and d. 20th day of 9th month, 1787; Anne Foulke b. 6th day of 6th month, 1788; Elizabeth Foulke b. 23rd day of 8th month, 1790 and d. 4th day of 10th month, 1791.

Children of Isacher and Jane Foulke, of Richland Tp: Priscilla Foulke b. 11th day of 8th month, 1793; Bathsheba Foulke b. 15th day of 11th month, 1794; Mary Foulke b. 3rd day of 8th month, 1797; Sarah Foulke b. 3rd day of 10th month, 1799; Rebecca Foulke b. 30th day of 5th month, 1801; Jane Foulke b. 1st day of 12th month, 1802; Aaron Foulke b. 26th day of 10th month, 1804; Mercy Foulke b. 25th day of 9th month, 1806 and d. 5th day of 11th month, 1806; Barton Foulke b. 22nd day of 5th month, 1808.

Children of Jesse and Sarah Foulke: Ellen Foulke b. 29th day of 9th month, 1798; Hannah Foulke b. 16th day of 7th month, 1800; Rachel Foulke b. 16th day of 9th month, 1802; William Foulke b. 6th day of 5th month, 1805.

Sarah Foulke, wife of Jesse, d. 21st day of 9th month, 1791.

Children of Benjamin and Martha Foulke, of Richland Tp: Hannah Foulke b. 25th day of 12th month, 1789, m. George Custard, and d. 11th day of 2nd month, 1859; Jane Foulke b. 25th day of 1st month, 1793, m. William L. Strawn, and d. 2nd month, 1859; Charles Foulke b. 14th day of 10th month, 1795; Rachel Foulke b. 16th day of 1st month, 1800 and d. 1803; Rachel Foulke, 2nd, b. 14th day of 3rd month, 1803.

Martha Foulke, wife of Benjamin, b. 25th day of 10th month, 1764 and d. 13th day of 8th month, 1831.

Children of Hugh and Sarah Foulke, of Richland Tp: Martha Foulke b. 1st day of 7th month, 1789 and d. 17th day of 10th month, 1868; Joseph Foulke b. 7th day of 9th month, 1791.

Children of Theophilus and Hannah Foulke, of Richland Tp: Antrim Foulke b. 21st day of 3rd month, 1793; Sarah Foulke b. 10th day of 1st month, 1797, m. Richard Moore, and d. 25th day of 10th month, 1852.

Hannah S. Foulke, widow of Theophilus, b. 2nd day of 2nd month, 1767 and d. 4th day of 7th month, 1850.
Theophilus Foulke d. 28th day of 7th month, 1798.

Children of Evan and Sarah Foulke: Olivia Foulke b. 27th day of 3rd month, 1796 and d. 13th day of 5th month, 1832; Charles Foulke b. 26th day of 2nd month, 1801; Asenath Foulke b. 26th day of 2nd month, 1808; Susanna L. Foulke b. 5th day of 10th month, 1810.

Jane Foulke, widow of Caleb, b. 8th day of 2nd month, 1785 and d. 3rd day of 3rd month, 1835.
Mariam Foulke, wife of David, b. 11th day of 1st month, 1782 and d. 14th day of 11th month, 1814.
Hannah S. Foulke, wife of James, b. 7th day of 3rd month, 1793 and d. 28th day of 5th month, 1859.
Ann Foulke, wife of Samuel, b. 11th day of 2nd month, 1790 and d. 28th day of 5th month, 1816.
Joshua Foulke, son of Edward and Ann, b. 12th day of 10th month, 1797.

Children of William and Elizabeth Fowler: Daniel Fowler b. 22nd day of 9th month, 1799; Jane B. Fowler b. 7th day of 12th month, 1801; William Fowler b. 16th day of 8th month, 1806; Mary Ann Fowler b. 8th day of 8th month, 1808; Elisa Fowler b. 4th day of 9th month, 1811.

Children of Benjamin and Sarah Gilbert: Rachel Gilbert b. 14th day of 11th month, 1732; Abigail Gilbert b. 3rd day of 9th month, 1734; Sarah Gilbert b. 24th day of 2nd month, 1737 and d. 23rd day of 8th month, 1738; Joseph Gilbert b. 10th day of 12th month, 1738; Benjamin Gilbert, Jr., b. 31st day of 1st month, 1741; John Gilbert b. 23rd day of 5th month, 1743; Sarah Gilbert b. 26th day of 4th month, 1745; Joshua Gilbert b. 3rd day of 3rd month, 1748;

Caleb Gilbert b. 19th day of 9th month, 1754.

Rachel Greasley, daughter of John and Ann Greasley, b. 30th day of 10th month, 1757.
Jane Greasley, wife of John Greasley and daughter of Hugh and Ann Foulke, d. 8th month, of 1771.

Children of Joseph and Catherine Green: Margaret Green b. 28th day of 11th month, 1744; Joseph Green, Jr., b. 23rd day of 12th month, 1745; Samuel Green b. 21st day of 10th month, 1748; Jane Green b. 27th day of 2nd month, 1750 and d. 2nd day of 2nd month, 1767; Benjamin Green (twin) b. 27th day of 2nd month, 1750 and d. 22nd day of 5th month, 1828; Ezekiel Green b. 14th day of 5th month, 1752; James Green b. 22nd day of 3rd month, 1754 and d. 10th day of 8th month, 1786, "much lamented."; Thomas Green b. 27th day of 7th month, 1756.

Joseph Green, Sr., the father, d. 26th day of 5th month, 1757, in his 40th year.
Catherine Green, widow of Joseph, d. 12th day of 7th month, 1770.

Children of Samuel and Rachel Green: Catherine Green b. 11th day of 3rd month, 1770; Mary Green b. 28th day of 8th month, 1771; Jane Green b. 5th day of 2nd month, 1773; Margaret Green b. 17th day of 8th month, 1774; Rachel Green b. 18th day of 6th month, 1776; Thomas Green b. 22nd day of 1st month, 1778; Alice Green b. 7th day of 8th month, 1781; Samuel Green b. 3rd day of 8th month, 1783.

Children of Benjamin and Jane Green: William Green b. 10th day of 11th month, 1776 and d. 24th day of 9th month, 1851; Hannah Green b. 29th day of 9th month, 1778, m. Thomas Lester, and d. 12th day of 4th month, 1828; Evan Green b. 10th day of 11th month, 1780; Benjamin Green b. 10th day of 12th month, 1782; Jane Green b. 8th day of 2nd month, 1785, m. Caleb Foulke, and d. 3rd day of 3rd month, 1835; James R. Green b. 4th day of 3rd month, 1787 and d. 27th day of 7th month, 1832; Lydia Green b. 20th day of 12th month, 1789 and d. 26th day of 10th month, 1850; Joseph Green b. 14th day of 2nd month, 1791; Martha Green b. 14th day of 2nd month, 1793; Abigail Green b. 18th day of 3rd month, 1797, m. Samuel Carey, and d. 21st day of 8th month, 1854.

Jane Green, widow of Benjamin, d. 18th day of 5th month, 1841, aged 88 yrs.

Children of James and Martha Green: Ann Green b. 10th day of 1st month, 1780; Elisabeth Green b. 1st day of 11th month, 1781; Thomas Green b. 7th day of 9th month, 1783; Margaret Green b. 5th day of 10th month, 1785.

Children of John and Ann Griffith: Hannah Griffith b. 14th day of 8th month, 1734; Sarah Griffith b. 16th day of 7th month, 1735.

Children of Isaac and Ann Griffith: Abraham Griffith b. 2nd day of 4th month, 1746; Rachel Griffith b. 23rd day of 9th month, 1747; Hannah Griffith b. 6th day of 7th month, 1749; Mary Griffith b. 28th day of 7th month, 1752; Ann Griffith b. 1st day of 2nd month, 1754; Sarah Griffith b. 15th day of 11th month, 1756; Joseph Griffith b. 22nd day of 11th month, 1758; Martha Griffith b. 23rd day of 8th month, 1760; Isaac Griffith, Jr., b. 7th day of 6th month 1764; John Griffith b. 29th day of 5th month, 1766; James Griffith b. 16th day of 1st month, 1769.

Children of Jonathan and Ann Griffith: Rachel Griffith b. 18th day of 10th month, 1752; Jonathan Griffith, Jr., b. 21st day of 9th month, 1754 and d. 18th day if 3rd month, 1809; John Griffith b. 1st day of 5th month, 1761.

Jonathan Griffith, Sr., d. 1st day of 8th month, 1767.
Abraham Griffith d. 3rd day of 10th month, 1760, in his 82nd year.

Children of John and Rachel Griffith: Jane Griffith b. 2nd day of 7th month, 1783, and m. Thomas Jackson; Hannah Griffith b. 12th day of 1st month, 1785 and m. Nathaniel Kinsey; John Greasley Griffith b. 12th day of 1st month, 1789; Thomas Griffith b. 3rd day of 3rd month, 1791; Abraham Griffith b. 9th day of 7th month, 1793; William Griffith b. 30th day of 6th month, 1795.

Children of Jonathan and Sarah Griffith: James Griffith b. 12th day of 3rd month, 1788; Joseph Griffith b. 29th day of 8th month, 1790; Mary Griffith b. 23rd day of 4th month, 1797 and d. 15th day of 9th month, 1799.

Walter Hadock, near kin of Samuel Clark, d. 22nd day of 1st month, 1789.

Children of Jesse and Tacy Heacock: John Heacock b. 28th day of 8th month, 1786; Jonah Heacock b. 18th day of 2nd month, 1788; William Heacock b. 19th day of 1st month, 1790; Ann Heacock b. 27th day of 12th month, 1791 and m. Samuel M. Foulke; Joel Heacock b. 26th day of 3rd month, 1794 and d. 17th day of 3rd month, 1853; Margaret Heacock b. 27th day of 3rd month, 1796 and m. 1st, John Good, 2nd, Jonathan Carr; Jesse Heacock b. 12th day of 6th month, 1798 and m. Elizabeth Rees or Reace; Joseph Heacock b. 26th day of 8th month, 1800, m. Esther Hallowell, of Abington, and d. 22nd day of 3rd month, 1883; Enos Heacock b. 20th day of 12th month, 1802 and m. Sarah Foulke; Nathan Heacock b. 27th day of 4th month, 1806 and m. Eliza Hallowell, of Abington; Aaron Heacock b. 27th day of 7th month, 1808.

Children of George and Sarah Hicks: Martha Hicks b. 25th day of 2nd month, 1728; Mary Hicks b. 6th day of 10th month, 1729; William Hicks b. 20th day of 7th month, 1732 and d. 19th day of 2nd month, 1800/1810?; Hannah Hicks b. 18th day of 11th month, 1734; George Hicks b. 31st day of 6th month, 1736; John Hicks b. 26th day of 2nd month, 1740.

Children of William and Margaret Hicks: Mary Hicks b. 21st day of 12th month, 1751; Abigail Hicks b. 21st day if 4th month, 1756 and d. 29th day of 5th month, 1820.

Margaret Hicks, wife of William Hicks, d. 29th day of 12th month, 1758.

Children of William and Hannah Hicks: Jesse Hicks b. 21st day of 9th month, 1761; Margaret Hicks b. 30th day of 11th month, 1762; Samuel Hicks b. 6th day of 9th month, 1764; George Hicks b. 12th day of 6th month, 1770 and d. 20th day of 8th month, 1847; William Hicks b. 6th day of 12th month, 1771; Hannah Hicks b. 11th day of 5th month, 1774; John Hicks b. 31st day of 7th month, 1776 and d. 14th day of 8th month, 1830.

Hannah Hicks, 2nd wife of William, b. 29th day of 7th month, 1738 and d. 24th day of 11th month, 1781.

Children of Jesse and ?Mary/Margaret (Ball) Hicks: Ann Hicks b. 23rd day of 9th month, 1787; Mahlon Hicks b. 9th day of 6th month, 1790; Hannah Hicks b. 6th day of 5th month, 1793; Rebecca Hacks b. 9th day of 8th month, 1795; Jesse Hicks b. 9th day of 3rd month, 1798; Thomas Hicks b. 31st day of 1st month, 1801.

Children of George and Ann Hicks: Rachel Hicks b. 26th day of 4th month, 1800; Penrose Hicks b. 9th day of 5th month, 1802, and m. 1st, Mary Edwards, m. 2nd, Elizabeth Foulke; William Hicks b. 21st day of 11th month, 1803; Peninah Hicks b. 25th day of 1st month, 1806; Martha Hicks b. 9th day of 10th month, 1807; Speakman Hicks b. 4th day of 10th month, 1809; Hannah Hicks b. 1st day of 8th month, 1811; Nathan P. Hicks b. 7th day of 9th month, 1813; Evan P. Hicks b. 20th day of 10th month, 1815; Anne R. Hicks b. 28th day of 11th month, 1817; Lacy Hicks b. 3rd day of 11th month, 1820 and d. 6th day of 11th month, 1821.

Ann Hicks, wife of George Hicks, b. 22nd day of 6th month, 1779.

Children of Hugh and Ann Hilles: Anne Hilles b. 11th day of 1st month, 1749; Mary Hilles b. 2nd day of 10th month, 1750; William Hilles b. 11th day of 10th month, 1752; David Hilles b. 11th day of 9th month, 1755.

Children of William and Ann Hoag (Hoge, Hogue), who m. 9th day of 2nd month, 1723: James Hoag b. 6th day of 12th month, 1724; William Hoag, Jr., b. 4th day of 1st month, 1726 and m. Esther Ewen; Solomon Hoag b. 21st day of 3rd month, 1729; George Hoag b. 6th day of 2nd month, 1733; Joseph Hoag b. 1st day of 12th month, 1735/6; Zebulon Hoag b. 15th day of 4th month, 1738; Ann Hoag b. 26th day of 12th month, 1740/1.

Ann Hoag, wife of William, d. 21st day of 2nd month, 1759.

Randal Iden, son of Randal and Margaret Iden, b. 4th day of 1st month, 1736 O.S., and d. 16th day of 5th month, 1812.

Children of Randal and Eleanor Iden: John Iden d. 4th day of 4th month, 1779; Margaret Iden b. 1st day of 9th month, 1774; Samuel Iden b. 2nd day of 2nd month, 1779 and m. Elizabeth Chapman; Jesse Iden b. 23rd day of 10th month, 1782; Jane Iden b. 24th day of 10th month, 1785; Sarah Iden b. 26th day of 10th month, 1789; Susanna Iden b. 8th day of 12th month, 1791; Albion Iden b. 29th day of 8th month, 1793 and d. 6th day of 10th month, 1806.

Eleanor Iden, widow of Randal, b. 5th day of 11th month, 1744 and d. 6th day of 7th month, 1833.

Children of George and Hannah Iden: Anne Iden b. 27th day of 9th month, 1782; Elizabeth Iden b. 29th day of 2nd month, 1784; Thomas Iden b. 25th day of 7th month, 1785; John Iden b. 16th day of 6th month, 1787; Greenfield Iden b. 6th day of 7th month, 1789; Paulina Iden b. 5th day of 5th month, 1792; Julia Iden b. 25th day of 8th month, 1794; Jacob Iden b. 26th day of 6th month, 1798.

Samuel Isaac d. 6th day of 4th month, 1781, in his 81st year.

James M. Jackson, son of Hugh and Rebecca Jackson, b. 11th day of 9th month, 1797.
Elizabeth Jackson d. 1779, aged 90 years.

Children of Isaias and Margaret Jamison: Joseph Jamison b. 22nd day of 5th month, 1799 and d. 13th day of 6th month, 1829; Margaret Jamison b. 1st day of 9th month, 1800 and d. 10th day of 3rd month, 1831; Mary Jamison b. 15th day of 11th month, 1802.

Children of Henry and Hannah Johnson: William Johnson b. 30th day of 3rd month, 1785; Benjamin Johnson b. 20th day of 5th month, 1787; Jane Johnson b. 26th day of 2nd month, 1790; Sarah Johnson b. 7th day of 4th month, 1793; Lydia Johnson b. 1st day of 4th month, 1795; Grey Johnson b. 28th day of 8th month, 1796; Hannah Johnson b. 24th day of 4th month, 1798; Henry Johnson b. 2nd day of 9th month, 1799.

Susan F. Johnson, wife of David, b. 18th day of 9th month, 1791.

Rachel Jones d. 8th month, 1767.

Children of Stephen and Phebe Kirk: Isaac Kirk b. 11th day of 1st month, 1762; Sarah Kirk b. 3rd day of 2nd month, 1764; Jonas Kirk b. 20th day of 10th month, 1766; Hannah Kirk b. 18th day of 1st month, 1769; Benjamin Kirk b. 26th day of 6th month, 1771; Elizabeth Kirk b. 19th day of 10th month, 1773; Rachel Kirk b. 2nd day of 6th month, 1776.

Thomas Lancaster, of Warwick, England, d. 9th month, 1750 O.S., in his 48th year. Came to this country with Ann Chapman.

Children of Benjamin and Rachel Lancaster: Jesse Lancaster b. 1st day of 1st month, 1751; Ann Lancaster b. 28th day of 6th month,

1753; Benjamin Lancaster b. 28th day of 2nd month, 1756 and d. 7th month, 1760; Joseph Lancaster b. 7th day of 11th month, 1758; Benjamin Lancaster b. 10th day of 10th month, 1761; Nathan Lancaster b. 8th day of 12th month, 1763.

Children of John and Elizabeth Lancaster: Abigail Lancaster b. 26th day of 8th month, 1754; Israel Lancaster b. 25th day of 7th month, 1756 and d. 7th day of 8th month, 1760; Jonah Lancaster b. 28th day of 3rd month, 1758; Anne Lancaster b. 27th day of 6th month, 1759; Israel Lancaster b. 22nd day of 5th month, 1761.

John Lancaster, the father, d. 26th day of 2nd month, 1791, about 59 years old.
Elizabeth Lancaster, widow of John, d. 11th day of 12th month, 1796, about 67 years of age.

Children of Israel and Hannah Lancaster: Harriet Lancaster b. 20th day of 1st month, 1799; John Lancaster b. 5th day of 4th month, 1801; William Lancaster b. 28th day of 10th month, 1802; Morris Lancaster b. 10th day of 3rd month, 1806.

Mary Lester, daughter of John and Catherine Lester, b. 1716 and d. 30th day of 5th month, 1761.
Catherine Lester, wife of John Lester, d. in the winter of 1732.

Children of John Lester and Dorothy, his 2nd wife: Catherine Lester b. 23rd day of 9th month, 1733; Priscilla Lester b. 18th day of 1st month, 1736 and m. Wm. Foulkes; John Lester b. 31st day of 1st month, 1738; William Lester b. 18th day of 3rd month, 1740

John Lester, the father, d. 27th day of 1st month, 1771, aged 82 years.

Children of Isaac and Elinor Lester: Margaret Lester b. 13th day of 11th month, 1749; Samuel Lester b. 6th day of 9th month, 1750; Joseph Lester b. 26th day of 2nd month, 1752; John Lester b. 19th day of 1st month, 1754; Elijah Lester b. 20th day of 11th month, 1755; Mary Lester b. 16th day of 7th month, 1757; Catherine Lester b. 10th day of 6th month, 1759; Isaac Lester b. 6th day of 1st month, 1761.

Children of John and Jane Lester: Sarah Lester b. 5th day of 4th month, 1763; Shipley Lester b. 23rd day of 11th month, 1764, m. Margaret Nixon, and d. 24th day of 3rd month, 1832; Hannah Lester b. 2nd day of 2nd month, 1767; Thomas Lester b. 1st day of 3rd month, 1769, m. 1st, Mary Stokes, m. 2nd Hannah Green, and d. 22nd day of 3rd month, 1828; Jane Lester b. 8th day of 9th month, 1771 and m. Moses Wilson; John Lester b. 11th day of 8th month, 1774 and m. Abigail Willson; Isaac Lester b. 20th day of 2nd month, 1777 and d. 18th day of 3rd month, 1780; Peter Lester b. 10th day of 9th month, 1779 and d. 22nd day of 8th month, 1785.

Jane Lester, wife of John Lester, b. 26th day of 10th month, 1739 and d. 26th day of 11th month, 1805.

Children of Shipley and Margaret Lester: Abel Lester b. 11th day of 10th month, 1792; Morris Lester b. 26th day of 4th month, 1794 and d. 10th day of 6th month, 1801; Samuel Lester b. 8th day of 15th month, 1795 and d. 10th day of 4th month, 1798; William Lester b. 29th day of 9th month, 1797; Albert Lester b. 15th day of 8th month, 1799; Jane Lester b. 5th day of 1st month, 1802 and d. 6th day of 10th month, 1809; Hannah Lester b. 23rd day of 7th month, 1804 and m. John Hampton Watson; Mary Ann Lester b. 15th day of 9th month, 1806; Shipley Lester b. 2nd day of 8th month, 1809.

Children of Thomas and Mary Lester: Peter Lester b. 17th day of 7th month, 1797; Jane Lester b. 20th day of 10th month, 1799 and d. 12th day of 7th month, 1801.

Mary Lester, wife of Thomas Lester, and daughter of John and Susanna Stokes, d. 3rd day of 4th month, 1803.
Isaac Lester d. 30th day of 1st month, 1762.

Children of Lewis and Ann Lewis: Elizabeth Lewis b. 5th day of 7th month, 1729; Hannah Lewis b. 5th day of 2nd month, 1730; Ellis Lewis b. 1st day of 3rd month, 1732 and d. 7th day of 12th month, 173_; Ellis Lewis, 2nd, b. 20th day of 5th month, 1734; Lewis Lewis, Jr., b. 30th day of 5th month, 1736 and d. 9th day of 5th month, 1738; Ann Lewis, Jr., b. 11th day of 8th month, 1738; Margaret Lewis b. 11th day of 12th month, 1741; Lewis Lewis b. 13th day of 9th month, 1744 and d. 15th day of 1st month, 1778; Joseph Lewis b. 3rd day of 9th month, 1746 and d. 5th month,. 1753; Jane Lewis b. 29th day of 11th month, 1748; Mary Lewis b. 20th day of 12th month, 1750 and d. 5th month, 1759; Martha Lewis b. 21st day of 3rd month, 1754.

Lewis Lewis, Sr., the father, d. 16th day of 2nd month, 1778, aged 72 years.
Ann Lewis, widow of Lewis Lewis, d. 8th day of 11th month, 1785.

Children of Lewis Lewis, Jr., and Mary, his wife : Sarah Lewis b. 27th day of 7th month, 1770 and d. 11th day of 5th month, 1771; James Lewis b. 30th day of 3rd month, 1772 and d. 11th day of 1st month, 1776; Lewis Lewis b. 10th day of 1st month, 1774; Joseph Lewis b. 9th day of 10th month, 1775; Jane Lewis b. 7th day of 11th month, 1777.

Children of Thomas and Elizabeth McCarty: Phebe McCarty b. 2nd day of 8th month, 1766, m. Levi Roberts, and d. 30th day of 3rd month, 1850; Samuel McCarty b. 8th day of 11th month, 1767; Silas McCarty b. 30th day of 11th month, 1768; Sarah and Mary McCarty (twins) b. 19th day of 12th month, 1769; Joel McCarty b. 16th day of 12th month, 1771; John McCarty b. 6th day of 5th month, 1773; James McCarty b. 11th day of 6th month, 1774; Jane McCarty b. 18th day of 9th month, 1775; Elizabeth McCarty b. 17th day of 9th month, 1776; Thomas McCarty b. 8th day of 3rd month, 1778; Job

McCarty b. 10th day of 8th month, 1779; Hannah McCarty b. 19th day of 2nd month, 1781; Benjamin McCarty b. 20th day of 7th month, 1783.

David Morris, son of Morris and Susanna Morris, d. 28th day of 5th month, 1752.
Susanna Morris, wife of Morris Morris, d. 28th day of 4th month, 1755.
Morris Morris d. 2nd day of 6th month, 1764.
Samuel Morris of Whitemarsh d. 31st day of 11th month, 1770.

William Newman b. 3rd day of 5th month, 1759.
Margaret Newman, wife of William Newman, b. 23rd day of 3rd month, 1759.

Children of William and Mary Nixon: Mary Nixon b. 27th day of 7th month, 1713; Samuel Nixon b. 30th day of 11th month, 1715, and d. 29th day of 1st month, 1747/8.

William Nixon (he came from England) d. 16th day of 12th month, 1747/8, in his 68th year.
Mary Nixon, widow of William, d. 21st day of 4th month, 1758, in her 78th year.

Children of Samuel and Susanna Nixon: Margaret Nixon b. 25th day of 2nd month, 1770 and m. Shipley Lester; Sarah Nixon b. 26th day of 8th month, 1771; William Nixon b. 29th day of 4th month, 1775; Hannah Nixon b. 27th day of 1st month, 1777; Mary Nixon b. 25th day of 1st month, 1779 and m. Isaac Parry; Abel Nixon b. 13th day of 4th month, 1783; Samuel Nixon b. 27th day of 12th month, 1785; Beulah Nixon b. 1st day of 1st month, 1790; Abigail Nixon b. 19th day of 3rd month, 1792.

Children of William and Martha Nixon: Hannah Nixon b. 13th day of 11th month, 1800; Sarah Nixon b. 16th day of 3rd month, 1802; Samuel Nixon b. 7th day of 4th month, 1805; Edward Roberts Nixon b. 5th day of 2nd month and d. 1st day of 3rd month, 1808.

Patrick Ogleby d. 23rd day of 7th month, 1760.

Owen Owens, of Sancon, d. 21st day of 8th month, 1742.
Mary Owens d. 14th day of 3rd month, 1760, in her 96th year.

Obadiah Palmer b. 15th day of 5th month, 1780.
Sarah V. Palmer, wife if Obadiah Palmer and daughter of Joseph and Susanna Van Vleet, b. 1st day of 9th month, 1784.
John Palmer b. 9th day of 4th month, 1794.

_ _ _ Parvin b. 16th day of 10th month, 1736.

Children of Samuel and Betty Peirson: George Peirson b. 27th day of 8th month, 1729; Hannah Peirson b. 20th day of 4th month, 1731 and d. 22nd day of 4th month, 1732; Samuel Peirson, Jr., b. 27th day of 7th month, 1733; Tom Peirson b. 15th day of 2nd month,

1736; Ann Peirson b. 12th day of 9th month, 1738 and d. 19th day of 12th month, 1739; Isabel Peirson b. 19th day of 10th month, 1740; Betty Peirson, Jr., b. 23rd day of 12th month, 1743.

Children of Robert and Mary Penrose: Jonathan Penrose b. 1st day of 1st month, 1735/6 and m. Martha Penrose; Joseph Penrose b. 10th day of 6th month, 1737; John Penrose b. 19th day of 11th month, 1739/40, m. Ann Roberts, and d. 12th day of 2nd month, 1813; William Penrose b. 15th day of 2nd month, 1742, m. Mary Roberts, Jr., and d. 26th day of 1st month, 1808; Robert Penrose, Jr., b. 6th day of 3rd month, 1744; Samuel Penrose b. 21st day of 6th month, 1748 and m. Sarah Roberts; Benjamin Penrose b. 30th day of 10th month, 1749/50; Mary Penrose b. 5th day of 6th month, 1753 N.S.; Jesse Penrose b. 2nd day of 5th month, 1755.

Children of John and Ann Penrose: Martha Penrose b. 13th day of 10th month, 1765, m. Amos Richardson, and d. 20th day of 3rd month, 1949; Enoch Penrose b. 1st day of 8th month, 1767, m. Martha Edwards, and d. 22nd day of 8th month, 1842; Nathan Penrose b. 1st day of 4th month, 1769; Rachel Penrose b. 7th day of 2nd month, 1771 and m. George Shaw; Jane Penrose b. 3rd day of 11th month, 1773 and d. 24th day of 5th month, 1848; Thomas Penrose b. 2nd day of 5th month, 1775 and m. Rachel Hillman; John Penrose b. 7th day of 2nd month, 1777; Ann Penrose b. 22nd day of 6th month, 1779 and m. George Hicks; Evan Penrose b. 2nd day of 4th month, 1782, m. Rebecca Ball, and d. 11th day of 2nd month, 1864; Mary Penrose b. 9th day of 5th month, 1785 and d. 10th day of 12th month, 1849.

Children of Joseph and Elinor Penrose: Israel Penrose b. 31st day of 12th month, 1768; Jane Penrose b. 7th day of 1st month, 1771; Benjamin Penrose b. 3rd day of 1st month, 1773 and d. 9th month, 1777; Joseph Penrose b. 27th day of 1st month, 1777.

Children of William and Mary Penrose: Abigail Penrose b. 11th day of 9th month, 1771; Margaret Penrose b. 5th day of 5th month, 1775 and d. 31st day of 10th month, 1826; Sarah Penrose b. 21st day of 11th month, 1778, m. Caleb Edwards, and d. 1860.

Mary Penrose, widow of William Penrose, d. 30th day of 11th month, 1843.

Children of Samuel and Sarah Penrose: Abel Penrose b. 7th day of 8th month, 1778, m. 1st, Kesiah Speakman, m. 2nd, Abigail Foulke and d. 7th day of 12th month, 1824; Gainor Penrose b. 14th day of 3rd month, 1780; William Penrose b. 14th day of 3rd month, 1782; Edward Penrose b. 7th day of 10th month, 1784; Mary Penrose b. 11th day of 5th month, 1787; Benjamin Penrose b. 16th day of 9th month, 1791; Susanna Penrose b. 21st day of 8th month, 1793; Samuel Penrose b. 10th day of 8th month, 1796; Margaret Penrose b. 20th day of 9th month, 1798; Morris Penrose b. 15th day of 6th month, 1801.

Children of Israel and Susanna Penrose: Elizabeth Penrose b. 25th day of 12th month, 1791 and m. W. Ambler; Edith Penrose b. 25th day of 6th month, 1794; Enos Penrose b. 15th day of 10th month, 1796; Jane Penrose b. 31st day of 1st month, 1801; Benjamin Penrose b. 9th day of 7th month, 1803; Edith Penrose b. 7th day of 10th month, 1806; Joseph Penrose b. 6th day of 9th month, 1808.

Children of Thomas and Rachel Penrose: Lydia Penrose b. 5th day of 2nd month, 1797; Hannah Penrose b. 16th day of 12th month, 1798, m. John Ball and d. 1st day if 7th month, 1865; Ann Penrose b. 6th day of 7th month, 1801; John Penrose b. 24th day of 3rd month, 1804; Elizabeth Penrose b. 27th day of 7th month, 1806 and m. Peter Lee; Clementine Penrose b. 30th day of 10th month, 1810.

Children of Nathan and Hannah Penrose: Martha Penrose b. 6th day of 6th month, 1795; Lavinia Penrose b. 5th day of 10th month, 1798 and m. William Heacock; Nathan Penrose b. 24th day of 11th month, 1800; Tacy Penrose b. 18th day of 3rd month, 1808; Washington Penrose b. 17th day of 9th month, 1809; William Penrose b. 18th day of 10th month, 1812.

Martha Penrose, wife of Enoch Penrose, b. 6th day of 7th month, 1776 and d. 8th day of 5th month, 1804.

Moses Phillips, son of Thomas and Sarah Phillips, of Solebury Tp., b. 24th day of 12th month, 1792.
Christiana Phillips, daughter of Thomas and Hannah Carey, b. 28th day of 3rd month, 1784.

Children of Thomas and Anne Rawlings: Joseph Rawlings b. 3rd day of 12th month, 17_ _ and d. 22nd day of 12th month, 1796; Margaret Rawlings b. 25th day of 1st month, 1786; Thomas Rawlings b. 23rd day of 12th month, 1787; Ann Rawlings b. 17th day of 10th month, 1789; Jane Rawlings b. 3rd day of 3rd month, 1792.

Children of Amos and Martha Richardson, of Rockhill Tp: Rebecca Richardson b. 7th day of 3rd month, 1796; Jane Richardson b. 27th day of 2nd month, 1798; Keziah Richardson b. 20th day of 2nd month, 1800 and d. 20th day of 10th month, 1844; John Richardson b. 4th day of 12th month, 1802 and d. 4th day of 9th month, 1822; Sarah Richardson b. 5th day of 3rd month, 1805 and d. 4th day of 9th month, 1867; Anne Richardson (twin) b. 5th day of 3rd month, 1805.

Children of Edward and Mary Roberts, who m. at Abington, Mont. Co., on 29th day of 10th month, 1714: Martha Roberts b. 16th day of 8th month, 1715 and d. 26th day of 1st month, 1768; Abel Roberts b. 23rd day of 8th month, 1717 and d. 5th day of 1st month, 1808; John Roberts b. 22nd day of 11th month, 1719; David Roberts b. 10th day of 1st month, 1722 and d. 14th day of 8th month, 1805; Everard Roberts b. 9th day of 3rd month, 1725; Nathan Roberts b. 13th day of 6th month, 1727 and d. 10th day of 12th month, 1806; Mary Roberts b. 6th day of 4th month, 1730, m. John Foulke, and d. 2nd day of 10th month, 1787; Jane Roberts b.

3rd day of 11th month, 1732, m. Thomas Foulke, and d. 25th day of 7th month, 1822.

Edward Roberts d. 25th day of 11th month, 1768, in his 82nd year.
Mary Roberts, widow of Edward, d. 22nd day of 7th month, 1784, aged 96-6-9.
William Roberts d. 13th day of 8th month, 1731.

Children of Thomas and Alice Roberts: John Roberts b. 6th month, 1716 and d. 2nd day of 2nd month, 1797; Ann Roberts b. 6th month, 1718; Thomas Roberts b. 2nd month, 1720 and d. 5th day of 6th month, 1767; Richard Roberts b. 12th month, 1722; Alice Roberts b. 2nd month, 1724, m. Edward Thomas and d. 6th day of 8th month, 1767; Rachel Roberts b. 2nd month, 1727; Abraham Roberts b. 14th day of 1st month, 1730.

Children of Abel and Gainer Roberts: Susanna Roberts b. 13th day of 12th month, 1748 and d. 26th day of 2nd month, 1818; Sidney Roberts b. 5th day of 7th month, 1756; Sarah Roberts b. 6th month, 1758.

Gainer Roberts, wife of Abel Roberts, d. 16th day of 1st month, 1779.

Children of Thomas Roberts, Jr., and Latitia, his wife: Abigail Roberts b. 28th day of 7th month, 1751; Martha Roberts b. 9th day of 3rd month, 1753; Alice Roberts b. 3rd day of 4th month, 1755; Israel Roberts b. 14th day of 1st month, 1757; Elizabeth Roberts b. 7th day of 8th month, 1759, m. Edward Foulke, and d. 25th day of 7th month, 1793; Isaac Roberts b. 25th day of 1st month, 1762.

Thomas Roberts, Jr., the father, d. 30th day of 5th month, 1786, about 65 years old.
Latitia Roberts, widow of Thomas, Jr., d. 12th day of 10th month, 1802.

Children of John and Margaret Roberts, of Milford Tp: Hannah Roberts b. 19th day of 4th month, 1754; Alriah Roberts b. 28th day of 10th month, 1755 and d. 14th day of 8th month, 1762; Enoch Roberts b. 28th day of 2nd month, 1757; David Roberts b. 27th day of 11th month, 1758; Samuel Roberts b. 13th day of 1st month, 1761 and d. 8th day of 8th month, 1762; Uriah Roberts b. 13th day of 11th month, 1762; Martha Roberts b. 25th day of 10th month, 1764, m. Benjamin Foulke, and d. 13th day of 8th month, 1831; Margaret Roberts b. 11th day of 8th month, 1768; Abel Roberts b. 27th day of 9th month, 1770.

John Roberts, the father, d. 8th day of 8th month, 1776.

Children of David and Phebe Roberts: Amos Roberts b. 1st day of 4th month, 1755; Mary Roberts b. 19th day of 4th month, 1758 and d. 22nd day of 8th month, 1760; Elizabeth Roberts b. 4th day of 7th month, 1760; Nathan Roberts b. 29th day of 6th month, 1762 and d. 28th day of 5th month, 1763; Jane Roberts b. 19th day of

12th month, 1764; Abigail Roberts b. 14th day of 2nd month, 1767; Nathan Roberts b. 24th day of 9th month, 1769; David Roberts b. 21st day of 9th month, 1772, m. Elizabeth Stokes, and d. 13th day of 11th month, 1856; Evan Roberts b. 20th day of 4th month, 1775 and d. 26th day of 3rd month, 1849.

Children of Amos and Margaret Roberts: Mordecai Roberts b. 29th day of 8th month, 1776; Mary Roberts b. 17th day of 3rd month, 1778; Alice Roberts b. 28th day of 4th month, 1780; Hugh Roberts b. 16th day of 2nd month, 1782; Andrew Roberts b. 31st day of 1st month, 1784; George Roberts b. 9th day of 1st month, 1786 and d. 17th day of 11th month, _ _ ; Phebe Roberts b. 7th day of 3rd month, 1788; Margaret Roberts b. 20th day of 2nd month, 1790.

Susan Roberts, daughter of Everard and Ann Roberts, b. 7th day of 2nd month, 1771 and d. 11th day of 4th month, 1854.
Edward Roberts b. 7th day of 11th month, 1743.
Mary Roberts b. 4th day of 12th month, 1752.

Children of Edward and Mary Roberts: Martha Roberts b. 24th day of 7th month, 1780 and m. Wm. Nixon; James Roberts b. 27th day of 11th month, 1783; Peninah Roberts b. 7th day of 4th month, 1788.

Children of Israel and Ann Roberts, Jr: Lidia Roberts b. 14th day of 4th month, 1783, m. Wm. Edwards and d. 5th day of 1st month, 1866; Jane Roberts b. 10th day of 3rd month, 1785; Thomas Roberts b. 16th day of 7th month, 1787; Latitia Roberts b. 21st day of 8th month, 1789; Lewis Roberts b. 21st day of 12th month, 1791.

Children of William and Rebecca Roberts: Joseph Roberts b. 7th day of 8th month, 1786; Sarah Roberts b. 18th day of 12th month, 1787; Maria Roberts b. 23rd day of 7th month, 1789; Martha Roberts b. 2nd day of 4th month, 1791; John and Rebecca (twins) Roberts b. 25th day of 12th month, 1796; Nathan Roberts b. 26th day of 2nd month, 1800 and d. 21st day of 10th month, 1805.

Children of Nathan and Margaret Roberts: Ashton Roberts b. 8th day of 3rd month, 1792; Theophilus Roberts b. 13th day of 3rd month, 1794; Guy Roberts b. 2nd day of 8th month, 1796.

Margaret Roberts, wife of Nathan, b. 24th day of 3rd month, 1765.

Children of Evan and Abigail Roberts: William Roberts b. 6th day of 9th month, 1800 and d. 4th day of 8th month, 1865; Hannah Roberts b. 17th day of 3rd month, 1802; Paulina Roberts b. 25th day of 3rd month, 1806; Maria Roberts b. 14th day of 3rd month, 1809.

Abigail Roberts, wife of Evan, b. 11th day of 9th month, 1771 and d. 12th day of 8th month, 1854.
Levi Roberts, son of Abraham and Peninah Roberts, b. 21st day of 10th month, 1759 and d. 4th day of 1st month, 1846.
Samuel Roberts, son of David and Elizabeth Roberts, b. 4th day of 5th month, 1782 and d. 14th day of 3rd month, 1856.

Jane Roberts, wife of Samuel Roberts, b. 24th day of 5th month, 1789.

Children of William and Mary Samuels, of Sancon Tp: Jane Samuels b. 18th day of 1st month, 1794; Jesse Samuels b. 17th day of 3rd month, 1795; Mary Samuels b. 10th day of 8th month, 1800; William Samuels b. 7th day of 8th month, 1806.

Children of Samuel and Mary Shaw: Hannah Shaw b. 29th day of 7th month, 1738; Mary Shaw b. 30th day of 5th month, 1740, m. Robert Miller, and d. 14th day of 11th month, 1779; John Shaw b. 16th day of 10th month, 1742 and d. 24th day of 9th month, 1826; Joseph Shaw b. 25th day of 6th month, 1744; William Shaw b. 23rd day of 2nd month, 1750 and d. 17th day of 6th month, 1818; Samuel Shaw b. 25th day of 8th month, 1756 and m. Susanna Rea; Moses Shaw b. 20th day of 8th month, 1758, m. Mary Carr, and d. 6th day of 9th month, 1826.

Samuel Shaw, the father, d. 21st day of 2nd month, 1781, in his 72nd year.
Mary Shaw, widow of Samuel Shaw, d. 23rd day of 12th month, 1794, aged 81 years, 2 weeks.

Children of John and Phebe Shaw: Israel Shaw b. 3rd day of 9th month, 1765 and d. 30th day of 9th month, 1833; Hannah Shaw b. 12th day of 12th month, 1766; Wm. Nixon Shaw b. 12th day of 11th month, 1769; Joseph Shaw b. 6th day of 2nd month, 1772 and d. 16th day of 2nd month, 1823; Gulielma Shaw b. 25th day of 9th month, 1774; Phebe Shaw b. 4th day of 1st month, 1778 and d. 1st day of 5th month, 1830; Mary Shaw b. 17th day of 1st month, 1780; Miriam Shaw b. 11th day of 1st month, 1782, m. David Foulke, and d. 14th day of 11th month, 1814; John Shaw b. 27th day of 7th month, 1783 and d. 17th day of 3rd month, 1839.

Children of William and Sarah Shaw: Mary Shaw b. 1st day of 12th month, 1778 and d. 21st day of 1st month, 1817; Jonathan Shaw b. 26th day of 9th month, 1781 and d. 1st month, 1859; Samuel Shaw b. 26th day of 2nd month, 1784, m. Sidney Foulke, and d. 6th day of 2nd month, 1863; Moses Shaw b. 24th day of 7th month, 1786; Abigail Shaw b. 3rd day of 7th month, 1789 and d. 29th day of 8th month, 1858; Hannah Shaw b. 7th day of 3rd month, 1793, m. James Foulke, and d. 28th day of 5th month, 1859.

Children of Samuel and Susanna Shaw: John Shaw b. 24th day of 11th month, 1780; Thomas Shaw b. 16th day of 10th month, 1782; Latitia Shaw b. 14th day of 12th month, 1784.

Susanna Shaw, wife of Samuel Shaw, d. 17th day of 6th month, 1788, aged 35 years, 2 months.

Children of Moses and Mary Shaw: Deborah Shaw b. 15th day of 12th month, 1782, m. _ _ Wood, and d. 10th day of 1st month, 1860; Sarah Shaw b. 30th day of 11th month, 1784 and m. Abner Dalbey; Mary Shaw b. 25th day of 1st month, 1787 and d. 29th day of 12th month, 1808; William Shaw b. 9th day of 10th month, 1790.

Mary Shaw, widow of Moses, d. 30th day of 4th month, 1833.

Children of Joseph and Hannah Shaw: Olivia Shaw b. 4th day of 2nd month, 1797; Ann Shaw b. 19th day of 7th month, 1800; Guli Shaw b. 23rd day of 6th month, 1804; Israel Shaw b. 22nd day of 4th month, 1809; Rebecca Shaw b. 11th day of 3rd month, 1815.

Children of Samuel and Patience Sleeper: Rebecca Sleeper b. 25th day of 7th month, 1796; Ketury Sleeper b. 17th day of 2nd month, 1801; Aves Sleeper b. 13th day of 1st month, 1804; Budell Sleeper b. 29th day of 7th month, 1806.

Children of Jacob and Staunchy Strawhent, now Strawn: William Strawn b. 17th day of 11th month, 1749; Daniel Strawn b. 27th day of 3rd month, 1752 and d. 10th day of 9th month, 1819; Mary Strawn b. 21st day of 2nd month, 1754; Hannah Strawn b. 8th day of 4th month, 1756; Josiah Strawn b. 28th day of 10th month, 1758; Job Strawn b. 12th day of 10th month, 1760; Jerusha Strawn b. 14th day of 12th month, 1762; Abel Strawn b. 12th day of 3rd month, 1765; Enoch Strawn b. 1st day of 9th month, 1768.

Mary Strawn, wife of Thomas, d. 27th day of 3rd month, 1770.

Children of Daniel and Eliza D. Stroud, of Stroudsburg: Charles Stroud b. 9th day of 4th month, 1793; Macdowel Stroud b. 12th day of 10th month, 1795; William Stroud b. 19th day of 8th month, 1797; Jacob D. Stroud b. 28th day of 3rd month, 1799; Jas. Hollinshead Stroud b. 12th day of 11th month, 1800; Susan Stroud b. 31st day of 3rd month, 1804; Simpson Stroud b. 31st day of 7th month, 1806; Elizabeth Stroud b. 5th day of 1st month, 1808.

Children of Edward and Alice Thomas, who m. 14th day of 10th month, 1749: Margaret Thomas b. 2nd day of 9th month, 1751; Miriam Thomas b. 2nd day of 9th month, 1753; Mary Thomas b. 2nd day of 10th month, 1755 and d. 19th day of 12th month, 1831; Martha Thomas b. 22nd day of 1st month, 1758; Samuel Thomas b. 15th day of 7th month, 1760 and d. 17th day of 5th month, 1847; Andrew Thomas b. 20th day of 1st month, 1764 and d. 15th day of 5th month, 1765.

Edward Thomas, the father, d. 4th day of 4th month, 1782, 59-2-13.

Children of William and Ann Thomas: Absalom Thomas b. 11th day of 7th month, 1761; Jane Thomas b. 8th day of 12th month, 1762.

Elizabeth Thomas, wife of Samuel, b. 17th day of 9th month, 1776.
Margaret Thomas, wife of Samuel, d. 24th day of 10th month, 1750, in her 57th yr.
Samuel Thomas d. 7th day of 5th month, 1755, in his 65th yr.
Mary Thomas, daughter of Samuel and Margaret, d. 27th day of 2nd month, 1756, in her 27th yr.

Thomas Thomas, son of Samuel and Margaret, d. 12th day of 10th month, 1780, aged 62 yrs.
Anne Thomas d. 14th day of 12th month, 1786.

Daniel Walton, son of Isaac Walton, b. 16th day of 4th month, 1754 and d. 1809.

Children of James and Margaret Walton: Ann Walton b. 15th day of 9th month, 1764; James Walton b. 22nd day of 7th month, 1776; Joseph Walton b. 27th day of 10th month, 1780; Ellis Walton b. 23rd day of 7th month, 1783.

Children of Daniel and Martha Walton: Jane Walton b. 24th day of 6th month, 1789; Mary Walton b. 6th day of 2nd month, 1791 and d. 12th day of 11th month, 1796; Edith Walton b. 13th day of 12th month, 1792 and d. 19th day of 11th month, 1796; David Walton b. 24th day of 1st month, 1795; Lydia Walton b. 25th day of 6th month, 1799 and d. 1809.

Children of Moses and Jane Wilson, Jr: Shipley Wilson b. 27th day of 7th month, 1798; Mark Wilson b. 27th day of 8th month, 1802.

Deborah Wood, daughter of Moses and Mary (Shaw) Wood, b. 15th day of 12th month, 1782 and d. 10th day of 1st month, 1860.

RICHLAND MONTHLY MEETING

MEN'S MINUTES

17/12/1742 - Complaint against Barnabas Murfin concerning several things laid to his charge such as clandestinely conveying things not his own. Diana Byran condemns her former misteps.
17/1/1743 - Barnabus Murfin condemns himself and his irregular conduct. Robert Penrose confessing his faults and irregular conduct in drinking to excess. Eleanor Williams condemns her outgoing in marriage.
21/2/1743 - Peter Ball requests a certificate to Buckingham monthly meeting.
16/4/1743 - John Stokes produced a certificate from Burlington monthly meeting on behalf of himself and wife.
21/5/1743 - Susanna Morris requests a certificate to visit friends in Long Island.
15/7/1743 - Samuel Foulke and Ann Grasley intend to marry.
20/8/1743 - Samuel Foulke and Ann Grasley clear to marry. Griffith David produced a certificate from Buckingham monthly meeting for himself, wife and children.
15/10/1743 - The marriage of Samuel Foulke and Ann Grasley orderly accomplished.
16/12/1743- Abel Roberts and Gainor Morris intend to marry. Willm. Shadeker produced a certificate from Chesterfield monthly meeting in behalf of himself and wife. Robert Penrose produced a paper wherein he confesseth his faults and irregular conduct.
15/1/1744 - Abel Roberts and Gainor Morris clear to marry. Jos. Green and Katherine Thomas intend to marry. Ann Parker produced a paper confessing her former missteps in going out in marriage.
19/2/1744 - Jos. Green and Katherine Thomas clear to marry.
17/3/1744 - The marriage of Jos. Green and Katherine Thomas orderly accomplished on the 10th day of this month. Margaret Thomas produced a certificate from Abington monthly meeting.
21/4/1744 - Our last meeting finding a shortness in Margaret Thomas's certif. in that there was no mention made of her children therefore this meeting appointed Edw. Roberts and Willm. Nisson to speak to the children and find whether they incline to friends or no. A complaint being brought to this meeting concerning the disorderly life and conversation of Benjamin Gilbert in his excessive drinking of strong liquors and extravagent expressions.
20/7/1744 - Tho. H _ _ produced a certificate from Buckingham monthly meeting on behalf of himself and wife. Isaac Griffith intends to marry with one belonging to Buckingham monthly meeting and requests a few lines by way of a certificate from this meeting.
15/9/1744 - There hath been repeated complaints of the extravigancy of Benj. Gilbert.
20/10/1744 - This meeting requires Walter McCoole to be present at the next monthly meeting to answer complaints made by Richard Lundy against him.

25/1/1745 - James Morgan requesting a few lines by way of a certificate from this meeting in order to marry with one belonging to Chester monthly meeting. Jontn. Heacock and Susanna Morgan declared their intentions to marry. He is required to produce a certificate from the monthly meeting to which he belongs.

18/2/1745 - Jontn. Heacock produced a certificate from Chester monthly meeting in order to be joined to this monthly meeting. Jontn. Heacock and Susanna Morgan clear to marry. Deborah Morgan having made application to this meeting signifying her desire to come under the care of Frds.

11/3/1745 - The marriage of Jonathan Heacock and Susanna Morgan orderly accomplished on the 9th of this instant.

17/8/1745 - Robert Penrose delivered a paper confessing his fault in drinking strong liquors.

21/9/1745 - Ann Morgan produced a certificate from Chester monthly meeting in order to be joined with us.

16/11/1745 - A motion being made in this meeting, concerning Sarah Banks, respecting her publick appearance in meetings, whether she may be worthy of recommendn. as a minister. This meeting having under consideration the sorrowful and afflicting case of Elizabeth Thomas, who hath a second time fallen into that great sin of fornication which is evident from her being lately delivered of an illegitimate child.

20/1/1746 - Informed that Walter McCoole hath taken some unwarrantable measures in taking up and disposing of strays as in giving people money for bringing in creatures and selling them.

17/2/1746 - David Davis having made application for a few lines by way of a certificate in order to proceed in marriage with one belonging to Gwinedd monthly meeting.

15/3/1746 - Debora Margan having delivered a paper acknowledging her former fault in marrying a man who had another wife. Elizabeth Walton having brought a paper confessing and condemning her fault in going out in marriage.

19/4/1746 - Walter McCoole appearing gave some satisfaction with respect to his proceedings in taking strays and promises to desist giving money for bringing in strays.

21/6/1746 - Thom. Foulk produces a certificate from Gwynedd monthly meeting in order to be joined with us.

18/7/1746 - Isaac Lester and Eleanor Thomas declare their intention to marry.

16/8/1746 - Isaac Lester and Elinor Thomas clear to marry. Application being made on behalf of Enos Ellis for a few lines by way of a certificate to Exeter monthly meeting. Repeated complaints being made against Robert Penrose with respect to his being time after time guilty of drinking strong liquor to excess.

20/9/1746 - The marriage of Isaac Lester and Ellinor Thomas orderly accomplished. David Owen having made breach of discipline in going out in marriage. James Sloan applying for a certificate on behalf of himself and wife to Hattonfield monthly meeting in New Jersey.

18/10/1746 - James Sloans certificate according to his own desire is deferred for some time.

15/11/1746 - Susanna Morris delivered in two certificates, one from London and the other from Wales giving a good account of her labours in the service of truth.

19/12/1746 - David Owen produced a paper confessing and condemning his faults of fornication and disorderly marriage. Patrick Ogilby produced a certificate from Abington monthly meeting on behalf of himself and wife.

16/2/1747 - Charles Dennis and Sarah Morgan declare their intention to marry.

20/3/1747 - Charles Dennis and Sarah Morgan clear to marry. A complaint being laid against Tho. Christy in respect of his disorderly conduct in playing at cards and he being present was treated gently but instead of complying with tender dealing he returned such insulting and reproachfull language and lightness of behavior as occationed much griefe and trouble.

18/4/1747 - The marriage of Charles Dennis and Sarah Morris orderly accomplished.

20/6/1747 - Elizabeth Blacklidge produced a certificate from Middletown monthly meeting on behalf of herself and children in order to be joined with us. Sarah Haisey who has lately gone out in marriage being also guilty of fornication. A complaint being brought against Barnabas Murfin in respect to him being often guilty of drinking strong liquors to excess and lately legally convicted of theft.

19/9/1747 - This meeting being informed of some disorderly behavior of Walter McCoole and Peter Lester at a public house.

1_/10/1747 - Application being made in behalf of Patrick Ogilby and wife for a certificate in order to join to Philad. monthly meeting. Thos. Christy making a complaint against Thomas Roberts and his son Richard for a slander.

21/11/1747 - Elizabeth Edwards brought in a paper wherein she confessed and condemned her faults of committing fornication and going out in marriage.

19/1/1748 - Jos. Ray requesting a certificate on behalf of himself and wife in order to be joined to Gwynnedd monthly meeting. The affair depending between Thos. Christy and Richard Roberts not being ended.

21/2/1748 - John Thomas and Elizabeth Lewis declare their intentions of marriage. Thos. Willson produced a certificate from Middletown monthly meeting. Walter McCoole, appearing, made an acknowledgement of his former misconduct.

19/3/1748 - John Thomas and Elizabeth Lewis clear to marry. Ann Griffith produced a certificate from Buckingham monthly meeting.

16/4/1748 - Joshua Scattergood produced a certificate from Burlington monthly meeting on behalf of himself and wife. Willm. Hogue produced a certificate from Hopewell monthly meeting at Opeçkan in Virginia on behalf of himself, wife and sons, Willm. and Solomon. The marriage of John Thomas and Elizabeth Lewis not yet being accomplished.

21/5/1748 - The marriage of John Thomas and Elizabeth Lewis orderly accomplished on the 23rd of last month. Thos. Christy requested a certificate in order to proceed in marriage with one belonging to Philada. monthly meeting. James Morgan requested a certificate on behalf of himself and wife in order to joyn to Derby monthly meeting.

18/6/1748 - Abel Roberts having made application for a certificate in order to joyn to Gwynedd monthly meeting.

15/7/1748 - Friends appointed find Richard Roberts to be clear of saying the slander complained of but has used too much freedom in speaking by information which he acknowledges and is sorry for. Therefore it is the judgement of this meeting that Thos. Christy ought to drop the affair and desist making any further complaint in that respect.

20/8/1748 - Martha ?Crew brought a paper in which she hath confessed and condemned her offence of fornication and disorderly marriage.

17/9/1748 - John Zelly and Rachel Griffith declare their intention of marriage.

15/10/1748 - John Zelley and Rachel Griffith clear to marry.

19/11/1748 - The marriage of John Zelly and Rachel Griffith orderly accomplished.

18/3/1749 - Hugh Hilles produced a certificate from Gwynedd monthly meeting on behalf of himself and wife.

15/4/1749 - Thos. Willson applying to this meeting for a certificate in order to joyn to Middletown monthly meeting. Mary Phillips brought in a paper in which she has confessed her offence in going out in marriage.

17/6/1749 - Benj. Gilbert produced a paper confessing and condemning his former misconduct and reproachfull practices.

21/7/1749 - Robert Penrose produced a paper acknowledging his former misconduct. Application being made on behalf of Benj. Lancaster for a few lines by way of a certificate in order to proceed in marriage with one belonging to Gwynedd monthly meeting.

19/8/1749 - Edward Thomas and Alice Roberts declared their intentions of marriage.

16/9/1749 - Edward Thomas and Alice Roberts clear to marry.

21/10/1749 - Tho. Lancaster Juner. produced a certificate from Buckingham monthly meeting. James Burson also produced a certificate from the same meeting.

18/11/1749 -Benj. Gilbert requested a certificate on behalf of himself, wife and family in order to join to Falls mo. meeting.

15/1/1750 - A complaint being laid against Thomas Roberts of his indecent and reproachfull behavior with Catherine Maycock which he has not hitherto been able to clear himself of.

19/2/1750 - Application being made on behalf of Griffith Davis for a certificate for himself, wife and children in order to joyn to Abington monthly meeting. John Stokes also requested a certificate for himself and wife in order to joyn to Burlington monthly meeting. Thos. Lancaster having acquainted this meeting with his concern to visit Frds. on the Islands of Barbadoes and Tortola requests a few lines by way of a certificate. The case of Mary Rains, who sometime past fell into the sin of fornication, was delivered of an illegitimate child and has since gone out in marriage.

16/6/1750 - Saml. Gaskill produced a certificate from Burlington monthly meeting in behalf of himself and wife. Mary Rains produced a paper in which she has confessed and condemned her late misconduct in committing fornication and going out in marriage. Joseph Ball and Sarah his wife produced a paper in condemnation of their late misconduct and disorderly proceeding in marriage. Thos. Roberts, Junr., and Letitia Rea declared their intentions of marriage. A complaint of Walter McCoole against Thos. Christy for a debt which has been long due.

18/8/1750 - Thos. Christy having made a complaint that Walter McCoole has deprived him of a piece of land and improvements which he has purchased. Thomas Roberts, Junr. and Letitia Rea clear to marry. Mary Roberts, formerly Jenkins, produced a paper in condemnation of her offence in going out in marriage. Application being made on behalf of Matthew Rea signifing his desire to be joyned with us.

15/9/1750 - The marriage of Thomas Roberts, Junr., and Letitia Rea orderly accomplished on the 14th? day of this month. A complaint being made some time past by Ingle Ingerloe against Walter McCoole in which Walter is charged with fraudulent dealing.

20/10/1750 - Frds. appointed to have a hearing of the difference between Thos. Christy and Walter McCoole have brought in their judgement, writing (viz) that Thomas ought to pay Walter the debt he owes him which he acknowledged to be just and that Walter ought to give the sd. Thos. Christy possession of the improvement which lies in dispute between them as far as he has power to do. The overseers having laid before this meeting the disorderly conduct of Isaac Lester in excessive drinking of strong liquors and other inordinate and scandalous practices.

18/2/1751 - Febe Lancaster delivered to this meeting two certificates on behalf of her dec'd. husband, one from Barbadoes and the other from Tortola.

16/3/1751 - Edmd. Phillips and Elizabeth his wife brought in a paper confessing and condemning their former misconduct and indecent behavior toward each other.

20/4/1751 - The overseers laid before this meeting the case of Wm. Hicks and Margaret Nixon who have for a considerable time cohabited together in the practice of uncleaness and fornication. The overseers also laid before this meeting the conduct of David Davies in excessive drinking of strong liquors and mispending his time and substance.

15/6/1751 - Jotha. Scattergood having made application for a certificate for himself and wife and family to Middletown monthly meeting.

19/7/1751 - David Davies appeared and confessed himself faulty in respect of drinking to excess. The misunderstanding still continuing between Thos. Christy and Walter McCoole.

17/8/1751 - Abner Rogers brought in a certificate from Burlington monthly meeting in behalf of himself and wife.

21/9/1751 - (Page very difficult to read) Abel Roberts produced a certificate from Gwynedd monthly meeting in behalf of himself and wife.

19/10/1751 - Abner Rogers brought in a paper signed by himself and wife wherein they confess their fault of unchastity before marriage. Application being made on behalf of Edmund Phillips and wife and children for a certificate to Goshen monthly meeting.

15/1/1752 - NEW STILE COMMENC'D. Isaac Walton produced a certificate from Abington monthly meeting on behalf of himself and wife. Susanna Morrice requests a certificate to cross the seas and visit Frds. in Great Britain.

19/3/1752 - Jos. Dennis, Junr. and Hannah Lewis declared their intention of marriage.

16/4/1752 - Jos. Dennis, Junr. and Hannah Lewis clear to marry. certificate approved for Edmd. Phillips, wife and three daughters.

21/5/1752 - The marriage of Joseph Dennis and Hannah Lewis was orderly accomplished on the thirteenth day of this month. Informed by the women overseers that the person formerly called Mary Rains who sometime past was testified against for having fallen into the sin of fornication and disorderly proceeding in marriage hath again gone out in marriage with another man.

20/8/1752 - Saml. Thomas and Febe Lancaster declared their intention of marriage. Wm. Hogue, Junr., and Esther Ewen declared their intention to marry. John Edwards, Junr., and wife brought in a paper in confession and condemnation of their going out in marriage. Willm. Hi_ _ and Margaret his wife delivered a paper in which they confessed their sin of cohabiting together a considerable time before marriage and condemned the same. Hannah Bittle produced a certificate from Philada. monthly meeting. Richard Roberts requested a certificate in order to proceed in marriage with one belonging to Abington monthly meeting. Thos. Christy entered a complaint against Walter McCoole that the sd. Walter refuse to deliver up his bond upon his tendering his payment or a balance.

21/9/1752 - Sam'l. Thomas and Febe Lancaster clear to marry. Wm. Hogue, Junr., and Esther Ewen clear to marry. Thos. Lancaster requesting a certificate in order to proceed in marriage with one belonging to Wrightstown meeting.

19/10/1752 - The marriage of Saml. Thomas and Febe Lancaster was orderly accomplished on the 17th of this month. The marriage of Wm. Hogue and Esther Ewen was orderly accomplished on the 12th of this month. Saml. Bevan produced a certificate from Chesterfield monthly meeting in New Jersy on behalf of himself and wife.

21/12/1752 - John Foulke intent of going on a trading voyage to Barbadoes, requests a few line by way of a certificate. Thomas Christy produced a written paper subscribed by David Herr in confirmation of his charge against Walr. McCoole in having offered inchastity to a woman in Macungee which was recd. as sufficient to make void the writing which the sd. Walter had before produced in order to clear himself from the charge.

18/1/1753 - Walter McCoole appearing acknowledged that some part of his past conduct has not been justifiable and promised to make restitution. The overseer of the women acquainting this meeting of the misconduct of Wm. Newman and his wife in drinking strong liquors to excess. Whereas Thos. Christy hath some time past charged Walter McCoole with having offered incivility and inchastity to a dutch woman in Macungie from which charge the sd. Walter has since produced a clearence in writing signed by both the woman and her husband.

15/3/1753 - Solomon Hogue and Ann his wife delivered a paper wherein they made confession of their sin of inchastity before marriage and condemn the same. John Roberts requested a few lines by way of a certificate in order to proceed in marriage with Margaret Gaskill belonging to Burlington monthly meeting.

19/4/1753 - Thos. Christy and Martha Ashton declared their intention to marry.

17/5/1753 - Thos. Christy and Martha Ashton clear to marry. The clerk reports that he has delivered to Walter McCoole a coppy of the meetings testification against him and that he has no intention of appealing.

19/7/1753 - Complaint of Wm. Hoge against Abrm. Griffith , the said Abrm. Griffith being present did acknowledge his fault in having publickly said without sufficient cause that he would not go to meeting at Wm. Hoges house if it were settled there. Complaint of Thomas Roberts against his son John Roberts for not performimg his engagement and covenant which he entered into by certain articles of agreement for the maintainance of his sd. father. The women Frds. laid before this meeting a testification against Rachel Roberts who fell into the sin of uncleaness and fornication.

20/9/1753 - John Roberts, being present, acquainted this meeting that he had endeavoured to satisfy his father but without the desired success. John Foulke requesting a certificate to the island of Barbadoes.

18/10/1753 - John Lancaster requesting a certificate to proceed in marriage with one belonging to Gwynnedd monthly meeting. Saml. Bevan entering a complaint against Thos. Head reflecting some dealings between them.

15/11/1753 - Received from Derby monthly meeting a certificate for James Morgan and wife who removed from thence and settled within the verge of our meeting a considerable time past and neglected applying for a certificate.

17/1/1754 - Susanna Morris being returned from a visit in several parts of Great Britain delivered to this meeting two certificates, one from London and the other from Bistol. Certiicate for Thos. Ashton to Wrightstown monthly meeting. Jos. Unthank and Saml. Pierson intending to go to North Carolina to see the country and try and look for a settlement there, are requesting our certificate for that purpose.

21/2/1754 - Complaint being made on behalf of Thos. Head against James Morgan for the detention of a certain sum of money.

21/3/1754 - David Roberts and Febe Lancaster declared their intention to marry.

18/4/1754 - David Roberts and Febe Lancaster clear to marry.

16/5/1754 - The marriage of David Roberts and Febe Lancaster orderly accomplished on the second day of this month. Application being made on behalf of Benjamin Lancaster and wife for a certificate in order to joyn to Gwynedd monthly meeting.

20/6/1754 - John Foulke produced a certificate from Bridgetown monthly meeting on the island of Barbadoes. The clerk is ordered to take care of and deliver [requested certificate] when Benjn. Lancaster comes to take up a bond which is lodged in his hand belonging to the gardian of the minor children of Thos. Lancaster, dec'd.

15/8/1754 - Thos. Foulk and Jane Roberts declared their intention of marriage.

19/9/1954 - Thos. Foulke and Jane Roberts clear to marry.

17/10/1754 - The marriage of Thos. Foulke and Jane Roberts orderly accomplished on the tenth day of this month. The clerk informed this meeting that he rec'd. the money due from Benjn. Lancasters bond to Wm. Edwards and sent his certificate by a safe hand to Gwynedd. A complaint being brought against John Lancaster of his refusing to perform his engagement to furnish his brother Jacob with freedom dues. The overseers laid before this meeting the disorderly conduct of David Davies by frequently drinking strong liquor to excess and behaving reproachfully at such times.

21/11/1754 - Abrm. Bond hath lately gone out in marriage and that with his first cousin.

Pages torn - Abrm. Bond not appearing. James Morgan not appearing to make satisfaction for his disorderly conduct. Abner Rogers requested a certificate for himself and wife to Burlington monthly meeting. Jos. Unthank and Saml. Pierson requested certificates for themselves and families to recom'd. them to Frds. in North Carolina.

17/4/1755 - Abrm. Bond delivered an acknowledgement in writing of his offence in going out in marriage with his first cousin.

15/5/1755 - Certificate for Abrm. Bond to Abington monthly meeting.

19/6/1755 - Thomas Jennings produced a certificate from Haddenfield monthly meeting in New Jersey on behalf of himself and wife. Dugald Cameron, having proposed being joyned to this meeting, produced a recomendation from some friends of Chester County. Thomas Jennings, intending to remove to North Carolina, requested our certificate to recommend him with his wife and children to Frds. there.

17/7/1755 - James Morgan having absconded from his family. Thos. Jennings having requested a certificate to remove to Carolina acquaints this meeting that he alters his intentions and defers it for some time.

2_/8/1755 - John Foulke and Mary Roberts declared their intentions to marry.

18/9/1755 - John Foulke and Mary Roberts clear to marry. Thomas Carrington produced a certificate from Abington monthly meeting on behalf of himself, wife Mary and children and his wifes daughter, Ester Walton. Application being made on behalf of Job Lancaster for a certificate to Abington monthly meeting.

16/10/1755 - Marriage of Jms. Foulke and Mary Roberts orderly accomplished on the 14th of this month. Jonathan Griffith produced a paper confessing his offence in going out in marriage.

20/11/1755 - Thomas Christy who is and has been above a year past mostly absent from his family and suffering his effects to be frequently seized by legal executions for debt, leaving his wife and children in a disconsolate condition at home.

19/2/1756 - On application of our women Frds. for our assistance in supporting and maintaining Susanna Davis, a poor infirm person. John Ashton produced a certificate from Exeter monthly meeting. Peter Ashton having some time past obtained a certificate to recommend his son Thomas to Frnds. at Wrightstown during his intended apprenticeship there, now returned the same, having found occasion to recall his son before the sd. certificate was entered there.

18/3/1756 - Saml. Doan produced a certificate from Abington monthly meeting. Thos. Jennings requested a certificate on behalf of himself, wife and children to Little Egg Harbour monthly meeting. Complaint against Benj. Griffith on behalf of a Frd. belonging to Abington monthly meeting for a debt unjustly detained by him.

15/4/1756 Application being made on behalf of Hezekiah, Humphry, Wm. and Driscilla Williams for a certificate to Gwynedd monthly meeting.

20/5/1756 - Thos. Carrington requested a certificate for himself, wife and children to recommend them back to Abington monthly meeting. There is a misunderstanding between Thos. Christy and Thos. Roberts concerning the removal of a fence.

15/7/1756 - Martha Christy sent a complaint against Wm. Foulke charging him with having falsely accused her to her husband. Susanna Morris deceased.

19/8/1756 - William Foulke clear in regard to Martha Christy. This meeting taking into consideration the case of several persons formerly belonging here /to wit/ William Shadocker, James Williams, Peter Lester and wife and Joseph Lester, who have several years past removed from among us in a disputable manner and there appearing at present no reason to expect them to return to make satisfaction for their misconduct it is the sense of this meeting they ought to be testified against.

16/9/1756 - Jno. Greasley and Jane Foulke declared their intention of marriage.

21/10/1756 - Jno. Greasley and Jane Foulke clear to marry. George Hoge and Eliz. Blacklidge declared their intention of marriage. Abrm. Roberts and Catherine Lester declared their intentions of marriage.

18/11/1756 - The marriage of Jno. Greasley and Jane Foulke orderly accomplished on the 17th day of this month. George Hoge and Elizabeth Blacklidge clear to marry. Abrm. Roberts and Katherine Lester clear to marry.

16/12/1756 - The marriages of Geo. Hoge and Eliz'th. Blacklidge and Abrm. Roberts and Catherine Lester accomplished on the 9th day of this month. Application being made on behalf of Thomas Lancaster to Gwynedd monthly meeting on behalf of himself,

wife and children.
20/1/1757 - Certificate for Thos. Lancaster not drawn by reason of some misunderstanding between the sd. Lancaster and one of his neighbors. Joseph Ball produced a paper containing a confession of his having taken an oath before a magistraite.
17/2/1757 - The case of Jos. Ball who has been seen reproachfully disguised with strong drink and made such equivocation and evasions concerning it.
17/3/1757 - Wilm. Foulke and Perscilla Lester declared their intentions of marriage.
21/4/1757 - Wilm. Foulke and Perscilla Lester clear to marry. Wilm. Blackledge and Ann Lewis declared their intentions of marriage.
19/5/1757 - The marriage of Wm. Foulke and Priscilla Lester orderly accomplished on the 12th day of this month. Willm. Blacklidge and Ann Lewis clear to marry. Application of Leonard Thomas for assistance to settle affairs between him and his mother, brother and sisters.
16/6/1757 - The marriage of Wm. Blackledge and Ann Lewis orderly accomplished on the 15th instant. Frds. appointed to assist the Widow Thomas and her children to settle their affairs. Margaret Walton, daughter of Isaac Walton, and Mercy Walton, daughter of Abrm. Walton, have both gone out in marriage.
18/8/1757 - Patrick Ogilby produced a certificate from Philada. monthly meeting on behalf of himself, wife Rebecca, son Joseph and daughter Rachel.
15/9/1757 - Benj. Fell and Sarah Rawlings declared their intentions of marriage. Theoph. Foulke and Margaret Thomas declared their intention of marriage.
20/10/1757 - Benjamin Fell and Sarah Rawlings clear to marry. Theophilus Foulke and Margaret Rawlings clear to marry. Joseph Rakestraw and Rachel Ogilby declared their intentions to marry.
17/11/1757 - Joseph Rakestran and Rachel Ogilby clear to marry. Marriage of Benjn. Fell and Sarah Rawlings orderly accomplished on the 3rd day of this month. The marriage of Theops. Foulke and Margaret Rawlings orderly accomplished on the 10th day of this month. Application made on behalf of George Hicks, Junr., to Middletown monthly meeting.
15/12/1757 - Marriage of Jos. Rakestran and Rachel Ogilvy orderly accomplished on the 17th day of last month.
19/1/1758 - George Hoge and Elizabeth, his wife, ...violation of their chastity before marriage and not appearing disposed to give any satisfaction. Simon Damson and John Loyd having a considerable time past gone out in marriage.
16/2/1758 - Simon Damson prepared a paper in condemnation of his outgoing in marriage. Everard Bolton deceased.
16/3/1758 - Thos. Blackledge and Margaret Wright declared their intentions of marriage. John Loyd produced a paper on behalf of himself and wife confessing their misconduct in going out to marry.
20/4/1758 - Thomas Blackledge and Margaret Wright clear to marry. Burlington monthly meeting informing us that Thomas Rawlings has lately sent them a paper condemning his misconduct when he

was a member of their meeting.

18/5/1758 - The marriage of Thomas Blackledge and Margaret Wright was orderly accomplished on the eleventh day of this month.

17/8/1758 - A certificate on behalf of Job Hughs from Exeter monthly meeting was read at this meeting. John Morgan signifying his desire to come under the care and notice of this meeting.

25/9/1758 - John Morgan and Mary Gaskill declared their intentions of marriage. Request of Tho. Edwards to come under the notice of Frds.

19/10/1758 - Jno. Morgan and Mary Gaskill clear to marry.

16/11/1758 - The marriage of Jno. Morgan and Mary Gaskill was orderly accomplished on the second day of this month. Application being made on behalf of Joseph Hoge for our certificate to Frds. in Virginia.

21/12/1758 - Mary Miller produced a paper in which she has confessed and condemned her misconduct and vice of inchastity and disorderly marriage. A certificate having been drawn for Rachel Burson to recommend her to Philada. monthly meeting.

15/2/1759 - Informed that Simon Adamson has absconded or removed in a clandestine manner out of the province leaving debts unpaid and taking no care to satisfy his creditors. There is a matter of controversy between Sollomon Hoge and Thomas Rawlings.

15/3/1759 - Jonathan Penrose and Martha James declared their intentions of marriage. Application being made on behalf of four orphan children, sons of Thomas Lancaster, deceased, who are put apprentice among frds. out of the limits of this meeting, for proper certificates to recommend them to the several meetings where they are respectively placed.

19/4/1759 - Jonathan Penrose and Martha James are clear to marry. Joseph Rawlings and Anne Hilles declared their intention to marry. Certificates drawn for Joseph, Jacob, Isaac and Aaron Lancaster.

17/5/1759 - Joseph Rawlings and Ann Hilles clear to marry. The marriage of Jonatn. Penrose and Martha James orderly accomplished on the 10th day of this month. William Hoge requesting our certificate in order to joyn Hopewell monthly meeting in Virginia.

21/6/1759 - The marriage of Joseph Rawlings and Ann Hilles orderly accomplished on the 20th day of this month.

19/7/1759 - Application being made on behalf of Solomon Hoge and George Hoge for our certificates, one to Hopewell monthly meeting and one to Fairfax monthly meeting in Virginia.

16/8/1759 - Certificates drawn for Solomon Hoge and George Hoge and their wives.

20/9/1759 - Robert Ashton and Sarah Thomas declared their intention to marry. Isaac Lester who has been _ _ _ of late frequently been _ _ _ with strong drink and mispending his time neglecting the care of his family. [Page faded and difficult to read]

1_/10/1759 - Robert Ashton and Sarah Thomas clear to marry. Thomas Stalford produced a certificate from Lisburn in the North of Ireland. Application being made on behalf of Thomas

Edwards for our certificate to Goshen monthly meeting.

17/1/1760 - Samuel Iden is removed with his family from among us and settled within the verge of Fairfax monthly meeting in Virginia without requesting a certificate.

21/2/1760 - Frds. appointed to inspect the affairs of Samuel Iden say that as they find he went away in debt without taking care to satisfy one of his creditors they could not properly draw a certificate for him. William Edwards laid before this meeting his concern to visit the meetings of Frds. in parts of the counties of Berks, Chester, Lancaster and York, requiring our concurrance and a few lines by way of a certificate.

20/3/1760 - Application being made on behalf of Willm. Hoge and wife for our certificate to Hopewell monthly meeting in Virginia. Also on behalf of Zebulon Hoge for our certificate to Burlington monthly meeting in New Jersey.

17/4/2760 - The clerk having been desired to draw two certificates, the one to Warrington monthly meeting in York County on behalf of the younger children of Edmund Philips, the other to Burlington monthly meeting on behalf of Abner Rogers and wife.

15/5/1760 - Ann Hays, formerly Hoge, has gone out in marriage. Samuel Walton has enlisted in order to go into Military Service but his father is gone over to New Jersey in order to see him, with some hopes of procuring his releasement.

19/6/1760 - Abraham Walton reported that he had made a journey to visit his son Samuel who is enlisted in the Army and that he is likely to continue in Military Service for some time. John Lester reported that he had spoken to his son Isaac and he has some hopes of his reforming his life and overcoming his weakness in drinking to excess. The case of Samuel Shaw, who has for a considerable time past taken too much liberty in censuring and openly reproaching of William Edwards and Samuel Foulke, accusing them with having acted fraud and injustice to him in the settlement of affairs relating to the estate of William Nixon, deceased, of which they were appointed Exect's.

17/7/1760 - John Lester reports he has spoke to his son Isaac and that there seems to be some hopes of amendment in him.

21/8/1760 - William Thomas and Ann Foulke declared their intentions of marriage.

18/9/1760 - William Thomas and Ann Foulke clear to marry. William Hicks and Hannah Shaw declared their intentions to marry. Saml. Shaw being present expressed his desire that the committee appointed to settle the controversy between him and the Executors of his father in law should meet here rather than elsewhere. From Wrightstown monthly meeting was adduced a certificate on behalf of John Chapman and his wife Mary and their children (viz) Mary, John, James, Elizabeth, Robert, Sarah, Mira, Charles, Susanna and Abraham. Robert Burr produced a certificate from Burlington monthly meeting on behalf of himself and Mercy his wife.

16/10/1760 - William Hicks and Hannah Shaw clear to marry. The marriage of Willm. Thomas and Ann Foulke orderly accomplished on the 9th day of this month. William Edwards and Samuel Foulke are clear of having acted unjustly in the settlement of the affairs they were intrusted with as Executors and that Saml. Shaw had charged them unjustly.

20/11/1760 - The marriage of Willm. Hicks and Hannah Shaw was orderly accomplished on the thirteenth instant. Sarah Rees delivered in a paper confessing her outgoing in marriage. Joseph Ball who some time past has been seen reproachfully disguised with excessive drinking of strong liquor.

19/2/1761 - Anne Hole had made application to come under the care and notice of Frds.

19/3/1761 - Joseph Ball being present delivered to this meeting a paper in which he confest himself guilty of drinking spiritous liquors to excess and of having made false excuses and evasions to conceal his faults.

16/4/1761 - Everard Roberts and Ann Hole declared their intentions of marriage. A certificate from Abington monthly meeting was given in, recommending to our care four of the minor children of John Loyd, deceased, (to wit) Rachel, Debora, Ann and Martha, who are placed with their relations among us.

21/5/1761 - Everard Roberts and Ann Hole clear to marry. Thomas Casner and Ann Thomas declared their intention to marry. John Hicks has of late egregiously misbehaved himself not only in a loose life and conversation but in violently breaking the windows of his house which was proved against him, soon after which he enlisted and entered into military service.

18/6/1761 - Thomas Casner and Anne Thomas clear to marry. Application being made on behalf of Moses Lancaster who is removed from among us and placed among Frds. in Philada. for our certificate. And likewise on behalf of the children of Hugh Hilles, deceased, one of whom, named William, being placed with a Friend belonging to Goshen monthly meeting, the others named Anne, Mary and David being placed among Frds. belonging to Gwynedd monthly meeting. The marriage of Everard Roberts and Ann Hole orderly accomplished on the eleventh day of this month. A certificate from Buckingham monthly meeting on behalf of one Joseph Townsend and family who are settled in the forks of the Delaware, having been under our consideration and the overseers having visited the sd. family report that they do not incline to be joyned to us as they cannot conveniently attend our meetings but intend to return again to the place from whence they came.

16/7/1761 - The marriage of Thomas Casner and Ann Thomas was orderly accomplished on the 2nd day of this month. Abraham Griffith is deceased.

20/8/1761 - Testifications drawn against Isaac Lester and John Hicks have been published. Joseph Austin produced a certificate from Abington monthly meeting on behalf of himself and Susanna his wife.

17/9/1761 - John Chapman, with his wife and several of his children, have removed and settled again within the limits of Wrightstown monthly meeting.

19/11/1761 - Application being made on behalf of John Morgan and wife for our certificate to Kennet monthly meeting.

18/2/1762 - Saml. Iden, who removed from among us and settled in

Virginia several years since without requesting a certificate or settling his affairs, has misbehaved in excessive drinking of strong liquors sundry times since he removed.

18/3/1762 - A certificate from the monthly meeting at Buckingham on behalf of Benjamin Lancaster and wife with their children.

20/5/1762 - Jos. Dennis, Junr., and Debora his wife brought in a paper containing a confession of their going out in marriage. The case of John Edwards, of whom it is currently reported that he is married to his sisters daughter, but will neither confess the fact nor positively deny it.

17/6/1762 - John Edwards readily owned his marriage with his niece.

19/8/1762 - John Lester and Jane Antrim declared their intention of marriage. Application being made on behalf of Joseph Ogilby for our certificate to the monthly meeting of Frds. in Philad. where to he has some time past removed and settled. Certificate for Job Hughs to recommend him to Exeter monthly meeting.

16/9/1762 - John Lester, Junr., and Jane Antrim clear to marry. Testification against John Edwards published. A certificate on behalf of Rebecca Ogilby to the monthly meeting in Philada. being prepared. As was also a certificate in like manner prepared on behalf of Mary Penrose recommending her to the monthly meeting at Warrington.

21/10/1762 - The marriage of John Lester and Jane Antrim orderly accomplished on the seventh day of this month.

18/11/1762 - Thomas Ashton and Mary Chapman declared their intention of marriage. William Burr produced a certificate from Philad. monthly meeting.

16/12/1762 - Thomas Ashton and Mary Chapman clear to marry.

18/1/1763 - The marriage of Thomas Ashton and Mary Chapman orderly accomplished on the 13th day of this month. Application being made on behalf of John McCool who is placed an apprentice within the limits of Abington monthly meeting for our certificate.

17/2/1763 - Stephen Kirk produced a certificate from Wrightstown monthly meeting and also his wife Phebe Kirk brought a certificate from Buckingham.

17/3/1763 - Thomas Stalford and Elizabeth Wright declared their intentions to marry.

21/4/1763 - Thomas Stalford and Elia'th. Wright clear to marry. Ellis Lewis and wife [Mary] who have a considerable time past gone out in marriage.

19/5/1763 - The marriage of Thomas Stalford and Elizabeth Wright was orderly accomplished on the 12th day of this month. Edward Evans and Jane his wife brought in a certificate from Gwynedd monthly meeting recommending them, with their four children, viz, Catherine, Jane, Joel and Sarah.

16/6/1763 - William Burr and Ann Edwards declared their intention of marriage.

21/7/1763 - William Burr and Ann Edwards clear to marry. The case of Robert Penrose who lies under the imputation of the crimes of drunkeness and adultry was laid before this meeting.

18/8/1763 - The marriage of William Burr and Ann Edwards was

orderly accomplished on the 3rd day of this month.
15/9/1763 - Abraham Ball and Ann Adamson declared their intention of marriage.
20/10/1763 - Abraham Ball and Ann Adamson clear to marry. Isaac Samuels and Ellinor Lester declared their intention to marry. James Walton and Margaret Lewis declared their intentions to marry.
17/11/1763 - Isaac Samuels and Elinor Lester clear to marry. James Walton and Margaret Lewis clear to marry. The marriage of Abraham Ball and Ann Adamson orderly accomplished on the tenth instant. Testification made against Robert Penrose.
15/12/1763 - The marriage of Isaac Samuels and Elinor Lester orderly accomplished on the 23rd of last month. The marriage of James Walton and Margaret Lewis orderly accomplished on the 8th instant.
19/4/1764 - Application being made on behalf of Robert Blackley for a certificate to Philadelphia.
17/5/1764 - Application being made on behalf of John Greasley and Jane his wife with their family for a certificate to Abington monthly meeting. Application being made on behalf of Job Hughs for a certificate to Exeter monthly meeting, he having some time past obtained one, which was lost.
21/6/1764 - A certificate brought in for Robert Tompkins and Elizabeth his wife from Abington monthly meeting.
20/9/1764 - John Penrose and Ann Roberts declared their intentions to marry.
18/10/1764 - John Penrose and Ann Roberts clear to marry. John Scarbrough produced a certificate from Buckingham monthly meeting on behalf of himself and wife.
15/11/1764 - The marriage of John Penrose and Ann Roberts orderly accomplished on the eighth day of this month.
20/12/1764 - A letter from Wilmington monthly meeting acquainting us of the miscarriage of the certificate sent for Martha Christy, which unhappily getting into the hands of her husband, could by no means be obtained from him again.
21/2/1765 - The clerk has sent a coppy of the certificate heretofore granted for Martha Christy. Samuel Bevan and wife who have a considerable time past removed to Virginia without a certificate by reason of the said Samuel's failure of satisfying his creditors.
21/3/1765 - Susanna Davis is much dissatisfied with the method which Friends have hitherto taken for maintaining her and several others not well satisfied therewith it is agreed that she be placed for one quarter under the care of John Ball, he to be paid for her board at the rate of ten pounds per annum and she to be at liberty to do what work she can for herself.
20/6/1765 - John Ball expressing an unwillingness to keep Susanna Lewis another quarter. Morris Morris and William Edwards are deceased.
18/7/1765 - Thomas McCarty signifying his desire to come under the notice of Friends.
16/8/1765 - Elizabeth Walton has lately had a bastard child. A motion being made concerning Nathan Walton, son of Abraham Walton, deceased, who is to be placed an apprentice to a

friend in Phila., and wants some assistance to cloathe him, his mother not being able to do it herself. The case of Samuel Clark and Mary his wife, who have lately separated and behaved in a manner very scandallous and reproachful was laid before this meeting.

19/9/1765 - Joseph Carnaghan produced a certificate from the monthly meeting of Ballenderry in the North of Ireland. The case of William Lester and Robert Burr, who have for a considerable time past, too much indulged themselves in a course of intemperance, idleness and profaness and of late have been frequently guilty of the crime of fornication with a certain young woman, who utterly denies the charge and asserts her innocence.

17/10/1765 - The case of William Chilcot was laid before this meeting, who a considerable time past has fallen into inchastity and gone out in marriage.

21/11/1765 - The meeting resuming the consideration of Thomas McCarty's application and it now appearing that he has imposed a fained shew of religion when some of his actions were quite inconsistant with his pretentions. John Shaw delivered a paper, on behalf of himself and Phebe and his wife, containing a confession and condemnation of their sin of inchastity and going out in marriage. Margaret Lester has gone out in marriage with one not of our society.

19/12/1765 - A certificate for Abigail Clark having been prepared by the womens meeting and some friends not being fully satisfied it should pass without acquainting her father with the contents. A certificate from the monthly meeting at Newtown on Long Island on behalf of Elizabeth Lancaster was brought in and read. The case of Joseph Damson who some time past feel into the sin of inchastity and went out in marriage with one communion. Application being made on behalf of Benjamin Lancaster and Rachel his wife with their children for our certificate to Deer Creek monthly meeting in Maryland. Friends appointed to draw a certificate for John Edwards children by his former wife produced one but it appearing necessary to make some alterations therein.

15/5/1766 - The marriage of William Clark and Hannah Loyd was orderly accomplished on the first day of this month. The marriage of William Edwards and Meribah Gaskill was orderly accomplished on the 24th day of last month. Everard Bolton, father of Isaac Bolton, is deceased.

19/6/1766 - A certificate from Abington monthly meeting on behalf of Benjamin Tomkins and wife with two of their children. Application being made on behalf of Robert Tomkins and wife for our certificate to recommend them to Abington monthly meeting.

18/9/1766 - Application being made on behalf of Joseph Carnaghen for our certificate to the monthly meeting at Crosswicks in West Jersey.

16/10/1766 - David Walton and Margaret Green declared their intentions to marry. Application being made on behalf of John Ball, son of Joseph Ball, who is placed an apprentice to a Friend in Philadelphia.

20/11/1766 - David Walton and Margaret Green clear to marry.

18/12/1766 - The marriage of David Walton and Margaret Green was orderly accomplished on the fourth day of this month. James Brown and Evan Jones from Uwchland monthly meeting acquainted this meeting that Abigail Clark who some time past removed from hence and had our certificate to that meeting, hath not given in her certificate but went out in marriage with one who is not of our communion.

19/2/1767 - Application being made on behalf of Michael Clark for a few lines to the monthly meeting at Uwchland.

19/3/1767 - Application being made on behalf of James Chapman for a certificate to the monthly meeting at Philadelphia. A motion being made respecting Mary Clark, who has sometime past removed from among us and resides within the limits of Uwchland monthly meeting. Joseph Dennis, being about to remove with his family to settle within the limits of Kingwood monthly meeting in New Jersey requested our certificate. Nathan Walton who is to be placed an apprentice to William Burr and is in need of some assistance to cloath him. A certificate being brought from Wrights Town monthly meeting recommending Samuel Hilborn with his wife and children, to our care. The meeting was informed that they have some time past settled beyond the Kittalinny Mountains on the Frontiers of Northampton County.

16/4/1767 - Joseph Shaw and Rachel Griffith declared their intentions of marriage.

21/5/1767 - Joseph Shaw and Rachel Griffith clear to marry. Application being made on behalf on Benjamin Penrose, placed as apprentice within the limits of Abington monthly meeting, for a few lines to recommend him to the care of friends there.

18/6/1767 - The marriage of Joseph Shaw and Rachel Griffith orderly accomplished on the 4th day of this month.

16/7/1767 - Jeremiah Heacock and Sarah his wife who being first cousins went out in marriage.

20/8/1767 - Jeremiah Heacock and Sarah, his wife, being present offered a paper of acknowledgement of their transgressions.

17/9/1767 - Benjamin Walton who stands charged with the sin of inchastity and going out in marriage.

15/10/1767 - Application being made on behalf of Sarah Chapman for a certificate to Wrights Town monthly meeting. Friends appointed to provide some cloathing for Nathan Walton have performed the service.

21/1/1768 - Benjamin Walton offered a paper in which he made confession of his sin of fornication and going out in marriage.

18/2/1768 - Robert Blackledge produced a certificate from the monthly meeting at Philadelphia on behalf of himself and Joanna, his wife, with their two children Elizabeth and Thomas. Elizabeth McCoole has turned from friends and joyned another society. Thomas Strahan desires to be received under the notice of Friends.

21/4/1768 - A Friend on behalf of Joseph Austin and Susanna his wife requested our certificate to Abington monthly meeting.

19/5/1768 - John Ball requesting some money for keeping Susanna

Davies.

16/6/1768 - A certificate prepared for Mary McCoole and two of her children named Catherine and Samuel being read and approved.

18/8/1768 - The case of Elizabeth Thomas and Ann Casner, the first being charged with stealing, the other being privy thereto, from which they have not been able to clear themselves.

15/6/1769 - The marriage of Robert Fisher and Martha Edwards was orderly accomplished on the 18th day of last month. The marriage of Thomas Strawhen and Mary Heacock was orderly accomplished on the 8th day of this month. Jacob Strawhen and Christiana his wife [and son John] request to be received into religious fellowship.

17/8/1769 - Lewis Lewis, Junr., and Mary Burson declared their intentions of marriage. Abraham Walton and Rachel Heacock declared their intentions to marry. Joseph Penrose brought a paper confessing his sin of inchastity before marriage. Samuel Green on behalf of self and his wife Rachel brought in a paper confessing their transgression in going out to marry.

21/9/1769 - Lewis Lewis and Mary Burson clear to marry. Abraham Walton and Rachel Heacock clear to marry. George Michener and Hannah Carr declared their intentions of marriage.

19/10/1769 - George Michener and Hannah Carr clear to marry. John Chapman and Hannah Antram declared their intentions of marriage. The marriage of Lewis Lewis and Mary Burson orderly accomplished on the twelfth of this month. The marriage of Abraham Walton and Rachel Heacock orderly accomplished on the same day. Friends are of the opinion that it may be best to leave the three eldest of Jacob Strawhens children (to wit) William, Daniel and Mary, until they come to make application for themselves and that all the younger ones to be taken under the care of Friends with their parents.

16/11/1769 - John Chapman and Hannah Antram clear to marry. The marriage of George Michener and Hannah Carr orderly accomplished on the 19th day of last month. The case of Robert Thomas who for a considerable time past hath fallen into a course of intemperance in the use of spirituous liquors and behaving in a manner very unbecoming a member of our society. The case of Hannah Kearney who for some time past has entertained a man in her house.

21/12/1769 - The marriage of John Chapman and Hannah Antram orderly accomplished on the 30th of last month. Rachel Lancaster gave in a paper confessing her sin of inchastity which occasioned her going out in marriage. Application being made on behalf of Samuel Clark, Junior, to Uwchland monthly meeting.

18/1/1770 - A certificate for Hannah Michener to Buckingham monthly meeting. Edward Roberts is deceased.

15/2/1770 - A certificate for Abigail Roberts brought in for the womens meeting was read and approved.

15/3/1770 - John Straham and Kezia Dennis, Junr., declared their intentions of marriage. Application being made by Thomas Stalford on behalf of himself, wife and children for our certificate to Sadsbury monthly meeting in Lancaster County. John Ball, Junr., applying for a few lines to recommend him to Gunpowder monthly meeting in Maryland. Certificate for Jane Adams to the monthly meeting at Hardwick in New Jersey. The case of Joseph Ball, Junr., who for some time past has taken undue liberty in company keeping, mispending his time and has lately fell into the sin of inchastity.

19/4/1770 - A certificate from Kennet monthly meeting recommending back to the care of this meeting John Edwards three children.

17/5/1770 - A certificate from Philada. monthly meeting for Joseph Parr a youth put apprentice to a member of this meeting.

21/6/1770 - The case of John Strahen continued, they report that he, with Kezia Dennis, Junr., have fell into the sin of inchastity yet stood in denial thereof until at or near the birth of their child. The cases of Abrahm. Walton and Rachel his wife, and Ezekiel Dennis and Ann his wife who also fell into the sin of inchastity before marriage, were laid before this meeting.

19/7/1770 - Robert Thomas still continues his disorderly conduct in drinking to excess and other reproachful behavior.

16/8/1770 - Joseph Shaw intends to remove with his family [wife Rachel and two children George and David] to settle within the compass of Gunpowder monthly meeting in Maryland and requests our certificate.

20/9/1770 - John Roberts and Martha Edwards declared their intentions of marriage. William Penrose and Mary Roberts, Junr., declared their intentions of marriage.

18/10/1770 - John Roberts and Martha Edwards clear to marry. William Penrose and Mary Roberts, Junr., clear to marry. A certificate from Warrinton monthly meeting in York County for William Penrose, Junr., who is placed as apprentice to a member of this meeting. John Ball, Junr. produced a certificate from Philada. monthly meeting. Moses Lancasetr produced a certificate from Philada. monthly meeting.

15/11/1770 - The marriage of John Roberts and Martha Edwards orderly accomplished the first of this month. The marriage of William Penrose and Mary Roberts, Junr., orderly accomplished on the eighth instant.

20/12/1770 - Application being made on behalf of Amos Dennis to Kennet monthly meeting, he being placed an apprentice to a member of that meeting.

17/1/1771 - A paper subscribed by Mary Adamson the Younger confessing her having fell into the sin of inchastity was brought in by the womens meeting.

18/4/1771 - John Stokes, Junr., produced a certificate from Burlington monthly meeting for himself, his wife Susanna and son William. James Chapman produced a certificate from Philada. monthly meeting recommending him back to our care and requests a few lines in order to proceed in marriage with a young woman belonging to Burlington monthly meeting.

16/5/1771 - Testification against Robert Thomas published. Abraham Walton and Rachel his wife offered a paper confessing their having fell into the sin of inchastity before marriage. Ezekiel Dennis and Ann his wife also offered a paper confessing their sin of inchastity and having gone out in marriage. A certificate for Debora Loyd to recommend her to Abington monthly meeting. William Shaw, inclining to remove to Maiden Creek, requested our certificate to Exeter monthly meeting.

20/6/1771 - Moses Lancaster, being removed from among us and settled within the compass of Abington monthly meeting, requests our certificate on behalf of himself and Rachel his wife with their daughter Meribah. The case of Hannah Morrison concerning some disagreeable reports of her behavior.

18/7/1771 - Friends appointed to visit Hannah Morrison report that she could by no means clear herself from the matter, to wit, unseemly company keeping, and entertaining men of loose characters at unseasonable times in her house.

15/8/1771 - Testification against Hannah Morrison published.

21/11/1771 - Randal Iden and Eleanor Foulke, Junr. declared their intentions to marry. A certificate from Burlington monthly meeting for Rebecca Chapman.

19/12/1771 - Randal Iden and Eleanor Foulke clear to marry. Isaac Walton and Martha his wife brought in a paper confessing their having fell into the sin of inchastity which occasioned their going out in marriage.

16/1/1772 - The marriage of Randal Iden and Eleanor Foulke orderly accomplished on the ninth day of this month.

20/2/1772 - A motion made on behalf of William Penrose, Junr., for a few lines to recommend him back to Warrington monthly meeting. The testification against John Strahan and Kezia his wife and Hannah Morrison has been published.

19/3/1772 - Joseph Ball, Junr., has taken undue liberty in drinking spirituous liquors to excess, disorderly company keeping and has fallen into the sin of fornication. There is some impediment in the way of William Penrose, Junior's, certificate.

21/5/1772 - The case of Isaac Walton, Senior, who has for some time past taken undue liberty in drinking spirituous liquors and disorderly company keeping and some part of his behavior of late having been extremly and reproachful.

18/6/1772 - Testification against Isaac Walton, Senior, published. A certificate for Mary Morgan, daughter of James Morgan, to Abington monthly meeting.

20/8/1772 - A motion being made on behalf of Susanna Ray, who desires to come under the notice of friends. John Roberts requesting our certificate for his son William who he has placed an apprentice with a Friend belonging to Concord monthly meeting.

15/10/1772 - William Edwards is deceased.

19/11/1772 - David Burson intends to proceed in marriage with a young woman belonging to Kingwood monthly meeting in New Jersey and requests our certificate.

18/2/1773 - John Thomson, son of William Thomson of Abington monthly meeting and Abigail Roberts, daughter of Thomas Roberts, declared their intentions of marriage, his father expressing his consent. The said John is required to produce a certificate from the meeting to which he belongs.

18/3/1773 - John Thomson and Abigail Roberts clear to marry, John having produced a certificate from Abington monthly meeting.

15/4/1773 - John Greasley being returned with his family to settle among us produced a certificate from Abington monthly meeting on behalf of himself and his daughter Rachel.

20/5/1773 - A certificate for Abigail Roberts to Abington monthly meeting. Debora Cohoe laid before this meeting a paper confessing her sin of inchastity and disorderly marriage.

17/6/1773 - Joseph Green produced a paper confessing his outgoing in marriage. Thomas Edwards and Hannah, his wife, laid before the meeting a paper confessing their sin of inchastity and disorderly marriage.

15/7/1773 - A certificate from Hopewell monthly meeting in Virginia recommending Sollomon and James Hoge was read and received.

19/8/1773 - Elizabeth Ray received into membership.

16/9/1773 - Eleanor Penrose received into membership. Amos Dennis produced a certificate from Kennet monthly meeting, he having served out his apprenticeship there. A certificate for Phebe Smith to Philadelphia monthly meeting. The case of William Heacock, Junior, and Miriam, his wife, who being first cousins have fell into the sin of inchastity and married contrary to the good order of Friends.

21/10/1773 - A certificate for Hannah Chapman to the monthly meeting of the Northern District of Philadelphia.

18/11/1773 - Application being made on behalf of Moses Walton for a certificate to Uwchland monthly meeting.

17/3/1774 - The case of Ezekiel Green who has some time since fallen into the sin of fornication. Hannah Adamson offered a paper confessing her having fallen into the sin of fornication.

19/5/1774 - Testification against Ezekiel Green published. A motion made on behalf of Thomas Strahan who desires to go to North Carolina to see his friends and relations requesting a few lines of recommendation.

16/6/1774 - Solomon Hoge and Hester his wife produced a paper confessing their transgression in accomplishing their marriage contrary to good order.

21/7/1774 - The case of James Hoge who has for a considerable time past totally neglected attending our meetings and taken many wrong liberties in company keeping and mispending his time.

15/9/1774 - John Hallowell, son of William Hallowell, of Abington monthly meeting and Martha Roberts, daughter of Thomas Roberts, declared their intentions of marriage, he with consent of his parents. Jeremiah Heacock and Sarah his wife laid before this meeting a paper confessing their breach of order in their marriage, desiring Friends to receive them again with their young children.

20/10/1774 - John Hallowell and Martha Roberts clear to marry. Edward Fell and Mary Penrose, Junior, declared their intentions of marriage, he required to produce a certificate from the monthly meeting to which he belongs. Joseph Ball, Junior, offered a paper confessing his former intemperance of drinking spirituous liquors and his having fallen into the sin of inchastity. Mary Ball also offered a paper confessing her outgoing in marriage.

17/11/1774 - Edward Fell and Mary Penrose clear to marry. The marriage of John Hallowell and Martha Roberts orderly accomplished on the third day of this month. A certificate for Martha Loyd to the monthly meeting at Abington.

15/12/1774 - Application being made on behalf of Jonathan Heacock, son of Wm. Heacock, and John Heacock, son of Jonathan Heacock, deceased, for certificates to recommend the first to Chester monthly meeting and the latter to Derby monthly meeting, they being placed apprentice within the verge of the said meetings.

19/1/1775 - A certificate for Martha Hallowell to Abington monthly meeting.

16/2/1775 - A certificate for Mary Fell to Chester monthly meeting. Application made for a certificate for Joseph Ball, Junr., and wife to the monthly meeting at Gunpowder in Maryland.

4/20/1775 - Moses Ray desires to be received into membership.

15/6/1775 - A certificate for Martha Christy and her daughter Mary to the monthly meeting of the Southern District of Philadelphia. Also a certificate for Hannah Edwards to Kennet monthly meeting.

17/8/1775 - Application made on behalf of Joseph Parr for a few lines to recommend him to Philadelphia monthly meeting, he being an apprentice formerly recommended from that meeting to this, who being freed from his late master is returned therein again, to finish his apprenticeship.

21/9/1775 - Benjamin Green and Jane Roberts declared their intentions to marry. Jesse Penrose having removed from among us and settled within the verge of Exeter monthly meeting requests our certificate.

19/10/1775 - Benjamin Green and Jane Roberts clear to marry. Amos Roberts and Margaret Thomas declared their intentions to marry. Mary Philips, wife of William Phillips, having a considerable time past removed from among us and settled within the compass of Kingwood monthly meeting, has now sent a request for our certificate.

16/11/1775 - The marriage of Benjamin Green and Jane Roberts was orderly accomplished on the ninth day of this month. Amos Roberts and Margaret Thomas clear to marry.

12/21/1775 - The marriage of Amos Roberts and Margaret Thomas was orderly accomplished the 30th of last month. Application being made on behalf of Hannah Bucher for a certificate to the monthly meeting at Pipe Creek in Maryland. The case of Samuel Lester who some time past fell into the sin of inchastity and married contrary to good order.

18/1/1776 - Isaac Burson and Elizabeth Blackledge declared their intentions of marriage.

15/2/1776 - Isaac Burson and Elizabeth Blackledge clear to marry. David Carr has expressed a desire to come under the notice of

Friends.

21/3/1776 - The marriage of Isaac Burson and Elizabeth Blackledge was orderly accomplished the 29th of last month. Hannah Chapman produced a certificate from the monthly meeting of the Northern District of Philadelphia.

18/4/1776 - Abel Roberts acquainted the meeting that David Carr, being removed from among us and settled within the limits of Buckingham monthly meeting, requests a certificate to Friends there.

20/6/1776 - A certificate from Abington monthly meeting on behalf of Ann Morgan was received and read.

18/7/1776 - A certificate for Hannah Chapman recommending her to Burlington meeting. Debora Johnson confesses her breach of order in her marriage.

15/8/1776 - Lydia Burson, wife of David Burson, produced a certificate from Kingwood monthly meeting.

19/9/1776 - Joseph Speakman of the City of Philadelphia and Catherine Dennis declared their intentions of marriage. John Roberts and Thomas Foulke are appointed to make inquiry for a suitable place for Susanna Davids for the ensuing winter season.

17/10/1776 - Joseph Speakman and Catherine Thomas clear to marry, he having produced a certificate from the monthly meeting of the Southern District of Philadelphia. Our antient Friend Phebe Way produced a certificate from Wrightstown monthly meeting.

21/11/1776 - The marriage of Joseph Speakman and Catherine Dennis was orderly accomplished on the fourteenth instant. William Thomas has joined the Military Association. Benjamin Gilbert produced a certificate from Abington monthly meeting on behalf of himself and wife, Elizabeth, with four of their children named Jesse, Rebecca, Abner and Elizabeth.

16/1/1777 - Mary Edwards, Hannah Adamson and Eleanor Dennis, late Sacheveril have severally gone out in their marriages.

20/2/1777 - William Shaw and Sarah Carr declared their intentions of marriage. John Ball, Junr., offered a paper confessing his breach of good order in accomplishing his marriage.

17/4/1777 - William Shaw and Sarah Carr clear to marry. A certificate from Concord monthly meeting on behalf of William Roberts, he having served out the term of his apprenticeship amongst them.

15/5/1777 - The Friends appointed to draw testifications against Hannah Stroud, late Adamson, and Mary Ehrhard, late Edwards, have performed the service.

19/6/1777 - Thomas Owen and Margaret, his wife, offered to this meeting a paper confessing their breach of good order by accomplishing their marriage thereto.

17/7/1777 - A certificate from the monthly meeting of the Northern District of Philadelphia on behalf of Hannah and Ann Biles, minor children of John and Ruth Biles of the said city.

21/8/1777 - Samuel Penrose and Sarah Roberts declared their intention of marriage. A certificate for our friend Phebe Way to Gwynedd monthly meeting, she having removed from us and settled within the limits of that meeting. A certificate from

Abington monthly meeting on behalf of Mary Morgan recommending her back to this meeting. John Lester, Junr., and Hannah his wife offered a paper confessing their having fallen into the sin of fornication which occasioned their going out to be married.

18/9/1777 - Samuel Penrose and Sarah Roberts clear to marry. Ann Strahan, wife of Daniel Strahan, confesses her breach of good order in going out in her marriage.

16/10/1777 - The marriage of Samuel Penrose and Sarah Roberts orderly accomplished on the ninth day of this month.

20/11/1777 - The Friends appointed to prepare a suitable place for Susanna Davis have agreed with Martha Richards to keep her the ensuing winter for 20 shillings per month.

16/7/1778 - Joseph Speakman produced a certificate from the monthly meeting of the Southern District of Philadelphia.

20/8/1778 - Several members of this meeting have (to wit) John Dennis, John Chilcot, Thomas Green, Daniel Walton, Thomas Walton and John Collard, have absconded and it's supposed they are gone off with the English army. Thomas Strawhen, having sometime past received a few lines recommending him to Friends in Carolina, returned the same to this meeting.

15/10/1778 - Susanna Davids is reduced to some difficulty in procuring the necessaries of life.

19/11/1778 - A certificate from Gunpowder monthly meeting in Maryland on behalf of Joseph Ball, Junr.

17/12/1778 - A certificate recommending Mary Penrose to the monthly meeting at Providence in Chester County.

21/1/1779 - Testification published against John Dennis, Junr., John Chilcot, Thomas Green, Daniel Walton, Thomas Walton and John Collard. Theophilius Foulke has joined in military services tending to encourage the present unnatural war.

18/2/1779 - A certificate from Gwinedd monthly meeting recommending Phebe Way to this meeting.

18/3/1779 - James Green and Martha Foulke declared their intentions of marriage. Jeremiah Williams and Mary Blackledge declared their intentions of marriage.

15/4/1779 - James Green and Martha Foulke clear to marry. Jeremiah Williams and Mary Blackledge clear to marry.

20/5/1779 - The marriage of James Green and Martha Foulke orderly accomplished on the sixth day of this month. The marriage of Jeremiah Williams and Mary Blackledge orderly accomplished on the twenty second day of last month. Testification against Tamar Thomas who has gone out in marriage with a man who is not a member of our society. Testification against Catherine Evans for the sin of fornication. A paper signed by Alice Wilson signifying her having gone out in marriage with a man not in unity.

19/8/1779 - Abraham Roberts and Peninnah Thomas declared their intentions of marriage. Edward Roberts and Mary Lewis declared their intentions of marriage. A certificate from the monthly meeting of the Southern District of Philadelphia recommending Hannah Rook to the care and notice of this meeting.

16/9/1779 - Abraham Roberts and Peninnah Thomas clear to marry. Edward Roberts and Mary Lewis clear to marry. Asher Foulke and

Alice Roberts declared their intentions of marriage. Elijah Lester and Anne his wife who have gone out in marriage.

21/10/1779 - Asher Foulke and Alice Roberts clear to marry. Samuel Shaw and Susanna Rea declared their intentions to marry. The marriage of Edward Roberts and Mary Lewis orderly accomplished on the thirteenth day of last month. The marriage of Abraham Roberts and Peninnah Thomas orderly accomplished on the seventh day of this instant.

18/11/1779 - Samuel Shaw, Junr., and Susanna Rea clear to marry. The marriage of Asher Foulke and Alice Roberts orderly accomplished on the eleventh day of this month.

16/12/1779 - The marriage of Samuel Shaw and Susanna Rea orderly accomplished on the fifth day of last month. Joseph Speakman requests a certificate to recommend him, his wife and children to Wrightstown monthly meeting.

16/3/1780 - Testification against Elijah Lester and wife has been published. A certificate from the womens meeting recommends Mary Carr to this meeting. Cases of complaint brought forward from the quarterly meeting against the following Friends, to wit: Enoch Roberts for taking a Test of Alegiance and abjuration under the present unsettled state of public affairs, for paying substitute fines and other fines and taxes imposed for the support of war, for his marriage before an hireling priest with a young woman in membership with Friends, their inchaste conduct, she being pregnant before marriage; William Edwards on account of taking a Test of Allegiance and abjuration and paying fines in lieu of personal service; Thomas Edwards for taking a like test, paying a substitute fine and taxes; Everard Foulke for paying a substitute fine and muster fines and joining in marriage with a woman not in membership with Friends before a hireling priest and contrary to the advice of his parents; Leonard Thomas for paying a tax to which was added a fine for his neglect of taking a Test of Alegiance and abjuration and neglecting to attend our religious meeting and drinking strong liquors to excess; Robert Thomas, Junr., on account of taking a test of Alegiance and abjuration, paying substitute and other fines and going out in marriage with his first cousin.

20/4/1780 - Moses Shaw and Mary Carr declared their intentions of marriage. A certificate from Gunpowder monthly meeting in Maryland recommending Rachel Shaw with four of her children, (to wit), George, David, Samuel and Anne.

18/5/1780 - Moses Shaw and Mary Carr clear to marry. Testification published against Thomas Edwards. Myra Chapman [otherwise Myra Vance] having gone out in marriage with a man not in membership with Friends. Elizabeth Potts having detained some negroes in bondage.

15/6/1780 - The marriage of Moses Shaw and Mary Carr orderly accomplished on the first day of this month. Testification against Leonard Thomas has been published. Testification published against Enoch Roberts and wife. Elizabeth Smith having gone out in marriage with a man not in membership with Friends. The case of Hannah Strawhen [now White] going out in marriage being considered. The case of Levi Dennis considered, he having taken an oath of Alegiance and abjuration under the present unsettled state of public affairs and has gone out in marriage with a young woman belonging to Wrightstown monthly meeting and paid fines imposed for the support of war. Ezekiel Walton has gone out in marriage and has taken an attest of Alegiance and Abjuration required by those in power and paid fines imposed for the support of war.

17/8/1780 - A certificate recommending Hannah Rork to the monthly meeting of the Southern District of Phila. Abigail Dalby acknowledges having fallen into the sin of fornication and going out in marriage.

21/9/1780 - A certificate from Abington monthly meeting recommending Moses Lancaster and Rachel his wife and their three children (to wit) Meraba, Thomas and Martha to this meeting. Testification against Elizabeth Smith published. A motion made concerning John Scarboroughs children who are separated one from another and placed within the limits of several meetings.

19/10/1780 - George Williams and Abigail Lancaster declared their intentions of marriage. Amos Dennis and Jane Heacock declared their intention to marry. The following cases of complaint were laid before the meeting: John Loyd has for many years been neglectful of attending our religious meetings and latteraly has paid fines demanded for the support of war; Thomas Loyd has committed fornication and gone out in marriage and paid fines imposed for the support of war; Amos Chilcot has gone out in marriage and also paid fines imposed for the support of war.

16/11/1780 - George Williams and Abigail Lancaster clear to marry, he having produced a certificate from Abington monthly meeting. Amos Dennis and Jane Heacock clear to marry.

16/11/1780 - Margaret Roberts condemns her conduct in consenting to the payment of military fines.

21/12/1780 - The marriage of George Williams and Abigail Lancaster orderly accomplished on the seventeenth day of last month. The marriage of Amos Dennis and Jane Heacock orderly accomplished the thirtieth day of last month. Request was made on behalf of Cadwalader Foulke for a few lines to recommend him to Gwinedd monthly meeting.

18/1/1781 - A certificate from the womens meeting recommending Abigail Williams to Gwynedd monthly meeting. Hannah Penrose acknowledges falling into the sin of fornication.

16/2/1781 - Testification published against Thomas Loyd. Moses Rea brought in a paper on account of him having paid a substitute fine.

19/3/1781 - Hannah Foulke condemns that part of her conduct which for several years past tended to the encouragement of the payment of fines and other military services.

19/4/1781 - Jonathan Griffith sent a request desiring to come under the notice of Friends. John Edwards, Junr., has fallen into the practice of drinking strong liquors to excess and into the sin of fornication and went out in marriage and joined in military matters.

17/5/1781 - Mary Lowright has gone out in marriage. Thomas

Roberts handed in a paper signifying his sorrow for receiving a currency which was made for the purpose of carrying on war and paying substitute fines.

21/6/1781 - A certificate from the monthly meeting at Pipe Creek in Maryland recommending Hannah Bougher back to this meeting. Ezekiel Green acknowledges having fallen into the sin of fornication and latterally had taken the Test of Allegiance and Abjuration required by those in power and paid fines. Ezekiel Green made application for a certificate to Hopewell monthly meeting in Frederick County in Virginia.

16/8/1781 - Thomas Blackledge, Junr., acknowledges and condemns his error in paying fines and taking an attest of Allegiance under the present unsettled state of Government and also requested a certificate for himself and family to Hopewell monthly meeting in Frederick County in Virginia.

20 /9/1781 - Edward Foulke and Elizabeth Roberts declared their intentions of marriage. A certificate from the womens meeting recommending Rebecca Blackledge to Philada. monthly meeting was approved and signed.

18/10/1781 - Edward Foulke and Elizabeth Roberts clear to marry. Nathan Ball, intending marriage with a young woman belonging to Middletown monthly meeting, desires a few lines to that meeting.

15/11/1781 - George Iden and Hannah Foulke declared their intentions of marriage. The marriage of Edward Foulke and Elizabeth Roberts orderly accomplished on the first of this month. The cases of Thomas Strawhen and Isaiah Strawhen, Thomas having gone out in marriage and taken an attest of Allegiance under the present unsettled state of Government and Isaiah hath gone out in marriage, paid substitute and other military fines and hath been charged with circulating counterfeit paper currancy.

20/12/1781 - Moses Rea requested a certificate to Uwchlan monthly meeting. James Burson sent a request for our certificate to Wrightstown monthly meeting in his weighty undertaking of marriage with Sarah Twining.

17/1/1782 - George Iden and Hannah Foulke clear to marry. Isaac Burson having given Assurance of Alegiance under the present unsettled state of government, paid substitute and military fines and has too frequently misspent his time in attending at horse races.

21/2/1782 - The marriage of George Iden and Hannah Foulke orderly accomplished on the 24th day of last month. Application for a certificate for Isaac Roberts to recommend him to Uwchlan meeting. Robert Chapman, having removed from among us sometime since, Samuel Nixon and Joseph Lester are appointed to make enquiry and prepare a certificate to recommend him to Friends where he is.

21/3/1782 - A certificate from Wrightstown for Mary Ball. The case of Thomas Blackledge and family being revived, it is thought expedient the family (except himself and his son Enoch) be recommended to Hopewell monthly meeting in Virginia. A letter from Redstone Settlement informs that Martha Adamson has gone out in marriage. Request was made on behalf of John

Morgan for a certificate to Chester monthly meeting held at Providence.

18/4/1782 - Israel Roberts and Anne Foulke declared their intentions to marry. Testification prepared against Martha Hatfield (late Adamson). A certificate from Chester monthly meeting for Jonathan Heacock.

16/5/1782 - Israel Roberts and Anne Foulke clear to marry. A certificate from Wrightstown monthly meeting for Sarah Dennis. A certificate also for Elizabeth Tyson from Abington monthly meeting. A certificate for Mary Adamson and such of the family as may be properly recommended [her children (to wit) Thomas, James and Sarah] to Hopewell monthly meeting in Virginia.

20/6/1782 - The marriage of Israel Roberts and Anne Foulke orderly accomplished on the sixth day of this month. A certificate from Wrightstown monthly meeting recommending Sarah Burson and her two children, Mary Twining and Stephen Twining, to this meeting. The case of Richard Roberts, he having paid military fines. The case of David Roberts, Junr., he having gone out in marriage with a member of this meeting, attended the military exercise, paid military fines and attended horse races.

18/7/1782 - Enoch Blackledge's case being revived, his father signified that his son did not incline to condemn his conduct in taking the attest of Allegiance because he was terrified into it in the time of his minority. Thomas Blackledge applied for a certificate to recommend him with his wife and children to Hopewell monthly meeting in Virginia. Martha Roberts is deceased.

[Several pages are faded and difficult to readl.]

_/8/1782 - A certificate recommending Elizabeth Mason to Hopewell monthly meeting in Virginia. A certificate from Gwinedd monthly meeting recommending Phebe Wey back again. Elizabeth Roberts condemns her misconduct in going out in marriage. John Scarbrough having gone out in marriage and paid military fines.

19/9/1782 - Israel Foulks and Elizabeth Roberts declared their intentions of marriage. A certificate for Margaret Thomas to the Northern District of Philadelphia. Martha Worrel acknowledges and condemns her misconduct in going out in marriage. Application made on behalf of Benjamin Tomkins, his wife and such of his children as have a right, for a certificate to Horsham monthly meeting. Solomon Hoge requests a certificate for himself, wife and their children to Fairfax monthly meeting. John Griffith requests to come under the care of Friends.

17/10/1782 - Israel Foulke and Elizabeth Roberts clear to marry. William Loyd and Susanna his wife have gone out in marriage.

19/12/1782 - John Griffith and Rachel Greasley declared their intentions of marriage. Solomon Hoge has been taking the test of Elegiance to one party in contention and Abjuration to the other and paid military fines and his wife is party concerned with him. William Roberts confesses taking a test of Eligiance and paid military fines. A certificate recommending Elizabeth Gilbert with her three children, namely Rebeckah, Abner and Elizabeth.

16/1/1783 - The marriage of John Griffith and Rachel Greasley was orderly accomplished on the second of this month. Abraham Roberts has paid substitute and muster fines and justifies same. Testification published against John Scarborough.

20/2/1783 - The certificate prepared for Elizabeth Gilbert and her three minor children recommending them to Horsham monthly meeting at Byberry being returned because it now appears that her daughter Rebeckah is arrived to mature age and is settled in the northern District of Philadelphia. The sd. certificate is now transcribed to recommend Elizabeth and her two minor children, Abner and Elizabeth, to the monthly meeting at Byberry and the sd. Rebeckah to the Northern District of Philad.

20/3/1783 - Phebe Wilson acknowledges she has gone out in marriage and accomplished it by the assistance of a hireling priest.

17/4/1783 - Robert Chapman having given assurance of Allegiance to the present ruling power in the time of the unsettled state and also paid a militia fine.

15/5/1783 - Benjamin Tomkins acknowledges his deviation in taking the attest of Allegiance and abjuration required by those in power and also in paying military fines.

19/6/1783 - Solomon Hoge and wife are moved out of our neighborhood and have not taken any care to satisfy the meeting on account of their misconduct. Sarah Philips has gone out in marriage with a man not in membership.

17/7/1783 - Abraham Roberts acknowledges his transgression of paying military fines. Diana Walker acknowledges her transgression in going out in marriage. David Owen having neglected to attend meetings and taking an attest of Allegiance and abjuration in a time of strife and contention. John Lester, Junr., has also been treated with an account of taking an attest of Allegiance and abjuration in time of strife and contention and paying military fines.

21/8/1783 - Nathan Ball has taken an attest of Allegiance and Abjuration and paid military fines. Application made on behalf of Jonathan Heacock for a few lines to recommend him to Haverford monthly meeting in his undertaking of marriage with Hannah Davis, a member of that meeting.

18/9/1783 - A certificate from Philada. monthly meeting recommending Mary Coset to this meeting. John Griffith has fallen into the sin of inchastity with the woman who is now his wife. Samuel Shaw condemns his paying military fines.

16/10/1783 - Application made on behalf of Jonas Kirk, minor child of Steven Kirk of Springfield, dec'd., for a few lines to recommend him to Buckingham monthly meeting.

20/11/1783 - Nathan Walton has gone out in marriage. Martha Hatfield condemns her going out in marriage.

18/12/1783 - A certificate for Anne Thomas and several of her minor children (to wit) Daniel, Anne, Thomas and Edward to Gwynedd monthly meeting. Also a certificate for Jane Thomas was brought with it. Martha Scot condemns her going out in marriage. A paper was signed by Thomas Adamson clearing himself of the charge of taking the attest and confessing to the payment of a fine.

15/1/1784 - Nathan Ball condemns his taking the attest, paying military fines and training with the militia.

19/2/1784 - Testification has been published against John and Rachel Griffith.

18/3/1784 - David Stokes and Anne Lancaster declared their intentions of marriage. A paper was offered by Nathan Walton signifying his sorrow for going out in marriage with a young woman that was not a member.

15/4/1784 - David Stokes and Anne Lancaster clear to marry, he having produced a certificate from Burlington monthly meeting in New Jersey. John Foreman produced a certificate from Gwinnedd monthly meeting.

20/5/1784 - The marriage of David Stokes and Anne Lancaster orderly accomplished on the fifteenth of last month. A certificate recommending Martha Worrall to friends at Providence in Chester County. A paper was signed by Elizabeth McCarty expressing her sorrow for her past misconduct. James Loyd having been treated with on account of going out in marriage and training with the militia.

17/6/1784 - A certificate recommending Anne Stokes to Burlington monthly meeting in West Jersey. A certificate recommending Hannah Heacock from Haverford monthly meeting.

15/7/1784 - Jane Quinn treated with on account of going out in marriage with a man not of our society. A few lines from Wrightstown informs us that Jacob Verity hath sometime past removed from thence and settled within the verge of this meeting without requesting a certificate.

19/8/1784 - Jerusha Reed has gone out in marriage with a man not of our society. A certificate recommending Cadwalader Foulke from Gwynedd monthly meeting. A certificate recommending Isaac Roberts from Uwchland.

21/10/1784 - Joseph Rawlings and Anne Heacock declared their intentions of marriage. Mary Penrose having fallen into the sin of fornication. Thomas McCarty and Elizabeth his wife are desirous that their children (to wit) Samuel, Silas, Sarah, Mary, Joel, John, James, Elizabeth, Thomas, Job, Hannah and Benjamin be considered as members. John Roberts requested a few lines to recommend him to Gwynedd monthly meeting in order to accomplish his marriage with a friend of that meeting. Joseph Hester having a desire to come under the notice of friends.

18/11/1784 - Joseph Rawlings and Anne Heacock clear to marry. Robert Penrose having been treated with on account of drinking to excess and paying military fines.

16/12/1784 - The marriage of Joseph Rawlings and Anne Heacock was orderly accomplished the twenty fifth day of last month. John Dennis, Junr., offered a paper condemning his going to the British army for protection and falling into the sin of fornication and going out in marriage by the assistance of a hireling priest. A paper signed by Hannah Johnson expressing her sorrow for her going out in marriage.

20/1/1785 - Testification against Mary Penrose has been published. Application made on behalf of Isaac Kirk for a certificate to Wrightstown monthly meeting.

17/2/1785 - Request was made for a few lines to recommend John Dennis, Junr., to Kingwood monthly meeting held at Hardwick. Jesse Gilbert having removed from amongst us and settled within the verge of Horsham monthly meeting without applying for a certificate.

17/3/1785 - John Greasley and Margaret Roberts declared their intentions of marriage. Hugh Foulke and Sarah Roberts declared their intentions of marriage. A request on behalf of Joseph Burr for a certiicate to Burlington monthly meeting in his weighty undertaking of marriage with a friend of that meeting.

21/4/1785 - John Greasley and Margaret Roberts clear to marry. Hugh Foulke and Sarah Roberts clear to marry. Jesse Hicks and Mary Ball declared their intentions of marriage. Jacob Verity brought a certificate from Wrightstown monthly meeting. A certificate recommending Mary Roberts from Gwynedd monthly meeting. Jonathan Heacock having been treated with on account of training with the militia and going out in marriage and of Mary his wife, she having married contrary to good order.

19/5/1785 - Jesse Hicks and Mary Ball clear to marry. The marriage of John Greasley and Margaret Roberts orderly accomplished on the fifth day of this month. The marriage of Hugh foulke and Sarah Roberts orderly accomplished on the twenty eighth day of last month. Testification against Robert Penrose published. A certificate recommending Martha Scott to Uwchland monthly meeting. Elizabeth Tyson having been treated with on account of committing fornication.

16/6/1785 - The marriage of Jesse Hicks and Mary Ball was accomplished on the twenty sixth day of last month, but not so orderly as could have been desired, the company being so large. Jesse Gilbert offered a paper condemning his disorderly marriage. A certificate recommending Ann Roberts to Abington monthly meeting. The certificate recommending Isaac Kirk to Wrightstown monthly meeting was returned, he being returned within the limits therein.

18/8/1785 - Testification against Elizabeth Tyson published. George Iden and Hannah his wife have fallen into the sin of fornication. Certificate for Jesse Gilbert to Horsham monthly meeting held at Byberry.

15/9/1785 - Application made on behalf of William Roberts for a certificate in order to join in marriage with a friend of Gwynedd monthly meeting. Anne Foulke being privy to the disorderly conduct of her daughter and suffering her marriage to be imposed upon the meeting.

20/10/1785 - William Burr has raised a charge against John Lancaster which he utterly denies.

17/11/1785 - A certificate recommending Elizabeth Burr from Burlington monthly meeting.

15/12/1785 - A request on behalf of Phebe McCarty, she having expressed a desire of coming under the notice of friends. Jonathan Penrose having been treated with on account of drinking spiritous liquor to excess.

19/1/1786 - Testification has been published against George Iden and his wife. William Burrs charge against John Lancaster of robbing him of his grain and stove appears not to be founded in truth.

16/2/1786 - A certificate recommending Rebecka Roberts from Gwynedd monthly meeting.

20/4/1786 - Eli Kennard and Elizabeth Blackledge declared their intentions of marriage.

18/5/1786 - Eli Kennard and Elizabeth Blackledge clear to marry.

15/6/1786 - The marriage of Eli Kennard and Elizabeth Blackledge orderly accomplished on the eighth day of this month. A certificate recommending Martha Hatfield to Westland monthly meeting. Theophilus Foulke having joined the militia and excepting of the office of a Captain amongst them.

20/7/1786 - Application made on behalf of Sarah Burson, she having a desire to come under the notice of friends.

16/11/1786 - The marriage of Jonathan Griffith and Sarah Burson was orderly accomplished on the second day of his month. The marriage of Joseph Custer and Amelia Foulke was orderly accomplished on the twentieth day of last month. The marriage of Judah Foulke and Sarah McCarty was orderly accomplished on the twentieth day of last month.

18/1/1787 - William Burr acknowledges his offense respecting the difference between him and John Lancaster. Margaret Owen having fallen into the sin of fornication. A request made on behalf of Robert Blackledge for a certificate in order to proceed in marriage with a friend of Buckingham monthly meeting.

15/2/1787 - John Forman produced a certificate from Gwynedd monthly meeting. Samuel Hicks having fallen into the sin of fornication and going out in marriage and joining the militia.

15/3/1787 - A paper signed by Anne Foulke, expressing her sorrow for and condemning that part of her conduct which she was some time past disowned for. A paper signed by Hannah Walton, expressing her sorrow for her breach of order in going out in marriage with a man not in membership. Application made on behalf of William Burr for a certificate to recommend himself and family to Exeter monthly meeting. Mirriam Seagle having gone out in marriage. Martha Green having gone out in marriage with her first cousin.

19/4/1787 - Testification against Margaret Owen published. Jesse Heacock offered a paper acknowledging and condemning his going out in marriage. Hannah Edwards, having charged her brother on affirmation with greviously abusing her, which appears to have been more in envy and to gain her unjustifiable attempt of freeing her son, than any just cause given.

17/5/1787 - Daniel Walton acknowledges and condemns his offences which he was some time past disowned for. Joseph Lester acknowledges and condemns his going out in marriage.

21/6/1787 - A certificate recommending Ruth Blackledge from Buckingham monthly meeting. John Foulke, father of Edward Foulke, is lately deceased. Application made on behalf of Joseph Walton, he having a desire to come under the care of friends. Motion made for a certificate for Joseph Heacock and wife and children, they having some time past moved and settled within the limits of Haverford monthly meeting.

19/7/1787 - Testification against Samuel Hicks published. Application made on behalf of Benjamin Walton for a certificate to recommend himself and family to Westland monthly meeting.

20/9/1787 - A certificate for Isaac Walton and wife and family, who are removed and settled within the limits of Buckingham monthly meeting. Aaron Ball having fallen into the sin of fornication and training with the militia and Margaret, his wife, she having fallen into the sin of fornication.

18/10/1787 - Jonathan Heacock condemns the paying of military fines. A request on behalf of Richard Roberts for a certificate to Abington monthly meeting.

15/11/1787 - Testification against Jonathan Penrose published.

20/12/1787 - Jesse Heacock condemns his going out in marriage and paying military fines.

17/1/1788 - A certificate recommending Mary, Lavinia, Rachel and Elizabeth Hoge, minor children of Solomon and Hester Hoge, to Westland monthly meeting. Margaret Ball condemns her falling into the sin of fornication and going out in marriage. Anne Blackledge having been labored with on account of refusing to answer a demand of James Waltons which appears to be just and he also charged her with falsly accusing him.

21/2/1788 - Abel Strawhen having gone out in marriage and training with the military.

20/3/1788 - Thomas Adamson and his son John Adamson having settled within the limits of Westland monthly meeting. A certificate recommending Joseph Ball to Westland monthly meeting.

17/4/1788 - Peter Ashton having gone out in marriage and neglected to attend religious services.

15/5/1788 - Joseph Dennis and Ezekiel Dennis having a desire to remove with their families to Niagara.

19/6/1788 - A certificate from Buckingham for Ezra Kinsey. Application on behalf of Isaac Dennis for a certificate to Chester monthly meeting held at Providence.

17/7/1788 - Abigail Walton having gone out in marriage. An account of some uneasiness between Moses Lancaster and wife and David Roberts charges them with endeavouring to defraud him.

21/8/1788 - Daniel Walton and Martha Green declared their intentions of marriage. Testification against Aaron Ball and wife published. Tace Heacock having a desire to come under the notice of friends with her two children. Joseph Tomkins acknowledges and condemns his going out in marriage. A certificate for Micajah and John Stevenson from Burlinton monthly meeting.

18/9/1788 - Daniel Walton and Martha Green clear to marry.

16/10/1788 - The marriage of Daniel Walton and Martha Green orderly accomplished on the second day of this month. A certificate for Phebe Wilson to Abington monthly meeting. Amy Crawford having fallen into the sin of fornication and going out in marriage. Peter Ashton acknowledges his error in accomplishing his marriage contrary to good order.

20/11/1788 - Hannah Denny having fallen into the sin of fornication before marriage.

18/12/1788 - The matter between David Roberts and Moses Lancaster is settled but it appears that Moses and his wife have spread an evil report concerning David Roberts and have falsly accused him. Joseph Tomkins condemns his going out in marriage and training with the militia. Catherine and Abigail Roberts, minor children of Abraham Roberts, having given way to the temptation of theft so as to take that which was not their own property. Jane Evans having moved from friends and as they have understood joined with another society.

15/1/1789 - Edward Roberts having trained with the militia and gone out in marriage. John and William Shaw having paid military fines.

19/2/1789 - Benjamin Foulke and Martha Roberts declared their intentions of marriage. Two papers, one signed by Catherine Roberts and the other by her sister Abigail, expressing their sorrow for their past misconduct of theft. Aquilia Foulke having been treated with on account of training with the militia and going out in marriage. A request on behalf of Joseph Tomkins for a certificate to Gwynnedd monthly meeting.

19/3/1789 - Benjamin Foulke and Martha Roberts clear to marry. Testification against Amy Crawford and Hannah Denny. A paper signed by George and Hannah Iden expressing their sorrow for their past misconduct which they were disowned for. John Shaw condemns the payment of military fines.

16/4/1789 - The marriage of Benjamin Foulke and Martha Roberts orderly accomplished on the 26th of last month. A certificate recommending Jane Evans to Gwynedd monthly meeting. William Shaw condemns the payment of military fines. Israel and Jane Penrose having the desire to come under notice of friends.

21/5/1789 - Jonas Kirk produced a certificate recommending him back from Buckingham monthly meeting where he had been placed an apprentice. A request on behalf of John Iden, a minor child of George and Hannah Iden, they having a desire he should come under the notice of friends.

18/6/1789 - A paper signed by Mary McCarty expressing her sorrow for going out in marriage with a man not in membership. Joseph Burr acknowledges the payment of military fines.

20/8/1789 - Rachel Lancaster acknowledges and condemns her past misconduct which she was disowned for.

17/9/1789 - A certificate recommending Anne Thomas from Gwynedd monthly meeting. Joseph Heston and Anne Thomas declared their intentions of marriage, he required to produce a certificate from the monthly meeting where he belongs. John Foulke and Letticia Roberts declared their intentions of marriage. Joseph Burr acknowledges the paying of military fines and training with the militia. A request on behalf of Joseph Burr for a certificate to recommend him with his wife and children to friends at Mount Holly.

15/10/1789 - Joseph Heston and Anne Thomas clear to marry, he having produced a certificate from Gwynedd monthly meeting.

John Foulke and Letticia Roberts clear to marry. The certificate recommending Jane Evans to friends at Gwynedd was returned, she having moved out of the limits of that meeting.

19/11/1789 - The marriage of Joseph Heston and Anne Thomas orderly accomplished on the 15th day of last month. The marriage of John Foulke and Letitia Roberts orderly accomplished on the 29th day of last month. Jane Chilcot acknowledges her breach of order in going out in marriage with a man not in membership.

17/12/1789 - William Clark condemns his misconduct in paying a substitute fine.

21/1/1790 - Edward Foulke condemns the paying of military fines.

18/2/1790 - A certificate for Anne Heston to the monthly meeting at Indian Springs in Maryland. Abigail Johnson acknowledges her beach of order in going out in marriage. A request on behalf of Eleanor Dennis, she having a desire that her children may be taken under the notice of friends. Application made on behalf of Everard Bettle, he having a desire to come under the notice of friends. William Clark desires a certificate with several of his children to Exeter monthly meeting.

18/3/1790 - Application made on behalf of Thomas Heacock for a certificate to Buckingham, he being placed an apprentice within the limits of that meeting. Thomas Foulke is deceased.

15/4/1790 - A certificate for Martha Clark to Exeter. Everard Bettle, being present, as agreed to be received into membership and he expecting to remove from among us and settle within the limits of Westland monthly meeting, a certificate was prepared. A certificate recommending Thomas and Edward Thomas from Gwynedd monthly meeting. Application made on behalf of Jesse Foulke for a certificate to friends at Abington, in order to accomplish his marriage with a member of that meeting. Application made on behalf of David Shaw for a certificate to friends at Abington, he being placed an apprentice within the limits of that meeting.

15/7/1790 - Testification against Issachar Heacock published.

19/8/1790 - A certificate recommending Hannah Lester, with her three minor children (to wit) Mary, Eleanor and Elizabeth, to Westland monthly meeting.

16/9/1790 - Israel Penrose and Susanna Foulke declared their intentions of marriage. Application made on behalf of Anne Foulke, she having a desire to come under the notice of friends with her children (to wit) Abigail, Eleanor, Caleb, Samuel and Thomas.

21/10/1790 - Israel Penrose and Susanna Foulke clear to marry.

18/11/1790 - The marriage of Israel Penrose and Susanna Foulke orderly accomplished on the eleventh day of this month. A certificate recommending Mary McCarty to friends at Exeter. Everard Foulke acknowledges and condemns his past misconduct which he was disowned for.

16/12/1790 - Hannah Johnson having assisted her husband to defraud Joseph Shaw of his property.

20/1/1791 - A certificate recommending Priscilla Roberts to friends at Abington. Mary Frantz having gone out in marriage.

Sarah Brock acknowledges and condemns her fault in going out in marriage. John Penrose acknowledges and condemns paying military fines.

17/2/1791 - A certificate recommending Catherine Roberts to friends at Abington.

17/3/1791 - Nathan Roberts, Junr., and Margaret Ashton declared their intentions of marriage. A certificate recommending Elizabeth Kirk to friends at Wrightstown. Application made on behalf of Judah Foulke for a certificate to recommend himself and wife and children to Westland. Application made on behalf of Amos Roberts for a certificate to recommend himself and wife and children to friends at Abington.

24/3/1791 - Amos Roberts acknowledges and condemns his taking an attest of allegiance and paying military fines.

21/4/1791 - Nathan Roberts, Junr., and Margaret Ashton clear to marry. Judah Foulke, having altered his mind respecting the place he intended to remove to, now proposes to settle within the limits of Exeter monthly meeting. Jesse Hicks acknowledges and condemns his former conduct in paying of fines and training with the militia. Robert Blackledge acknowledges and condemns his paying of military fines. Robert Blackledge requested a certificate to recommend himself and wife and children to friends at Buckingham.

19/5/1791 - The marriage of Nathan Roberts, Junr., and Margaret Ashton was orderly accomplished on the fifth day of this month.

21/7/1791 - Application made on behalf of Evan Roberts for a certificate to friends at Gwynedd.

16/8/1791 - Application made on behalf of Moses Lancaster for a certificate for his son Thomas to friends at Buckingham.

15/9/1791 - A certificate recommending Jane Chilcot to friends at Goose Creek in Virginia. A certificate recommending Eli Kinnard and Elizabeth his wife and their children (to wit) William, Hannah, Thomas and Joseph from Buckingham. Jesse Foulke acknowledges and condemns the paying of military fines.

20/10/1791 - Shipley Lester and Margaret Nixson declared their intentions of marriage. Application made for a certificate for James Walton and wife and family to the monthly meeting at Exeter. There being a difference subsisting between Abrahm. Roberts and William Roberts.

17/11/1791 - Shipley Lester and Margaret Nixson clear to marry. Lydia Richardson having gone out in marriage with a man who is not in membership who is her first cousin.

15/12/1791 - The marriage of Shipley Lester and Margaret Nixson was accomplished on the 24th of last month and except for the reading of the certificate being done by a man that was not a member it appeared to be orderly conducted. A certificate recommending Ann Walton to friends at Exeter.

26/1/1792 - Mary Savits having gone out in marriage with a man who is not a member of our society and accomplished her marriage by the assistance of an hireling Minister. Application made on behalf of Evan Loyd for a certificate back to Gwynedd monthly meeting.

16/2/1792 - A testification of Rahway and Plainfield monthly meeting in the Jersey against Anne Brown late Biles disowning her for fornication and marrying a man whose former wife was his sister. Moses Shaw acknowledged the paying of military fines and training with the militia.

15/3/1792 - Testification published against Anne Brown. Application made on behalf of John Shaw and Moses Shaw with their wives and families to friends at Abington. Application made on behalf of Issachar Foulke for a certificate to the monthly meeting at Springfield in the Jersey, in order to accomplish his marriage with a member of that meeting.

17/4/1792 - Thomas Blackledge having fallen into the sin of fornication which occasioned his going out in marriage. David Penrose having fallen into the sin of fornicating which occasioned him going out in marriage.

17/5/1792 - Application made on behalf of Ezra Kinsey for a certificate to the monthly meeting at Fairfax in Virginia.

16/8/1792 - Mary Burson condemns her going out in marriage with a man not in membership with friends.

20/9/1792 - Testification against Thos. Blackledge published. A certificate recommending Jane Foulke from the monthly meeting at upper Springfield in the Jersey.

18/10/1792 - Samuel Shaw and Elizabeth Ball declared their intentions of marriage. Thos. Green acknowledges and condemns his past misconduct which he was disowned for and likewise his going out in marriage with his first cousin. Also, his wife condemns her going out in marriage with her first cousin. Application made on behalf of Thomas Roberts for a certificate to the monthly meeting at Abington. Enoch Strawhen having gone out in marriage with a young woman that was not a member of our society.

15/11/1792 -Saml. Shaw and Elizabeth Ball clear to marry. Sarah Nixson having fallen into the sin of fornication.

20/12/1792 - The marriage of Saml. Shaw and Elizabeth Ball orderly accomplished on the sixth day of this month. John Chapman having fallen into the sin of fornication and absconded out of the parts.

17/1/1793 - Isaac Roberts and Mary Green declared their intentions of marriage. Everard Bettle having some time past been recommended to friends at Westland but has not delivered his certificate and has since he removed from us gone out in marriage.

21/2/1793 - Isaac Roberts and Mary Green are clear to marry. A certificate recommending Catherine Roberts from Abington monthly meeting. Application made on behalf of Amos Richardson, he having a desire to come under the notice of friends.

21/3/1793 - William Samuels and Mary Foulke declared their intentions of marriage. The marriage of Isaac Roberts and Mary Green orderly accomplished on the 28th day of last month. Israel Shaw condemns his going out in marriage. Meribah Lancaster having fallen into the sin of fornication. Application on behalf of Joseph Blackledge for a certificate to friends at Buckingham.

18/4/1793 - William Samuels and Mary Foulke clear to marry.

Testification against Sarah Nixon published. Application made on behalf of Ann Ball, she having a desire to come under the notice of friends, her husband also with her requests that their children (to wit) Joel, Joseph, Margaret, Sarah, Jesse, James and Susanna, may be taken into membership. Application made on behalf of Isaac Roberts and Mary his wife for a certificate to friends at Exeter.

16/5/1793 - The marriage of William Samuels and Mary Foulke orderly accomplished on the twenty fifth day of last month. A certificate recommending Mary Shaw, Jur., to friends at Abington.

20/6/1793 - Cadwalader Foulke and Margaret, his wife, having joined in marriage, being first cousins.

18/7/1793 - Testification against Meribah Lancaster read. Application made on behalf of Saml. Green for a certificate to recommend him and his wife and children to friends at Exeter. Hannah Foulke expresses her sorrow for her breach in order in going out in marriage. Margaret Ball expresses her sorrow for her past misconduct which she was disowned for, and requests that her children might be taken into membership.

15/8/1793 - The children of Margaret Ball (to wit) Hannah, Rebecka, William and Aaron, taken into membership.

19/9/1793 - A certificate recommending Catherine Green to friends at Exeter. Mary Heacock having fallen into the sin of fornication.

17/10/1793 - Josiah Dennis and Alice Wilson declared their intentions of marriage.

21/11/1793 - Josiah Dennis and Alice Wilson clear to marry. Samuel Green acknowledges and condemns his taking an attest of Allegiance and Abjuration in the time of the unsettled state of government and paying military fines. A certificate granted in the fifth month last recommending Mary Shaw to friends at Abington was returned, she being still living amongst us.

19/12/1793 - The marriage of Josiah Dennis and Alice Wilson orderly accomplished on the 28th day of last month. Hannah Surns having gone out in marriage. A certificate recommending six minor children of Joseph Speakman, namely Townsend, Mary, Keziah, Hester, Lidia and John, from the monthly meeting of friends at the Falls.

16/1/1794 - Testification against Mary Heacock published. Sarah Jenkins condemns her going out in marriage. Margaret Gibson having gone out in marriage. Robert Penrose having fallen into the sin of fornication which occasioned his going out in marriage.

20/2/1794 - Josiah Heacock having fallen into the sin of fornication with her that is now his wife.

20/3/1794 - Margaret Penington having fallen into the sin of fornication with the man she has since married.

17/4/1794 - Nathan Penrose having fallen into the sin of fornication with her that is now his wife. A certificate recommending John Shaw and Phebe his wife with their minor children, namely, Phebe, Mariam and John, from Abington monthly meeting. Also a certificate recommending Moses Shaw and Mary his wife with their children, namely Deborah, Sarah,

Mary and William, from Abington. Also a certificate recommending Joseph Shaw, jur., from Abington. Job Strawhen having gone out in marriage with a young woman that was not a member among friends.

20/5/1794 - Asher Foulke requests a certificate to recommend himself and wife and children to Buckingham. A certificate recommending Mary Clark from Exeter monthly meeting.

5/6/1794 - Job Strawhen acknowledges and condemns his going out in marriage. William Hicks, Jur., having fallen into the sin of fornication with her that he has since married.

19/6/1794 - Application on behalf of Mary Walton, she having a desire to come under the notice of friends.

17/7/1794 - Nathan Penrose and Hannah his wife acknowledge and condemn their falling into the sin of fornication and going out in marriage. Application made on behalf of Isaac Kirk for a certificate to the monthly meeting at Bush River in South Carolina. George Thomas having fallen into the sin of fornication and marrying his first cousin.

21/8/1794 - A certificate for Sarah Jenkins to Gwynedd monthly meeting. The meeting agrees to consider Mary Walton as a member. A certificate recommending Jacob Pritter from the monthly meeting in Philadelphia for the Northern District.

18/9/1794 - A certificate recommending John Ross from the monthly meeting at Wrightstown.

16/10/1794 - A certificate recommending Hannah Kirk to friends at Wrightstown. Testification published against George Thomas.

28/11/1794 - Testification read against Margaret Penington and William Hicks, Jur.

18/12/1794 - Rachel Griffith acknowledges and condemns her past misconduct which she was disowned for.

15/1/1795 - Abigail Watson expresses her sorrow and condemns her past misconduct which she was condemned for.

19/2/1795 - Saml. Ashton and Jane Roberts declared their intentions of marriage. Lewis Lewis and Abigail Roberts declared their intentions of marriage. Isaiah Roberts having gone out in marriage with a man not in membership.

19/3/1795 - Samuel Ashton and Jane Roberts clear to marry. Lewis Lewis and Abigail Roberts clear to marry. Amos Richardson and Martha Penrose declared their intentions of marriage. Application on behalf of Silas, Joel, John and James McCarty for certificates to friends at Exeter. Application on behalf of Elizabeth McCarty requesting that her four youngest children, namely, Martha, David, Jesse and Lydia be received into membership.

16/4/1795 - The marriage of Samuel Ashton and Jane Roberts was orderly accomplished on the ninth day of this month. the marriage of Lewis Lewis and Abigail Roberts was orderly accomplished on the sixth day of last month. Amos Richardson and Martha Penrose clear to marry. Levi Roberts and Phebe McCarty declared their intentions of marriage. Samuel McCarty having gone out in marriage contrary to good order, and also the case of Margaret, his wife, for the same offense.

21/5/1795 - A certificate recommending Elizabeth Lancaster to friends at Abington. Amos Chilcot expressed his sorrow for his past misconduct which he was disowned for. Mary Lester having neglected the attendance of religious meetings and living in a public house and the meeting is informed she is since moved to Philadelphia without requesting a certificate. A certificate recommending Townsend and Esther Speakman from the monthly meeting at the Falls. A certificate recommending Elizabeth McCarty with four minor children (namely) Thomas, Job, Hannah and Benjamin, to friends at Exeter. Also two others, one for Elizabeth McCarty, Jun., and the other for Jane McCarty, recommending them to the same place. The marriage of Amos Richardson and Martha Penrose orderly accomplished on the 30th day of the 4th month. Levi Roberts and Phebe McCarty clear to marry.

18/6/1795 - Testification against Isaac Lester has been publicly read. The marriage of Levi Roberts and Phebe McCarty orderly accomplished on the fourth day of this month. Rachel Hillman having a desire to come under the notice of friends. A certificate recommending Evan Roberts from Gwynedd monthly meeting. Thomas and John Ashton having gone out in marriage and paid military fines.

16/7/1795 - A certificate recommending Mary Tyson from the monthly meeting at Horsham.

20/8/1795 - Ann Chilcot, having a desire to come under the notice of friends with her children, namely, Martha, Peninna, Mary , John, William, Rachel and Sarah.

17/9/1795 - Thomas Strawhen having gone out in marriage with a woman not a member of our society. David Loyd having gone out in marriage and meeting with the militia at their times of training.

15/10/1795 - A certificate recommending Rachel Blackledge from Buckingham. A certificate recommending Samuel Morris and Rachel his wife and their children, namely, Elizabeth More Morris, Thomas More Morris and Samuel Morris from the monthly meeting at Buckingham. George Shaw and Rachel Penrose declared their intentions of marriage.

19/11/1795 - An account received from the monthly meeting for the Northern District of Philadelphia respecting Mary Lester, signifying that she appears to be much in the neglect of attending religious meetings and not clear of intemperance in the use of strong drink. George Shaw and Rachel Penrose clear to marry.

17/12/1795 - David Loyd expresses his sorrow for going out in his marriage and attending with the militia at their times of training. Testification against Josiah Penrose published. The marriage of George Shaw and Rachel Penrose orderly accomplished on the 26th day of last month.

21/1/1796 - Lewis Lewis, having fallen into the sin of fornication, taken an oath and using prophane language and attending a horse race and laying wagers, and Abigail his wife having fallen into the sin of fornication. Evan Foulke having gone out in marriage and taken an oath. Everard Roberts having gone out in marriage with a woman not of our society and using prophane language and being concerned in the unjustifiable practice of horse racing.

18/2/1796 - Thomas Penrose and Rachel Hillman declared their intentions of marriage.

17/3/1796 - Testification against John Chapman was publicly read. Benjamin Kirk condemns his joining marriage with a woman not a member of our society. Thomas Penrose and Rachel Hillman clear to marry.

21/4/1796 - A certificate recommending Elizabeth Lancaster from the monthly meeting at Abington. A certificate recommending Eleanor Roberts to friends at Cattawissa. The marriage of Thomas Penrose and Rachel Hillman orderly accomplished on the thirty first day of last month. Application made on behalf of Abraham and Nathan Walton for certificates to recommend themselves and families to the monthly meeting at Westland.

19/5/1796 - A certificate recommending Abigail Walton to friends at Westland. Application made on behalf of Eli Kennard for a certificate to recommend himself and three of his minor children to Deer Creek monthly meeting.

16/6/1796 - Testification against Everard Roberts, Junr., has been publicly read. Abel Roberts, Junr., and Martha his wife having fallen into the sin of fornication and he having attended with the militia at their times of training.

18/8/1796 - Testifications against Mary Lester, and also against Lewis Lewis, have been publicly read. Joseph Shaw, Jun., and Hannah his wife having accomplished their marriage out of the unity of friends. Application on behalf of Joseph Lewis for a certificate to friends at Abington.

15/9/1796 - Ann McCord and Hannah Mannon having gone out in marriage with young men not members of our society.

20/10/1796 - Testification against Abel Roberts, Jun., and his wife has been publicly read. Ann McCord expresses her desire to be continued under the care of friends. Mary Heacock expresses her sorrow for her past misconduct which she was disowned for. A certificate recommending Rachel West from London Grove meeting. A certificate recommending Thomas Lancaster from the monthly meeting at Buckingham. Deborah Colp having gone out in marriage.

17/11/1796 - Thomas Lester and Mary Stokes declared their intentions of marriage.

15/12/1796 - Joseph Shaw, Jun., and Hannah, his wife, condemn their accomplishing their marriage out of unity of friends. Amos Evans having joined in marriage with the wife of another man and also attending with the militia at their times of training. Application on behalf of Benjamin Kirk for a certificate to friends at Buckingham. Thomas Lester and Mary Stokes clear to marry.

19/1/1797 - The marriage of Thomas Lester and Mary Stokes orderly accomplished on the 22nd day of last month.

16/2/1797 - Thomas Strawhen condemns his going out in marriage. Rachel Carr having gone out in marriage.

16/3/1797 - Testification against Amos Evans publicly read. Application made on behalf of Thomas Ball for a certificate to friends at Westland. Application made on behalf of Thomas Strawhen for a certificate to Westland.

20/4/1797 - A certificate recommending Mary Heacock to friends at

Cattawissa. A certificate recommending Thomas Heacock from the monthly meeting at Buckingham. Application made on behalf of Samuel Morris for a certificate to recommend himself and wife and children to the monthly meeting held in Philadelphia for the Northern District.

18/5/1797 - A certificate recommending Elizabeth Tucker from the monthly meeting at Gwynedd.

15/6/1797 - Application made on behalf of Isaiah Jemison, he having a desire to come under the notice of friends.

20/7/1797 - A certificate recommending Mary Clark to friends at Cattawissa. Application made on behalf of John Ball for a certificate to recommend himself and wife and children, namely, Joel, Joseph, Margaret, Jesse, Sarah, James, Susanna and Iden to friends at Westland. Thomas Roberts produced a certificate recommending him back from the monthly meeting in Philadelphia. Application made on behalf of Jesse Ball for a certificate to friends at Westland. Application likewise made on behalf of Samuel Shaw to recommend himself and wife and children, namely, John, Thomas, Lettitia, Susanna and Margaret to friends at Westland. Edward Foulke having fallen into the sin of fornication and joining in marriage with the sister of his former wife. Jacob Beans and Hannah Iden declared their intentions of marriage, he required to produce a certificate of his clearness.

17/8/1797 - Two certificates recommending Mary and Sarah Burson to friends at Wrightstown. A certificate recommending Joel Cadwalader from the monthly meeting at Abington. Jacob Beans and Hannah Iden clear to marry.

21/9/1797 - The marriage of Jacob Beans and Hannah Iden orderly accomplished on the thirty first day of last month. A certificate recommending Joseph Wilson from the monthly meeting at Catawissa. Moses Wilson and Jane Lester declared their intentions of marriage.

19/10/1797 - A certificate recommending Hannah Beans to friends at Buckingham. Abraham Ball having fallen into the sin of fornication. Thomas Lester and Mary his wife having fallen into the sin of fornication and imposing their marriage upon the meeting. Application made on behalf of Daniel Strawhen, he having a desire to come under the notice of friends. Application made on behalf of Jesse Foulke for a certificate to Catawissa in order to accomplish his marriage with a member of that meeting. Moses Wilson and Jane Lester clear to marry.

16/11/1797 - A certificate recommending Hannah Kennard to friends at Deer Creek in Maryland. The marriage of Moses Willson and Jane Lester, Jun., orderly accomplished on the second day of this month.

21/12/1797 - Testification against Edward Foulke publicly read. Hannah Paul having fallen into the sin of fornication with a young man who she has since married.

15/2/1798 - Application made on behalf of Job Strawhen for a certificate to the monthly meeting at Redstone. Application also made on behalf of Stephen Twyning for a certificate to friends at Wrightstown. Application likewise made on behalf of John Stephenson for a certificate to the monthly meeting at

Mount Holly in the Jersey. Israel Lancaster and Hannah Nixon declared their intentions of marriage. Sarah Santee having gone out in marriage with a man that is not a member of our society. Israel Lancaster and Hannah Nixon clear to marry.

15/3/1798 - The marriage of Israel Lancaster and Hannah Nixon orderly accomplished on the twenty second day of last month. Thomas Lancaster having absconded out of the neighborhood in a clandestine manner and left his creditors unsatisfied and the circumstances attending his elopement give strong reason to suspect that he has stolen a horse. Isaiah Jemison and Margaret Ball declared their intentions of marriage.

19/4/1798 - Testimony against Abraham Ball has been publicly read. Joseph Lewis having kept back his certificate, granted sometime past by this meeting, recommending him to friends at Abington, and there has also been a charge of fornication exhibited against him by a young woman in this neighborhood. Mary Tyson, alias Brown, having gone out in marriage with a man that it is said is another womans husband. Isaiah Jemison and Margaret Ball clear to marry.

17/5/1798 - Testimony against Thomas Lancaster publicly read. the testimony of Abington monthly meeting against Ann Foulke was publicly read. The marriage of Isaiah Jemison and Margaret Ball orderly accomplished on the 26th day of last month. A certificate recommending Sarah Foulke from the monthly meeting at Cattawissa. Also a certificate to recommend Elizabeth Tucker to friends at Wrightstown. And likewise a certificate recommending Cadwalader Child from the monthly meeting at Buckingham.

21/6/1798 - John Ross having gone out in marriage with a woman who is not a member of our society and accomplished his marriage before an hireling minister.

19/7/1798 - A certificate from the monthly meeting recommending Thomas Chapman to the care of this meeting.

16/8/1798 - Sarah Santee expresses condemns her going out in marriage with a man not a member of our society. Nathan Ball, Jun., having joined in marriage with a young woman that is not a member of our society.

20/9/1798 - Testimony against Hannah Paul publicly read.

18/10/1798 - Hannah Surns condemns her going out in marriage with a man that is not a member of our society. William Edwards, Jun., having gone out in marriage with a woman not in membership among friends.

15/11/1798 - Testimonies against John Ross and Joseph Lewis have been publicly read. Amy Crawford condemns her past misconduct which she was disowned for. Ann Roberts, Jun., having fallen into the sin of fornication. Rosamond Heacock having fallen into the sin of fornication. Hugh Foulke and Sarah Lester declared their intentions of marriage.

20/12/1798 - Nathan Ball, Jun., expresses his sorrow for and condemns his going out in marriage. William Edwards condemns his past misconduct which he was disowned for. Hugh Foulke and Sarah Lester clear to marry.

17/1/1799 - The marriage of Hugh Foulke and Sarah Lester orderly accomplished on the 27th day of last month.

21/2/1799 - A certificate recommending Mary Nixon to friends in Philadelphia. George Hicks and Ann Penrose declared their intentions of marriage.

21/3/1799 - George Hicks and Ann Penrose clear to marry. William Edwards and Susanna Nixon declared their intentions of marriage.

25/4/1799 - Testimony against Ann Roberts, Jun., has been publicly read. Rosamond Heacock acknowledges and condemns her falling into the sin of fornication. The marriage of George Hicks and Ann Penrose orderly accomplished on the fourth day of this month. William Edwards and Susanna Nixon clear to marry.

16/5/1799 - The marriage of William Edwards and Susanna Nixon orderly accomplished on the second day of this month. Samuel Shaw, Jun., having removed from among us and settled within the limits of Westland monthly meeting without applying for a certificate and we are informed that he has attended a marriage of a member accomplished out of unity and also attended at a military muster and answered to his name when called and has likewise accomplished his marriage out of unity with a woman that is not a member of our society.

20/6/1799 - A certificate recommending Rachel Foulke to friends at Gwynedd. Rachel Lancaster having spoken scandalous things of Jesse Heacock which he stands in denial of.

18/7/1799 - A certificate recommending Rachel Lancaster to the friends at Horsham. Joseph Walton having gone out in marriage with a woman not in membership.

15/8/1799 - Nathan Ball having fallen into the sin of fornication with a young woman whom he refuses to marry.

19/9/1700 - Application made on behalf of Abraham Shaw, minor son of Joseph Shaw, for a certificate to friends in Philadelphia.

17/10/1799 - A certificate recommending Dianna Walker to friends at Westland. Application made on behalf of Cadwalader Child for a certificate friends at Horsham.

21/11/1799 - In the case of Rachel Lancaster and Jesse Heacock, the matter has been tried at law and he has been acquitted by the court. The testimony against Nathan Ball has been publicly read. Deborah Care hath signified a desire to come under the notice of friends. William Nixon and Martha Roberts declared their intentions of marriage.

19/12/1799 - George Shaw having committed fornication with her that he hath since married. A certificate recommending Rachel Shaw and her daughter Sarah to the monthly meeting in Philadelphia for the Southern District. Also, one recommending Amy Crawford to Pelham monthly meeting in upper Canada. William Nixon and Martha Roberts clear to marry.

16/1/1800 - Rachel Lancaster has entered a complaint against Susanna Edwards wherein she charges her with taking a false qualification. The marriage of William Nixon and Martha Roberts orderly accomplished on the second day of this month. Thomas Heacock having fallen into the sin of fornication.

20/2/1800 - William Thomas, so far deviating from our testimony against war as to take up arms against civil government. David Thomas having for a considerable time past given way to a disposition of idleness and dissipation which has led him into unjustifiable and reproachful practices and lately accomplished his marriage out of the unity of friends. A certificate recommending Jane Foulke, daughter of Edward Foulke, to friends at Abington. Also, a certificate recommending Gaynor Thomson from the monthly meeting at Gwynedd. Josiah Heacock condemns his past misconduct which he was disowned for. Application made on behalf of Thomas Roberts for a certificate to friends at Buckingham.

17/4/1800 - Richard Heacock having joined in marriage with a young woman that is not a member of our society. A certificate recommending Abigail Wilson from the monthly meeting at Muncie.

15/5/1800 - Testimony against George Shaw has been publicly read.

19/6/1800 - A certificate recommending Keziah Speakman from the monthly meeting held in Philadelphia for the Northern District.

17/7/1800 - This meeting received a few lines from Westland monthly meeting respecting Gabriel Walton who has left that place some time since in a disreputable manner.

8/21/1800 - Richard Heacock also accomplished his marriage before an hireling minister. Evan Roberts having joined in marriage, they being in a degree of kindred between first and second cousins. Application made for a certificate to recommend Abel Nixon to friends at Darby, he being placed an apprentice to a man who resides within the limits of that meeting. A motion was made for sending a certificate to Philadelphia for Joseph Lester, he having removed within the limits of the North meeting.

18/9/1800 - A certificate recommending Sarah Dennis to friends at Cattawissee.

16/10/1800 - Application made on behalf of Hannah Johnson, she having a desire that her children might be taken under the notice of friends.

18/12/1800 - A certificate recommending Gulielma Watson from the monthly meeting at Abington.

BUCKINGHAM MONTHLY MEETING

BIRTHS AND DEATHS

Children of Samuel and Elizabeth Armitage: James Armitage b. 27th day of 1st month, 1749; John Armitage b. 23rd day of 2nd month, 1751.

Elizabeth Armitage, wife of Samuel, d. 29th day of 2nd month, 1751,O.S.

Children of Samuel and Mary Armitage: Jane Armitage b. 23rd day of 10th month, 1754, N.S: Sarah Armitage b. 19th day of 6th month, 1756; Mary Armitage b. 22nd day of 5th month, 1758; Samuel Armitage b. 16th day of 8th month, 1769; Amos Armitage b. 21st day of 7th month, 1764.

Samuel Armitage, father of the above, d. 29th day of 1st month, 1801.

Children of Amos and Martha (Doan) Armitage: Seba Armitage b. 11th day of 6th month, 1786; Anna Armitage b. 26th day of 9th month, 1787; Hervey Armitage b. 2nd day of 3rd month, 1789; Amos Armitage b. 18th day of 4th month, 1790; James Armitage b. 10th day of 10th month, 1792.

Mary Armitage, daughter of Samuel and Sarah (Foster) Armitage was b. 29th day of 10th month, 1782.

Children of James and Martha (Dennis) Armitage: Elizabeth Armitage b. 2nd day of 8th month, 1776; Hannah Armitage b. 2nd day of 5th month, 1778; John Armitage b. 12th day of 3rd month, 1780; Martha Armitage b. 9th day of 11th month, 1782; Henry Armitage b. 13th day of 1st month, 1785; Samuel Armitage b. 16th day of 10th month, 1786; Letitia Armitage b. 22nd day of 9th month, 1788; Charles Armitage b. 14th day of 2nd month, 1794, ?James Armitage b. 7th day of 1st month, 1796.

Sarah Atkinson, daughter of Joseph and Rachel (Child) Atkinson was b. 12th day of 2nd month, 1789.

Children of Nicholas and Susanna Austin: Elizabeth Austin b. 2nd day of 2nd month, 1784; Samuel Austin b. 22nd day of 4th month, 1786; Lydia Austin b. 4th day of 2nd month, 1788; Hannah Austin b. 26th day of 3rd month, 1790; Sarah Austin b. 15th day of 6th month, 1792, Isaac Austin b. 13th day of 6th month, 1796; Robert Austin b. 12th day of 2nd month, 1798; Martha Austin b. 10th day of 6th month, 1800; Mary Austin b. 16th day of 8th month, 1802; Latitia Austin b. 9th day of 5th month, 1805.

Isaac Austin d. 4th day of 7th month, 1796.

John Balderston, Sr., d. 9th day of 7th month, 1778.
Hannah Balderston, widow of John Balderston, Sr., d. 26th day of

5th month, 1792.
John Balderston, son of John and Hannah Balderston, b. 15th day of 3rd month, 1740.
Deborah Balderston, wife of John Balderston and daughter of Mark and Ann Watson, b. 23rd day of 3rd month, 1744 and d. 17th day of 4th month, 1794.

Children of John and Deborah Balderston: Ann Balderston b. 28th day of 9th month, 1768 and d. 1st day of 11th month, 1774; Mark Balderston b. 25th day of 7th month and d. 10th day of 8th month, 1770; Marah Balderston (twin) b. 25th day of 7th month, 1770; Hannah Balderston b. 30th day of 5th month, 1772; John W. Balderston b. 24th day of 2nd month, 1775 and d. 26th day of 2nd month, 1842; Mark Balderston b. 1st day of 5th month, 1778; Ann Balderston b. 15th day of 12th month, 1780; Ezra Balderston b. 13th day of 1st month and d. 27th day of 1st month, 1783.

Elisabeth Balderston, wife of John W. Balderston and daughter of William and Hannah Buckman, b. 2nd day of 11th month, 1777 and d. 6th day of 7th month, 1854.

Children of John and Martha Beale: Lydia Beale b. 9th day of 7th month, 1731; Phebe Beale b. 16th day of 9th month, 1733; Rachel Beale b. 8th day of 9th month, 1735; John Beale b. 16th day of 10th month, 1737.

John Beale, father of above, d. 4th day of 11th month, 1769.

Children of William and Grace (Gill) Beale: Sarah Beale b. 14th day of 8th month, 1743; Thomas Beale b. 17th day of 7th month, 1745; Grace Beale b. 7th day of 7th month, 1745; Joseph Beale b. 14th day of 10th month, 1747; Elisabeth Beale b. 23rd day of 3rd month, 1750 and d. 11th day of 11th month, 1751; William Beale b. 12th day of 8th month, 1752.

William Beale, father of above, d. 27th day of 10th month, 1751.

Children of John and Jane Beale: John Beale b. 21st day of 1st month, 1762; Joseph Beale b. 1st day of 3rd month, 1764; Martha Beale b. 2nd day of 4th month, 1766; William Beale b. 26th day of 2nd month, 1768; Elisabeth Beale b. 21st day of 5th month, 1770.

Children of Joseph and Hannah (Russel?) Beale: Thomas Beale b. 14th day of 3rd month, 1774; Elisabeth Beale b. 28th day of 10th month, 1776; Grace Beale b. 10th day of 10th month, 1778; Samuel Beale b. 20th day of 6th month, 1781; Hannah Beale b. 1st day of 5th month, 1783.

Children of William and Rachel E. (Parry) Beale: Mercy Beale b. 12th day of 10th month, 1779; Philip Beale b. 21st day of 3rd month, 1782; Sarah Beale b. 14th day of 9th month, 1784; Joseph Beale b. 18th day of 3rd month, 1787; William Beale b. 17th day of 8th month, 1789; Hannah Beale b. 7th day of 5th month, 1792.

Children of Matthew and Elisabeth (Rice, a widow) Beans, his 2nd wife: Aaron Beans b. 12th day of 3rd month, 1764; Elisabeth Beans b. 16th day of 8th month, 1766; a son b. 8th day of 10th month, 1769.

Children of Jacob and Sarah (Hartley) Beans: Hannah Beans b. 1st day of 2nd month, 1747 o.s.; Joseph Beans b. 6th day of 3rd month, 1750 o.s. and d. 8th day of 8th month, ?1835; Rachel Beans b. 19th day of 12th month, 1752 n.s.; Benjamin Beans b. 12th day of 5th month, 1758; Tamar Beans b. 13th day of 3rd month, 1761; Asenath Beans b. 9th day of 3rd month, 1764; Ann Beans b. 2nd day of 10th month, 1766; Mahlon Beans b. 29th day of 1st month, 1769.

Sarah Beans, wife of Jacob Beans, d. 29th day of 7th month, 1795, aged 69 years.
Sarah (Mitchener) Beans, 1st wife of Joseph Beans, d. 1st day of 6th month, 1784, aged 33 years, near 8 months.

Children of Joseph and Sarah (Smith) Beans, his 2nd wife: Samuel Beans b. 24th day of 2nd month, 1787; Jesse Beans b. 17th day of 3rd month, 1789; Sarah Beans b. 12th day of 4th month, 1793.

Children of Aaron and Mary (Burges) Beans: George Beans b. 27th day of 1st month, 1790; Levi Beans b. 26th day of 5th month, 1793; Hannah Beans b. 12th day of 1st month, 1795 and d. 28th day of 11th month, 1802; Mary Beans b. 10th day of 10th month, 1801 and d. 8th day of 12th month, 1802; Ann Beans b. 5th day of 1st month, 1804.

Children of Benjamin and Mary (Smith) Beans: Sarah Beans b. 7th day of 7th month, 1784; Rachel Beans b. 10th day of 3rd month, 1786; Charles Beans b. 27th day of 6th month, 1788; Jonathan Beans b. 19th day of 12th month, 1790.

Children of David and Sarah Beans: Isaac beans b. 3rd day of 9th month, 1776; Susanna Beans b. 4th day of 10th month, 1778; John Beans b. 9th day of 2nd month, 1781; Amos Beans b. 11th day of 12th month, 1783; Matthew Beans b. 2nd day of 2nd month, 1787; David Beans b. 5th day of 3rd month, 1790; Rebeckah Beans b. 25th day of 3rd month, 1793.

Children of Mahlon and Rachel (Hillbourn) Beans: Jacob Beans b. 21st day of 7th month, 1794; Jane Beans b. 7th day of 10th month, 1796; Oliver Beans b. 7th day of 7th month, 1799; Hannah Beans b. 6th day of 3rd month and d. 7th day of 11th month, 1802.

Children of Stephen and Hannah (Blackfan) Betts: William Betts b. 29th day of 1st month, 1787; Sarah Betts b. 1st day of 5th month, 1788; Martha Betts b. 3rd day of 5th month, 1790; Stephen Betts b. 19th day of 8th month, 1792; Hannah Betts b. 19th day of 7th month, 1794; Esther Betts b. 4th day of 2nd month, 1797; Anna Betts b. 25th day of 5th month, 1799; Latitia Betts b. 11th day of 11th month, 1801; John Betts b. 10th day of 8th month, 1804.

James P. Betts, son of Isaac and Tamar Betts, b. 17th day of 5th month, 1799.

Edward Blackfan, son of Crispin and Martha (Davis) Blackfan, of Solebury, b. 26th day of 10th month, 1760.
Miranda Blackfan, daughter of Joseph Moore and Christianna, his 2nd wife, of New Jersey, b. 5th day of 5th month, 1772.

Children of Edward and Mary (Smith) Blackfan, of Solebury: Crispin Blackfan b. 25th day of 9th month, 1784; Samuel Blackfan b. 11th day of 4th month, 1788; Joseph Blackfan b. 2nd day of 2nd month, 1792.

Children of Samuel and Sarah Blaker: Peter Blaker b. 3rd day of 1st month, 1722; Mary Blaker b. 1st day of 3rd month, 1723; Hannah Blaker b. 19th day of 5th month, 1724; Lydia Blaker b. 28th day of 2nd month, 1726; Sarah Blaker b. 23rd day of 12th month, 1728; Judith Blaker b. 30th day of 10th month, 1729.

William Blaker, son of Peter and Agnes Blaker, b. 30th day of 6th month, 1745.

Children of William and Hannah (Pennington) Bradfield: Abner Bradfield b. 21st day of 9th month, 1748; Jane Bradfield b. 24th day of 1st month, 1751 and d. 15th day of 6th month, 1752; John Bradfield b. 29th day of 3rd month, 1753 and d. 27th day of 8th month, 1798; Jane Bradfield b. 17th day of 3rd month, 1755; James Bradfield b. 28th day of 12th month, 1756; Hannah Bradfield b. 29th day of 11th month, 1758; Rachel Bradfield b. 14th day of 11th month, 1760; Jonathan and Benjamin Bradfield (twins) b. 5th day of 10th month, 1763; Elisabeth Bradfield b. 23rd day of 7th month, 1767; George Bradfield b. 14th day of 12th month, 1769.

Hannah Bradfield, wife of William Bradfield, d. 3rd day of 3rd month, 1784.
William Bradfield b. 8th day of 11th month, 1784.
Uri (McGill) Bradfield, wife of John Bradfield, d. 20th day of 11th month, 1796.

Children of David and Elisabeth (Carver) Bradshaw: Sarah Bradshaw b. 29th day of 9th month, 1780; William Bradshaw b. 8th day of 6th month, 1782; Sidney Bradshaw b. 10th day of 4th month, 1784; David Bradshaw b. 21st day of 4th month, 1786; Ruth Bradshaw b. 12th day of 9th month, 1789; James Bradshaw b. 13th day of 6th month, 1791; Elizabeth Bradshaw b. 25th day of 6th month, 1799.

Children of William and Sarah (Preston) Bradshaw: Ruth Bradshaw b. 9th day of 7th month, 1770; Sarah Bradshaw b. 5th day of 10th month, 1772; Martha Bradshaw b. 15th day of 11th month, 1775; James Bradshaw b. 11th day of 1st month, 1778; Mary Bradshaw b. 10th day of 15th month, 1780; William Bradshaw b. 23rd day of 6th month, 1784; Susanna Bradshaw b. 3rd day of 3rd month, 1788; Samuel Bradshaw b. 18th day of 12th month, 1794 and d. 18th day of 4th month, 1799.

Mary Bradshaw d. 10th day of 12th month, 1782, aged 22 years.
Sarah Bradshaw d. 24th day of 10th month, 1772.

Adam Brooks b. 2nd day of 5th month, 1788.
Hepsibah Brooks, wife of Adam Brooks, b. 11th day of 3rd month, 1796.

Children of Joseph and Mary (Preston) Brown: Ann Brown b. 11th day of 12th month, 1760; Sarah Brown b. 3rd day of 10th month, 1762.

Mary Brown, wife of Joseph Brown, d. 23rd day of 11th month, 1764.

Children of Joseph and Ann (Dawson) Brown: Abraham Brown b. 23rd day of 4th month, 1730; Isaac Brown b. 18th day of 6th month, 1731; Ann Brown b. 10th day of 2nd month, 1733; Joseph Brown b. 8th day of 7th month, 1737.

Joseph Brown, father of above, d. 27th day of 2nd month, 1748.

Children of George and Sarah Brown: John Brown b. 7th day of 2nd month, 1723; Jonathan Brown b. 23rd day of 8th month, 1724 and d. 9th month, 1748; Susanna Brown b. 23rd day of 9th month, 1726, m. Benj. Kinsey, and d. 24th day of 2nd month, 1765; Mary Brown b. 27th day of 7th month, 1728.

Moses Brown, son of Thomas and Elisabeth (Dawson) Brown, of Plumstead, b. 21st day of 10th month, 1727 and d. 26th day of 2nd month, 1758.

Children of Moses and Sarah Brown: Elisabeth Brown b. 1st day of 6th month, 1764; Thomas Brown b. 16th day of 7th month, 1757.

Children of Alexander and Esther (Dyer) Brown: Elisabeth Brown b. 22nd day of 7th month, 1736; Josiah Brown b. 28th day of 2nd month, 1738; Esther Brown b. 29th day of 2nd month, 1740; Thomas Brown b. 4th day of 1st month and d. 7th day of 9th month, 1742; Alexander Brown b. 15th day of 7th month, 1743; Mary Brown b. 13th day of 3rd month, 1745 and d. 21st day of 1st month, 1747; John Brown b. 24th day of 1st month, 1747; Martha Brown b. 13th day of 1st month, 1749; Mary Brown b. 17th day of 4th month, 1751; Jonathan Brown b. 1st day of 8th month, 1753; Thomas Brown b. 15th day of 12th month, 1755 and d. 27th day of 12th month, 1756; James Brown (twin) b. 15th day of 12th month, 1757 and d. 5th day of 2nd month, 1760.

Children of John and Jane (Harvey) Brown: Elisabeth Brown b. 4th day of 10th month, 1751 and d. 3rd day of 12th month, 1753; George Brown b. 15th day of 10th month, 1753; Sarah Brown b. 7th day of 4th month, 1756; Jane Brown b. 4th day of 12th month, 1759; Matthias Brown b. 10th day of 5th month, 1762; Jonathan Brown b. 1st day of 2nd month, 1766; Mary Brown b. 29th day of 5th month, 1769 and d. 14th day of 10th month, 1781; John Brown

b. 22nd day of 10th month, 1770; Amos Brown b. 7th day of 8th month, 1773.

Children of John and (2nd wife) Rachel (Child) Brown: Martha Brown b. 14th day of 6th month, 1779; Moses Brown b. 15th day of 7th month, 1782 and d. 1st day of 6th month, 1783.

Children of Alexander and Elisabeth (Kinsey) Brown: Levina Brown b. 30th day of 10th month, 1770; Sarah Brown b. 8th day of 8th month, 1772; Elisabeth Brown b. 23rd day of 7th month, 1774.

Children of Josiah and Deborah (Wilson) Brown, of Plumstead: Samuel Brown b. 20th day of 2nd month, 1785; Martha Brown b. 8th day of 2nd month, 1787, m. Charles Smith, and d. 22nd day of 2nd month, 1841; George Brown b. 21st day of 8th month, 1789; Moses Brown b. 11th day of 5th month, 1792; Esther Brown b. 14th day of 1st month, 1794 and d. 15th day of 2nd month, 1794; Thomas Brown b. 12th day of 4th month, 1795; Josiah Brown b. 28th day of 1st month, 1799.

Isaac Buckman, son of William and Esther (Penquite) Buckman, b. 29th day of 3rd month, 1729.

Rebecca Buckman, daughter of Thomas and Agnes (Penquite) Brown, b. 11th day of 1st month, 1727.

Children of Joseph and Deborah (Fisher) Burges: Elisabeth Burges b. 24th day of 12th month, 1758; Jonathan Burges b. 20th day of 5th month, 1760; Tace Burges b. 21st day of 6th month, 1761; Jesse Burges b. 3rd day of 10th month, 1762; Thomas Burges b. 21st day of 3rd month, 1764; Sarah Burges b. 3rd day of 10th month, Martha Burges b. 6th day of 9th month, 1767; John Burges b. 8th day of 8th month, 1769; Daniel Burges b. 8th day of 3rd month, 1771; Latitia Burges b. 4th day of 11th month, 1772; Joseph Burges b. 21st day of 8th month, 1774.

Children of Joseph and Rachel (Shepherd) Burges: Jesse Burges b. 4th day of 11th month, 1786; George Burges b. 5th day of 3rd month, 1789; John Burges b. 19th day of 2nd month, 1792; Jonathan Burges b. 21st day of 12th month, 1794 and d. 11th day of 10th month, 1805; Hiram Burges b. 6th day of 9th month, 1797; Aaron Burges b. 2nd day of 9th month, 1800; Phebe Burges b. 23rd day of 10th month, 1804 and d. 28th day of 8th month, 1805.

Children of John and Margaret (Michener) Burges: Ann Burges b. 26th day of 7th month, 1760; William Burges b. 27th day of 3rd month, 1763; Mary Burges b. 25th day of 12th month, 1766; George Burges b. 5th day of 11th month, 1769; Agness Burges b. 17th day of 1st month, 1772; Elisabeth Burges b., 23rd day of 12th month, 1774; Hannah Burges b. 6th day of 10th month, 1777; Rachel Burges b. 10th day of 12th month, 1779.

Enoch Bye, son of John and Sarah Bye, of Solebury, b. 6th day of 7th month, 1722.

Margaret Bye, wife of Thomas Bye, d. 6th day of 10th month, 1724. Thomas Bye d. 25th day of 6th month, 1726.

Children of Thomas and Elisabeth (Ross) Bye: Nathaniel Bye b. 22nd day of 3rd month, 1734; Martha Bye b. 21st day of 11th month, 1735; Margaret Bye b. 22nd day of 11th month, 1737; Thomas Bye b. 25th day of 3rd month, 1740; Elisabeth Bye b. 13th day of 7th month, 1742, m. Matthias Hutchinson, and d. 11th day of 5th month, 1805; Lydia Bye b. 22nd day of 7th month, 1744 and d. 5th month, 1748; Jane Bye b. 14th day of 11th month, 1746 and d. 5th month, 1748; Lydia Bye b. 3rd day of 3rd month, 1749.

Elisabeth Bye, wife of Thomas Bye, d. 6th day of 6th month, 1774. Thomas Bye d. 24th day of 2nd month, 1786, aged 77-10-8.
Hesekiah Bye, son of John and Sarah Bye, of Solebury, b. 27th day of 11th month, 1717.
Mary Bye, wife of Hesekiah Bye and daughter of ?Jonas Ingham, b. 28th day of 10th month, 1723.

Children of Hesekiah and Mary Bye: Rachel Bye b. 31st day of 8th month, 1743; John Bye b. 23rd day of 7th month, 1745; Jonas Bye b. 22nd day of 3rd month, 1748; Jemima Bye b. 16th day of 6th month, 1751; Hesekiah Bye b. 27th day of 3rd month, 1754; Enoch Bye b. 27th day of 9th month, 1757; Jonathan Bye b. 22nd day of 1st month, 1761; Samuel Bye b. 29th day of 1st month, 1764.

Children of Thomas Bye, Jr., and Mercy (Woolston), his wife: Elisabeth Bye b. 10th day of 5th month, 1769; Mary Bye b. 20th day of 12th month, 1770 and m. John Scholfield; Martha Bye b. 15th day of 10th month, 1772; Mercy Bye b. 1st day of 9th month, 1774; Sarah Bye b. 5th day of 7th month, 1776 and d. 11th day of 7th month, 1777; Lydia Bye b. 1st day of 9th month, 1778; Sarah Bye b. 7th day of 1st month, 1781, m. Josiah Shaw, and d. 29th day of 7th month, 1831; Thomas Bye b. 1st day of 1st month, 1783, m. Mary Carver, and d. 17th day of 11th month, 1856; John Bye b. 9th day of 1st month, 1785; Anne Bye b. 10th day of 3rd month, 1787.

Mercy Bye, wife of Thomas Bye, Jr., d. 26th day of 8th month, 1800.
Rebecca Bye, wife of Cyrus Bye and daughter of Joseph and Sarah Shepherd, d. 9th month, 1795.

Thomas Canby, son of Benjamin Canby of Thorn, Yorkshire, England, came from Walton, in Lancashire, with Henry Baker and family. They arrived in Philadelphia, 17th day of 7th month, 1684, in the "Nine" of Liverpool, William Preeson, Master, Dogelly, Merionethshire, Wales.

Thomas Canby m. Sarah Jarvis, 9th day of 2nd month, 1693.

Children of Thomas and Sarah (Jarvis) Canby: Benjamin Canby b. 24th day of 7th month, 1694; Sarah Canby b. 23rd day of 8th month, 1695 and m., 30th day of 7th month, 1719, John Hill;

Elisabeth Canby b. 24th day of 10th month, 1696 and m. Thomas Lacey; Mary Canby b. 14th day of 10th month, 1697 and m. Joseph Hampton; Phebe Canby b. 19th day of 7th month, 1699 and m. (1) 1719, Robert Smith, m. (2) Hugh _ _; Esther Canby b. 16th day of 12th month, 1700 and m. (1) John Stapler, m. (2) John White; Thomas Canby b. 12th day of 8th month, 1702; Benjamin Canby b. 18th day of 7th month, 1704, m. (1) 26th day of 3rd month, 1724, Martha Preston, m. (2) 1734, Sarah Yardley, and d. 17th day of -- month, 1748; Martha Canby b. 9th day of 3rd month, 1705 and m. (1) James Gillingham, m. (2) Joseph Duer.

Sarah Canby. wife of Thomas Canby, d. 8th day of 2nd month, 1708.

Children of Thomas and Mary (Oliver) Canby: Jane Canby b. 12th day of 4th month, 1710; Rebecca Canby b. 16th day of 12th month, 1711; Hannah Canby b. 3rd day of 11th month, 1712 and d. 25th day of 8th month, 1722; Joseph Canby b. 1st day of 1st month, 1714 and d. 4th day of 7th month, 1718; Rachel Canby b. 8th day of 7th month, 1715 and never married; Oliver Canby b. 24th day of 11th month, 1716; Ann Canby b. 26th day of 5th month, 1778 and never married; Lydia Canby b. 25th day of 10th month, 1720 and m. John Johnson.

Mary Canby, wife of Thomas Canby, d. 20th day of 10th month, 1721.
Thomas Canby m. (3) 9th day of 8th month, 1722, Jane Preston.
Thomas Canby b. 1667 and d. 20th day of 9th month, 1742.

Children of Benjamin and Martha (Preston) Canby: Thomas Canby b. 26th day of 1st month, 1725 and d. 11th day of 6th month, 1728; Joseph Canby b. 20th day of 8th month, 1726; Benjamin Canby b. 31st day of 5th month, 1728.

Martha Canby, wife of Benjamin Canby, d. 1st day of 9th month, 1729.

Children of Benjamin and Sarah (Yardley) Canby: Sarah Canby b. 4th day of 8th month, 1735; William Canby b. 6th day of 2nd month, 1737; Ann Canby b. 1st day if 9th month, 1738; Thomas Canby b. 26th day of 11th month, 1739; Zacheus Canby b. 16 day of __ month, 1743 and d. 14th day of 6th month, 1747; Samuel Canby b. 6th day of 4th month, 1745; Charles Canby b. 26th day of 8th month, 1747 and d. 9th month, 1748.

Children of Thomas and Mary (Skelton) Canby: Elisabeth Canby b. 7th day of 7th month, 1764; Thomas Canby b. 17th day of 12th month, 1766; Hannah Canby b. 28th day of 4th month, 1769; Ann Canby b. 8th day of 9th month, 1773 and d. 12th day of 5th month, 1777.

John Canby, son of John Canby, m. Eleanor Preston in 1786 and d. 14th day of 12th month, 1794.

Children of Thomas and Hannah (Moore) Canby: Joseph Canby b. 8th day of 7th month, 1788; Julia Canby b. 17th day of 9th month, 1790; John Canby b. 13th day of 5th month, 1792; Christianna Canby b. 29th day of 3rd month, 1794; Mary Canby b. 28th day of 7th month, 1796; Elisabeth Canby b. 4th day of 4th month, 1799 and d. 3rd day of 9th month, 1813; Moore Canby b. 8th day of 5th month, 1801; Anna Canby b. 9th day of 8th month, 1803; Hannah Canby b. 17th day of 1st month, 1806; Sarah Canby b. 18th day of 6th month, 1808; Rebecca Canby b. 30th day of 1st month, 1812; Thomas Canby b. 9th day of 6th month, 1814.

Elias Canby b. 23rd day of 6th month, 1749 and d. 28th day of 1st month, 1839.
Hannah Canby, wife of Elias Canby, b. 26th day of 5th month, 1754 and d. 4th day of 9th month, 1836.

Children of John and Sarah (Pennington) Carlile: Jonathan Carlile b. 25th day of 3rd month, 1754; Daniel Carlile b. 5th day of 1st month, 1756 and d. 22nd day of 2nd month, 1843, an elder; John Carlile b. 4th day of 2nd month, 1758; Elisabeth Carlile b. 1st day of 11th month, 1759; Sarah Carlile b. 12th day of 3rd month, 1764; Amos Carlile b. 12th day of 6th month, 1766; Benjamin Carlile b. 17th day of 7th month, 1768; Rachel Carlile b. 28th day of 4th month 1771; David Carlile b. 2nd day of 7th month, 17773 and d. 16th day of 12th month, 1775; Rebecca Carlile b. 24th day of 4th month, 1775.

Sarah Carlile, ?wife of Benjamin Carlile, d. 13th day of 9th month, 1785.

Children of Daniel and Elisabeth (Smith) Carlile, of Plumstead: Samuel Carlile b. 10th day of 5th month, 1783 and d. 1st day of 7th month, 1793; Ann Carlile b. 29th day of 9th month, 1784 and d. 30th day of 10th month, 1802.

Elisabeth Carlile, wife of Daniel Carlile and daughter of Samuel and Jane Smith, b. 4th day of 4th month, 1753.

Children of David and Hannah (Michener) Carr: Deborah Carr b. 3rd day of 9th month, 1778; Joseph carr b. 18th day of 11th month, 1780; Jonathan Carr b. 1st day of 5th month, 1783 and d. 17th day of 4th month, 1857; Grace Carr b. 1st day of 4th month, 1786; David Carr b. 28th day of 7th month, 1789; John Carr b. 23rd day of 2nd month, 1793 and d. 11th day of 12th month, 1799; Hannah Carr b. 5th day of 3rd month, 1797.

Children of Joseph and Hannah (Carey) Carver: Thomas Carver b. 9th day of 9th month, 1788; Henry Carver b. 8th day of 2nd month, 1790; Rachel Carver b. 24th day of 8th month, 1794; Mary carver b. 26th day of 2nd month, 1798; Anna Carver b. 26th day of 1st month, 1802; Eli Carver b. 4th day of 6th month, 1804.

Children of Cephus and Priscilla (Naylor) Child: Mary Child b. 31st day of 11th month, 1751; Joseph Child b. 29th day of 10th month , 1753; Cephus Child b. 10th day of 4th month, 1755;

William Child b. 9th day of 2nd month, 1757; Jane Child b. 20th day of 2nd month, 1759 and d. 16th day of 11th month, 1762; Richard Child b. 3rd day of 1st month, 1761; Naylor Child b. 15th day of 7th month, 1762.

Priscilla Child, wife of Cephus Child, d. 17th day of 8th month, 1768.

Children of Henry and Mary (Shoemaker) Child: Sarah Child b. 11th day of 5th month, 1751; John Child b. 24th day of 9th month, 1752; Isaac Child b. 3rd day of 4th month, 1755; George Child b. 5th day of 7th month, 1757; Thomas Child b. 5th day of 3rd month, 1760.

Henry Child, son of John and Sarah (Shoemaker) Child, b. 12th day of 10th month, 1752.
Cadwallader Child, son of Cephus and Mary (Cadwallader) Child, b. 18th day of 9th month, 1776.
Mary Child, wife of Cephus Child, d. 22nd day of 12th month, 1794.

Children of Jonathan and Deborah (Michener) Child, of Plumstead: Isaac Child b. 15th day of 12th month, 1799; George Child b. 27th day of 3rd month, 1801; Rachel Child b. 1st day of 4th month, 1803; Israel Child b. 16th day of 1st month, 1805; Jonathan Child b. 26th day of 5th month, 1807; Joshua Child b. 3rd day of 8th month, 1810 and d. 3rd day of 8th month, 1837.

Children of Richard and Sarah (Fell) Church: Moses Church b. 15th day of 4th month, 1736; Sarah Church b. 3rd day of 10th month, 1737; John Church b. 6th day of 11th month, 1739; Elisabeth Church b. 14th day of 3rd month, 1743; Rachel Church b. 5th day of 4th month, 1745; Millicent Church b. 8th day of 11th month, 1746; Abi Church b. 30th day of 8th month, 1746; Joseph Church b. 6th day of 1st month, 1751; Asenath Church b. 9th day of 1st month, 1753.

Richard Church d. 11th day of 6th month, 1776.
Sarah Church, wife of Richard Church, d. 11th day of 10th month, 1797.

Children of William Coats and Mary (Hambleton), his 2nd wife: Elisa Coats b. 3rd day of 3rd month, 1799; William Coats b. 6th day of 5th month, 1802 and d. 9th day of 10th month, 1808; Seneca Coats b. 27th day of 9th month, 1804; Moses Coats b. 26th day of 6th month, 1809; John Coats b. 11th day of 3rd month, 1812; Paxson Coats b. 24th day of 6th month, 1815.

John Comfort, son of Ezra and Alice (Fell) Comfort, b. 17th day of 9th month, 1775 and d. 20th day of 10th month, 1840.
Ann Comfort, wife of John Comfort and daughter of Robert and Elisabeth Eastburn, b. 2nd day of 12th month, 1774 and d. 19th day of 9th month, 1867.

Children of John and Ann (Eastburn) Comfort: Rachel Comfort b. 20th day of 7th month, 1799; Alice Comfort b. 1st day of 12th month, 1800; Elisabeth Comfort b. 21st day of 12th month, 1802; Mercy Comfort b. 24th day of 9th month, 1805; Ezra Comfort b. 31st day of 10th month, 1808; Ann Comfort b. 11th day of 5th month, 1815; Sarah Comfort b. 19th day of 4th month, 1818.

Jacob Cooper, son of Jonathan and Sarah Cooper, b. 29th day of 3rd month, 1727.

Children of Mahlon and Jane Cooper, of Solebury: John Cooper b. 5th day of 4th month, 1796; Esther Cooper b. 6th day of 9th month, 1797; Levi Cooper b. 7th day of 8th month, 1799; Charles Cooper b. 7th day of 12th month, 1802; Nancy Cooper b. 2nd day of 12th month, 1803.

Children of Abraham and Dorothy Cowgill: John Cowgill b. 4th day of 1st month, 1726 and d. 6th day of 9th month, 1737; Sarah Cowgill b. 11th day of 8th month, 1727; Ralph Cowgill b. 31st day of 10th month, 1729; Abraham Cowgill b. 10th day of 12th month, 1731 and d. 22nd day of 9th month, 1737; Nehemiah Cowgill b. 13th day of 4th month, 1734 and d. 4th day of 9th month, 1737; Mary Cowgill b. 1st day of 10th month, 1736 and d. 4th day of 9th month, 1737; Abraham Cowgill b. 25th day of 7th month, 1738; Isaac Cowgill b. 6th day of 8th month, 1740; Jacob Cowgill b. 24th day of 8th month, 1744 and d. 23rd day of 10th month, 1744.

Dorithy Cowgill, wife of Abraham Cowgill, d. 1st day of 4th month, 1744.

Martha Dennis, wife of Henry Dennis, d. 7th day of 12th month, 1744.

Joseph Dilworth, son of Amos and Hannah Dilworth, b. 6th day of 2nd month, 1787.
Mary Dilworth, wife of Joseph Dilworth and daughter of Moses and Mary Paxson, b. 21st day of 4th month, 1794 and d. 8th month, 1868.

Children of Mahlon and Rebecca (Hartley) Doan: Anna Doan b. 14th day of 2nd month, 1796; James Hartley Doan b. 31st day of 10th month, 1797; Agnes Doan b. 6th day of 10th month, 1799; Jonathan Doan b. 17th day of 9th month, 1801; Rebecca Doan b. 3rd day of 6th month, 1804; Elizabeth Balderston Doan b. 19th day of 7th month, 1806.

Ebeneser Doan, son of Ebeneser and Anna Doan, b. 9th day of 9th month, 1772.

Eleaser Doan b. 10th day of 12th month, 1742.

Children of Eleaser and Mary Doan: Eleaser Doan b. 10th day of 12th month, 1742; Susanna Doan b. 11th day of 8th month, 1770; Jonas Doan b. 28th day of 2nd month, 1773; Rebeckah Doan b. 22nd day of 1st month, 1775; Jonathan Doan b. 19th day of 1st month, 1777; Mercy Doan b. 27th day of 12th month, 1780; Joshua Doan b. 26th day of 4th month, 1783; Jemima Doan b. 2nd day of 8th month, 1785 and d. 2nd day of 5th month, 1802; Joel Doan b. 1st day of 3rd month, 1788; Mary Doan b. 9th day of 9th month, 1791; Hannah Doan b. 29th day of 5th month, 1796.

Children of Joseph and Ann (Hampton) Duer: James Hampton Duer b. 10th day of 4th month, 1792; Mary Duer b. 25th day of 5th month, 1794 and d. 26th day of 9th month, 1795.

Ann Duer, wife of Joseph Duer, d. 25th day of 10th month, 1798.
Sarah Duer, wife of Joseph Duer and daughter of William and Ann Kitchen, b. 19th day of 1st month, 1777.

Children of Hosiah and Esther (Brown) Dyer: Joseph Dyer b. 30th day of 9th month, 1729; Josiah Dyer b. 14th day of 10th month, 1731; Thomas Dyer b. 26th day of 3rd month, 1734; John Dyer b. 1st day of 9th month, 1736; Mary Dyer b. 1st day of 7th month, 1740.

John Dyer d. 31st day of 11th month, 1738.
Elisabeth Dyer, widow of John Dyer, d. 29th day of 1st month, 1755.

Children of Samuel and Elisabeth Eastburn: Benjamin Eastburn b. 11th day of 2nd month, 1729; Joseph Eastburn b. 18th day of 12th month, 1730 and d. 28th day of 12th month, 1780; Ann Eastburn b. 23rd day of 7th month, 1732; Mary Eastburn b. 16th day of 2nd month, 1734; Benjamin Eastburn b. 21st day of 11th month, 1735; Sarah Eastburn b. 14th day of 4th month, 1736; Robert Eastburn b. 23rd day of 6th month, 1739.

Children of Joseph and Mary (Wilson) Eastburn: Joseph Eastburn b. 16th day of 7th month, 1754; Benjamin Eastburn b. 4th day of 7th month, 1756; Samuel Eastburn b. 20th day of 6th month, 1758; John Eastburn b. 28th day of 4th month, 1760 and d. 5th day of 4th month, 1833; Rebeckah Eastburn b. 4th day of 4th month, 1762; Thomas Eastburn b. 14th day of 5th month, 1764; Mary Eastburn b. 22nd day of 6th month, 1766; James Eastburn b. 27th day of 8th month, 1768 and d. 4th day of 7th month, 1792; Amos Eastburn b. 25th day of 12th month, 1770; David Eastburn b. 7th day of 4th month, 1773; Elisabeth Eastburn b. 22nd day of 4th month, 1776.

Joseph Eastburn, son of Samuel Eastburn, Jr., and Maire, his wife, b. 13th day of 1st month, 1782.
Maire Eastburn, wife of Samuel Eastburn, d. 30th day of 4th month, 1782, aged 22 years.
Elisabeth Eastburn, daughter of John and Elisabeth (Wiggins) Eastburn, b. 21st day of 8th month, 1788.

Children of Benjamin and Kezia (Ross) Eastburn: Mary Eastburn b. 19th day of 7th month, 1783; Ann Eastburn b. 24th day of 9th month, 1784; Rachel Eastburn b. 31st day of 1st month, 1787;

Martha Eastburn b. 8th day of 3rd month, 1789 and d. 15th day of 12th month, 1793; Sarah Eastburn b. 17th day of 2nd month, 1792.

Children of Robert and Elisabeth (Duer) Eastburn: Sarah Eastburn b. 12th day of 1st month, 1766, m. Thomas Philips, and d. 12th month, 1828; Moses Eastburn b. 1st day of 4th month, 1768; Elisabeth Eastburn b. 6th day of 9th month, 1770 and d. 6th day of 12th month, 1775; Aaron Eastburn b. 10th day of 1st month, 1773 and d. 24th day of 3rd month, 1846; Ann Eastburn b. 27th day of 12th month, 1774.

Elisabeth Eastburn, wife of Robert Eastburn, d. 14th day of 11th month, 1780.

Children of Aaron and Mercy (Bye) Eastburn, of Solebury: Elisa Eastburn b. 15th day of 10th month, 1797; Mercy Eastburn b. 11th day of 8th month, 1799 and d. 11th day of 12th month, 1801; Martha Eastburn b. 2nd day of 10th month, 1801, m. John D. Balderston, and d. 8th day of 7th month, 1859; Anna Eastburn b. 5th day of 11th month, 1803 and d. 15th day of 8th month, 1804; Mary Eastburn b. 25th day of 11th month, 1805 and d. 12th day of 5th month, 1866, widow of John Brown; Rachel Eastburn b. 21st day of 2nd month, 1808 and d. 8th day of 3rd month, 1860; Sarah Eastburn b. 29th day of 1st month, 1810 and d. 23rd day of 5th month, 1873.

Children of Joseph Eastburn, Jr., and Rebecca (Kitchen), his wife: Elisabeth Eastburn b. 13th day of 9th month, 1778; Latitia Eastburn b. 31st day of 7th month, 1780; Sarah Eastburn b. 11th day of 12th month, 1782; Charles Eastburn b. 12th day of 4th month, 1785 and d. 13th day of 8th month, 1785; Mercy Eastburn b. 13th day of 7th month, 1787 and d. 10th day of 4th month, 1791; Hannah Eastburn b. 19th day of 9th month, 1791; Mary Eastburn b. 2nd day of 11th month, 1795.

Children of Moses and Rachel (Knowles) Eastburn, of Solebury: John Eastburn b. 5th day of 8th month, 1791; Elisabeth Eastburn b. 3rd day of 1st month, 1793; Robert Eastburn b. 29th day of 10th month, 1794; Charles Eastburn b. 20th day of 10th month, 1796 and d. 30th day of 8th month, 1799; Jacob Eastburn b. 14th day of the _ month, 1798; Mary Eastburn b. 13th day of 9th month, 1800; Rachel Eastburn b. 12th day of 3rd month, 1803 and d. 2nd day of 3rd month, 1804; Sarah Eastburn b. 15th day of 11th month, 1804; Elias Eastburn b. 21st day of 11th month, 1806.

Joseph Ellicott, son of Andrew Ellicott, Jr., and Ann (Bye), his wife, b. 8th day of 8th month, 1773.
Andrew Ellicott b. 22nd day of 1st month, 1734.
Nathaniel Ellicott b. 17th day of 2nd month, 1736.
Thomas Ellicott b. 16th day of 3rd month, 1738 and d. 25th day of 1st month, 1799.
John Ellicott b. 28th day of 12th month, 1739.
Andrew Ellicott d. 6th month, 1740.

Children of Andrew and Elisabeth (Brown) Ellicott: Jonathan Ellicott b. 9th day of 11th month, 1756; Elias Ellicott b. 27th day of 12th month, 1757 and d. 2nd month, 1758; Elias Ellicott b. 4th day of 1st month, 1759; George Ellicott b. 28th day of 3rd month, 1760; Benjamin Ellicott b. 16th day of 10th month, 1761; Nathaniel Ellicott b. 10th day of 1st month, 1763; Andrew Ellicott b. 9th day of 12th month, 1764 and d. 31st day of 5th month, 1766; Elisabeth Ellicott b. 18th day of 1st month, 1766 and d. 23rd day of 5th month, 1766.

Elisabeth Ellicott, wife of Andrew Ellicott, d. 19th day of 4th month, 1766.

Children of Thomas and Ann (Ely) Ellicott: Ruth Ellicott b. 4th day of 10th month, 1764; John Ellicott b. 23rd day of 5th month, 1766; Sarah Ellicott b. 7th day of 4th month, 1768; Ann Ellicott b. 13th day of 4th month, 1770; Pamela Ellicott b. 15th day of 7th month, 1773; Thomas Ellicott b. 15th day of 4th month, 1778; Joseph Ellicott b. 31st day of 3rd month, 1780; Latitia Ellicott b. 27th day of 11th month, 1781.

Ann Ellicott, wife of Thomas Ellicott and daughter of Thomas Ely, b. 4th day of 5th month, 1742 and d. 2nd day of 12th month, 1781.

Children of Thomas Ellicott and Rebecca, his 2nd wife: George Ellicott b. 20th day of 2nd month, 1785; Rachel Ellicott b. 18th day of 4th month, 1787.

Rachel Ellicott, 2nd wife of Thomas Ellicott, d. 23rd day of 2nd month, 1790.
Hannah Ellicott, daughter of Thomas Ellicott and Jane (Kinsey), his 3rd wife, b. 15th day of 10th month, 1792.

Phebe Ely, wife of Hugh Ely and widow of _ _ , d. 1774.

Children of Hugh and Elisabeth (Wilson) Ely: Rebeckah Ely b. 25th day of 8th month, 1765; Sarah Ely b. 2nd day of 5th month, 1768; Hannah Ely b. 30th day of 6th month, 1771; John Ely b. 19th day of 12th month, 1773 and d. 31st day of 1st month, 1778; John Ely b. 9th day of 4th month, 1778.

Children of Joseph and Mary (Wilson) Ely: Anne Ely b. 1st day of 8th month, 1785; Charles Ely b. 4th day of 3rd month, 1787; Thomas Ely b. 1st day of 9th month, 1788.

Children of John and Sarah (Simcock) Ely: Mary Ely b. 21st day of 6th month, 1766; Asher Ely b. 11th day of 7th month, 1768; Elisabeth Ely b. 7th day of 3rd month, 1770; Merab Ely b. 29th day of 5th month, 1771; Sarah Ely b. 27th day of 3rd month, 1773 and d. 5th day of 6th month, 1773.

Sarah Ely, wife of John Ely, d. 13th day of 4th month, 1773.

Children of John and Mary (Richards), his 2nd wife: Phineas Ely

b. 18th day of 3rd month, 1779; Samuel Ely b. 23rd day of 10th month, 1780; Sarah Ely b. 27th day of 11th month, 1781; Hugh Ely b. 5th day of 11th month, 1783.

Children of Hugh and Elisabeth (Blackfan) Ely: John Ely b. 19th day of 3rd month, 1748; William Ely b. 7th day of 4th month, 1750; Elisabeth Ely b. 29th day of 11th month, 1755; Hugh Ely b. 6th day of 3rd month, 1760; Jesse Ely b. 26th day of 3rd month, 1765; Joseph Ely b. 3rd day of 5th month, 1771.

Hugh Ely d. 28th day of 4th month, 1791.
Elisabeth Ely, widow of Hugh Ely, d. 7th day of 5th month, 1796.

Children of John and Hannah (Austin) Ely: Seneca Ely b. 18th day of 7th month, 1777 and d. 14th day of 6th month, 1805; Elisabeth Ely b. 22nd day of 12th month, 1778; Latitia Ely b. 10th day of 11th month, 1780 and d. 2nd day of 1st month, 1803; Samuel Ely b. 17th day of 8th month, 1782; John Ely b. 8th day of 4th month, 1784; Hannah Ely b. 28th day of 3rd month, 1787 and d. 11th day of 12th month, 1814; James Ely b. 19th day of 4th month, 1789 and d. 1st day of 3rd month, 1810; Thomas Ely b. 8th day of 9th month, 1791.

Children of Jesse and Rachel (Carver) Ely: Hugh Ely b. 3rd day of 11th month, 1792; Charles Ely b. 24th day of 6th month, 1794; Joseph Ely b. 14th day of 6th month, 1797; William Ely b. 17th day of 3rd month, 1801; Alfred Ely b. 11th day of 10th month, 1809; Henry Ely b. 8th day of 10th month, 1811; Alfred Ely b. 11th day of 10th month, 1813; Joseph Ely b. 31st day of 8th month, 1814.

Rachel Ely, wife of Jesse Ely, b. 10th day of 5th month, 1769.
George Ely, son of Joshua and Elisabeth Ely, b. 9th day of 9th month, 1733 o.s.
Sarah Ely, wife of George Ely and daughter of William and Sarah Magill, b. 9th day of 9th month, 1742.

Children of George and Sarah Ely: Joseph Ely b. 13th day of 8th month, 1761 n.s; Jane Ely b. 5th day of 1st month, 1764; Joshua Ely b. 4th day of 7th month, 1766 and d. 5th day of 8th month, 1775; Amos Ely b. 6th day of 2nd month, 1769; George Ely b. 25th day of 7th month, 1772 and m. Sarah Smith; William Ely b. 26th day of 11th month, 1774; Aaron Ely b. 24th day of 7th month, 1777; Joshua Ely b. 24th day of 10th month, 1779 and d. 26th day of 11th month, 1779; Mark Ely b. 18th day of 9th month, 1781; Mathias Ely b. 5th day of 9th month, 1783; Amasa Ely b. 12th day of 11th month, 1787.

Children of Amos and Deborah (Whitson) Ely: Latitia Ely b. 8th day of 5th month, 1792; Elisabeth Ely b. 12th day of 1st month, 1794; George Ely b. 30th day of 1st month, 1796; Thomas Ely b. 1st day of 2nd month, 1798; Whitson Ely b. 6th day of 1st month, 1800; Seth Ely b. 14th day of 2nd month, 1802 and d. 4th day of 12th month, 1808; Deborah Ely b. 3rd day of 8th month, 1804 and

d. 12th day of 12th month, 1808; Anne Ely b. 3rd day of 12th month, 1806 and d. 19th day of 12th month, 1808; Amos Ely b. 22nd day of 1st month, 1809.

Children of Joshua and Sarah (Griffith) Ely, of Solebury: J. Moore Ely b. 28th day of 1st month, 1785 and d. 5th day of 3rd month, 1808; Elisabeth Ely b. 26th day of 6th month, 1786; Joshua Ely b. 19th day of 10th month, 1788; Sarah Ely b. 30th day of 7th month, 1792; Nathan Ely b. 22nd day of 11th month, 1797.

Ruth Ely, wife of Hugh Ely and daughter of Oliver and Ruth Paxson, of Solebury, b. 16th day of 2nd month, 1769 and d. 18th day of 3rd month, 1851.
Elias Ely, son of Hugh and Ruth (Paxson) Ely, b. 2nd day of 9th month, 1795 and d. 15th day of 2nd month, 1836.
Sarah M. Ely, wife of Elias Ely and daughter of John and Margaret Wilson, b. 19th day of 5th month, 1800.

Children of Joseph and Elisabeth Fell: Sarah Fell b. 26th day of 8th month, 1713; Titus Fell b. 7th day of 5th month, 1722.

Children of Joseph and Bridget (Wilson) Fell: Joseph Fell b. 29th day of 4th month, 1704 and d. 26th day of 2nd month, 1777; Benjamin Fell b. 1st day of 9th month, 1703; Tamer Fell b. 25th day of 1st month, 1706; Mary Fell b. 26th day of 4th month, 1708.

Joseph Fell, son of John and Margaret Fell, d. 3rd day of 2nd month, 1748.
Bridget Fell, wife of Joseph Fell, d. 7th day of 5th month, 1708.

Children of Joseph and (2nd wife) Elisabeth (Doyle) Fell: John Fell b. 7th day of 5th month, 1712 and d. 20th day of 11th month, 1762; Sarah Fell b. 26th day of 8th month, 1713 and d. 11th day of 10th month, 1797; Isaac Fell b. 17th day of 6th month, 1715; Rachel Fell b. 7th day of 10th month, 1716; Titus Fell b. 7th day of 5th month, 1722; Thomas Fell b. 9th day of 6th month, 1725; George Fell b. 13th day of 7th month, 1728.

Elisabeth Fell, widow of Joseph Fell, d. 17th day of 4th month, 1784.

Children of Joseph Fell, Jr., and Mary (Kinsey), his wife: Elisabeth Fell b. 4th day of 10th month, 1736 and d. 21st day of 11th month, 1752; Joseph Fell b. 31st day of 8th month, 1738 and d. 26th day of 3rd month, 1789; Sarah Fell b. 9th day of 12th month, 1740; Rachel Fell b. 16th day of 5th month, 1744; Mary Fell b. 19th day of 10th month, 1746 and d. 20th day of 11th month, 1753; David Fell b. 9th day of 10th month, 1750; Martha Fell b. 1st day of 2nd month, 1756.

Mary Fell, wife of Joseph Fell, d. 29th day of 12th month, 1769.

Children of Benjamin and Hannah (Scarborough) Fell: John Fell b. 1st day of 4th month, 1730; Hannah Fell b. 15th day of 6th month,

1731 and d. 5th day of 7th month, 1731; Asa Fell b. 18th day of 11th month, 1732;1 Sarah Fell b. 11th day of 6th month, 1734 and d. 12th day of 12th month, 1734; Phebe Fell b. 27th day of 1st month, 1736; Benjamin Fell b. 11th day of 2nd month, 1739.

Hannah Fell, 1st wife of Benjamin Fell and daughter of John Scarborough, b. 31st day of 8th month, 1704 and d. 21st day of 2nd month, 1743.

Children of Benjamin and Hannah Fell: Thomas Fell b. 11th day of 1st month, 1746; Deborah Fell b. 14th day of 7th month, 1747; Levi Fell b. 23rd day of 6th month, 1749.
Hannah Fell, 2nd wife of Benjamin Fell, d. 27th day of 11th month, 1755.

Maurice Fell, son of Benjamin and (3rd wife) Sarah (Rollins) Fell, b. 26th day of 8th month, 1758.

Children of John and Elisabeth (Watson) Fell: Ann Fell b. 6th day of 10th month, 1739 o.s. and d. 20th day of 3rd month, 1828; Jonathan Fell b. 2nd day of 12th month, 1740; Elisabeth Fell b. 25th day of 3rd month, 1743 and d. 6th month, 1748; Sarah Fell b. 25th day of 6th month, 1745; John Fell b. 8th day of 5th month, 1748; Elisabeth Fell b. 18th day of 7th month, 1751; Alice Fell b. 3rd day of 9th month, 1753 n.s; Watson Fell b. 28th day of 9th month, 1756; Thomas Fell b. 14th day of 5th month, 1759; Jane Fell b. 24th day of 10th month, 1761.

Elisabeth Fell, widow of John Fell and daughter of Dr. John Watson, b. 1717/18 and d. 13th day of 3rd month, 1812, in her 94th year.

Children of Jonathan Fell and Rebecca, his wife, daughter of Samuel and Rebecca Wilson: Ann Fell b. 29th day of 9th month, 1768; Jonathan Fell b. 13th day of 1st month, 1771.

Children of Joseph and Rachel (Wilson) Fell: Mary Fell b. 14th day of 7th month, 1768 and d. 19th day of 1st month, 1781; Joseph Fell (twin) b. 14th day of 7th month, 1768; John Fell b. 5th day of 9th month, 1770, m. B. Scholfield, and d. 11th day of 12th month, 1848; David Fell b. 1st day of 7th month, 1774 and d. 22nd day of 2nd month, 1856; Jonathan Fell b. 5th day of 5th month, 1776; Martha Fell b. 17th day of 4th month, 1772 and m. B. Scholfield; Rebeckah Fell b. 18th day of 4th month, 1778 and d. 14th day of 6th month, 1788; Rachel Fell b. 2nd day of 12th month, 1783.

Rachel Fell, widow of Joseph Fell, b. 5th day of 4th month, 1741 and d. 8th day of _ month, 1810.

Children of John Fell and Sarah, his wife, daughter of Jonathan Palmer: Alice Fell b. 8th day of 6th month, 1776 and d. 29th day of 6th month, 1778; John Fell b. 10th day of 4th month, 1778; Mark Fell b. 23rd day of 10th month, 1779; Elisabeth Fell b. 16th day of 6th month, 1781; Moses Fell b. 13th day of 12th month, 1782 and d. 2nd day of 5th month, 1783; Ezra Fell b. 4th day of 6th month, 1784; Ann Fell b. 19th day of 7th month, 1786; Moses Fell b. 9th day of 6th month, 1788; Richard Fell b. 3rd day of 4th month, 1790.

Children of George and Martha (Bradshaw) Fell: Mary Fell b. 22nd day of 11th month, 1797; Rachel Fell b. 26th day of 1st month, 1801; Elisabeth Fell b. 6th day of 5th month, 1804; Phebe Fell b. 17th day of 7th month, 1807.

Children of Thomas and Jane (Kirk) Fell: Jesse F. Fell b. 16th day of 4th month, 1751; Joseph Fell b. 2nd day of 11th month, 1752; Samuel Fell b. 4th day of 8th month, 1756; Sarah Fell b. 6th day of 11th month, 1758 and d. 27th day of 3rd month, 1838; Amos Fell b. 1st day of 11th month, 1762; Abi Fell b. 18th day of 12th month, 1770.

Children of John and Edith (Smith) Fell: Ann Fell b. 20th day of 7th month, 1796; Samuel Fell b. 31st day of 10th month, 1798; Hannah Fell b. 23rd day of 10th month, 1800 and d. 13th day of 9th month, 1879; Martha Fell b. 23rd day of 8th month, 1802; Jane Fell b. 20th day of 9th month, 1804.

Edith Fell, wife of John Fell and daughter of Samuel and Jane Smith, b. 23rd day of 9th month, 1767 and d. 17th day of 4th month, 1839.

Children of Jonathan and Sarah (Balderson) Fell: Jane Fell b. 20th day of 4th month, 1800; Rebecca Fell b. 13th day of 8th month and d. 17th day of 9th month, 1802.

Children of John and Elisabeth Fisher: Robert Fisher b. 19th day of 7th month, 1720; Sarah Fisher b. 11th day of 2nd month, 1722 and d. 6th day of 6th month, 1812; John Fisher b. 25th day of 10th month, 1723 and d. 9th day of 4th month, 1752; Elisabeth Fisher b. 14th day of 7th month, 1725; Hannah Fisher b. 13th day of 4th month, 1727; Joseph Fisher b. 24th day of 7th month, 1729; Deborah Fisher b. 5th day of 1st month, 1734; Sarah Fisher b. 19th day of 2nd month, 1736; Samuel Fisher b. 29th day of 3rd month, 1738; Katherine Fisher b. 28th day of 4th month, 1740.

Elisabeth Fisher, wife of John Fisher, d. 20th day of 1st month, 1742.
John Fisher d. 12th day of 2nd month, 1765.

Children of Joseph and Ann (Carey) Fisher: Betty Fisher b. 5th day of 9th month, 1751; John Fisher b. 8th day of 8th month, 1743 and d. 16th day of 4th month, 1773; Joseph Fisher b. 20th day of 2nd month, 1746; Elias Fisher b. 10th day of 5th month, 1768; Robert Fisher b. 1st day of 11th month, 1770; John Fisher b. 10th day of 4th month, 1773; Barah Fisher b. 6th day of 4th month, 1775; Samuel Fisher b. 12th day of 12th month, 1777; Hannah Fisher b. 23rd day of 12th month, 1779; Ann Fisher b. 3rd day of

4th month, 1782.

Children of Barah and Mary (Butler) Fisher: John Fisher b. 1st day of 2nd month, 1762; Thomas Fisher b. 18th day of 11th month, 1763.

Children of Samuel and Margaret (Daws) Fisher: Ruth Fisher b. 27th day of 6th month, 1763; Samuel Fisher b. 31st day of 1st month, 1765; Joseph Fisher b. 7th day of 10th month, 1767; Eunice Fisher b. 1st day of 7th month, 1769; Josiah Fisher b. 7th day of 7th month, 1772.

Children of Asher and Alice Foulke: Elisabeth Foulke b. 15th day of 8th month, 1792; William Roberts Foulke b. 30th day of 6th month, 1795; Latitia Foulke b. 5th day of 10th month, 1797; Euphemia Foulke b. 22nd day of 7th month, 1799; Shipley Foulke b. 2nd day of 2nd month, 1802.

Children of Thomas and Lydia Gilbert: Thomas Gilbert b. 11th day of 1st month, 1726; Joseph Gilbert B. 26th day of 9th month, 1727; Sarah Gilbert b. 31st day of 5th month, 1730; William Gilbert b. 19th day of 4th month, 1732; David Gilbert b. 8th day of 9th month, 1734 and d. 15th day of 8th month, 1799; Jonathan Gilbert b. 22nd day of 1st month, 1737; Caleb Gilbert b. 14th day of 11th month, 1739; Joshua Gilbert b. 3rd day of 3rd month, 1742; Daniel Gilbert b. 22nd day of 11th month, 1745 and d. 1st day of 11th month, 1746.

Children of David and Sarah (Bradshaw) Gilbert: Lydia Gilbert b. 20th day of 2nd month, 1771; Patience Gilbert b. 15th day of 7th month, 1772; Sarah Gilbert b. 16th day of 5th month, 1774; David Gilbert b. 8th day of 5th month, 1776; James Gilbert b. 1st day of 9th month, 1777; Amos Gilbert b. 8th day of 10th month, 1781?; Sarah Gilbert b. 29th day of 10th month, 1781,

Alice Gill, wife of Thomas Gill, d. 26th day of 9th month, 1759, aged about 62 years.

Children of James and Martha (Canby) Gillingham: John Gillingham b. 19th day of 1st month, 1731?; Yeamans Gillingham b. 15th day of 8th month, 1734; James Gillingham b. 30th day of 6th month, 1736; Martha Gillingham b. 9th day of 8th month, 1738; Thomas Gillingham b. 16th day of 1st month, 1740; Joseph Gillingham b. 14th day of 5th month, 1743; Mary Gillingham b. 26th day of 5th month, 1746.

James Gillingham, father of above, d. 4th day of 11th month, 1745.
William Gillingham, son of Yeamans Gillingham and Ruth (Preston), his 1st wife, b. 12th day of 3rd month and d. 18th day of 4th month, 1765.
Ruth Gillingham, 1st wife of Yeamans Gillingham, d. 25th day of 3rd month, 1765.

Children of Yeamans Gillingham and Bridget (Moore), his 2nd wife: James Gillingham b. 27th day of 12th month, 1768; Thomas Gillingham b. 15th day of 10th month, 1770; Moses Gillingham b. 4th day of 9th month, 1772; John Gillingham b. 30th day of 9th month, 1774; Matthias Gillingham b. 25th day of 2nd month, 1776; Yeamans Gillingham b. 9th day of 2nd month, 1778; Joseph Gillingham b. 3rd day of 8th month, 1780; Mahlon Gillingham b. 27th day of 7th month, 1782; Stacy Gillingham b. 16th day of 11th month, 1784.

Children of John and Sarah (Taylor) Gillingham: Mary Gillingham b. 7th day of 9th month, 1755; James Gillingham b. 26th day of 8th month, 1757.

Sarah Gillingham, wife of John Gillingham, d. 7th day of 9th month, 1757.

Children of John and Sarah (White) Gillingham: Samuel Gillingham b. 30th day of 12th month, 1762; Martha Gillingham b. 18th day of 7th month, 1764 and d. 7th day of 9th month, 1777; John Gillingham b. 6th day of 2nd month, 1766; Joseph Gillingham b. 10th day of 7th month, 1768 and d. 17th day of 5th month, 1794; Benjamin Gillingham b. 10th day of 4th month, 1770 and d. 6th day of 11th month, 1851; Jonathan Gillingham b. 6th day of 4th month, 1772 and d. 15th day of 9th month, 1777; Sarah Gillingham b. 9th day of 3rd month, 1774; Esther Gillingham b. 6th day of 10th month, 1776; Amos Gillingham b. 28th day of 10th month, 1778 and d. 28th day of 3rd month, 1801; David Gillingham b. 20th day of 12th month, 1780 and d. 3rd day of 6th month, 1804.

Sarah Gillingham, wife of John Gillingham, d. 12th day of 6th month, 1799, aged 58-3-6.

Children of John and Ann (Preston) Gillingham: Martha Gillingham b. 6th day of 6th month, 1788; Jonathan P. Gillingham b. 12th day of 8th month, 1789; John P. Gillingham b. 12th day of 3rd month, 1791; Anne Gillingham b. 12th day of 9th month, 1792; Elisabeth Gillingham b. 13th day of 7th month, 1794; William P. Gillingham b. 25th day of 8th month, 1796; Jesse Gillingham b. 13th day of 3rd month, 1798; Sarah Gillingham b. 13th day of 9th month, 1799; Amos Gillingham b. 21st day of 8th month, 1801; David Gillingham b. 18th day of 4th month, 1804; Mary Gillingham b. 26th day of 3rd month, 1808 and d. 27th day of 7th month, 1808.

Children of Samuel and Margaret (Jenks) Gillingham: Elisabeth Gillingham b. 21st day of 11th month, 1784; William Gillingham b. 20th day of 9th month, 1786; Jonathan Gillingham b. 3rd day of 6th month, 1788; Joseph Gillingham b. 20th day of 9th month, 1793; Jenks Gillingham b. 22nd day of 7th month, 1798.

Phebe Gillingham, wife of Joseph Gillingham, d. 16th day of 11th month, 1795.
Sarah Gillingham, wife of Benjamin Gillingham and daughter of Amos and Sarah Austin, b. 8th month, 1784 and d. 4th month, 1858.

Children of Edward and Elinor (Harris) Goode: Gainor Goode b. 22nd day of 12th month, 1766; Hannah Goode b. 27th day of 9th month, 1768; Jonathan Goode b. 12th day of 8th month, 1772; Margaret Goode b. 11th day of 10th month, 1773; Mary Goode b. 21st day of 10th month, 1775; Eleanor Goode b. 16th day of 10th month, 1777; John Goode b. 3rd day of 9th month, 1779 and d. 14th day of 5th month, 1844; Edward Goode b. 1st day of 9th month, 1781; Jane Goode b. 30th day of 3rd month, 1783; Nathan Goode b. 10th day of 7th month, 1785.

Thomas Goode b. 14th day of 8th month, 1735.

Children of Thomas and Esther (Lewis) Goode: Jesse Goode b. 14th day of 4th month, 1768; Rebecca Goode b. 13th day of 10th month, 1769; Miriam Goode b. 9th day of 12th month, 1771 and d. 20th day of 9th month, 1775; Joseph Goode b. 26th day of 10th month, 1773; Miriam Goode b. 6th day of 1st month, 1779; Hannah Goode b. 14th day of 3rd month, 1781; Mary Goode b. 20th day of 7th month, 1783; Thomas Goode b. 19th day of 11th month, 1785 and d. 16th day of 8th month, 1788; Robert Goode b. 5th day of 7th month, 1788; Thomas Goode b. 8th day of 7th month, 1791.

Children of Francis and Sarah (Roberts) Goode: Ann Goode b. 11th day of 3rd month, 1763; Mary Goode b. 10th day of 1st month, 1765; Margaret Goode b. 13th day of 1st month, 1767, m. Silas Preston, and d. 28th day of 2nd month, 1858; Thomas Goode b. 26th day of 6th month, 1769; Francis Goode b. 8th day of 6th month, 1771; Sarah Goode b. 18th day of 1st month, 1774; Thomas Goode b. 17th day of 1st month, 1776; Rebecca Goode b. 24th day of 4th month, 1776?; Joseph Goode b. 12th day of 7th month, 1780.

Children of George and Martha (Smith) Grubum: Elisabeth Grubum b. 19th day of 9th month, 1796; George Grubum b. 26th day of 8th month, 1799; Thomas Grubum (twin) b. 26th day of 8th month, 1799; John Grubum b. 30th day of 7th month, 1802 and d. 23rd day of 6th month, 1805.

Children of Matthew and Sarah (Hayworth) Hall: David Hall b. 7th day of 7th month, 1732; Mahlon Hall b. 12th day of 11th month, 1733; Margery Hall b. 23rd day of 1st month, 1735; Sarah Hall b. 24th day of 11th month, 1736.

Sarah Hall, wife of Matthew Hall, d. 4th day of 3rd month, 1748.

Children of James and Elisabeth (Paxson) Hambleton: Peninah Hambleton b. 17th day of 4th month, 1780; Hannah Hambleton b. 8th day of 5th month, 1781; Mercy Hambleton b. 14th day of 4th month, 1783; Alice Hambleton b. 10th day of 1st month, 1785; Elisabeth Hambleton b. 14th day of 5th month, 1786; Rachel Hambleton b. 23rd day of 5th month, 1787; Mary Hambleton b. 2nd day of 10th month, 1788; John Hambleton b. 2nd day of 2nd month, 1790; Joseph Hambleton b. 10th day of 5th month, 1791; Stephen Hambleton b. 30th day of 7th month, 1793; Sarah Hambleton b. 17th day of 5th month, 1795.

Children of Stephen and Hannah (Paxson) Hambleton: James Hambleton b. 5th day of 1st month, 1754; John Hambleton b. 14th day of 6th month, 1755; Jane Hambleton b. 9th day of 3rd month, 1757; William Hambleton b. 23rd day of 10th month, 1758; Jonas Hambleton b. 17th day of 10th month, 1760; Joseph Hambleton b. 2nd day of 12th month, 1762; Rachel Hambleton b. 7th day of 3rd month, 1765; Moses Hambleton b. 27th day of 1st month, 1768; Aaron Hambleton b. 21st day of 1st month, 1770; Margaret Hambleton b. 19th day of 1st month, 1772; Mary Hambleton b. 13th day of 2nd month, 1774.

Hannah Hambleton, widow of Stephen Hambleton, b. 28th day of 12th month, 1731 and d. 21st day of 11th month, 1812.

Children of Aaron and Hannah Hambleton: Charles Hambleton b. 19th day of 3rd month, 1795; Moses Hambleton b. 25th day of 12th month, 1796; Samuel Hambleton b. 14th day of 7th month, 1798; Aaron Hambleton b. 14th day of 9th month, 1801 and d. 13th day of 3rd month, 1806; Elihu Hambleton b. 7th day of 7th month, 1803; Josiah L. Hambleton b. 30th day of 9th month, 1805; Elisa P. Hambleton b. 11th day of 7th month, 1807.

Charles Hampton, son of Oliver and Hannah (Dennis) Hampton, b. 17th day of 3rd month, 1792.

Children of Oliver Hampton and Hannah (Kitchen), his 2nd wife: James Hampton b. 31st day of 8th month, 1796; Hannah Hampton (twin) b. 31st day of 8th month, 1796; Elisabeth Hampton b. 6th day of 3rd month, 1798 and d. 22nd day of 9th month, 1799; Ann Hampton b. 10th day of 7th month and d. 15th day of 9th month, 1800; Ann Hampton b. 28th day of 3rd month, 1802 and d. 11th day of 4th month, 1804; Elisabeth Hampton b. 1st day of 9th month, 1803; Martha Hampton b. 29th day of 4th month, 1805; Oliver Hampton b. 28th day of 9th month, 1807.

Children of Roger and Rebecca Hartley: Janey Hartley b. 27th day of 7th month, 1728; Bathsheba Hartley b. 14th day of 10th month, 1729 and d. 8th day of 6th month, 1731; Ann Hartley b. 14th day of 5th month, 1732; Roger Hartley b. 19th day of 1st month, 1734; James Hartley b. 11th day of 9th month, 1735; Bathsheba Hartley b. 25th day of 4th month, 1737; Benjamin Hartley b. 2nd day of 12th month, 1740; Rebecca Hartly b. 25th day of 10th month, 1743.

Roger Hartley, father of above, d. 3rd day of 7th month, 1743, in his 41st year.

Children of Thomas and Elisabeth (Paxson) Hartley: Sarah Hartley b. 7th day of 10th month, 1726; Mary Hartley b. 19th day of 11th month, 1727 and d. 15th day of 7th month, 1746; Thomas Hartley b. 6th day of 5th month, 1729 and d. 2nd day of 2nd month, 1736; Anthony Hartley b. 3rd day of 10th month, 1730; William Hartley b. 15th day of 2nd month, 1732 and d. 1st day of 1st month, 1808; Elisabeth Hartley b. 16th day of 11th month, 1733; Martha Hartley b. 26th day of 6th month, 1735; Anne Hartley b. 28th day of 5th month, 1738; Rachel Hartley b. 2nd day of 5th month, 1740; Joseph Hartley b. 18th day of 8th month, 1742; Benjamin Hartley b. 6th day of 10th month, 1745 and m. Elisabeth Simcocks; Mahlon Hartley b. 21st day of 5th month, 1749.

Elisabeth Hartley, wife of Thomas Hartley, d. 4th day of 12th month, 1786.

Children of Anthony and Elisabeth (Smith) Hartley: Thomas Hartley b. 27th day of 12th month, 1756 and m. Elisabeth Bradfield; Samuel Hartley b. 30th day of 3rd month, 1758 and m. Lavinia Bradfield; Mary Hartley b. 20th day of 8th month, 1759; Jonathan Hartley b. 21st day of 10th month, 1761; William Hartley b. 22nd day of 3rd month, 1763 and d. 3rd day of 6th month, 1775; Sarah Hartley b. 11th day of 11th month, 1765; Elisabeth Hartley b. 2nd day of 8th month, 1769.

Elisabeth Hartley, wife of Anthony Hartley, d. 3rd day of 8th month, 1769, aged 35-3-11.

Children of Anthony Hartley and Sarah (Betts), his 2nd wife: Ann Hartley b. 6th day of 3rd month, 1772 and d. 3rd day of 6th month, 1775; Rachel Hartley b. 23rd day of 12th month, 1773; William Hartley b. 11th day of 7th month, 1776; Jane Hartley b. 1st day of 4th month, 1779; Hannah Hartley b. 30th day of 1st month, 1781; Amy Hartley b. 2nd day of 4th month, 1788.

Sarah Hartley, 2nd wife of Anthony Hartley, d. 6th day of 8th month, 1797.

Children of Thomas and Mary (Bye) Head: John Head b. 4th day of 5th month, 1706; Barbara Head b. 1st day of 10th month, 1708; Ruth Head b. 16th day of 7th month, 1712.

Mary Head, wife of Thomas Head, d. 1st day of 2nd month, 1727.

Children of John and Sarah (Canby) Hill: William Hill b. 24th day of 7th month, 1720; Thomas Hill b. 29th day of 2nd month, 1722; Hannah Hill b. 23rd day of 10th month, 1723 and d. 18th day of 6th month, 1751; John Hill b. 9th day of 11th month, 1725; Joseph Hill b. 14th day of 9th month, 1727; Benjamin Hill b. 4th day of 11th month, 1729; James Hill b. 9th day of 11th month, 1731; Samuel Hill b. 4th day of 2nd month, 1734; Moses Hill b. 27th day of 2nd month, 1736; Aaron Hill b. 2nd day of 3rd month, 1739.

John Hill, father of above, d. 17th day of 11th month, 1748.

Children of John and Elisabeth (Smith) Hill: Ezekiel Smith Hill b. 3rd day of 4th month and d. 3rd day of 7th month, 1758; Ezekiel Hill b. 22nd day of 5th month, 1759; Joseph Hill b. 16th day of 4th month, 1761; Deborah Hill b. 23rd day of 1st month, 1763; Margaret Hill b. 24th day of 3rd month, 1765; John Hill b. 7th day of 12th month, 1766; Benjamin Hill b. 19th day of 9th month, 1768; Moses Hill b. 17th day of 9th month, 1770.

Children of John and Ellinor (Sands) Hough: Mary Hough b. 4th day of 7th month, 1715 and d. 5th day of 11th month, 1782; John Hough b. 21st day of 12th month, 1716; Jane Hough b. 10th day of 10th month, 1718; Stephen Hough b. 27th day of 1st month, 1721; William Hough b. 16th day of 12th month, 1722; Daniel Hough b. 5th day of 2nd month, 1725; Joseph Hough b. 10th day of 7th month, 1727; Richard Hough b. 3rd day of 3rd month, 1730.

Children of Matthew and Elisabeth Hughes: Matthew Hughes b. 3rd day of 1st month, 1734; George Hughes b. 17th day of 8th month, 1735; Elisabeth Hughes b. 21st day of 1st month, 1738; Isaac Hughes b. 15th day of 4th month, 1740; Hannah Hughes b. 7th day of 3rd month, 1742; Sarah Hughes b. 3rd day of 10th month, 1744; Humphrey Hughes b. 9th day of 3rd month, 1747; Mary Hughes b. 6th day of 9th month, 1749; Thomas Hughes b. 10th day of 1st month, 1752 n.s; Constantine Hughes b. 8th day of 9th month, 1754.

Matthew Hughes d. 23rd day of 10th month, 1755.
Elisabeth Hughes, widow of Matthew Hughes, d. 17th day of 1st month, 1767.

Matthias Hutchinson, son of Thomas and Ann (Cary Walker) Hutchinson, b. 24th day of 12th month, 1795.

Children of Matthias and Elisabeth (Bye) Hutchinson: Thomas Hutchinson b. 20th day of 2nd month, 1766; Martha Hutchinson b. 16th day of 10th month, 1767, m. Samuel Johnson, and d. 11th day of 12th month, 1840; Matthias Hutchinson b. 25th day of 9th month and d. 27th day of 9th month, 1775; Elisabeth Hutchinson b. 19th day of 6th month, 1779 and d. 13th day of 5th month, 1780.

Samuel Johnson, son of William and Ruth Johnson, b. 17th day of 7th month, 1763 and d. 12th day of 11th month, 1843.

Children of Samuel and Martha (Hutchinson) Johnson: Elisabeth Johnson b. 7th day of 6th month, 1790; Ann Johnson b. 23rd day of 1st month, 1792; William Hutchinson Johnson b. 18th day of 6th month, 1794.

Children of Jonathan and Hannah (Pickering) Johnson: Jesse Johnson b. 29th day of 11th month, 1779; Hannah Johnson b. 8th day of 2nd month, 1782; John Pickering Johnson b. 17th day of 3rd month, 1784; Sarah Ann Johnson b. 3rd day of 6th month, 1786.

Hannah Johnson, wife of Jonathan Johnson and daughter of John and Hannah Pickering, b. 11th day of 4th month, 1754 and d. 19th day of 7th month, 1834.
Jonathan Johnson d. 1st day of 11th month, 1786.

Children of Isaiah and Elisabeth (Watson) Jones: Ezra Jones b. 27th day of 9th month, 1799 and d. 27th day of 2nd month, 1822; Sarah Jones b. 17th day of 5th month, 11802 and d. 27th day of 8th month, 1820; Elisabeth Jones b. 28th day of 4th month and d. 12th day of 11th month, 1804.

Elisabeth Jones, wife of Isaiah Jones and daughter of Thomas and Sarah Watson, b. 6th day of 1st month, 1764 and d. 16th day of 3rd month, 1806.
Jesse Jones, son of John and Huldah (Fenton) Jones, b. 29th day of 2nd month, 1782 and d. 22nd day of 4th month, 1861.
Sarah Jones, wife of Jesse Jones, b. 20th day of 10th month, 1780.

Children of Jesse and Sarah Jones: Hiram Jones b. 17th day of 10th month, 1800; Amos Jones b. 15th day of 1st month, 1803; Harriet B. Jones b. 25th day of 3rd month, 1805; Priscilla M. Jones b. 31st day of 7th month, 1807; John Jones b. 19th day of 4th month, 1809; Aaron W. Jones b. 23rd day of 7th month, 1811; Mary Ann Jones b. 17th day of 10th month, 1813; Jemima D. Jones b. 1st day of 5th month, 1816; Sarah D. Jones b. 14th day of 10th month, 1818.

Nathan Kinman, son of John and Margaret Kinman, b. 17th day of 2nd month, 1763.

Children of Samuel and Sarah (Ingham) Kinsey: Ulysses Kinsey b. 18th day of 10th month, 1763; Jonas Kinsey b. 18th day of 10th month, 1766; Ingham Kinsey b. 3rd day of 4th month, 1769.

David Kinsey, son of Edmund and Sarah Kinsey, b. 3rd day of 7th month, 1712.

Tamar Kinsey, wife of David Kinsey, b. 25th day of 1st month, 1706.

Children of David and Tamar (Fell) Kinsey: David Kinsey b. 20th day of 12th month, 1736; Rachel Kinsey b. 21st day of 7th month, 1738 and d. 2nd day of 7th month, 1740; George Kinsey b. 12th day of 7th month, 1740; John Kinsey b. 5th day of 2nd month, 1742; Isaac Kinsey b. 4th day of 12th month, 1743.

Benjamin Kinsey, son of Edmund and Sarah Kinsey, b. 22nd day of 8th month, 1727 and d. 12th day of 7th month, 1789.
Susanna Kinsey, wife of Benjamin Kinsey and daughter of George and Sarah Brown, b. 23rd day of 10th month, 1726 and d. 24th day of 2nd month, 1765.

Children of Benjamin and Susanna (Brown) Kinsey: Martha Kinsey b. 4th day of 1st month, 1750 and d. 1st day of 9th month, 1769; George Kinsey b. 21st day of 3rd month, 1752 and m. Mary Gillingham; Jonathan Kinsey b. 9th day of 11th month, 1753; Susanna Kinsey b. 9th day of 11th month, 1756; Sarah Kinsey b. 1st day of 11th month, 1758 and d. 12th day of 8th month, 1764; Mary Kinsey b. 2nd day of 10th month, 1760; Lucretia Kinsey b. 16th day of 10th month, 1762; Benjamin Kinsey b. 18th day of 2nd month and d. 8th day of 3rd month, 1765.

Children of Benjamin and Martha (White) Kinsey: Joseph Kinsey b. 8th day of 11th month, 1767; Sarah Kinsey b. 23rd day of 6th month, 1770; Benjamin Kinsey b. 7th day of 5th month, 1772 and m. Margaret Hambleton; Martha Kinsey b. 9th day of 3rd month, 1774; Abi Kinsey b. of 5th month, 1776; Alcesta Kinsey b. 2nd day of 10th month, 1779; Esther Kinsey b. 20th day of 12th month, 1781; Edmund Kinsey b. 25th day of 1st month, 1784; Ann Kinsey b. 7th day of 4th month, 1786.

Children of Joseph and Hannah (Adeste) Kinsey: John Kinsey b. 4th day of 12th month, 1749 and m. Mary Rice; Isaac Kinsey b. 21st day of 9th month, 1751 and m. Mary Bradshaw; Sarah Kinsey b. 3rd day of 6th month, 1753 and d. 24th day of 2nd month, 1754; Jane Kinsey b. 23rd day of 12th month, 1754; Joseph Kinsey b. 11th day of 6th month, 1757 and m. Ann Plunket; Jacob Kinsey b. 6th day of 6th month, 1759; James Kinsey b. 22nd day of 12th month, 1761 and m. Mary Hunt; Joshua Kinsey b. 17th day of 1st month, 1764.

Joseph Kinsey, father of above, d. 17th day of 9th month, 1764.

Children of John and Mary (Rice) Kinsey: Alice Kinsey b. 27th day of 1st month, 1775; Elisabeth and Hannah (twins) Kinsey b. 7th day of 3rd month, 1777; Abel Kinsey b. 13th day of 6th month, 1779; Phebe Kinsey b. 18th day of 6th month, 1782; Seth Kinsey b. 23rd day of 1st month, 1785; Elam Kinsey b. 9th day of 4th month, and d. 15th day of 10th month, 1787; Asher Kinsey (twin) b. 9th day of 4th month, 1787.

Children of Isaac and Mary (Bradshaw) Kinsey: Ruth Kinsey b. 3rd day of 8th month, 1777 and d. 13th day of 4th month, 1788; James Kinsey b. 11th day of 12th month, 1778; Isaac Kinsey b. 17th day of 10th month, 1780; Mary Kinsey b. 20th day of 1st month, 1782; Jacob Kinsey b. 4th day of 2nd month, 1783; Joseph Kinsey b. 15th day of 4th month, 1784; Hannah Kinsey b. 3rd day of 6th month, 1786; Israel Kinsey b. 30th day of 10th month, 1787 and d. 16th day of 4th month, 1788; Oliver Kinsey b. 24th day of 11th month, 1788; Rachel Kinsey b. 9th day of 11th month, 1792; Mary Kinsey b. 11th day of 3rd month, 1794.

Children of Joseph and Ann (Plunket) Kinsey: Jane Kinsey b. 21st day of 4th month, 1785; John Kinsey b. 5th day of 3rd month, 1788; Robert Kinsey b. 2nd day of 2nd month, 1791 and d. 4th day of 8th month, 1793; Joseph Kinsey b. 13th day of 11th month, 1795.

Ann Kinsey, wife of Joseph Kinsey, d. 13th day of 11th month, 1795.

Children of Edmund and Sarah Kinsey: Samuel Kinsey b. 20th day of 10th month, 1710; David Kinsey b. 3rd day of 9th month, 1712; Mary Kinsey b. 20th day of 2nd month, 1715; Elisabeth Kinsey b. 23rd day of 9th month, 1717; John Kinsey b. 5th day of 2nd month, 1719; Joseph Kinsey b. 21st day of 6th month, 1722; Sarah Kinsey b. 13th day of 11th month, 1724; Benjamin Kinsey b. 22nd day of 10th month, 1727; Jonathan Kinsey b. 12th day of 3rd month, 1731.

Children of Robert and Hannah (Bidgood) Kirkbride: Mary Kirkbride b. 1st day of 10th month, 1759; Esther Kirkbride b. 24th day of 10th month, 1761; Mahlon Kirkbride b. 18th day of 2nd month, 1765 and d. 27th day of 9th month, 1777; Hannah Kirkbride b. 16th day of 1st month, 1767; Sarah Kirkbride b. 22nd day of 2nd month, 1769; Latitia Kirkbride b. 15th day of 4th month, 1771; Robert Kirkbride b. 10th day of 3rd month, 1773; David Kirkbride b. 17th day of 3rd month, 1775; Ann Kirkbride b. 22nd day of 1st month, 1782.

Hannah Kirkbride, wife of Robert Kirkbride, d. 6th day of 10th month, 1784.

Ann Kitchen, wife of William Kitchen and daughter of Thomas and Sarah Paxson, b. 3rd day of 7th month, 1757.

William Kitchen, son of William and Ann Kitchen, b. 26th day of 7th month, 1792.
Eleanor Kitchen, wife of William Kitchen and daughter of Ellis and Hannah Carey, b. 24th day of 8th month, 1794.

Children of Thomas and Elisabeth (Canby) Lacey: Thomas Lacey b. 14th day of 2nd month, 172_; William Lacey b. 6th day of 11th month, 1726 and d. 10th day of 9th month, 172_; Barbary Lacey b. 26th day of 1st month, 173_; Benjamin Lacey b. 6th day of 8th month, 173_.

Tamar Lacey, wife of Jesse Lacey and daughter of Richard and Mary Wirthington, b. 20th day of 10th month, 1763 and d. 11th month,, 1846.

Joseph Large b. 23rd day of 1st month, 1746.

Children of Eleneser and Hannah (Knowles) Large: Jacob Large b. 27th day of 8th month and d. 12th day of 10th month, 1791; Mary Large b. 24th day of 10th month, 1792 and d. 11th day of 2nd month, 1793; William Large b. 21st day of 3rd month and d. 23rd day of 8th month, 1794; Joseph Large b. 13th day of 11th month, 1795; Isaiah Large b. 23rd day of 10th month, 1797; Anne Large b. 23rd day of 3rd month, 1801; Samuel Large b. 1st day of 1st month, 1804.

Children of Joseph and Mary Lupton: Ann Lupton b. 16th day of 3rd month, 1733; Mercy Lupton b. 16th day of 3rd month, 1735; Jonathan Lupton b. 11th day of 2nd month, 1739.

Children of Robert and Hannah McDowell: William McDowell b. 17th day of 10th month, 1785; Mary McDowell b. 1st day of 8th month, 1787; Ann McDowell b. 17th day of 1st month, 1790; Sarah McDowell b. 31st day of 5th month, 1793; George McDowell b. 1st day of 6th month, 1796 and d. 12th day of 2nd month, 1797; Eleaser McDowell b. 1st day of 9th month, 1798; Robert McDowell b. 24th day of 12th month, 1803.

Children of Jacob and Rebecca (Paxson) Magill: Mary Magill b. 18th day of 5th month, 1797; Jonathan P. Magill b. 3rd day of 10th month, 1798; Susan Magill b. 12th day of 5th month, 1800; Charles Magill b. 25th day of 3rd month, 1805; Sarah Magill b. 4th day of 9th month, 1809.

Rebecca Magill, wife of Jacob Magill and daughter of Jonathan and Rachel Paxson, b. 11th day of 7th month, 1772 and d. 16th day of 6th month, 1855.

Children of John and Agness (Whitson) Magill: Jacob Magill b. 2nd day of 11th month, 1766; Jane Magill b. 24th day of 5th month, 1769; Rachel Magill b. 25th day of 2nd month, 1772; William Magill b. 24th day of 3rd month, 1774; David Magill b. 6th day of 8th month, 1776; John Magill b. 12th day of 7th month, 1779.

Children of John and Rebecca (Goode) Malone: Mary Malone b. 6th day of 12th month, 1770; Hannah Malone b. 27th day of 12th month, 1772; John Malone b. 13th day of 12th month, 1774; Sarah Malone b. 12th day of 2nd month, 1777 and d. 5th day of 9th month, 1793; Alice Malone b. 11th day of 3rd month, 1779; James Malone b. 8th day of 11th month, 1780; Rebeckah Malone b. 22nd day of 12th month, 1782 and d. 29th day of 1st month, 1792; Levi Malone b. 6th day of 10th month, 1785 and d. 13th day of 7th month, 1793; Phebe Malone b. 12th day of 10th month, 1787; Francis Malone b. 15th day of 9th month, 1790 and d. 22nd day of 7th month, 1793; Rachel Malone b. 26th day of 12th month, 1793.

Children of John and Sarah (Armitage) Merrick: Elisabeth Merrick b. 3rd day of 7th month, 1778; Sarah Merrick b. 23rd day of 1st month, 1780; Amos Merrick b. 3rd day of 8th month, 1781; John Merrick b. 7th day of 4th month, 1783; David Merrick b. 15th day of 5th month, 1786.

Children of William and Mary Michener: John Michener b. 2nd day of 3rd month, 1721; Mordecai Michener b. 30th day of 1st month, 1723; Sarah Michener b. 29th day of 4th month, 1725 and d. 29th day of 12th month, 1747; Mary Michener b. 4th day of 1st month, 1728; William Michener b. 8th day of 6th month, 1729; Joseph Michener b. 10th day of 4th month, 1732; Elisabeth Michener b. 7th day of 11th month, 1734; Meshach Michener b. 22nd day of 4th month, 1737 and d. 9th day of 1st month, 1826; Margaret Michener b. 4th day of 2nd month, 1741; George Michener b. 10th day of 6th month, 1744 and d. 14th day of 11th month, 1820.

Mary Michener, wife of William Michener, d. 24th day of 4th month, 1758.

Children of Mordecai and Sarah (Fisher) Michener: William Michener b. 20th day of 8th month, 1749; John Michener b. 21st day of 12th month, 1750; Sarah Michener b. 2nd day of 10th month, 1752, m. Joseph Beans, and d. 1st day of 6th month, 1784; Barah Michener b. 17th day of 3rd month, 1754; Hannah Michener b. 16th day of 10th month, 1755 and d. 4th day of 1st month, 1760;

Deborah Michener b. 23rd day of 4th month, 1757; Mordecai Michener b. 28th day of 1st month, 1759; Hannah Michener b. 22nd day of 9th month, 1760; Elisabeth Michener b. 18th day of 3rd month, 1762; Robert Michener b. 15th day of 10th month, 1763; Katherine Michener b. 8th day of 11th month, 1766.

Children of John and Mary (Haworth) Michener: George Michener b. 15th day of 8th month, 1747 and d. 12th day of 10th month, 1827; Mahlon Michener b. 5th day of 10th month, 1748; William Michener b. 20th day of 6th month, 1750 and d. 2nd day of 3rd month, 1771; Arnold Michener b. 28th day of 1st month, 1752; Mary Michener b. 25th day of 11th month, 1754; Absalom Michener b. 12th day of 9th month, 1756; Sarah Michener b. 13th day of 11th month, 1759; John Michener b. 14th day of 11th month, 1761 and d. 15th day of 2nd month, 1762; David Michener b. 9th day of 11th month, 1766.

Children of William and Esther (Vickers) Michener: Rebeckah Michener b. 21st day of 10th month, 1769; Sarah Michener b. 20th day of 10th month, 1771; John Michener b. 10th day of 2nd month, 1774; William Michener b. 15th day of 8th month, 1776.

Cynthia Michener, daughter of Mahlon and Sarah (Day) Michener, b. 11th day of 5th month, 1774.

Children of Meshach and Sarah (Trego) Michener: Isaiah Michener b. 7th day of 11th month, 1762; Joyce Michener b. 10th day of 11th month, 1764 and d. 12th day of 9th month, 1770; Mary Michener b. 16th day of 2nd month, 1767; Rachel Michener b. 11th day of 2nd month, 1769; Mary Michener b. 5th day of 5th month, 1770; Meshach Michener b. 30th day of 4th month, 1771; Elisha Michener b. 1st day of 10th month, 1773; Nathan Michener b. 26th day of 11th month, 1775; Thomas Michener b. 21st day of 8th month, 1778; Marmaduke Michener b. 18th day of 12th month, 1780; Hannah Michener b. 22nd day of 8th month, 1783.

Mercy Michener, daughter of Robert and Sarah (Stradling) Michener, b.2nd day of 12th month, 1800.

Children of John and Esther (Dyer) Michener: Absalom Michener b. 5th day of 3rd month, 1798; Joseph Michener b. 6th day of 8th month, 1800 and d. 15th day of 10th month, 1812; John D. Michener b. 30th day of 12th month, 1802; Josiah Michener b. 13th day of 8th month, 1807; John? Michener b. 23rd day of 9th month, 1813.

Esther Michener, wife of John Michener, b. 27th day of 2nd month, 1772 and d. 15th day of 3rd month, 1855.

Children of George and Hannah Michener, of Plumstead: Grace Michener b. 15th day of 2nd month, 1776 and d. 29th day of 9th month, 1851; George Michener b. 10th day of 11th month, 1777; Abraham Michener b. 21st day of 8th month, 1782 and d. 23rd day of 4th month, 1857.

Children of George and Hannah Michener: Deborah Michener b. 22nd day of 7th month, 1770; John Michener b. 26th day of 8th month, 1773 and d. 12th day of 3rd month, 1837; Mary Michener b. 12th day of 1st month, 1775; Joshua Michener b. 27th day of 7th month, 1777 and d. 9th day of 2nd month, 1850; Hannah Michener b. 2nd day of 6th month, 1779.

Hannah Michener, wife of George Michener, b. 24th day of 3rd month, 1749 and d. 16th day of 2nd month, 1829.

Elisabeth Michener, wife of Joshua Michener and daughter of John and Sarah Shaw, b. 6th day of 12th month, 1780 and d. 31st day of 3rd month, 1833.

Children of David and Rebecca Michener: Jacob Michener b. 8th day of 8th month, 1791; Mary Michener b. 2nd day of 7th month, 1793; James Michener b. 4th day of 11th month, 1799.

William Henry Morris b. 20th day of 10th month, 1799.

Children of Robert and Jane Nary: Margaret Nary b. 22nd day of 5th month, 1742; Jane Nary b. 22nd day od 12th month, 1743; William Nary b. 15th day of 6th month, 1745.

Children of Phillip and Rachel Parry: Hannah Parry b. 1st day of 12th month, 1740; John Parry b. 10th day of 9th month, 1743; Jane Parry b. 10th day of 3rd month, 1745 and m. Mahlon Paxson; Thomas Parry b. 3rd day of 2nd month, 1747; Grace Parry b. 21st day of 2nd month, 1749; Rachel Parry b. 31st day of 1st month, 1751; Mary Parry b. 10th day of 1st month, 1753; Philip Parry b. 25th day of 5th month, 1755 and d. 7th day of 2nd month, 1818; David Parry b. 5th day of 7th month, 1760.

Philip Parry, father of above, d. 16th day of 1st month, 1785.

Children of John and Rachel (Fell) Parry: Elisabeth Parry b. 12th day of 3rd month, 1772; Joyce Parry b. 5th day of 2nd month, 1774; Mercy Parry b. 15th day of 3rd month, 1776; David Parry b. 20th day of 10th month, 1778; Charity Parry b. 30th day of 10th month, 1781; Tacy Parry b. 18th day of 4th month, 1783 and d. 18th day of 2nd month, 1870; Rachel Parry b. 8th day of 12th month, 1786; John Parry b. 31st day of 7th month, 1788; Thomas Parry F. b. 8th day of 7th month, 1791.

Rachel Parry, wife of John Parry and daughter of Titus and Elisabeth Fell, b. 9th day of 8th month, 1751.

Children of Philip and Mary (Armitage) Parry: Sarah Parry b. 18th day of 12th month, 1779; Samuel Parry b. 25th day of 12th month, 1780; Susanna Parry b. 11th day of 5th month, 1784 and d. 2nd day of 9th month, 1785; Charles Parry b. 11th day of 10th month, 1785; Seneca Parry b. 3rd day of 6th month, 1789; Rachel Parry b. 25th day of 7th month, 1793; Philip Parry b. 28th day of 2nd month, 1801.

Daniel Parry, son of John and Margaret Parry, b. 21st day of 4th month, 1774 and d. 16th day of 7th month, 1856.
Martha Parry, wife of Daniel Parry and daughter of Amos and Hannah Dilworth, b. 12th day of 5th month, 1777 and d. 3rd day of 4th month, 1831.

Children of Benjamin and Jane (Paxson) Parry: Ruth Parry b. 4th day of 1st month, 1797; Jane Parry b. 27th day of 8th month, 1799 and d. 28th day of 9th month, 1879; Margaret Parry b. 7th day of 12th month, 1804 and d. 26th day of 7th month, 1880.

Children of Henry and Ann (Plumly) Paxson: William Paxson b. 31st day of 11th month, 1707 and d. 7th day of 5th month, 1731; Elisabeth Paxson b. 11th day of 4th month, 1709; Mary Paxson b. 24th day of 2nd month, 1711 and d. 31st day of 6th month, 1719; Sarah Paxson b. 25th day of 11th month, 1712; Jane Paxson b. 14th day of 11th month, 1714; Margery Paxson b. 24th day of 9th month, 1716; Ann Paxson b. 8th day of 11th month, 1718; Rebecca Paxson b. 5th day of 9th month, 1720; Henry Paxson b. 28th day of 6th month, 1722 and d. 2nd day of 8th month, 1799; James Paxson b. 8th day of 6th month, 1724 and d. 1st day of 9th month, 1743; Thomas Paxson b. 17th day of 4th month, 1726 and d. 13th day of 1st month, 1764; Martha Paxson b. 4th day of 12th month, 1728.

Ann Paxson, wife of Henry Paxson, d. 10th day of 12th month, 1728, aged 40 years.
Henry Paxson, the father, d. 5th day of 9th month, 1756, aged 73-115.

Jane Paxson, wife of James Paxson, d. 7th day of 2nd month, 1710.
James Paxson d. 29th day of 7th month, 1722.

Children of Thomas and Sarah (Harvey) Paxson: Abraham Paxson b. 19th day of 4th month, 1749; Aaron Paxson b. 4th day of 6th month, 1757 and d. 15th day of 10th month, 1827; Moses Paxson b. 13th day of 8th month, 1754 and d. 26th day of 2nd month, 1826; Ann Paxson b. 3rd day of 6th month, 1757.

Sarah Paxson, wife of Thomas Paxson, d. 16th day of 6th month, 1762, aged 32 years.

Children of James and Mary (Horsman) Paxson: William Paxson b. 20th day of 12th month, 1724/5; Abigail Paxson b. 23rd day of 6th month, 1726.

Mary Paxson, wife of James Paxson, d. 23rd day of 6th month, 1726.

Children of James and Mary (Hodge) Paxson: Thomas Paxson b. 16th day of 7th month, 1731; Hannah Paxson b. 27th day of 10th month, 1732; Jonas Paxson b. 25th day of 4th month, 1735; James Paxson b. 11th day of 2nd month, 1738; Jane Paxson b. 3rd day of 6th month, 1739 and m. Joseph Pickering; Mary Paxson b. 22nd day of 1st month, 1743; Margaret Paxson b. 24th day of 8th month, 1745.

Children of ?Thomas and ?Abigail Paxson: Joseph Paxson b. 10th day of 9th month, 1733; Benjamin Paxson b. 1st day of 8th month, 1739 and d. 29th day of 3rd month, 1814; Oliver Paxson b. 9th day of 7th month, 1741; Rachel Paxson b. 6th day of 3rd month, 1744 and m. John Watson of Middletown; Jacob Paxson b. 6th day of 11th month, 1745, m. (1) 29th day of 6th month, 1769, Lydia Blakey, m. (2) 13th day of 11th month, 1777, Mary Shaw, and d. 13th day of 7th month, 1832; Jonathan Paxson b. 14th day of 11th month, 1748.

Children of Jacob and Lydia (Blakey) Paxson: Joshua Paxson b. 22nd day of 4th month, 1770; Lydia Paxson b. 29th day of 11th month, 1771.

Lydia Paxson, wife of Jacob Paxson, d. 3rd day of 8th, 1772.

Children of Aaron and Latitia (Knowles) Paxson: Phineas Paxson b. 26th day of 3rd month, 1776 and d. 6th day of 8th month, 1777; Ezra Paxson b. 1st day of 7th month, 1780; Eliada Paxson b. 2nd day of 3rd month, 1782; Aaron Paxson b. 13th day of 5th month, 1785.

Children of Benjamin and Deborah (Taylor) Paxson: Timothy Paxson b. 27th day of 5th month, 1764 and d. 21st day of 4th month, 1839; Hannah Paxson b. 19th day of 2nd month, 1766; Thomas Paxson b. 2nd day of 9th month, 1769 and d. 7th day of 6th month, 1843; Benjamin Paxson b. 22nd day of 4th month, 1776; Deborah Paxson b. 3rd day of 9th month, 1780; Rachel Paxson b. 28th day of 7th month, 1783 and d. 24th day of 1st month, 1860; Charles Paxson b. 16th day of 11th month, 1787.

Deborah Paxson, wife of Benjamin Paxson and daughter of Benjamin Taylor, d. 20th day of 8th month, 1792.
Rachel Paxson, 2nd wife of Benjamin Paxson and daughter of _ _ Newbold, d. 22nd day of 10th month, 1798.
Mary Paxson, 3rd wife of Benjamin Paxson and daughter of Elihu and Ann Pickering, d. _ _.

Children of Oliver and Ruth (Watson) Paxson: Jane Paxson b. 24th day of 1st month, 1767; Ruth Paxson b. 16th day of 2nd month, 1769; William Paxson b. 19th day of 8th month, 1771 and d. 17th day of 1st month, 1774; Oliver Paxson b. 16th day of 4th month, 1773 and d. 3rd day of 7th month, 1773;

Ruth Paxson, wife of Oliver Paxson, d. 17th day of 9th month, 1774, aged 34 years.

Children of Abraham and Elisabeth (Brown) Paxson: Elias Paxson b. 22nd day of 9th month, 1776; Sarah Paxson b. 1st day of 7th month, 1779; Elisabeth Paxson b. 10th day of 8th month, 1783; Martha Paxson b. 23rd day of 12th month, 1785 and d. 6th day of 8th month, 1793; Hannah Paxson b. 12th day of 2nd month, 1788; Abraham Paxson b. 1st day of 5th month, 1790 and d. 7th day of 7th month, 1791; Mary Paxson b. 4th day of 10th month, 1792 and d. 17th day of 12th month, 1792; Martha Paxson b. 7th day of 3rd month, 1794.

Elisabeth Paxson, wife of Abraham Paxson, d. 7th day of 6th month, 1797.

Children of Joseph and Mary (Heston) Paxson: Joseph Paxson b. 30th day of 10th month, 1759; Benjamin Paxson b. 10th day of 11th month, 1761; Jacob Paxson b. 4th day of 3rd month, 1763; Mary Paxson b. 14th day of 1st month, 1765; Rachel Paxson b. 8th day of 12th month, 1766; Amelia Paxson b. 22nd day of 9th month, 1768; Sarah Paxson b. 19th day of 4th month, 1770; Aaron Paxson b. 3rd day of 5th month, 1772 and d. 26th day of 1st month, 1773; Aaron Paxson b. 16th day of 11th month, 1773; Jonathan Paxson b. 26th day of 5th month, 1775; Abigail Paxson b. 23rd day of 7th month, 1776; Hester Paxson b. 20th day of 12th month, 1777; Oliver Paxson b. 15th day of 8th month, 1780 and d. 1st day of 9th month, 1780; Jane Paxson b. 19th day of 11th month, 1781; Ann Paxson b. 15th day of 11th month, 1783.

Children of Henry and Elisabeth (Lupton) Paxson: Mahlon Paxson b. 4th day of 3rd month, 1746; Rachel Paxson b. 30th day of 5th month, 1747; Isaac Paxson b. 29th day of 9th month, 1748; Henry Paxson b. 17th day of 8th month, 1750; Elisabeth Paxson b. 15th day of 2nd month, 1752; Joseph Paxson b. 1st day of 1st month, 1754; Sarah Paxson b. 1st day of 12th month, 1755; Mary Paxson b. 5th day of 2nd month, 1758; Mercy Paxson b. 25th day of 8th month, 1759; Ann Paxson b. 12th day of 8th month, 1761; Amy Paxson b. 6th day of 8th month, 1763; John Paxson b. 27th day of 7th month, 1766.

Children of Mahlon and Jane (Parry) Paxson: Alice Paxson b. 9th day of 8th month, 1774 and d. 20th day of 5th month, 1809; Asher Paxson b. 4th day of 3rd month, 1776 and d. 23rd day of 3rd month, 1869; Phinehas Paxson b. 27th day of 7th month, 1778 and d. 7th day of 9th month, 1802; Jane Paxson b. 25th day of 3rd month, 1782.

Children of Moses and Mary Paxson: Charles Paxson b. 28th day of 8th month, 1781; Ann Paxson b. 4th day of 9th month, 1783; Hannah Paxson b. 21st day of 11th month, 1785; Robert Paxson b. 27th day of 4th month, 1788; Thomas Paxson b. 30th day of 12th month, 1790 and d. 6th day of 4th month, 1817, at New Albany; Mary Paxson b. 21st day of 4th month, 1794; Moses Paxson b. 18th day of 9th month, 1801 and d. 14th day of 9th month, at New Orleans.

Children of Reuben and Elisabeth Paxson: Rachel Paxson b. 16th day of 3rd month, 1793; Samuel Paxson b. 5th day of 9th month, 1794; Anna Paxson b. 16th day of 5th month, 1794; William Paxson b. 1st day of 10th month, 1798.

Children of Elias and Catherine (Rice) Paxson: Elisabeth Paxson b. 11th day of 11th month, 1799; Abraham Paxson b. 17th day of 7th month, 1802.

Hannahmeel Paxson, wife of Thomas Paxson and daughter of Thomas and Beulah Canby, b. 13th day of 1st month, 1787 and d. 13th day of 5th month, 1857.
Sarah Paxson, daughter of Jonathan and Rachel (widow of Moses Paxson) Paxson.

Children of Enoch and Margaret (Smith) Pearson: William Pearson b. 9th day of 8th month, 1713; Thomas Pearson b. 9th day of 12th month, 1714; Mary Pearson b. 26th day of 11th month, 1716; Thomas Pearson b. 4th day of 2nd month, 1719; Enoch Pearson b. 25th day of 3rd month, 1718; Sarah Pearson b. 9th day of 2nd month, 1720; Phebe Pearson b. 5th day of 10th month, 1721; Margaret Pearson b. 6th day of 5th month, 1723; Rachel Pearson b. 4th day of 7th month, 1724; Elisabeth Pearson b. 8th day of 12th month, 1726; John Pearson b. 27th day of 4th month, 1728; Samuel Pearson b. 2nd day of 3rd month, 1730.

Children of William and Elisabeth (Duer) Pearson: Margaret Pearson b. 17th day of 7th month, 1741; Elisabeth Pearson b. 3rd day of 9th month, 1744.

Elisabeth Pearson, wife of William Pearson, d. 11th day of 2nd month, 1791.

Children of Joseph and Elisabeth Pearson: Sarah Pearson b. 30th day of 3rd month, 1742; Ann Pearson b. 5th day of 10th month, 1743; Mary Pearson b. 14th day of 8th month, 1745; Elisabeth Pearson b. 10th day of 3rd month, 1747; Enoch Pearson b. 22nd day of 1st month, 174_; Lawrence Pearson b. 31st day of 12th month, 1752; John Pearson b. 8th day of 11th month, 1756.

Children of John and Sarah (Hall) Pearson: Enoch Pearson b. 18th day of 4th month, 1757; Margaret Pearson b. 16th day of 3rd month, 1759.

Children of Nicholas and Abigail Penquite: Gorshom Penquite b. 13th day of 6th month, 1725; Esther Penquite b. 21st day of 12th month, 1727; Thomas Penquite b. 28th day of 8th month, 1736 and d. 6th day of 1st month, 1757; Abigail Penquite b. 27th day of 8th month, 1739.

Abigail Penquite, wife of Nicholas Penquite, d. 25th day of 3rd month, 1740.

Children of Aaron and Mary (Clauson) Phillips: Rebecca Phillips b. 29th day of 5th month, 1757; Thomas Phillips b. 25th day of 11th month, 1758; Elisabeth Phillips b. 25th day of 7th month, 1762.

Children of Thomas and Sarah (Eastburn) Phillips: Elisabeth Phillips b. 5th day of 12th month, 1786; Mary Phillips b. 13th day of 9th month, 1788; Aaron Phillips b. 28th day of 8th month, 1790; Moses Phillips b. 24th day of 12th month, 1792; Thomas Phillips b. 7th day of 3rd month, 1795; Robert Phillips b. 1st day of 6th month, 1797; Rachel Philips b. 27th day of 3rd month, 1800; Samuel Phillips b. 1st day of 7th month, 1802; Mercy Phillips b. 8th day of 4th month, 1804.

Isaac Pickering, son of Samuel Pickering and Mary, his wife, daughter of John Scarborough, b. 23rd day of 12th month, 1716. Samuel Pickering d. 10th day of 1st month, 1727.

Children of Isaac and Sarah (Lupton) Pickering: Joseph Pickering b. 9th day of 5th month, 1739 and d. 13th day of 2nd month, 1792; Sarah Pickering b. 27th day of 2nd month, 1741; Mary Pickering b. 13th day of 5th month, 1743 and d. 14th day of 1st month, 1787; Mercy Pickering b. 27th day of 8th month, 1745; Isaac Pickering b. 24th day of 1st month and d. 21st day of 5th month, 1748; Samuel Pickering (twin) b. 24th day of 1st month, 1748 and d. 29th day of 8th month, 1749; Jonathan Pickering b. 15th day of 3rd month, 1750 and d. 9th day of 7th month, 1804; Rachel Pickering b. 17th day of 2nd month, 1752; Esther Pickering b. 6th day of 6th month, 1755 and d. 9th day of 10th month, 1755.

Sarah Pickering, wife of Isaac, d. 27th day of 5th month, 1778.

Children of John and Hannah (Daws) Pickering: John Pickering b. 27th day of 7th month, 1748; Jesse Pickering b. 10th day of 12th month, 1751 O.S; Hannah Pickering b. 11th day of 4th month, 1754 N.S.

John Pickering d. 1st day of 2nd month, 1787, upwards of 71 years.
Hannah Pickering, wife of John Pickering, d. 14th day of 12th month, 1796, about 85 years.

Children of Samuel and Grace (Stackhouse) Pickering: Mary Pickering b. 30th day of 10th month, 1748; Jacob Pickering b. 4th day of 9th month, 1750 O.S: Benjamin Pickering b. 1st day of 9th month, 1752 N.S; Sarah Pickering b. 2nd day of 9th month, 1754; Samuel Pickering b. 5th day of 2nd month, 1757; Isaac Pickering b. 18th day of 5th month, 1759; Jonathan Pickering b. 28th day of 3rd month, 1761.

Children of John and Rachel (Duer) Pickering: Joseph Pickering b. 26th day of 3rd month, 1772; Mercy Pickering b. 25th day of 1st month, 1774; Benjamin Pickering b. 8th day of 10th month, 1775; John Pickering b. 9th day of 9th month, 1777 and d. 8th day of 10th month, 1831; Phineas Pickering b. 2nd day of 4th month, 1780 and d. 25th day of 10th month, 1818; William Pickering b. 26th day of 5th month, 1782; Yeamans Pickering b. 12th day of 5th month, 1784; Martha Pickering b. 7th day of 10th month, 1786; Stacy Pickering b. 1st day of 4th month, 1789.

Children of Jonathan and Mary (Williams) Pickering: Anna Pickering b. 12th day of 4th month, 1775 and m. David Parry; Elihu Pickering b. 29th day of 1st month, 1777; Isaac Pickering b. 4th day of 3rd month, 1779; Sarah Pickering b. 4th day of 5th month, 1782; Charles Pickering b. 23rd day of 2nd month, 1784 and d. 18th day of 9th month, 1788; Mercy Pickering b. 25th day of 10th month, 1786; Jonathan Pickering b. 27th day of 9th month, 1788 and m. Elisabeth Johnson; Charles Pickering b. 19th day of 3rd month, 1790 and d. 9th day of 8th month, 1803; Samuel Pickering b. 19th day of 8th month, 1791; Joseph Pickering b. 25th day of 11th month, 1792; George Pickering b. 28th day of 9th month, 1794.

Children of Joseph and Ann (Watson) Pickering: Benjamin Pickering b. 17th day of 1st month, 1798; Watson Pickering b. 15th day of 2nd month, 1800.

Children of Isaac and Elisabeth (Carey) Pickering: Joseph Pickering b. 12th day of 7th month, 1787; Thomas Pickering b. 16th day of 10th month, 1789; John Pickering b. 3rd day of 10th month, 1791; Isaac Pickering b. 21st day of 1st month, 1794; James Pickering b. 22nd day of 2nd month, 1796; Stephen Pickering b. 3rd day of 8th month, 1798; Mary Pickering b. 10th day of 10th month, 1800; Mahlon Pickering b. 9th day of 10th month, 1803.

Children of William and Jane Preston, of Bradley, in the Parish of Huddersfield, in old England: John Preston b. 12th day of 2nd month, 1699; Martha Preston b. 30th day of 7th month, 1700; Joseph Preston b. 28th day of 12th month, 1702 and d. 30th day of 5th month, 1716; Sarah Preston b. 6th day of 4th month, 1706; William Preston b. 7th day of 6th month, 1708; Jonas Preston b. 19th day of 11th month, 1710; Mary Preston b. 13th day of 7th month, 1713 and d. 2nd day of 7th month, 1731.

Children of Jonas and Jane (Paxson) Preston: William Preston b. 25th day of 12th month, 1732; Mary Preston b. 24th day of 9th month, 1734.

Children of Henry and Rachel (Beeks) Preston: Henry Preston b. 14th day of 9th month, 1743; Amos Preston b. 19th day of 2nd month, 1746; Sarah Preston b. 30th day of 1st month, 1748 and d. 28th day of 2nd month, 1751; Esther and Rachel (twins) Preston b. 20th day of 2nd month, 1750.

Nathan Preston, son of Amos and Esther (Large) Preston, b. 28th day of 2nd month, 1711 and d. 28th day of 4th month, 1778.

Children of Nathan and Mary (Hough) Preston: Mary Preston b. 13th day of 10th month, 1739 and d. 7th day of 7th month, 1795; Martha Preston b. 31st day of 6th month, 1743 and d. 4th day of 6th month, 1747; Ellinor Preston b. 30th day of 3rd month, 1748.

Mary Preston, wife of Nathan Preston, d. 5th day of 11th month, 1782, aged 67 years, 2 months.

Children of Paul and Hannah (Fisher) Preston: Deborah Preston b. 2nd day of 9th month, 1754 and d. 15th day of 10th month, 1837, a single woman of Doylestown; Samuel Preston b. 17th day of 6th month, 1756; Ann Preston b. 3rd day of 3rd month, 1758 and d. 4th day of 1st month, 1845, a minister at Plumstead; Naomi Preston b. 1st day of 3rd month, 1762; Euphemia Preston b. 15th day of 2nd month, 1765 and d. 25th day of 9th month, 1837, a single woman of Doylestown; Paul Preston b. 10th day of 3rd month, 1767; Silas Preston b. 20th day of 6th month, 1769 and d. 20th day of 2nd month, 1855.

Children of William and Deborah (Chesman) Preston: Martha Preston b. 27th day of 5th month, 1737; Mary Preston b. 17th day of 2nd month, 1740; Ruth Preston b. 15th day of 9th month, 1742; Sarah Preston b. 3rd day of 6th month, 1745; Joseph Preston b. 11th day of 1st month, 1748.

Deborah Preston, wife of William Preston, d. 29th day of 11th month, 1749.

Children of Silas and Margaret (Good) Preston: Francis Preston b. 15th day of 5th month, 1797; Nathan Preston b. 22nd day of 2nd month, 1802; Sarah Preston b. 22nd day of 2nd month, 1806; Margaret Preston b. 13th day of 1st month, 1767 and d. 28th day of 2nd month, 1858.

Children of James and Naomi (Preston) Price: Phebe Price b. 26th day of 9th month, 1786 and d. 27th day of 10th month, 1837; Samuel Price b. 26th day of 5th month, 1789; Joseph Price b. 15th day of 4th month, 1791; Hannah Price b. 24th day of 2nd month, 1797 and d. 9th day of 6th month, 1801; Esther Price b. 13th day of 12th month, 1803.

Children of Moses Quinby, son of Isaiah Quinby, and Jane (Fell), his wife: Josiah Quinby b. 14th day of 6th month, 1783 and d. 10th month, 1802; John Quinby b. 7th day of 12th month, 1784; Elisabeth Quinby b. 18th day of 1st month, 1786; Joseph Quinby b. 8th day of 10th month, 1787; Moses Quinby b. 12th day of 7th month, 1789; Rachel Quinby b. 1st day of 2nd month, 1793; Ann Quinby b. 10th day of 2nd month, 1795.

Richard Randolph, son of Edward and Julianna Randolph, b. 24th day of 1st month, 1791 and d. 15th day of 12th month, 1863. Elizabeth E. Randolph, wife of Richard Randolph and daughter of Hugh and Ruth Ely, b. 28th day of 2nd month, 1794 and d. 12th day of 10th month, 1831.

Children of Joseph and Latitia (Hartley) Rice: Catherine Rice b. 17th day of 2nd month, 1780; William Rice b. 30th day of 4th month, 1782; James Rice b. 7th day of 8th month, 1785; Latitia Rice b. 7th day of 7th month, 1788; James Rice b. 7th day of 2nd month, 1791; Joseph Rice b. 2nd day of 6th month, 1792.

Rachel Rich, wife of John Rich and daughter of Jonathan and Abi Carlile, b. 3rd day of 4th month, 1790.

Children of Alexander and Mary (Michener) Rich: John Rich b. 21st day of 2nd month, 1784 and d. 25th day of 12th month, 1863; Joseph Rich b. 4th day of 6th month, 1788; William Rich b. 4th day of 12th month, 1795.

Richard Roberts, son of Henry and Mary Roberts, b. 8th day of 2nd month, 1730.
Mercy Roberts, wife of Richard Roberts and daughter of Thomas and
Henry Roberts, son of Richard and Mercy (Betts) Roberts, b. 5th day of 6th month, 1760.

Elisabeth Robinson, daughter of Thomas and Elisabeth (Brown) Robinson, b. 30th day of 2nd month, 1727.
Elisabeth Robinson, wife of Thomas Robinson, d. 19th day of 4th month, 1727.

Children of Thomas and Rebecca Rose: Sarah Rose b. 19th day of 10th month, 1768; Thomas Rose b. 5th day of 3rd month, 1731; Ann Rose b. 8th day of 6th month, 1773; Rebecca Rose b. 22nd day of 7th month, 1775; James Rose b. 25th day of 3rd month, 1779; John Rose b. 25th day of 10th month, 1781; Miriam Rose b. 29th day of 12th month, 1783; Deborah Rose b. 23rd day of 3rd month, 1786; Amos Rose b. 26th day of 6th month, 1788.

Children of Thomas and Kesia (Wilkinson) Ross: Mary Ross b. 27th day of 1st month, 1733; John Ross b. 11th day of 11th month, 1734; Kesia Ross b. 4th day of 1st month, 1737.

Rachel Ross, daughter of Thomas and Rachel (Longstreth) Ross, b. 23rd day of 3rd month, 1782.
Rachel Ross, wife of Thomas Ross, 30th day of 5th month, 1782.

Children of John and Mary (Duer) Ross: Sarah Ross b. 1st day of 10th month, 1755; Thomas Ross b. 24th day of 6th month, 1757; Kesia Ross b. 3rd day of 6th month, 1760; John Ross b. 2nd day of 5th month, 1762; Joseph Ross b. 29th day of 5th month, 1764; Isaiah Ross b. 18th day of 12th month, 1766; Mary Ross b. 21st day of 4th month, 1769.

Children of Thomas and Sarah Ruckman: Jonathan Ruckman b. 12th day of 12th month, 1747; Sarah Ruckman b. 8th day of 7th month, 1749.

Children of Joseph and Sarah (White) Ruckman: Achsah Ruckman b. 18th day of 8th month, 1752 and d. 23rd day of 9th month, 1759; Hannah Ruckman b. 20th day of 3rd month, 1754; Mehetable Ruckman b. 21st day of 11th month, 1755 and d. 5th day of 10th month, 1758; Martha Ruckman b. 29th day of 5th month, 1757; Isaiah Ruckman b. 9th day of 1st month, 1759; Sarah Ruckman b. 23rd day of 5th month, 1761.

Children of Robert and Elisabeth Scarborough: John Scarborough b. 28th day of 11th month, 1734; Mary Scarborough b. 18th day of 9th month, 1736.

Children of Robert and Ann (Paxson) Scarborough: Elisabeth Scarborough b. 27th day of 2nd month, 1788; Anne Scarborough b. 9th day of 4th month, 1791; Henry Scarborough b. 12th day of 11th month, 1792 and m. Elisabeth Skelton; Mahlon Scarborough b. 21st day of 7th month, 1794; Mary Scarborough b. 22nd day of 1st month, 1801.

Children of John and Margaret Scarborough: John Scarborough b. 6th day of 5th month, 1761; Robert Scarborough b. 9th day of 3rd month, 1763; Rachel Scarborough b. 8th day of 5th month, 1765; Isaac Scarborough b. 8th day of 5th month, 1769; Elisabeth Scarborough b. 30th day of 11th month, 1772; Charity Scarborough b. 5th day of 11th month, 1774; Joseph Scarborough b. 6th day of 10th month, 1776 and d. 21st day of 6th month, 1813.

Children of John and Ann Scholfield: John Scholfield b. 2nd day of 3rd month, 1725; Jane Scholfield b. 30th day of 6th month, 1726; Isaac Scholfield b. 29th day of 9th month, 1728; David Scholfield b. 9th day of 3rd month, 1730 and d. 6th month, 1733; Thomas Scholfield b. 22nd day of 2nd month, 1732; Samuel Scholfield b. 18th day of 5th month, 1734 and d. 4th day of 9th month, 1801; David Scholfield b. 10th day of 2nd month, 1736; Phebe Scholfield b. 16th day of 5th month, 1739; Jonathan Scholfield b. 24th day of 7th month, 1742.

Children of Benjamin and Martha (Fell) Scholfield: Joseph Scholfield b. 25th day of 5th month, 1794; Edith Scholfield b. 29th day of 7th month, 1796; Samuel Scholfield b. 12th day of 7th month, and d. 25th day of 12th month, 1800; Sarah Scholfield b. 16th day of 7th month, 1802.

John Scholfield, son of Samuel and Edith (Marshall) Scholfield, b. 16th day of 9th month, 1763 and d. 9th day of 5th month, 1848. Edith Scholfield, wife of John Scholfield and daughter of William and Esther Blackfan, b. 10th day of 3rd month, 1769 and d. 4th day of 4th month, 1804.

Elisabeth Scholfield, 2nd wife of John Scholfield and daughter of Thomas and Mercy Bye, b. 5th day of 10th month, 1769 and d. 18th day of 8th month, 1830.

Jane Scott, wife of John Scott of Wrightstown, d. 25th day of 6th month, 1730.
Jane Scott, Jr., d. 25th day of 6th month, 1730.

Children of James and Mary Shaw: Elisabeth Shaw b. 6th day of 10th month, 1719; Joseph Shaw b. 29th day of 10th month, 1721; James Shaw b. 27th day of 1st month, 1724; John Shaw b. 6th day of 3rd month, 1728 and d. 11th day of 11th month, 1740; Jonathan Shaw b. 15th day of 6th month, 1730, m. Sarah Goode, and d. 24th day of 5th month, 1790; Alexander Shaw b. 24th day of 9th month, 1734.

Children of Jonathan and Sarah (Goode) Shaw: Jonathan Shaw b.

18th day of 4th month, 1755 and d. 17th day of 4th month, 1852; Sarah Shaw b. 18th day of 5th month, 1757; Mary Shaw b. 28th day of 5th month, 1759 and m. Jacob Paxson; John Shaw b. 9th day of 1st month, 1761 and m. Elisabeth Brown; Thomas Shaw b. 13th day of 12th month, 1762; Rebeckah Shaw b. 7th day of 5th month, 1765; Elisabeth Shaw b. 29th day of 12th month, 1766; Joseph Shaw b. 5th day of 8th month, 1768; James Shaw b. 22nd day of 1st month, 1771; Anna Shaw b. 15th day of 10th month, 1773.

Children of John and Sarah (Skelton) Shaw: Anna Shaw b. 8th day of 7th month, 1778; Elisabeth Shaw b. 6th day of 12th month, 1780; Mary Shaw b. 1st day of 5th month, 1783.

John Shaw, the father, d. 19th day of 6th month, 1783.

Children of Alexander and Sarah (Brown) Shaw: George Shaw b. 2nd day of 4th month, 1760; James Shaw b. 14th day of 5th month, 1762 and d. 29th day of 10th month, 1765; Mary Shaw b. 8th day of 11th month, 1764; Alexander Shaw b. 6th day of 9th month, 1767 and m. Martha Wilson; John Shaw b. 28th day of 4th month, 1769 and m. Martha Brown; Hannah Shaw b. 29th day of 2nd month, 1772; Sarah Shaw b. 18th day of 10th month, 1774; Aaron Shaw b. 19th day of 8th month, 1778 and m. Susanna Brown.

Alexander Shaw, the father, d. 11th day of 1st month, 1790.

Children of Joseph and Mary (Pryor) Shaw: Charles Shaw b. 21st day of 12th month, 1787, m. Martha Pettit, and d. 6th day of 12th month, 1828; James Shaw b. 25th day of 6th month, 1790 and m. Elisabeth Watson; John Shaw b. 22nd day of 6th month, 1792; Joseph P. Shaw b. 4th day of 7th month, 1794; Susanna Shaw b. 15th day of 6th month, 1797 and d. 13th day of 8th month, 1801; David Shaw b. 24th day of 1st month, 1799; Jesse Shaw b. 12th day of 2nd month, 1801; Mathias Shaw b. 29th day of 11th month, 1802; Mary Shaw b. 4th day of 8th month, 1805.

Children of Joseph and Elisabeth Shaw: Sarah Shaw b. 17th day of 7th month and d. 31st day of 7th month, 1796; Jonathan Tyson Shaw b. 21st day of 11th month, 1797; Maria Shaw b. 16th day of 11th month, 1799; William Shaw b. 12th day of 3rd month, 1802 and d. 13th day of 8th month, 1803; Rebecca Shaw b. 1st day of 6th month, 1804.

Children of John and Martha (Brown) Shaw: Elia Shaw b. 10th day of 7th month, 1700; Robert Shaw b. 14th day of 4th month, 1801; Sarah Shaw b. 15th day of 3rd month, 1805.

Children of Alexander and Martha (Wilson) Shaw: Sarah Shaw b. 18th day of 10th month, 1799; Hannah Shaw b. 27th day of 4th month, 1801; George Shaw b. 10th day of 4th month, 1806 and d. 29th day of 11th month, 1811; Stephen Shaw b. 9th day of 3rd month, 1811; Rebecca Shaw b. 3rd day of 9th month, 1813.

Sarah B. Shaw, 2nd wife of Josiah Shaw, of Solebury, and daughter

of Thomas and Mercy Bye, b. 7th day of 1st month, 1781 and d. 29th day of 7th month, 1831.
Martha Shaw, wife of Charles Shaw and daughter of William and Lydia Pettit, b. 6th day of 12th month, 1788 and d. 17th day of 9th month, 1849.

Children of Cornelius and Catherine Shepherd: Rachel Shepherd b. 3rd day of 7th month, 1762 and m. Joseph Burges; Joseph Shepherd b. 31st day of 5th month, 1764; Margaret Shepherd b. 14th day of 10th month, 1766 and m. Isaiah Michener; Jonathan Shepherd b. 8th day of 6th month, 1771; Mary Shepherd b. 9th day of 6th month, 1774.

John Simpson b. 23rd day of 10th month, 1739.
Ruth Simpson, wife of John Simpson and daughter of David Whitson, b. 23rd day of 1st month, 1733 and d. 21st day of 3rd month, 1805.

Children of John and Ruth Simpson: David Simpson b. 4th day of 4th month, 1765 and d. 5th day of 6th month, 1831; Hannah Simpson b. 20th day of 4th month, 1767; John Simpson b. 5th day of 8th month, 1769 and m. Elisabeth Blackfan; Ruth Simpson b. 21st day of 12th month, 1772; James Simpson b. 17th day of 6th month, 1775.

Children of David and Agnes (Wiggins) Simpson: Ruth Simpson b. 3rd day of 4th month, 1795 and d. 16th day of 3rd month, 1856; Sarah Simpson b. 13th day of 10th month, 1797 and d. 7th day of 4th month, 1856; John Simpson b. 19th day of 4th month, 1799 and d. 31st day of 1st month, 1878; Rachel Simpson b. 20th day of 7th month, 1802 and d. 23rd day of 2nd month, 1828; Hannah Simpson b. 8th day of 2nd month, 1804 and d. 30th day of 12th month, 1868; Agnes Simpson b. 6th day of 8th month, 1808 and d. in 1868.

Children of Samuel and Mary (Lowther) Simson: Joel Simson b. 16th day of 5th month, 1746, O.S, and d. 27th day of 8th month, 1752, N.S; James Simson b. 7th day of 1st month, 1748, O.S; Martha Simson b. 13th day of 3rd month, 1750, O.S., and d. 1st day of 9th month, 1752, N.S: Benjamin Simson b. 25th day of 7th month, 1752, N.S; Samuel Simson b. 12th day of 10th month, 1754; William Simson b. 15th day of 9th month, 1756; Amos Simson b. 26th day of 10th month, 1760.

Children of William and Susanna (Beck) Skelton: Rachel Skelton b. 19th day of 6th month, 1749; Susanna Skelton b. 16th day of 8th month, 1751, O.S; William Skelton b. 8th day of 7th month, 1753, N.S; Jane Skelton b. 15th day of 3rd month, 1755; Ann Skelton b. 15th day of 9th month, 1757; Jonathan Skelton b. 16th day of 4th month, 1760; Jesse Skelton, b. 9th day of 10th month, 1763; Sarah Skelton b. 18th day of 12th month, 1765; Robert Skelton b. 9th day of 6th month, 1769.

John Skelton, Jr., son of John and Jane Skelton, b. 2nd day of 1st month, 1736.

Margaret Skelton m. John Townsend.

Children of Joseph and Mary (Townsend) Skelton: John Skelton b. 14th day of 10th month, 1752 and m. Sarah Kimble; Joseph Skelton b. 8th day of 5th month, 1754 and m. Elisabeth J. Johnson; Mary Skelton b. 29th day of 4th month, 1756 and m. Joseph White; Sarah Skelton b. 3rd day of 11th month, 1758 and m. John Shaw; Martha Skelton b. 29th day of 4th month, 1761 and m. Benjamin White.

Joseph Skelton, the father, d. 5th day of 3rd month, 1762.

Children of Robert and Jane (Beck) Skelton: Sarah Skelton b. 18th day of 6th month, 1745; Ellinor Skelton b. 12th day of 7th month, 1749.

Children of Joseph and Mary (Casey) Skelton: Mary Skelton b. 19th day of 2nd month, 1778; Joseph Skelton b. 25th day of 1st month, 1780; Jason Skelton b. 28th day of 6th month, 1781; Rhoda Skelton b. 29th day of 2nd month, 1784; Elisabeth Skelton b. 30th day of 7th month, 1785.

Children of Robert and Phebe (Canby) Smith: Thomas Smith b. 13th day of 6th month, 1720 and d. 15th day of 3rd month, 1806; Timothy Smith b. 29th day of 1st month, 1722 and d. 14th day of 5th month, 1798; Robert Smith b. 11th day of 12th month, 1724; John Smith b. 20th day of 12th month, 1726; Joseph Smith b. 1st day of 8th month, 1728 and d. 16th day of 8th month, 1729.

Robert Smith, the father, d. 26th day of 6th month, 1745.

Children of Wm. Smith, Jr., and Rebecca (Wilson), his wife: Sarah Smith b. 12th day of 3rd month, 1724; Wm. Smith b. 12th day of 5th month, 1726; Thomas Smith b. 30th day of 10th month, 1728.

Children of Thomas and Elisabeth (Lana_ _?) Smith: Thomas Smith b. 13th day of 6th month, 1728; Samuel Smith b. 17th day of 1st month, 1730; Wm. Smith b. 6th day of 1st month, 1732.

Children of Thomas and Elisabeth (Kinsey) Smith: Robert Smith b. 16th day of 6th month, 1743 and d. 6th day of 6th month, 1745; Phebe Smith (twin) b. 16th day of 6th month, 1743 and d. 13th day of 6th month, 1745; Edmund Smith b. 3rd day of 4th month, 1745 and m. (1) Sarah Dawson, (2) Deborah Fell, (3) Mary (Story) Briggs; Thomas Smith b. 22nd day of 4th month, 1747; Elisabeth Smith b. 2nd day of 7th month, 1749; Sarah Smith b. 5th day of 11th month, 1752; Ellen Smith b. 11th day of 11th month, 1754; John Smith b. 8th day of 1st month, 1757 and d. 14th day of 3rd month, 1763; Martha Smith b. 24th day of 11th month, 1758; David Smith b. 11th day of 12th month, 1761 and m. Eleanor Blackfan.

Elizabeth Smith, wife of Thomas Smith, d. 16th day of 5th month, 1790, aged 73 years.
Thomas Smith, son of John and Sarah Smith, b. 8th day of 8th month, 1730.

Children of Samuel Smith, son of John Smith (formerly of Cold Spring, near Bristol) and Elisabeth, his wife: John Smith b. 13th day of 2nd month, 1742; Abraham Smith b. 6th day of 4th month, 1744; Thomas Smith b. 12th day of 3rd month, 1746; Henry Smith b. 27th day of 7th month, 1748.

Children of Timothy and Sarah (Kinsey) Smith: Jonathan Smith b. 1st day of 7th month, 1746 and d. 2nd day of 1st month, 1767; Robert Smith b. 22nd day of 5th month, 1749; Sarah Smith b. 22nd day of 1st month, 1752 and d. 3rd day of 4th month, 1752; Joseph Smith b. 7th day of 7th month, 1753; Sarah Smith b. 9th day of 11th month, 1755; Mary Smith b. 25th day of 7th month, 1758; Jane Smith b. 12th day of 6th month, 1761 and d. 8th day of 5th month, 1806.

Children of Henry and Alice (Hill) Smith: Sam'l Smith b. 17th day of 4th month, 1754; George Smith b. 20th day of 8th month, 1756; John Smith b. 7th day of 7th month, 1760; Thomas Smith b. 24th day of 7th month, 1762.

Children of Thomas and Sarah (Townsend) Smith: John Smith b. 18th day of 12th month, 1753 and d. 31st day of 7th month, 1785; Aaron Smith b. 9th day of 10th month, 1755; Nehemiah Smith b. 23rd day of 3rd month, 1757; Sarah Smith b. 29th day of 12th month, 1758; Dorothy Smith b. 27th day of 7th month, 1760 and d. 12th day of 5th month, 1775; Ann Smith b. 21st day of 7th month, 1762; Mary Smith b. 12th day of 8th month, 1764; Prudence Smith b. 17th day of 2nd month, 1766; Hannah Smith b. 27th day of 11th month, 1767; Rachel Smith b. 20th day of 5th month, 1769; Leah Smith b. 19th day of 4th month, 1771 and d. 19th day of 9th month, 1777; Tamar Smith b. 16th day of 6th month, 1773 and d. 3rd day of 9th month, 1777.

Thomas Smith, the father, d. 30th day of 9th month, 1777.
Sarah Smith, wife of Thomas Smith, d. 2nd day of 12th month, 1776.

Children of Wm. and Ann (Williams) Smith: Ezekiel Smith b. 30th day of 11th month, 1755; Mahlon Smith b. 20th day of 4th month, 1757; Sarah Smith b. 2nd day of 2nd month, 1759; Wm. Smith b. 11th day of 3rd month, 1761; Edith Smith b. 9th day of 8th month, 1765; Ann Smith b. 29th day of 10th month, 1770; Jane Smith b. 4th day of 2nd month, 1773.

Children of Robert and Elisabeth (Hughes) Smith: Sarah Smith b. 31st day of 5th month, 1771; Timothy Smith b. 26th day of 9th month, 1772; Rebeckah Smith b. 16th day of 4th month, 1774; Mary Smith b. 27th day of 12th month, 1775 and d. 10th day of 8th month, 1782; Benjamin Smith b. 28th day of 12th month, 1777; Esther Smith b. 11th day of 4th month, 1780 and d. 5th day of 11th month, 1780; Robert Smith b. 15th day of 1st month, 1783 and m. Mary Canby; Elias H. Smith b. 2nd day of 6th month, 1786 and d. 17th day of 7th month, 1814; Cyrus Smith b. 6th day of 3rd month, 1788.

Children of David and Eleanor (Blackfan) Smith: Robert Smith b. 10th day of 7th month, 1791; David Smith b. 10th day of 2nd month, 1793; Jonathan Smith b. 17th day of 3rd month, 1796 and m. Elisabeth Smith; John Smith b. 18th day of 1st month, 1799; Hannah Smith b. 8th day of 10th month, 1803.

Jonathan Smith, son of Edmund and Sarah (Dawson) Smith, b. 31st day of 1st month, 1768.
Sarah Smith, wife of Edmund Smith, d. 19th day of 3rd month, 1770.

Children of Edmund Smith and Deborah (Fell), his 2nd wife: Samuel Smith b. 3rd day of 5th month, 1777; Edmund Smith b. 22nd day of 12th month, 1778; Benjamin Smith b. 26th day of 9th month, 1780; Joshua Smith b. 25th day of 5th month, 1782; Jesse Smith b. 12th day of 3rd month, 1784.

Children of Thomas and Elisabeth (Ely) Smith: Hannah Smith b. 4th day of 7th month, 1777; John Smith b. 9th month, 1779; Hugh Smith b. 28th day of 8th month, 1781 and m. (1) Rebecca Smith, (2) Elisabeth Heston; Thomas Smith b. 15th day of 1st month, 1784; Ely Smith b. 5th day of 2nd month, 1786 and d. 1st day of 4th month, 1790; Elisabeth Smith b. 17th day of 9th month, 1788 and d. 20th day of 2nd month, 1789; Samuel Smith b. 20th day of 12th month, 1793.

Children of Joseph and Ann Smith: Jonathan Smith b. 2nd day of 12th month, 1775; Joseph Smith b. 9th day of 9th month, 1777 and m. Hannah Smith; William Smith b. 3rd day of 6th month, 1779; George Smith b. 20th day of 4th month, 1781 and d. 30 day of 4th month, 1870; Mahlon Smith b. 5th day of 6th month, 1783 and m. Deborah Kinsey; Amos Smith b. 20th day of 12th month, 1785; Charles Smith b. 25th day of 9th month, 1788 and m. Martha Brown; Jonas Smith b. 29th day of 9th month, 1790 and m. Miriam Paxson; Albert Smith b. 2nd day of 1st month, 1793; Daniel Smith b. 2nd day of 3rd month, 1795 and m. Hannah Betts; Phebe Smith b. 4th day of 6th month, 1797; Sarah Smith b. 29th day of 4th month, 1800.

Children of Joseph and Elisabeth (Smith) Stockdale: Sarah Stockdale b. 20th day of 11th month, 1771; Elisabeth Stockdale b. 18th day of 7th month, 1773; John Stockdale b. 14th day of 9th month, 1774; Mary Stockdale b. 27th day of 8th month, 1777.

Joseph Stockdale, the father, d. 5th day of 8th month, 1777.

David Story, son of John and Elisabeth Story, b. 20th day of 4th month, 1760 and d. 23rd day of 3rd month, 1833.
Rachel Story, wife of David Story and daughter of William and Elisabeth Richardson, b. 21st day of 11th month, 1765 and d. 9th day of 11th month, 1844.

Children of David and Rachel Story: Hannah Story b. 23rd day of 3rd month, 1794; John Story b. 15th day of 1st month, 1796 and d.

22nd day of 10th month, 1844; Mary Story b. 23rd day of 3rd month, 1800; Elisabeth Story b. 6th day of 3rd month, 1807.

Children of Thomas and Lydia Stradling: Joseph Stradling b. 16th day of 9th month, 1726; Lydia Stradling b. 15th day of 6th month, 1729; Mehetable Stradling b. 2nd day of 1st month, 1732.

Children of Joseph and Hannah Stradling: Daniel Stradling b. 11th day of 3rd month, 1780; Joseph Stradling b. 3rd day of 12th month, 1781; Sarah Stradling b. 23rd day of 9th month, 1783; Hannah Stradling b. 13th day of 7th month, 1785; Elisabeth Stradling b. 20th day of 8th month, 1787 and d. 19th day of 4th month, 1789; Deborah Stradling b. 12th day of 11th month, 1789.

Hannah Stradling, wife of Joseph Stradling, d. 28th day of 5th month, 1790.

Children of Joseph and Sarah (Shaw) Stradling: John Stradling b. 12th day of 8th month, 1792; Thomas Stradling b. 15th day of 9th month, 1794 and m. Marg. ?Shaw; William Stradling b. 5th day of 11th month, 1796; Samuel Stradling b. 26th day of 8th month, 1798; Martha Stradling b. 21st day of 12th month, 1801.

Daniel Stradling, Sr., d. 29th day of 1st month, 1796.

Banner Taylor, son of Joseph and Martha Taylor, b. 4th day of 9th month, 1789.
Elisabeth Taylor, wife of Banner Taylor, b. 19th day of 11th month, 1790.

Children of Jonah and Ann Thompson: Sarah Thompson b. 1st day of 3rd month, 1798; John Thompson b. 14th day of 2nd month, 1801; Mark Thompson b. 29th day of 11th month, 1802; Jonathan Thompson b. 29th day of 4th month, 1806.

Children of Joseph and Mary Thornton: Elisabeth Thornton b. 1st day of 7th month, 1786; Beulah Thornton b. 4th day of 7th month, 1788; Samuel Carey Thornton b. 14th day of 1st month, 1791; Ann W. Thornton b. 16th day of 12th month, 1793; John Pearson Thornton b. 15th day of 3rd month, 1798; Carey Thornton b. 3rd day of 10th month, 1800; Rutledge Thornton b. 31st day of 1st month, 1806; Mary Thornton b. 26th day of 12th month, 1809; Wm. Pearson Thornton b. 29th day of 9th month, 1813.

Children of William and Margaret (Paxson) Townsend: John Townsend b. 9th day of 8th month, 1764; Joseph Townsend b. 13th day of 8th month, 1766; Stephen Townsend b. 2nd day of 5th month, 1768.

Children of William and Elisabeth (Watson) Townsend: Mary Townsend b. 22nd day of 12th month, 1774; William Townsend b. 22nd day of 7th month, 177_; Elisabeth Townsend b. 19th day of 7th month, 1779; Thomas Townsend b. 5th day of 4th month, 1781.

Children of John and Rebecca (Shaw) Townsend: Sarah Townsend b.

8th day of 10th month, 1792; Aaron Townsend b. 14th day of 2nd month, 1794; Jonathan Townsend b. 26th day of 2nd month, 1796; Joseph Townsend b. 17th day of 10th month, 1800; Elisabeth Townsend b. 4th day of 11th month, 1802; Moses Townsend b. 25th day of 4th month, 1806 and d. 19th day of 9th month, 1817.

Children of Joseph and Mary (Hartley) Townsend: David Townsend b. 2nd day of 1st month, 1791; Joseph Townsend b. 20th day of 2nd month, 1792; Elisabeth Townsend b. 13th day of 2nd month, 1793; Anne Townsend b. 6th day of 5th month, 1794; Stephen Townsend b. 25th day of 5th month, 1795; John Townsend b. 6th day of 7th month, 1797; Charles Townsend b. 31st day of 8th month, 1798; Levi Townsend b. 26th day of 8th month, 1799; Amos Townsend b. 26th day of 1st month, 1801; Sarah Townsend b. 29th day of 9th month, 1802; Mahlon Townsend b. 4th day of 12th month, 1803; Samuel H. Townsend b. 2nd day of 11th month, 1805; Senecca P. Townsend b. 14th day of 1st month, 1810.

Ann Townsend, wife of Jonathan Townsend, b. 20th day of 7th month, 1796.

Sarah Tucker, wife of Nicholas Tucker, d. 11th day of 9th month, 1768.

Children of Robert and Lydia (Allen) Tucker: James Tucker b. 6th day of 10th month, 1739; Mary Tucker b. 1st day of 10th month, 1741.

Robert Tucker b. 1st day of 8th month, 1744.
Lydia Tucker b. 20th day of 7th month, 1747.

Children of Jacob and Phebe (Tucker) Twining: Malachi Twining b. 3rd day of 1st month, 1794; Mary Twining b. 2nd day of 11th month and d. 2nd day of 12th month, 1795; Phebe Twining b. 7th day of 5th month, 1798; Joseph Twining b. 10th day of 1st month, 1800; John Twining b. 22nd day of 3rd month, 1802; Sarah Twining b. 1st day of 1st month, 1804; Hannah Twining b. 12th day of 4th month, 1807.

Jacob Twining, son of Jacob and Sarah Twining, b. 30th day of 6th month, 1786 and d. 22nd day of 2nd month, 1871.
Priscilla Twining, wife of Jacob Twining and daughter of Thomas and Mary Buckman, b. 6th day of 7th month, 1787 and d. 26th day of 9th month, 1876.

Elisabeth (Duckworth) Verity, wife of John Verity, d. 6th day of 10th month, 1726.
Jacob Verity, son of John and Elisabeth (Bye) Verity, b. 8th day of 5th month, 1728.

Children of Thomas and Rebecca (Dillon) Vickers: Esther Vickers b. 9th day of 4th month, 1747; John Vickers b. 3rd day of 8th month, 1749; Mary Vickers b. 3rd day of 9th month, 1752; Rebecca Vickers b. 1st day of 7th month, 1754; Thomas Vickers b. 8th day of 3rd month, 1757; Rachel Vickers b. 6th day of 9th month, 1759; Abraham Vickers b. 17th day of 1st month, 1762; Mercy Vickers b. 19th day of 8th month, 1764.

Children of Robert and Mary Walker: Robert Walker b. 3rd day of 10th month, 1761; Joseph Walker b. 27th day of 9th month, 1763 and d. 30th day of 8th month, 1790; Mary Walker b. 13th day of 1st month, 1766; Randall Walker b. 19th day of 6th month, 1768; Mahlon Walker b. 9th day of 6th month, 1769 and d. 23rd day of 9th month, 1777; Jesse Walker b. 8th day of 9th month, 1771 and d. 18th day of 4th month, 1776; David Walker b. 6th day of 1st month, 1774 and d. 7th day of 9th month, 1777; Phineas Walker b. 18th day of 9th month, 1776; Benjamin Walker b. 12th day of 3rd month, 1779; Sarah Walker b. 18th day of 4th month, 1784.

Mary Walker, wife of Robert Walker, d. 30th day of 1st month, 1790.

Children of Robert Walker and Asenath (Beans), his 2nd wife: Ann Walker b. 17th day of 8th month, 1792; Amos Walker b. 22nd day of 11th month, 1794; Stacy Walker b. 25th day of 2nd month, 1797; John Walker b. 6th day of 4th month, 1799; Elisabeth Walker b. 27th day of 9th month, 1802.

Children of Jacob and Ann Walton: John Walton b. 17th day of 12th month, 1742; Mary Walton b. 23rd day of 1st month, 1744.

Children of Jacob Walton and Mary (Holcomb), his 2nd wife: Jacob Walton b. 6th day of 8th month, 1751 and d. 1st day of 10th month, 1817; Jesse Walker b. 8th day of 3rd month, 1754; Ann Walker b. 6th day of 8th month, 1755; Isaac Walton b. 17th day of 12th month, 1756; Rachel Walton b. 14th day of 4th month, 1758; William Walker b. 27th day of 9th month, 1759; Joseph Walker b. 11th day of 12th month, 1761; Amos Walker b. 1st day of 4th month, 1763.

Jacob Walton, the father, d. 7th day of 10th month, 1776.

Children of Joshua and Elisabeth Walton: Isaac Walton b. 17th day of 12th month, 1770; Thomas Walton b. 12th day of 11th month, 1772; Joshua Walton b. 6th day of 1st month, 1777; Elisabeth Walton b. 3rd day of 11th month, 1787; Nathan Walton b. 26th day of 11th month, 1789.

Elisabeth Walton, wife of Joshua (a minister), d. 7th day of 5th month, 1790, aged 43 years.

Children of Jacob and Lydia (Gilbert) Walton: Jacob Walton b. 22nd day of 9th month, 1779; Thomas Walton b. 19th day of 6th month, 1781; Alice Walton b. 16th day of 5th month, 1783; Sarah Walton b. 20th day of 12th month, 1786.

Children of John and Hannah (Carey) Walton: Mary Walton b. 29th day of 10th month, 1771 and d. 14th day of 8th month, 1777;

Jonathan Walton b. 30th day of 7th month, 1773 and d. 19th day of 8th month, 1777; David Walton b. 21st day of 1st month, 1776 and d. 9th day of 8th month, 1778; Jacob Walton b. 14th day of 12th month, 1778; John Walton b. 16th day of 9th month, 1781; Jesse Walton b. 24th day of 9th month, 1784; Samuel Walton b. 19th day of 4th month, 1788 and d. 14th day of 6th month, 1801.

Susanna Warner, daughter of John and Susanna (Buckman) Warner, b. 17th day of 8th month, 1775.

Children of John and Ann (Biles) Watson: Elisabeth Watson b. 22nd day of 12th month, 1717, m. John Fell, and d. 13th day of 3rd month, 1812; Joseph Watson b. 21st day of 11th month, 1718; Thomas Watson b. 22nd day of 8th month, 1721 and d. 31st day of 1st month, 1787.

Ann Watson, wife of John Watson, d. 12th day of 9th month, 1787, aged 53 years.
John Watson, Practitioner of Physics, d. 22nd day of 10th month, 1760, aged 64 years.
John Watson, son of Joseph and Alice (Mitchell, Jr.) Watson, b. 12th day of 6th month, 1746 O.S. and d. 23rd day of 10th month, 1817.

Children of Thomas and Sarah (Woolston) Watson: Thomas Watson b. 2nd day of 7th month, 1761; Elisabeth Watson b. 6th day of 1st month, 1764, m. Isaiah Jones and d. 16th day of 3rd month, 1806; Joseph Watson b. 27th day of 1st month, 1766 and d. 2nd day of 7th month, 1786; Sarah Watson b. 4th day of 14th month, 1767; Ann Watson b. 1st day of 1st month, 1771 and d. 20th day of 9th month, 1777.

Sarah Watson, widow of Thomas Watson, d. 14th day of 9th month, 1792.

Children of John and Mary (Hampton, Jr.) Watson: Alice Watson b. 4th day of 12th month, 1772; John Watson b. 25th day of 8th month, 1774; Frances Watson b. 7th day of 6th month, 1777 and d. 25th day of 5th month, 1790; Ann Watson b. 12th day of 9th month, 1778 and d. 28th day of 12th month, 1812; Rachel Watson b. 15th day of 1st month, 1781; Joseph Watson b. 16th day of 9th month, 1783; Mary Watson b. 18 day of 3rd month, 1787 and d. 21st day of 5th month, 1790; Sarah Watson (twin) b. 18th day of 3rd month, 1787.

Mary Watson, wife of John Watson, d. 29th day of 12th month, 1788.

Children of Thomas and Mary (Verree) Watson: Anne Watson b. 21st day of 8th month, 1791; Mary Watson b. 2nd day of 7th month, 1794; Sarah Watson b. 30th day of 12th month, 1796; Thomas Watson b. 13th day of 4th month, 1800; Elisabeth Watson b. 1st day of 12th month, 1802; Robert Watson b. 14th day of 9th month, 1805.

Children of John and Mary Watson: Sarah Watson b. 4th day of 10th month, 1779 and d. 21st day of 10th month, 1784; William Watson b. 25th day of 10th month, 1781; Aaron Watson b. 2nd day of 11th month, 1783; Hannah Watson b. 14th day of 11th month, 1785, Wm. M. Gillingham, and d. 12th day of 9th month, 1822; Joseph Watson b. 31st day of 12th month, 1787; Charles Watson b. 18th day of 10th month, 1790; Sarah Watson b. 5th day of 11th month, 1792; Elisabeth Watson b. 20th day of 4th month, 1795 and d. 28th day of 12th month, 1812; Elisa Ann Watson b. 31st day of 7th month, 1797 and d. 28th day of 12th month, 1812; Marmaduke Watson b. 3rd day of 1st month, 1800; Mary Watson b. 28th day of 6th month, 1802; John Emley Watson b. 7th day of 2nd month, 1805.

Children of John and Euphemia (Ingham) Watson: Frances Watson b. 24th day of 5th month, 1796; Jonathan Watson b. 10th day of 10th month, 1797; Joseph Watson b. 17th day of 12th month, 1799; Isaiah Watson b. 29th day of 8th month, 1801 and d. 29th day of 12th month, 1822; Hannah Watson b. 26th day of 4th month, 103; John Hampton Watson b. 30th day of 12th month, 1804; Euphemia Ann Watson b. 28th day of 9th month, 1806; Anthony Harris Watson b. 28th day of 4th month, 1809; Sam'l. Ingham Watson b. 26th day of 4th month, 1816.

Euphenia Watson, wife of John Watson and daughter of Jonathan and Anna Ingham, b. 29th day of 3rd month, and d. 5th day of 6th month, 1816.

Daniel White m. Ann Dillon, 24th day of 9th month, 1747.
Amos White b. 14th day of 5th month, 1748.

Children of Joseph and Mary (Skelton) White: Joseph White b. 16th day of 1st month, 1777; Sarah White b. 21st day of 7th month, 1780; Daniel White b. 26th day of 10th month, 1782; Thomas White b. 9th day of 11th month, 1785; Martha White b. 11th day of 11th month, 1788; Martha White b. 28th day of 3rd month, 1792; Mary White b. 14th day of 5th month, 1795; Mercy white b. 1st day of 9th month, 1798.

Children of Benjamin and Martha (Skelton) White: Mary White b. 1st day of 4th month, 1781; Joseph White b. 4th day of 11th month, 1782 and d. 2nd day of 12th month, 1783; Job White b. 29th day of 11th month, 1784; Hannah White b. 27th day of 12th month, 1786; Sarah White b. 16th day of 2nd month, 1789; Rachel White b. 15th day of 6th month, 1791; Latitia White b. 27th day of 3rd month, 1794; Mercy White b. 25th day of 3rd month, 1796; Deborah White b. 6th day of 6th month, 1798 and d. 1799.

Benjamin Wiggins, son of Benjamin and Sarah Wiggins, b. 26th day of 3rd month, 1774 and d. 31st day of 8th month, 1863.
Margaret Wiggins, wife of Benjamin Wiggins and daughter of John and Susanna Buckman, b. 29th day of 3rd month, 1774 and d. 1st day of 9th month, 1840.
Sarah Wiggins, daughter of Benjamin and Sarah Wiggins, b. 3rd day of 6th month, 1782 and d. 13th day of 11th month, 1857.

Children of Joseph and Sarah (Paxson) Wilkinson: Rachel Wilkinson b. 4th day of 11th month, 1779; Elisabeth Wilkinson b. 28th day of 12th month, 1780; Henry Wilkinson b. 29th day of 10th month, 1783; Joseph Wilkinson b. 15th day of 4th month, 1785.

Children of Samuel and Rebecca (Canby) Wilson: Thomas Wilson b. 19th day of 1st month, 1731 and d. 23rd day of 7th month, 1803; Mary Wilson b. 2nd day of 10th month, 1732 and d. 19th day of 11th month, 1805; Sarah Wilson b. ?10/16th day of 8th month, 1734 and d. 23rd day of 10th month, 1809; Samuel Wilson b. 20th day of 10th month, 1736 and d. 13th day of 12th month, 1813; Elisabeth Wilson b. 10th day of 6th month, 1739 and d. 28th day of 1st month, 1821; Rachel Wilson b. 5th day of 4th month, 1741 and d. 8th day of 3rd month, 1810; Rebecca Wilson b. 7th day of 6th month, 1743 and d. 22nd day of 6th month, 1814; John Wilson b. 15th day of 5th month, 1745; Hannah Wilson b. 2nd day of 5th month, 1747 and d. 16th day of 7th month, 1826; Stephen Wilson b. 2nd day of 7th month, 1749 and d. 9th day of 4th month, 1818; Oliver Wilson b. 17th day of 10th month, 1751 and d. 15th day of 9th month, 1846; David Wilson b. 23rd day of 8th month, 1754 and d. 25th day of 4th month, 1826; Isaac Wilson b. 14th day of 3rd month, 1757 and d. 8th day of 5th month, 1827

Children of Thomas and Margaret (Bye) Wilson: Joseph Wilson b. 25th day of 3rd month, 1757; Jonathan Wilson b. 24th day of 2nd month, 1759 and d. 11th day of 12th month, 1764; Benjamin Wilson b. 27th day of 3rd month, 1761.

Margaret Wilson, wife of Thomas Wilson, d. 11th day of 12th month, 1763.

Children of Thomas Wilson and Maire (Croasdale), his 2nd wife: Grace Wilson b. 22nd day of 5th month, 1766; Thomas Wilson b. 14th day of 12th month, 1768; Ezra Wilson b. 7th day of 9th month, 1771.

Children of Samuel and Mary (Baily) Wilson: John Wilson b. 27th day of 4th month, 1766; Samuel Wilson b. 4th day of 7th month, 1768; Thomas Wilson b. 21st day of 6th month, 1770; Mary Wilson b. 10th day of 2nd month, 1773; Joseph Wilson b. 8th day of 12th month, 1775; Mercy Wilson b. 14th day of 12th month, 1778.

Children of John and Elisabeth (Fell) Wilson: John Wilson b. 2nd day of 5th month, 1772; Rebecca Wilson b. 8th day of 10th month, 1773; Hannah Wilson b. 10th day of 1st month, 1775 and d. 23rd day of 8th month, 1777; Jonathan Wilson b. 23rd day of 9th month, 1776; Joel Wilson b. 23rd day of 9th month and d. 29th day of 10th month, 1779; Amos Wilson (twin) b. 23rd day of 9th month, 1779; Hannah Wilson b. 21st day of 11th month, 1781 and d. 3rd day of 3rd month, 1782.

Children of Oliver and Sarah Wilson: Ann Wilson b. 21st day of 1st month, 1781; John Wilson b. 27th day of 8th month, 1783.

Children of Stephen and Sarah (Blackfan) Wilson: Martha Wilson b. 9th day of 3rd month, 1780; Rachel Wilson b. 17th day of 7th month, 1781 and m. Seneca Ely; Rebeckah Wilson b. 5th day of 4th month, 1783, m. Samuel Ely and d. 16th day of 5th month, 1818; Hannah Wilson b. 1st day of 1st month and d. 5th day of 1st month, 1785; Samuel Wilson b. 1786 and d. 28th day of 1st month, 1859; Hannah Wilson b. 15th day of 3rd month, 1788 and d. 25th day of 10th month, 1822; Elisabeth Wilson b. 13th day of 11th month, 1789; Stephen Wilson b. 5th day of 5th month, 1792; Oliver Wilson b. 13th day of 2nd month, 1796, m. Ann W. Thornton and d. 27th day of 8th month, 1822.

Children of Jesse and Amy Wilson: Isaac Wilson b. 28th day of 7th month, 1791 and d. 22nd day of 2nd month, 1800; Rachel Wilson b. 28th day of 9th month, 1793; Elisabeth Wilson b. 11th day of 11th month, 1796; Amos Wilson b. 15th day of 1st month, 1799; Grace Wilson b. 16th day of 8th month, 1802.

Children of Jonathan and Mary (Child) Worthington: Zenas Worthington b. 1st day of 12th month, 1783; Cephus Worthington b. 19th day of 1st month, 1786; Jane Worthington b. 27th day of 10th month, 1787; Maire Worthington b. 23rd day of 10th month, 1789; William Worthington b. 8th day of 7th month, 1792.

Joseph Worthington b. 1753 and d. 27th day of 10th month, 1829. Jonathan Worthington b. 31st day of 12th month, 1766 and d. 13th day of 3rd month, 1837.

Children of Solomon and Rachel (Pickering) Wright: Sidney Wright b. 14th day of 8th month, 1788; Isaac Wright b. 20th day of 10th month, 1789; Sarah Wright b. 12th day of 5th month, 1791; John Wright b. 27th day of 12th month, 1792; Solomon Wright b. 20th day of 3rd month, 1794.

MAKEFIELD MONTHLY MEETING

BIRTHS AND DEATHS

Children of Thomas and Mary Linton, of Northampton Tp., Bucks Co; Asa Cary Linton b. 1st day of 5th month, 1797; Isaiah Linton b. 3rd day of 7th month, 1798; Mary Linton b. 20th day of 10th month, 1803; Silas Linton b. 21st day of 6th month, 1806; Thomas Linton b. 2nd day of 1st month, 1807 and d. 13th day of 7th month, 1824.

Joseph Flowers, son of William and Elisabeth Flowers, b. 27th day of 12th month, 1799 and d. 8th day of 6th month, 1867.

Children of Joseph and Elisabeth Buckman, of Newtown Tp: Sarah Buckman b. 12th day of 3rd month, 1793; Martha Buckman b. 23rd day of 12th month, 1795; Joseph Buckman b. 26th day of 1st month, 1799 and d. 8th day of 9th month, 1828; Linton Buckman b. 26th day of 12th month, 1801 and d. 25th day of 7th month, 1827; Letitia Buckman b. 22nd day of 3rd month, 1804; Elizabeth Buckman b. 17th day of 9th month, 1806; George Buckman b. 28th day of 11th month, 1808 and d. 6th day of 4th month, 1809; Levi Buckman b. 16th day of 6th month, 1810.

Joseph Buckman d. 16th day of 9th month, 1828, aged 76 yrs., 16 days.
Elisabeth Buckman, wife of Joseph Buckman, d. 16th day of 3rd month, 1832, aged 63-3-13.

Children of Benjamin and Mary Field, of Lower Makefield Tp: William Field, Jr. b. 23rd day of 10th month, 1799; Joseph Field b. 6th day of 6th month, 1801; Hannah Field, Jr. b. 3rd day of 7th month, 1803; Elizabeth Field b. 18th day of 11th month, 1805; Cyrus Field b. 26th day of 9th month, and d. 22nd day of 12th month, 1807.

Oliver Hough, Jr., of Upper Makefield Tp., was b. 27th day of 8th month, 1763 and d. 18th day of 1st month, 1804.

William Field, Sr. was b. 6th day of 8th month, 1751 and d. 25th day of 12th month, 1799.

Children of Thomas and Susan Yardley, of Lower Makefield Tp: Elizabeth Yardley b. 9th day of 5th month, 1787; Mary Yardley b. 6th day of 12th month, 1788; William Yardley b. 20th day of 12th month, 1791; Mercy Yardley b. 29th day of 10th month, 1793; Sarah B. Yardley b. 1st day of 3rd month, 1796; George Yardley b. 24th day of 5th month, 1798; Thomas H. Yardley b. 3rd day of 12th month, 1800; Edward Yardley b. 6th day of 11th month, 1802; Susannah Letitia Yardley b. 16th day of 6th month, 1806.

Mary Lownes, wife of William Lownes, of Upper Makefield Tp., d. 23rd day of 8th month, 1807, in her 71st year.

Children of John and Sarah Scott, of Upper Makefield Tp: John Scott, Jr. b. 8th day of 6th month, 1786; Samuel Scott b. 13th day of 4th month, 1788; Abraham Scott b. 10th day of 9th month, 1791 and d. 17th day of 9th month, 1801.

Jacob Cadwallader, son of Jacob and Phebe Cadwallader, b. 21st day of 11th month, 1768.
Ann Cadwallader, daughter of Timothy and Ann (Taylor) Cadwallader, b. 23rd day of 8th month, 1773.

Children of Joseph and Sarah Yardley, of Lower Makefield Tp: Isaac Yardley b. 30th day of 7th month, 1799; Mary Yardley b. 20th day of 10th month, 1801; Susannah Yardley b. 29th day of 9th month, 1803; Letitia Yardley b. 13th day of 1st month, 1807.

Children of Jonathan and Sarah Buckman, of Lower Makefield Tp: Stacy Buckman b. 28th day of 1st month, 1779; Mahlon Buckman b. 18th day of 4th month, 1781; Mary Buckman b. 21st day of 11th month, 1783; Jonathan Buckman b. 26th day of 4th month, 1786; Amos Buckman b. 21st day of 7th month, 1789; Sarah Buckman b. 17th day of 12th month, 1791; Frances Buckman b. 9th day of 6th month, 1795; Ascah Buckman b. 8th day of 8th month, 1797.

John Worstall, son of James and Esther Worstall, of Middletown Tp., b. 3rd day of 9th month, 1765.
Ruth Worstall, wife of John Worstall and daughter of Samuel and Ruth Hillborn, b. 5th day of 3rd month, 1772.

Children of John and Ruth Worstall, of Upper Makefield Tp: Samuel Worstall b. 14th day of 11th month, 1797; Rachel Worstall b. 24th day of 11th month, 1799; Robert Worstall b. 8th day of 9th month, 1801; Joseph Worstall b. 21st day of 8th month, 1803 and d. 2nd day of 10th month, 1803; Jonathan Worstall b. 13th day of 8th month, 1804; James Worstall b. 22nd day of 3rd month, 1807.

Children of John and Mary Knowles, of Upper Makefield Tp: Robert Knowles b. 21st day of 4th month, 1759; Mary Knowles b. 10th day of 10th month, 1768.

Joseph Winder, son of Thomas and Elizabeth Winder, of Lower Makefield Tp., b. 8th day of 3rd month, 1764.
Ruth Winder, daughter of John and Eleanor (Buckman) Winder, b. 3rd day of 2nd month, 1766.

Children of Joseph and Ruth Winder, of Lower Makefield Tp: Elizabeth Winder b. 25th day of 1st month, 1793; John Winder b. 5th day of 7th month, 1794 and d. 14th day of 11th month, 1814; Rachael Winder b. 28th day of 2nd month, 1796; Joseph Winder b. 5th day of 3rd month, 1798; Thomas Winder b. 16th day of 1st month, 1800; Amos Winder b. 19th day of 3rd month, 1802.

Children of Jonathan and Rachael Paxson, of Upper Makefield Tp: Rebeckah Paxson b. 11th day of 7th month, 1772; Jane Paxson b. 26th day of 2nd month, 1774; Sarah Paxson b. 27th day of 12th month, 1775; Rachael Paxson b. 4th day of 10th month, 1778; Deborah Paxson b. 21st day of 10th month, 1780; Betsy Paxson b. 13th day of 10th month, 1782; Mary Paxson b. 17th day of 11th month, 1784; Letitia Paxson b. 17th day of 1st month, 1787; Esther Paxson b. 15th day of 10th month, 1789; Jonathan Paxson b. 21st day of 8th month, 1791.

Children of John and Hannah Stapler, of Lower Makefield Tp: Elizabeth Stapler b. 15th day of 7th month, 1799 and d. 23rd day of 1st month, 1817; Christianna Stapler b. 23rd day of 9th month, 1803.

Charles Buckman, son of Samuel and Rachael Buckman, b. 13th day of 5th month, 1785.

Children of Mahlon and Elizabeth Yardley, of Makefield: Sarah Yardley b. 16th day of 4th month, 1788; Ann Yardley b. 6th day of 2nd month, 1790; Acsah Yardley b. 1st day of 9th month, 1792; John Yardley b. 9th day of 12th month, 1794; Hannah Yardley b. 25th day of 4th month, 1797; Robert Yardley b. 18th day of 11th month, 1799; Charles Yardley b. 4th day of 8th month, 1802; Elizabeth Yardley b. 21st day of 7th month, 1807.

Children of Phineas and Sarah (Taylor) Briggs: William T. Briggs b. 21st day of 12th month, 1800; Susanna Briggs b. 6th day of 2nd month, 1802 and d. 19th day of 1st month, 1803; Samuel Briggs b. 29th day of 11th month, 1803; Yardly Briggs b. 21st day of 9th month, 1805; James Briggs b. 29th day of 10th month, 1807; Sarah Ann Briggs b. 2nd day of 9th month, 1810; Theodore L. Briggs b. 7th day of 1st month, 1812; Mary Briggs b. 29th day of 3rd month, 1816 and d. 6th day of 10th month, 1822.

Phineas Briggs d. 22nd day of 11th month, 1823.
Sarah Briggs, widow of Phineas Briggs, mar. Micajah Speakman.

Jonathan Buckman, of Newtown Tp., b. 29th day of 4th month, 1755 and d. 4th day of 10th month, 1826, aged 71-5-5-.

Sarah Buckman, of Philadelphia, b. 11th day of 9th month, 1757 and d. 27th day of 2nd month, 1840.

SOLEBURY MONTHLY MEETING

BIRTHS AND DEATHS

Children of George and Sarah Ely: Robert Ely b. 19th day of 10th month, 1799; Timothy Ely b. 8th day of 5th month, 1801 and d. 13th day of 9th month, 1813; Jervis Ely b. 5th day of 12th month, 1803; Esther Ely b. 18th day of 5th month, 1805 and d. 14th day of 9th month, 1813; Smith Ely b. 28th day of 2nd month, 1807; Matilda Ely b. 7th day of 5th month, 1809 and d. 27th day of 9th month, 1813; George Ely b. 11th day of 1st month, 1815.

Children of Benajah and Martha Hayhurst: Sarah Hayhurst b. 6th day of 3rd month, 1798; Abi Hayhurst b. 8th day of 9th month, 1799; Rachel Hayhurst b. 25th day of 4th month, 1801; Marmaduke Hayhurst b. 5th day of 9th month, 1804 and d. 28th day of 7th month, 1826; Ethelbert Hayhurst b. 3rd day of 12th month, 1806; Kesia Hayhurst b. 14th day of 8th month, 1810; Ann Hayhurst b. 10th day of 9th month, 1817; Laman Hayhurst b. 3rd day of 4th month, 1823.

Surnames were recorded with various spellings; consider all possible variations. The name may appear more than once on the page; check the entire page.

-A-

ABBET, Catherine, 69
ABBETT, Catherine, 57, 59
ADAMS, Jane, 114
  Judadiah, 44
  Rebekah, 47
ADAMSON, Ann, 74, 110
  Betty, 74
  Deborah, 74
  Esther, 74
  Hannah, 74, 116, 118
  Hester, 74
  James, 74, 123
  John, 74, 128
  Joseph, 74
  Martha, 74, 122, 123
  Mary, 74, 114, 123
  Rachel, 74
  Sarah, 74, 123
  Simon, 106
  Susanna, 74
  Thomas, 74, 123, 125, 128
ALLIBONE, Esther, 65
  Hester, 64
  Mary, 64
AMBLER, Joseph, 59
  W., 90
ANTRAM, Hannah, 113
ANTRIM, Jane, 109
ARBUCKLE, James, 39
ARMITAGE, Amos, 141
  Anna, 141
  Charles, 141
  Elizabeth, 141
  Hannah, 141
  Henry, 141
  Hervey, 141
  James, 141
  Jane, 141
  John, 141
  Letitia, 141
  Martha, 141
  Martha Dennis, 141
  Martha Doan, 141
  Mary, 141
  Samuel, 141
  Sarah, 61, 141
  Sarah Foster, 141
  Seba, 141
ASHTON, Abigail, 74
  Eleanor, 74
  Eliza Roberts, 74
  Jane, 74
  John, 104, 135
  Margaret, 74, 131
  Martha, 102
  Mary, 56, 59, 74
  Peter, 74, 104, 128, 129
  Phebe, 74
  Robert, 74, 106
  Samuel, 74, 134
  Sarah, 74
  Thomas, 74, 102, 104, 109, 135
ASTON, Isaac, 39
ATKINSON, Benjamin, 55
  Cephas, 43, 59, 65
  Cephus, 11
  Christopher, 11, 43, 50, 56
  Edmund L., 20
  Eleanor, 7, 54
  Elizabeth, 7, 11
  Ezekiel, 11, 55, 68
  Ezekiell, 44
  Isaac, 7, 27, 72
  Jane, 35, 59
  John, 7, 11, 16, 30, 35, 50, 54, 64, 65, 67
  Jonathan, 16
  Joseph, 7, 16, 141
  Mahlon, 16
  Margaret, 59
  Mary, 5, 7, 11, 16, 33, 34, 44, 50, 52
  Moses, 56
  Phebe, 7
  Rachel, 55
  Rachel Child, 141
  Sarah, 5, 7, 16, 54, 63, 141
  Thomas, 5, 7, 11, 16, 30, 33, 41, 54, 55, 62, 63
  Timothy, 16
  Watson, 55
  William, 7, 11, 14, 31, 34, 72
AUSTIN, Amos, 160
  Elizabeth, 141
  Hannah, 141
  Isaac, 141
  Joseph, 108, 112
  Latitia, 141
  Lydia, 141
  Martha, 141
  Mary, 141
  Nicholas, 141
  Robert, 141
  Samuel, 141
  Sarah, 141, 160
  Susanna, 108, 112, 141

-B-

BACON, Joseph, 66
BAINS, Tamar, 62
BAKER, Henry, 147
  Margret, 43
BALANCE, Dorothy, 24
BALDERSON,

Bartholomew, 8
Hannah, 8
Isaiah, 8, 52
Jacob, 8, 52
John, 8, 52
Jonathan, 8, 55
Lydia, 8, 52
Mary, 8, 52
Mordaicai, 8
Mordicah, 52
Rachel, 28
Sarah, 8, 52
Timothy, 8, 57
BALDERSTON, Ann, 142
David, 27
Deborah, 36, 37, 142
Elizabeth, 27, 142
Ezra, 142
Hannah, 52, 141, 142
Isaiah, 27
John, 27, 31, 36, 37, 51, 52, 141, 142
John D., 153
John W., 142
Lydia, 27
Marah, 142
Mark, 142
Mary, 27
Rachael, 27
Sarah, 27
Timothy, 27, 31
BALDWIN, William, 41
BALL, Aaron, 75, 128, 133
Abraham, 74, 110, 137, 138
Ann, 75, 133
Catherine, 74
Elizabeth, 74, 132
Hannah, 75, 133
Iden, 75, 137
James, 75, 133, 137
Jesse, 74, 75, 133, 137
Joel, 75, 133, 137
John, 74, 75, 90, 110, 111, 112, 114, 118, 137
Joseph, 74, 75, 100, 105, 108, 111, 114, 115, 117, 119, 128, 133, 137
Margaret, 74, 75, 128, 133, 137, 138
Margret, 128
Martha, 30
Mary, 51, 64, 117, 122, 126
Nathan, 122, 124, 125, 138, 139
Peter, 39, 48, 96
Petter, 43
Rebecca, 75, 89
Rebecka, 133
Sarah, 74, 75, 100, 133, 137
Susanna, 75, 133, 137
Thomas, 136
William, 133
William H., 75
BALLANCE, Anna, 29, 65
Catherine, 29
Dorathy, 71
Dorithy, 10
Dorothy, 63
John, 10, 29
Joseph, 10, 29, 64
Mary, 29
Rachel, 29
Simeon, 29
Susanna, 29
Thomas, 10
BANKS, Sarah, 97
BARCRAFT, John, 72
Lydia, 72
BARCROFT, Lydia, 70
BEALE, Elizabeth, 142
Grace, 142
Grace Gill, 142
Hannah, 142
Hannah Russel, 142
Jane, 142
John, 142
Joseph, 142
Lydia, 142
Martha, 142
Mercy, 142
Phebe, 142
Philip, 142
Rachel, 142
Rachel E. Parry, 142
Samuel, 142
Sarah, 142
Thomas, 142
William, 142
BEANS, Aaron, 143
Amos, 143
Ann, 143
Asenth, 143
Benjamin, 143
Charles, 143
David, 143
Elizabeth, 143
Elizabeth Rice, 143
George, 143
Hannah, 55, 137, 143
Isaac, 10, 143
Jacob, 35, 137, 143
Jane, 143
Jesse, 143
John, 143
Jonathan, 143
Joseph, 143, 168
Levi, 143
Mahlon, 35, 143
Mary, 143
Mary Burges, 143
Mary Smith, 143
Matthew, 143
Oliver, 143
Rachael, 26
Rachel, 143
Rachel Hillbourn, 143
Rebeckah, 143
Samuel, 143
Sarah, 143
Sarah Hartley,

143
Sarah Mitchener, 143
Sarah Smith, 143
Susanna, 143
Tamar, 143
William, 52
BEAUMONT, Jane, 63
John, 31, 32, 41, 46, 63, 66
Mercy, 32
Rebeckah, 31
Sarah, 32, 55
BENDER, Susannah, 59
BETTLE, Everard, 130, 132
BETTS, Ann, 5, 60
Anna, 143
Bethula, 55
Cyrus, 20
Esther, 24, 70, 143
Hannah, 143, 184
Hannah Blackfan, 143
Isaac, 5, 144
James P., 144
Jesse, 23, 70
John, 5, 36, 65, 143
Latitia, 143
Mariam, 24, 34
Martha, 143
Mary, 5, 70
Mercy, 24, 70
Miriam, 70
Phebe, 5
Rachael, 24
Rachel, 70
Rebecca, 53
Rebekah, 5
Richard, 42, 58, 62, 65
Samuel, 24, 70
Sarah, 5, 31, 36, 143
Stephen, 5, 143
Susanna, 32, 62, 64
Susannah, 5, 47, 49, 63
Tamar, 144
Thomas, 5, 24, 31, 32, 33, 36, 41, 70
William, 5, 59, 143
Zachariah, 5, 24, 32, 49, 50, 51, 54, 64, 70
BEVAN, Samuel, 101, 102, 110
BIGGS, Jane, 32
Thomas, 10
BILES, Ann, 118
Anne, 132
Hannah, 118
John, 118
Ruth, 118
BILLS, Rachel, 53, 54
Rebecca, 54
Rebekah, 53
BITTLE, Hannah, 101
BLACKFAN, Crispin, 32, 144
Edward, 32, 144
Eleanor, 182
Elisabeth, 181
Esther, 179
Joseph, 144
Martha Davis, 144
Mary, 65
Mary Smith, 144
Miranda, 144
Samuel, 144
William, 179
BLACKFANN, Latitia, 66
BLACKLEDGE, Anne, 128
Elizabeth, 112, 118, 127
Enoch, 122
Joanna, 112
Joseph, 132
Mary, 119
Rachel, 135
Rebecca, 122
Robert, 112, 127, 131
Ruth, 127
Thomas, 105, 106, 112, 122, 132
William, 105
BLACKLEY, Robert, 110
BLACKLIDGE, Elizabeth, 75, 98, 104
Rachel, 75
Thomas, 75
William, 75, 105
BLACKSON, William, 17
BLACKSTON, Crispin, 18
Martha, 18
BLAKER, Abraham, 25
Achilles, 61
Agnes, 144
Alice, 59
Amos, 25
David, 25
Hannah, 144
John, 9, 25, 30, 31, 34, 38, 46, 53, 58
Joseph, 25
Judith, 144
Lydia, 144
Mary, 31, 47, 144
Paul, 56, 64
Peter, 25, 50, 53, 144
Phebe, 34
Samuel, 40, 144
Sarah, 25, 30, 61, 144
William, 52, 144
BLAKEY, Lydia, 172
BOAMAN, Jeremiah, 57
BOLTON, Everard, 105, 111
Isaac, 111
BOND, Abraham, 75, 103
Benjamin, 75
Edward, 75
Hannah, 75
John, 75
Joshua, 75
Mary, 75
Rebecca, 75
Sarah Cadwalter,

75
BOON, James, 75
John, 75
____, 78
BOUGHER, Hannah, 122
BOWMAN, Jeremiah, 46
BRADFIELD, Abner, 144
Benjamin, 144
Elisabeth, 163
Elizabeth, 144
George, 144
Hannah, 144
Hannah Pennington, 144
James, 144
Jane, 144
John, 144
Jonathan, 144
Lavinia, 163
Rachel, 144
Uri McGill, 144
William, 144
BRADSHAW, David, 144
Elizabeth, 144
Elizabeth Carver, 144
James, 144
Martha, 144
Mary, 144, 145, 167
Ruth, 144
Samuel, 144
Sarah, 144, 145
Sarah Preston, 144
Sidney, 144
Susanna, 144
William, 144
BRIGGS, Amos, 15, 28
Ann, 15, 33, 51
Benjamin, 43, 45
David, 15
Deidamia, 60
Dudamia, 34
Edmund, 34
Elennor, 42
Elinor, 9
Elizabeth, 15, 33
James, 14, 15, 33, 40, 42, 46, 52, 194
John, 15, 37, 51, 54, 64
Joseph, 44, 46, 53, 56
Letitia, 37
Margret, 47
Mary, 15, 36, 46, 49, 52, 55, 194
Mary Story, 182
Phineas, 15, 194
Rachael, 15
Rachel, 56
Samuel, 46, 49, 194
Sarah, 37, 194
Sarah Ann, 194
Sarah Taylor, 194
Susanna, 194
Theodore L., 194
Thomas, 15
William, 12, 24, 39, 41, 43, 59, 62, 71
William T., 194
Yardly, 194
BROCK, Sarah, 131
BROOKS, Adam, 145
Hepsibah, 145
BROWN, Abraham, 145
Agnes Penquite, 146
Alexander, 145, 146
Amos, 146
Ann, 145
Ann Dawson, 145
Anne, 132
Deborah Wilson, 146
Elisabeth, 146, 180
Elisabeth Kinsey, 146
Elizabeth, 145
Elizabeth Dawson, 145
Esther, 145, 146
Esther Dyer, 145
George, 145, 146, 165
Isaac, 145
James, 112, 145
Jane, 63, 145
Jane Harvey, 145
John, 145, 146, 153
Jonathan, 145
Joseph, 145
Josiah, 145, 146
Levina, 146
Martha, 145, 146, 180, 184
Mary, 138, 145
Mary Preston, 145
Matthias, 145
Moses, 145, 146
Rachel Child, 146
Samuel, 146
Sarah, 145, 146, 165
Susanna, 145, 180
Thomas, 145, 146
BRUNDAGE, Bartlet, 14
BUCHER, Hannah, 117
BUCKMAN, Abdon, 9
Abner, 12, 13, 60, 62
Abraham, 69
Acsah, 193
Agnes, 10, 33, 38, 56
Aldon, 28
Amos, 13, 28, 193
Ann, 13, 68
Anna, 16, 29
Asceneth, 70
Asenath, 10
Benjamin, 16, 24, 29, 64, 71
Cadwalader, 16
Chapman, 13
Charles, 16, 69, 194
Cyrus, 23
David, 9, 16, 29, 41, 45, 46,

52, 54, 57, 58, 65, 67, 69
Deborah, 16, 29, 65, 69
Dilworth, 13
Edmund, 16, 29
Elinor, 9
Elisabeth, 192
Elizabeth, 10, 12, 13, 16, 30, 32, 33, 36, 37
Ellin, 12
Esther, 16, 29, 62, 67
Esther Penquite, 146
Ezra, 13
Frances, 193
George, 13, 192
Hannah, 13, 16, 23, 55, 56, 59, 67, 71, 142
Hester, 10, 12, 16
Isaac, 16, 30, 44, 63, 65, 69, 146
Jacob, 12, 13, 22, 46, 63
James, 12, 28, 64
Jane, 12, 13, 23, 28, 64
Jesse, 23, 70, 71
John, 9, 13, 16, 29, 34, 36, 37, 41, 57, 58, 64, 67, 189
Joice, 63
Jonathan, 9, 62, 65, 193, 194
Joseph, 10, 31, 33, 41, 42, 52, 192
Joyce, 16, 65, 69
Joyce Fell, 16
Julian, 28
Latitia, 192
Letitia, 10, 54
Levi, 192
Lidia, 13
Linton, 192
Lydia, 28
Mahlon, 65, 193
Margaret, 9, 13, 58, 59
Martha, 10, 13, 192
Mary, 10, 12, 16, 31, 37, 69, 186, 193
Oliver, 16, 29
Phineas, 25, 28, 72
Phinias, 12
Rachael, 9, 16, 28, 29
Rachel, 67, 194
Rebecca, 146
Ruth, 9, 25
Samuel, 9, 194
Sarah, 10, 12, 13, 28, 34, 40, 62, 63, 64, 65, 192, 193, 194
Stacy, 65, 193
Susanna, 13, 25, 189
Susannah, 13, 36, 37
Thomas, 23, 46, 54, 61, 66, 69, 186
William, 12, 13, 14, 30, 32, 34, 36, 37, 55, 142, 146
Zenas, 16
BUDD, Joseph, 26
BURGES, Aaron, 146
Agness, 146
Ann, 146
Daniel, 146
Deborah Fisher, 146
Elisabeth, 146
George, 146
Hannah, 146
Hiram, 146
Jesse, 146
John, 146
Jonathan, 146
Joseph, 146, 181
Latitia, 146
Margaret Michener, 146
Martha, 146
Mary, 146
Phebe, 146
Rachel, 146
Rachel Shepherd, 146
Sarah, 146
Tace, 146
Thomas, 146
William, 146
BURGESS, Ann, 41
Martha, 43
Mary, 44
Sarah, 46
BURR, Ann, 75
David, 75
Elizabeth, 126
Henry, 75
Jane, 75
Joseph, 126, 129, 130
Martha, 75
Mercy, 107
Reuben, 75
Robert, 75, 107, 111
Samuel, 75
Timothy, 75
William, 75, 109, 112, 126, 127
BURROUGHS, Sarah, 64
BURSON, David, 115, 118
Isaac, 118, 122
James, 33, 99, 122
Joseph, 33
Lydia, 118
Mary, 113, 132, 137
Rachel, 106
Sarah, 65, 123, 127
Sarh, 137
BUTLER, Grace, 2
Isaac, 3
John, 2, 3, 32, 48
Mary, 2, 3
Thomas, 2, 38
BYE, Anne, 147
Cyrus, 147

Elisabeth, 147
Elisabeth Ross, 147
Enoch, 146, 147
Hesekiah, 147
Jane, 147
Jemima, 147
John, 146, 147
Jonas, 147
Jonathan, 147
Lydia, 147
Margaret, 147
Martha, 147
Mary, 147
Mercy, 147, 179, 181
Mercy Woolston, 147
Nathaniel, 147
Rachel, 147
Rebecca, 147
Samuel, 147
Sarah, 146, 147
Thomas, 147, 179, 181
BYRAN, Diana, 96

-C-

CADWALADER, Joel, 137
CADWALLADER, Ann, 193
Ann Taylor, 193
Jacob, 193
Phebe, 193
Timothy, 193
CAMERON, Dugald, 103
CANBY, Ann, 148
Anna, 149
Benjamin, 147, 148
Beulah, 174
Charles, 148
Christianna, 149
Elias, 149
Elisabeth, 149
Elizabeth, 148
Esther, 148
Hannah, 148, 149
Hannah Moore, 148
Jane, 148
John, 148, 149
Joseph, 148
Julia, 149
Lydia, 50, 148
Martha, 148
Martha Preston, 148
Mary, 148, 149, 183
Mary Oliver, 148
Mary Skelton, 148
Moore, 149
Oliver, 148
Phebe, 148
Rachel, 148
Rebecca, 148, 149
Samuel, 148
Sarah, 147, 148, 149
Sarah Jarvis, 147
Sarah Yardley, 148
Thomas, 3, 147, 148, 149, 174
William, 148
Zacheus, 148
CARE, Deborah, 139
CAREY, Ellis, 167
Hannah, 90, 167
Samuel, 82
Thomas, 90
CARLILE, Abi, 177
Amos, 149
Ann, 149
Benjamin, 149
Daniel, 32, 149
David, 149
Elisabeth, 149
Elisabeth Smith, 149
Elizabeth, 65
John, 32, 149
Jonathan, 149, 177
Rachel, 149
Rebecca, 149
Samuel, 149
Sarah, 149
Sarah Pennington, 149
CARLISLE, John, 62
CARNAGHAN, Joseph, 111
CARR, David, 118, 149
Deborah, 149
Dorathy, 39
Elizabeth, 61
Grace, 149
Hannah, 113, 149
Hannah Michener, 149
John, 10, 149
Jonathan, 83, 149
Joseph, 149
Martha, 10, 42
Mary, 93, 120
Rachel, 136
Sarah, 42, 118
CARRINGTON, Mary, 103
Thomas, 103, 104
CARTER, Agness, 51
Rachel, 47
William, 49, 50
CARVER, Ann, 69
Anna, 149
Eli, 149
Hannah Carey, 149
Henry, 45, 149
Joel, 32, 69
John, 31
Joseph, 69, 149
Martha, 69
Mary, 57, 147, 149
Rachel, 69, 149
Robert, 69
Sarah, 47
Thomas, 149
William, 45
CARY, Barthula, 54
Rachel, 61, 62
Samuel, 62
Thomas, 56, 58
CASNER, Ann, 113
Thomas, 108
CAWLEY, Sarah, 49
CHAPMAN, Aaron, 14
Abbott, 76
Abigail, 76
Abraham, 1, 11, 13, 30, 32, 46, 49, 65, 68, 73,

107
Abrahanm, 33
Alice, 53, 60
Amos, 17, 65
Ann, 10, 11, 12, 17, 47, 48, 53, 60, 85
Benjamin, 1, 12, 26, 70
Charles, 1, 12, 17, 26, 32, 49, 107
David, 14, 65
Edward, 11, 17
Elisa, 1
Elizabeth, 1, 11, 12, 26, 30, 49, 76, 85, 107
Hannah, 75, 76, 116, 118
Isaac, 11, 44
Isaiah, 12, 26
Jacob, 76
James, 1, 32, 76, 107, 112, 114
Jane, 1, 32, 33, 53, 76
Jesse, 17
John, 1, 12, 17, 32, 35, 36, 48, 49, 50, 51, 71, 75, 76, 107, 108, 113, 132, 136
Jonathan, 11
Joseph, 1, 2, 11, 12, 26, 27, 36, 46, 53
Latitia, 26
Letitia, 12
Margaret, 1, 29, 60
Margery, 71
Martha, 17
Mary, 1, 12, 26, 45, 49, 57, 107, 109
Mercy, 12, 26, 30, 35, 36
Miles, 53, 60
Mira, 1, 49, 60, 107
Myra, 120
Penquite, 14
Rachael, 14, 17
Rebecca, 17, 26, 76, 115
Rebeckah, 12
Robert, 1, 107, 122, 124
Ruth, 32
Samuel, 12
Sarah, 1, 12, 14, 35, 36, 40, 53, 107, 112
Seth, 24, 72
Stephen, 12, 26
Susanna, 26, 58, 107
Susannah, 1, 12, 34, 49
Tamar, 14
Thomas, 1, 11, 28, 42, 51, 53, 60, 138
William, 1, 12, 13, 14, 34, 41, 56
William Ross, 17
CHAPMANN, Jonathan, 12
CHILCOT, Amos, 121, 134
Ann, 135
Jane, 130, 131
John, 119, 135
Martha, 135
Mary, 135
Peninna, 135
Rachel, 135
Sarah, 135
William, 111, 135
CHILD, Cadwalader, 138, 139
Cadwallader, 150
Cephas, 38
Cephus, 149, 150
Deborah Michener, 150
George, 150
Henry, 150
Isaac, 150
Israel, 150
Jane, 150
John, 150
Jonathan, 150
Joseph, 149
Joshua, 150
Mary, 149, 150
Mary Cadwallader, 150
Mary Shoemaker, 150
Naylor, 150
Priscilla, 150
Priscilla Naylor, 149
Rachel, 150
Richard, 150
Sarah, 150
Sarah Shoemaker, 150
Thomas, 150
William, 150
CHRISTY, Martha, 104, 110, 117
Mary, 117
Thomas, 98, 99, 100, 101, 102, 104
CHURCH, Abi, 150
Asenath, 150
Elisabeth, 150
John, 150
Joseph, 150
Millicent, 150
Moses, 150
Rachel, 150
Richard, 150
Sarah, 150
Sarah Fell, 150
CLARK, Abigail, 76, 111, 112
Abraham, 19
Ann, 19
Benjamin, 19
Eleazer, 76
Elizabeth, 19, 76
Esther, 19
Gabriel, 76
Hannah, 19, 76
Jane, 19
Joseph, 19
Martha, 76, 130
Mary, 19, 61, 66, 76, 111, 112, 134, 137
Michael, 76, 112
Samuel, 76, 83, 111, 113
Samuel J., 76

Sarah, 19, 76
Solomon, 19
Thomas, 76
Walter, 76
William, 76, 111, 130
CLARKE, Ann, 51
CLERK, Ann, 51
CLOAK, Petter, 40
CLOSON, Elizabeth, 34, 66
John, 34
COATS, Elisa, 150
John, 150
Mary Hambleton, 150
Moses, 150
Paxson, 150
Seneca, 150
William, 150
COHOE, Debora, 116
COLLARD, John, 119
COLLINS, Andrew, 20, 21, 33, 65
Esther, 21
Joseph, 21
Martha, 21
Mary, 21
Rachael, 21
Rebecca, 55
COLP, Deborah, 136
COMFORT, Alice, 151
Alice Fell, 150
Ann, 150, 151
Ann Eastburn, 151
Elisabeth, 151
Ezra, 150, 151
Jesse, 68
John, 150, 151
Mercy, 151
Rachel, 151
Robert, 46, 51
Sarah, 151
Stephen, 40, 45
COMFORTE, Robert, 42, 44
Stephen, 45
COMLEY, Isaac, 61
COMLY, Abigaile, 31
Asceneth, 56
Elizabeth, 55, 60
Isaac, 56
Joseph, 31
CONRAD, Deidamy, 25
Dennis, 25
CONROD, Dennis, 34
COOP, Jonathan, 41
COOPER, Amos, 27
Caroline, 29
Charles, 151
Chilion, 69
Elizabeth, 29
Esther, 30, 69, 151
Henry, 29, 69
Jacob, 42, 69, 151
James, 29
Jane, 151
Jeremiah, 40, 55
Job, 59
John, 29, 30, 38, 52, 54, 69, 151
Jonathan, 8, 151
Levi, 151
Levy, 30
Mahlon, 30, 69, 151
Margaret, 69
Martha, 69
Mary, 29, 54
Nancy, 151
Phebe, 53
Rachael, 29
Rachel, 59
Sarah, 28, 69, 151
Thomas, 53, 54
William, 29, 45, 50, 52, 55
COSET, Mary, 124
COWGILL, Abraham, 151
Dorithy, 151
Dorothy, 151
Isaac, 151
Jacob, 151
John, 151
Mary, 151
Nehemiah, 151
Ralph, 151
Sarah, 151
CRAWFORD, Amy, 128, 129, 138, 139
CREW, Martha, 99
CROASDALE, Ann, 40, 42
Jeremiah, 4, 42
Mare, 50
CROSDALE, Macre, 32
Mary, 41
CUNNARD, Edward, 56
CURRY, Mary, 25, 61
CUSTARD, Amelia, 76
Ann, 76
George, 76, 81
Joseph, 76
Mary, 76
CUSTER, Joseph, 78, 127
CUTLER, Benjamin, 31
Mary, 54
Mercy, 31
CUTTER, Sarah, 30
Thomas, 30

-D-

DALBEY, Abner, 93
DALBY, Abigail, 121
DAMSON, Joseph, 111
Simon, 105
DAVID, Griffith, 96
DAVIDS, Hugh, 26
Susanna, 118, 119
DAVIES, David, 100, 103
John, 76
Mary, 76
Susanna, 76, 113, 119
DAVIS, David, 24, 68, 72, 97
Griffith, 32, 99
Hannah, 124
Lidia, 18
Morris, 18

Samuel, 18, 35
Sarah, 32
Seth, 18
Susanna, 104, 110
DAWES, Alice, 55
David, 40
Elizabeth, 42
John, 54
Rebeckah, 43
Sarah, 40
DAWS, Adrian, 38
David, 46
DAWSON, Sarah, 182
DEAN, Alexander, 40, 41
Eleaser, 44
James, 39, 41
John, 42
Joseph, 41
Katherine, 39
Ruth, 47
Samuel, 39
Samuell, 40, 41
DENNIS, Amos, 114, 116, 121
Ann, 114, 115
Anne, 76
Catherine, 76, 118
Charles, 98
Debora, 109
Eleanor, 118, 130
Ezekiel, 76, 114, 115, 128
Hannah, 76
Henry, 151
Isaac, 128
Jesse, 76
John, 76, 119, 125, 126
Joseph, 76, 101, 109, 112, 128
Josiah, 133
Kezia, 76, 113, 114
Levi, 120
Lewis, 76
Martha, 151
Sarah, 65, 76, 123, 140
Tamar, 76
DENNY, Hannah, 129
DERBORAH, Mary, 55
DILLON, Ann, 66, 189
Bridgget, 63
Deborah, 50, 51
Hannah, 48, 53, 66
James, 14, 48, 50
John, 14, 43, 45, 66
Josiah, 50, 66
Moses, 14
Rebecca, 14
Sarah, 66
William, 44, 45, 50
DILWORTH, Amos, 151, 171
Hannah, 55, 151, 171
Joseph, 151
Mary, 151
DOAN, Abegale, 49
Abigail, 60
Agnes, 151
Amos, 71
Ann, 1, 24, 65, 70, 72
Anna, 151
Benjamin, 34, 47
Daniel, 46, 49
Ebeneser, 151
Ebenezer, 11
Eleaser, 151
Eleazer, 14, 43, 55, 62
Elijah, 1
Elizabeth, 49, 59
Elizabeth Balderston, 151
Grace, 11, 50
Hannah, 152
James, 11
James Hartley, 151
Jemima, 152
Joel, 152
Johannah, 1
John, 11, 39, 63
Jonas, 62, 151
Jonathan, 62, 151, 152
Joseph, 11
Joshua, 152
Katherine, 1
Mahittable, 11
Mahlon, 151
Martha, 11, 44
Mary, 1, 11, 62, 151, 152
Mercy, 34, 152
Miriam, 47
Nathan, 63
Rachel, 61
Rebecca, 62, 151
Rebecca Hartley, 151
Rebeckah, 151
Rebekah, 1, 48
Samuel, 67, 104
Sarah, 63
Susanna, 62, 151
Titus, 1
DUBRE, Armella, 23, 29
Esther, 23
Hannah, 57
James, 23, 57, 59, 62
Joseph, 23
Lemiramis, 23
Martha, 23
Mary, 23
Rachael, 23
Sarah, 23, 29, 62
DUCKWORTH, Elizabeth, 7
DUER, Ann, 152
Ann Hampton, 152
James Hampton, 152
Joseph, 26, 148, 152
Mary, 152
Sarah, 152
DUNGAN, Sarah, 48, 53, 56, 67
DYER, Elisabeth, 152
Esther Brown, 152
Hosiah, 152
John, 152
Joseph, 152
Josiah, 152

Mary, 152
Thomas, 152

-E-

EASTBURN, Aaron, 153
Amos, 152
Ann, 152, 153
Anna, 153
Barzalleel, 19
Benjamin, 152
Charles, 153
David, 152
Elias, 153
Elisa, 153
Elisabeth, 150, 152, 153
Elisabeth Duer, 153
Elisabeth Wiggins, 152
Elizabeth, 18, 19
Hannah, 153
Jacob, 153
James, 152
Jane, 19
John, 18, 19, 68, 152, 153
Joseph, 152, 153
Kezia Ross, 152
Latitia, 153
Maire, 152
Martha, 153
Mary, 152, 153
Mary Wilson, 152
Mercy, 153
Mercy Bye, 153
Moses, 153
Rachel, 152, 153
Rachel Knowles, 153
Rebecca Kitchen, 153
Rebeckah, 152
Robert, 150, 152, 153
Samuel, 17, 152
Sarah, 152, 153
Thomas, 152

EDWARDS, Abel, 77
Amos, 77
Ann, 77, 109
Caleb, 77, 89
Elizabeth, 98
Hannah, 77, 116, 117, 127
Hugh, 77
Joel, 77
John, 77, 101, 109, 111, 114, 121
Lydia R., 77
Margaret, 77
Martha, 76, 77, 89, 113, 114
Mary, 76, 77, 84, 118
Meribah, 77
Nathan, 77
Samuel, 77
Sarah, 77
Susanna, 77, 139
Thomas, 77, 106, 107, 116, 120
William, 76, 77, 92, 103, 107, 110, 111, 115, 120, 138

EHRHARD, Mary, 118

ELLICOTT, Andrew, 153, 154
Ann, 154
Ann Bye, 153
Ann Ely, 154
Benjamin, 154
Elias, 154
Elisabeth, 154
Elisabeth Brown, 154
George, 154
Hannah, 154
Isaac, 66
Jane Kinsey, 154
John, 153, 154
Jonathan, 154
Joseph, 153, 154
Latitia, 154
Nathaniel, 153, 154
Pamela, 154
Rachel, 154
Rebecca, 154
Ruth, 64, 154
Sarah, 154
Thomas, 66, 153, 154

ELLIS, Enos, 97

ELY, Aaron, 155
Alfred, 155
Amasa, 155
Amos, 155, 156
Anne, 154, 156
Asher, 154
Charles, 154, 155
Deborah, 155
Deborah Whitson, 155
Elias, 156
Elisabeth, 154, 155, 156
Elisabeth Blackfan, 155
Elisabeth Wilson, 154
Esther, 195
George, 33, 155, 195
Hannah, 154, 155
Hannah Austin, 155
Henry, 155
Hugh, 154, 155, 156, 177
J. Moore, 156
James, 155
Jane, 155
Jervis, 195
Jesse, 155
John, 154, 155
Joseph, 33, 154, 155
Joshua, 155, 156
Latitia, 155
Mark, 155
Mary, 66, 154
Mary Richards, 154
Mary Wilson, 154
Mathias, 155
Matilda, 195
Merab, 154
Nathan, 156
Phebe, 154
Phineas, 154
Rachel, 57, 155
Rachel Carver, 155
Rebeckah, 154
Robert, 195
Ruth, 156, 177

Ruth Paxson, 156
Samuel, 155, 191
Sarah, 46, 154, 155, 156, 195
Sarah Griffith, 156
Sarah Limcock, 154
Sarah M., 156
Seneca, 155, 191
Seth, 155
Smith, 195
Thomas, 154, 155
Timothy, 195
Whitson, 155
William, 155
EVANS, Amos, 136
Catherine, 109, 119
Edward, 109
Jane, 109, 129, 130
Joel, 109
Sarah, 109
EWEN, Esther, 84, 101
EWERS, George, 53, 59
Hammah, 59

-F-

FASTE, Robert, 26
FAULKE, Ann, 76
Samuel, 76
FELL, Aaron, 25, 72
Abi, 158
Alice, 157
Amos, 158
Ann, 25, 46, 72, 157, 158
Asa, 157
Benjamin, 105, 156, 157
Bridget, 156
Bridget Wilson, 156
David, 156, 157
Deborah, 157, 182
Edith, 158
Edith Smith, 158
Edward, 116, 117
Elisabeth, 156, 157, 158, 170
Elisabeth Doyle, 156
Elisabeth Watson, 157
Elizabeth, 23, 25, 68, 70, 72
Ezra, 25, 63, 72, 158
George, 43, 156, 158
Hannah, 156, 157, 158
Hannah Scarborough, 156
Isaac, 156
Jane, 157, 158
Jane Kirk, 158
Jesse F., 158
John, 11, 33, 35, 156, 157, 158, 188
Jonathan, 157, 158
Joseph, 35, 156, 157, 158
Joyce, 63
Levi, 157
Mahlon, 25, 63, 69, 72
Margaret, 156
Mark, 157
Martha, 156, 157, 158
Martha Bradshaw, 158
Mary, 117, 156, 157, 158
Mary Kinsey, 156
Maurice, 157
Morris, 77
Moses, 25, 72, 158
Phebe, 157, 158
Rachael, 25, 35
Rachel, 63, 72, 156, 157, 158
Rachel Wilson, 157
Rebecca, 157, 158
Rebeckah, 157
Richard, 158
Samuel, 158
Sarah, 33, 60, 77, 156, 157, 158
Sarah Balderston, 158
Sarah Rollins, 157
Tamer, 156
Thomas, 23, 42, 70, 156, 157, 158
Titus, 42, 156, 170
Watson, 157
FEREBY, Benjamin, 39
FIELD, Benjamin, 192
Cyrus, 192
Elisabeth, 192
Hannah, 192
Joseph, 192
Margaret, 25, 53, 61
Mary, 192
Stephen, 25, 61, 64
William, 192
FIPPS, Petter, 45
FISHER, Ann, 158
Ann Carey, 158
Barah, 158, 159
Betty, 158
Deborah, 158
Elias, 158
Elisabeth, 158
Elizabeth, 41
Eunice, 159
Hannah, 158
John, 158, 159
Joseph, 158, 159
Josiah, 159
Katherine, 158
Margaret Daws, 159
Mary, 33
Mary Butler, 159
Robert, 113, 158
Ruth, 159
Samuel, 158, 159
Sarah, 158
Thomas, 159
FLAGLER, John L., 77
Zachariah, 77
FLOWERS,

Elisabeth, 192
Joseph, 192
William, 192
FORCE, Prudence, 68
FOREMAN, John, 125
FORMAN, John, 127
FORSTER, Mary, 48
FOULK, Thomas, 97
FOULKE, Aaron, 80
Abigail, 79, 80, 89, 130
Agnes, 79
Alice, 80, 159
Amelia, 78, 80, 127
Amos, 79
Ann, 78, 79, 80, 81, 82, 107, 126, 138
Anna, 80
Anne, 78, 80, 123, 127, 130
Anthony, 80
Antrim, 81
Aquila, 78
Aquilia, 129
Asemath, 81
Asher, 79, 80, 119, 120, 134, 159
Barton, 80
Bathsheba, 80
Benjamin, 81, 91, 129
Cadwalader, 121, 125, 133
Cadwallader, 78, 79, 80
Caleb, 80, 81, 82, 130
Charles, 81
David, 79, 81, 93
Deborah, 79
Edward, 78, 79, 81, 91, 122, 127, 130, 137, 140
Eleanor, 78, 79, 80, 115, 130
Elinor, 78
Elisabeth, 159
Elizabeth, 79, 80, 84
Ellen, 80
Euphemia, 159
Evan, 78, 81, 135
Everard, 78, 80, 120, 130
Grace, 80
Hannah, 78, 80, 81, 121, 122, 133
Hannah S., 81
Hugh, 78, 79, 81, 82, 126, 138
Isacher, 79, 80
Israel, 78, 79, 123
Issachar, 132
James, 80, 81, 93, 104
Jane, 78, 79, 80, 81, 104, 132, 140
Jesse, 79, 80, 130, 137
John, 78, 79, 80, 90, 101, 102, 103, 127, 130
Joseph, 81
Joshua, 81
Judah, 78, 79, 127, 131
Kezia, 80
Latitia, 80, 159
Lydia, 78
Margaret, 78, 79, 80, 133
Martha, 78, 81, 119
Mary, 78, 79, 80, 132, 133
Mary R., 79
Mercy, 80
Miriam, 81
Olivia, 81
Phebe, 79, 80
Priscilla, 79, 80
Rachel, 80, 81, 139
Rebecca, 80
Rowland, 79
Samuel, 78, 79, 80, 81, 96, 107, 130
Samuel M., 77, 83
Sarah, 79, 80, 81, 83, 138
Shipley, 159
Sidney, 80, 93
Silas, 80
Susanna, 79, 80, 130
Susanna L., 81
Theophilous, 105
Theophilus, 78, 79, 81, 119, 127
Thomas, 78, 79, 80, 91, 103, 118, 130
William, 78, 79, 80, 104, 105
William Roberts, 159
FOULKES, William, 86
FOULKS, Israel, 123
FOWLER, Daniel, 81
Elisa, 81
Elizabeth, 81
Jane B., 81
Mary Ann, 81
William, 81
FRANTZ, Mary, 130
FURNIS, Thomas, 38, 41

-G-

GARNER, Phebe, 50
GASKILL, Margaret, 102
Mary, 106
Meribah, 111
Samuel, 100
GEASLEY, Ann, 82
Jane, 82
John, 82
Rachel, 82
GIBSON, John, 50
Margaret, 133
GILBERT, Abigail, 81
Abner, 118, 124
Amos, 159
Benjamin, 81, 96, 99, 118
Caleb, 82, 159
Daniel, 159

David, 159
Elizabeth, 118, 124
James, 159
Jesse, 118, 126
John, 81
Jonathan, 159
Joseph, 81, 159
Joshua, 81, 159
Lydia, 159
Patience, 159
Rachel, 81
Rebecca, 118
Rebeckah, 124
Sarah, 81, 159
Sarah Bradshaw, 159
Thomas, 159
William, 159
GILBIRD, Rachel, 44
GILL, Alice, 159
Thomas, 159
GILLAM, Rebeckah, 23
GILLINGHAM, Amos, 160
Ann Preston, 160
Anne, 160
Benjamin, 160
Bridget Moore, 160
David, 160
Elisabeth, 160
Esther, 160
James, 148, 159, 160
Jenks, 160
Jesse, 160
John, 159, 160
John P., 160
Jonathan, 160
Jonathan P., 160
Joseph, 159, 160
Mahlon, 160
Margaret Jenks, 160
Martha, 159, 160
Martha Canby, 159
Mary, 159, 160, 165
Matthias, 160
Moses, 160
Phebe, 160
Ruth, 159
Ruth Preston, 159
Samuel, 160
Sarah, 160
Sarah Taylor, 160
Sarah White, 160
Stacy, 160
Thomas, 159, 160
William, 159, 160, 189
William P., 160
Yeamans, 159, 160
GILLUM, Rebecca, 69
GLULMA, Benjamin, 24
Elizabeth, 24
John, 24
Thomas, 24
GOMERY, Ann, 57
Joseph, 57
GOOD, Francis, 30
John, 83
Sarah, 58
GOODE, Ann, 161
Edward, 161
Eleanor, 161
Elinor Harris, 161
Esther Lewis, 161
Francis, 161
Gainor, 161
Hannah, 161
Jane, 161
Jesse, 161
John, 161
Jonathan, 161
Joseph, 161
Margaret, 161
Mary, 161
Miriam, 161
Nathan, 161
Rebecca, 161
Robert, 161
Sarah, 161, 179
Sarah Roberts, 161
Thomas, 161
GOURLEY, Elizabeth, 6, 30, 60
John, 6, 42
Joseph, 6
Margaret, 6
Mary, 6
Samuel, 6
Sarah, 6
GOURLY, Margaret, 60
Samuel, 55
GRASLEY, Ann, 96
GREASLEY, Ann, 78
Jane, 110
John, 78, 104, 110, 116, 126
Rachel, 116, 123, 124
GREEN, Abigail, 82
Alice, 82
Ann, 82
Benjamin, 82, 117
Catherine, 82, 133
Elizabeth, 82
Evan, 82
Ezekiel, 82, 116, 122
Hannah, 82, 86
James, 82, 119
James R., 82
Jane, 82
Joseph, 82, 96, 116
Lydia, 82
Margaret, 82, 111, 112
Martha, 82, 127, 128
Mary, 82, 132
Rachel, 82, 113
Samuel, 82, 113, 133
Thomas, 82, 119, 132
William, 82
GRIFFITH, Abraham, 82, 83, 102, 108
Ann, 82, 83, 98
Benjamin, 104
Hannah, 82, 83
Isaac, 82, 83, 96

James, 83
Jane, 83
John, 82, 83, 123, 124, 125
John Greasley, 83
Jonathan, 83, 104, 121, 127
Joseph, 83
Martha, 83
Mary, 83
Rachel, 83, 99, 112, 125, 134
Sarah, 82, 83
Thomas, 83
William, 83
GRUBUM, Elisabeth, 161
George, 161
John, 161
Martha Smith, 161
Thomas, 161

-H-

HADOCK, Walter, 83
HAIR, John, 54, 58
HAISEY, Sarah, 98
HALL, David, 161
Mahlon, 18, 161
Margery, 161
Matthew, 161
Sarah, 161
Sarah Hayworth, 161
HALLOWELL, David, 31
Eliza, 83
Esther, 83
John, 116
Martha, 117
William, 31, 116
HAMBLETON, Aaron, 162
Alice, 161
Charles, 162
Elihu, 162
Elisa P., 162
Elisabeth, 161
Elisabeth Paxson, 161
Hannah, 161, 162
Hannah Paxson, 162
James, 161, 162
Jane, 162
John, 161, 162
Jonas, 162
Joseph, 161, 162
Josiah L., 162
Margaret, 162, 167
Mary, 161, 162
Mercy, 161
Moses, 162
Peninah, 161
Rachel, 161, 162
Samuel, 162
Sarah, 161
Stephen, 161, 162
William, 162
HAMPTON, Abner, 26
Amos, 26
Ann, 26, 162
Benjamin, 12, 31
Charles, 162
David, 26
Elisabeth, 162
Elizabeth, 26
Hannah, 26, 162
Hannah Dennis, 162
Hannah Kitchen, 162
James, 24, 162
John, 26, 29
Jonathan, 26
Joseph, 3, 26, 39, 148
Martha, 162
Mary, 3, 26, 31
Oliver, 27, 162
Samuel, 26
HAMTON, Abner, 9
Amos, 9
Ann, 4, 5, 18, 61, 63, 67, 69, 71, 72
Asceneth, 56
Asenath, 4
Benjamin, 4, 5, 18, 30, 57, 68, 71
David, 4, 9, 60
Elizabeth, 5
Esther, 4
Hannah, 4, 9, 18
James, 5, 68, 69, 72
Jane, 4, 27, 53
John, 4, 9, 16, 31, 42, 65
Jonathan, 4, 65
Joseph, 4, 7, 9, 18, 31, 47, 53, 54
Katherine, 18
Margaret, 18, 69
Mary, 4, 9, 18, 54, 70
Mercy, 26
Moses, 18
Oliver, 5, 23, 67, 68, 69, 72
Rachell, 4
Rebecca, 26
Samuel, 9
Sarah, 4, 5, 18, 33, 56, 68, 71
HARDING, Phebe, 62, 63, 66
Rachel, 68
HARE, John, 57
HARKER, Adam, 45
Amy, 45
Ann, 38
James, 45
HARPER, Nathan, 26
HARTLEY, Amy, 163
Ann, 162, 163
Anne, 162
Anthony, 31, 162, 163
Bathsheba, 162
Benjamin, 162, 163
Elisabeth, 162, 163
Elisabeth Paxson, 162
Elisabeth Smith, 163
Hannah, 163
James, 162
Jane, 163
Janey, 162
Jonathan, 163
Joseph, 163
Mahlon, 163
Martha, 162
Mary, 162, 163

Rachel, 163
Rebecca, 162
Roger, 162
Samuel, 163
Sarah, 56, 162, 163
Sarah Betts, 163
Thomas, 31, 162, 163
William, 162, 163
HARTLY, Anthony, 45
HARVEY, Elizabeth, 61, 67
Ellenor, 71
Mathias, 60, 61
Matthias, 64
Rachel, 71
HATFIELD, Martha, 123, 124, 127
HAYHURST, Abi, 195
Ann, 195
Bazaleel, 15
Benajah, 36, 195
Benjamin, 15, 21
Bezaleel, 26, 70
Cuthbert, 31
Elizabeth, 15, 36
Esther Kinsey, 21
Ethelbert, 21, 195
Isaac Wiggins, 21
John, 15, 20, 21, 31, 36, 46
Kesia, 195
Kezia, 21
Laman, 195
Lamar Wells, 21
Margery, 15
Margery Ann, 21
Marmaduke, 195
Marmaduke Kinsey, 21
Martha, 21, 195
Mary, 15, 36
Rachael, 21
Rachel, 15, 38, 68, 195
Ruth, 15, 43
Sarah, 21, 195
Susanna, 26
Thomas, 26
William, 26
HAYS, Ann, 107
HEACOCK, Aaron, 83
Ann, 83
Anne, 125
Enos, 83
Hannah, 125
Issachar, 130
Jane, 121
Jeremiah, 112, 116
Jesse, 83, 127, 128, 139
Joel, 83
John, 83, 117
Jonah, 83
Jonathan, 97, 117, 123, 124, 126, 128
Joseph, 83, 128
Josiah, 133, 140
Margaret, 83
Mary, 113, 126, 133, 136
Miriam, 116
Nathan, 83
Rachel, 113
Richard, 140
Rosamond, 138, 139
Sarah, 112, 116
Tace, 128
Tacy, 83
Thomas, 130, 137, 139
William, 83, 90, 116, 117
HEAD, Barbara, 163
John, 163
Mary, 163
Mary Bye, 163
Ruth, 163
Thomas, 102, 163
HEADLEY, Mary, 54
HEATON, Joseph, 45
Lydia, 58
William, 45
HERR, David, 101
HESTAN, Joseph, 130
HESTER, Joseph, 125
HESTON, Abner, 69
Abraham, 27
Amos, 24, 70
Ann, 11, 27, 53
Anne, 130
Benjamin, 18
David, 5, 23, 29, 36, 56, 68
Dorothy, 8
Eber, 34
Ebor, 27
Edward, 51
Edward Warner, 10
Elisabeth, 184
Elizabeth, 5, 18, 28, 29, 42
Elizabeth Buckman, 5
Esther, 22
Hannah, 8, 22, 23, 28, 55, 59, 69, 72
Isaac, 8, 10, 11, 60
Isaiah, 5, 28, 53
Jacob, 8, 10, 11, 16, 18, 35, 37, 51, 67
James, 3
Jane, 24, 71
Jarret, 59
Jemima, 5, 8, 43
Jesse, 10, 11, 19, 29, 34, 35, 36, 51
John, 5, 8, 11, 22, 24, 36, 55, 59, 72
Jonathan, 3, 11
Joseph, 32, 68, 129
Latitia, 27
Levi, 59
Mahlon, 24, 34, 71
Mary, 5, 10, 11, 27, 29, 30, 33, 34, 51, 61
Mercy, 22, 24, 28, 70
Phebe, 29
Phineas, 24

Phinehas, 70
Rachael, 11, 22, 23, 29
Rachel, 8, 10, 43, 52, 69, 71
Rachell, 5
Rebecca, 23, 69
Rebeckah, 22, 28
Rebekah, 5, 72
Sarah, 23, 27, 28, 69, 72
Stephen, 8
Tacey, 23, 29
Thomas, 8, 10, 51
William, 5, 24, 31, 51, 64, 70
Zebulon, 5, 8, 23, 27, 28, 30, 31, 32, 34, 36, 46, 48, 60, 65, 69, 72
HIBBS, Abraham, 25, 56, 58, 64
Benjamin, 25
Elizabeth, 59, 60, 65
Hannah, 25, 57
Isaac, 51
James, 30
John, 50
Joseph, 42, 43, 46, 65
Mary, 25, 58, 65
Phebe, 25
Rachael, 3, 33
Rachell, 44
Rebecca, 53
Rebeckah, 10, 31
Ruth, 71
Sarah, 50, 65
Susanna, 25
Thomas, 58
William, 30, 31, 65, 67
HIBRON, Elizabeth, 67
HICKS, Abigail, 84
Ann, 84
Anne R., 84
Evan P., 84
George, 83, 84, 89, 105, 139
Hannah, 83, 84
Jesse, 84, 126, 131
John, 83, 84, 108
Lacy, 84
Mahlon, 84
Margaret, 84
Margaret Ball, 84
Martha, 83, 84
Mary, 83, 84
Mary Ball, 84
Nathan P., 84
Peninah, 84
Penrose, 84
Rachel, 84
Rebecca, 84
Samuel, 84, 127, 128
Sarah, 83
Speakman, 84
Thomas, 84
William, 83, 84, 100, 107, 108, 134
HILBORN, Amos, 29
Ann, 63
Elizabeth, 66
Hannah, 70
Jane, 29, 54
John, 29, 39
Mary, 60, 70
Ruth, 29, 70
Samuel, 38, 58, 112
Sarah, 62
Thomas, 62
HILBOURN, Amos, 26, 36
John, 26
Joseph, 26
Phebe, 26
Rachael, 26
Robert, 36
Ruth, 35
Samuel, 35
Stephen, 26
Thomas, 26
HILL, Aaron, 163
Benjamin, 163
Deborah, 163
Elisabeth Smith, 163
Ezekiel, 163
Ezekiel Smith, 163
Hannah, 163
James, 163
John, 147, 163
Joseph, 163
Margaret, 163
Moses, 163
Samuel, 163
Sarah Canby, 163
Thomas, 163
William, 163
HILLBORN, Hannah, 48
Joseph, 31
Mary, 29
Rachel, 35
Robert, 35, 49
Ruth, 193
Samuel, 31, 38, 48, 51, 193
Thomas, 71, 72
HILLBORNE, Rachel, 38
HILLBOURN, Anna, 26
Elizabeth, 26
HILLES, Ann, 84
Anne, 84, 106, 108
David, 84, 108
Hugh, 84, 99, 108
Mary, 84, 108
William, 84, 108
HILLMAN, Rachel, 89, 135, 136
HIRST, Ann, 59
David, 59
Jesse, 8, 59
John, 8, 13, 30, 52, 57, 59
Judith, 54, 56
Mary, 8, 59
Rebecca, 59
Rebeckah, 8
Sarah, 8, 32, 59
Thomas, 59
HOAG, Ann, 84
George, 84
James, 84
Joseph, 84
Solomon, 84
William, 84

Zebulon, 84
HOGE, Ann, 84, 107
Elizabeth, 105, 128
George, 84, 104, 105, 106
Hester, 116, 128
James, 84, 116
Joseph, 84, 106
Lavinia, 128
Mary, 128
Rachel, 128
Sollomon, 106, 116
Solomon, 84, 106, 116, 123, 124, 128
William, 47, 84, 106, 107
Zebulon, 84, 107
HOGUE, Ann, 84, 102
George, 84
James, 84
Joseph, 84
Solomon, 84, 98, 102
William, 84, 98, 101, 102
Zebulon, 84
HOLE, Ann, 108
HOLLINGSWORTH, Isaac, 47
HOLLOWELL, Abigail, 55
HOLMES, Benjamin, 71
Elizabeth, 71
John, 71
Ruth, 71
Thomas, 71
HOPKINS, Elizabeth, 67
Samuel, 34
William, 34
HOUGH, Daniel, 164
Ellinor Sands, 164
Jane, 164
John, 164
Joseph, 164
Mary, 164
Oliver, 192
Rachel, 71
Richard, 164
Stephen, 164
William, 164
HOWELL, Arthur, 66
HUFF, Rachel, 71
HUGHES, Abraham, 55
Constantine, 164
Deborah, 53, 55
Elisabeth, 164
George, 164
Hannah, 164
Humphrey, 164
Isaac, 164
James, 53, 55
Mary, 164
Matthew, 164
Sarah, 55, 164
Thomas, 164
Ursella, 53
Ursula, 55
HUGHS, Job, 106, 109. 110
HULME, Elizabeth, 58
George, 58
HUMMER, Nathan, 57
HUNT, Mary, 167
HUTCHINSON, Ann Cary Walker, 164
Elisabeth, 164
Elisabeth Bye, 164
John, 36
Martha, 164
Mary, 25, 34, 71
Matthias, 147, 164
Michael, 34
Rebecca, 17
Rebekah, 36
Thomas, 164

-I-

IDEN, Albion, 85
Anne, 85
Eleanor, 85
Elizabeth, 85
George, 85, 122, 126, 127, 129
Greenfield, 85
Hannah, 85, 126, 129, 137
Jacob, 85
Jane, 85
Jesse, 85
John, 85, 129
Julia, 85
Margaret, 84, 85
Paulina, 85
Randal, 78, 84, 85, 115
Samuel, 76, 85, 107, 108
Sarah, 85
Susanna, 85
Thomas, 85
INGHAM, Anna, 189
Jonas, 147
Jonathan, 189
INGLELOE, Ingle, 100
INK, Sobiah, 56
ISAAC, Samuel, 85

-J-

JACKSON, Elizabeth, 85
Hugh, 85
James M., 85
Rebecca, 85
Thomas, 83
JAMES, Martha, 106
JAMISON, Isaias, 85
Joseph, 85
Margaret, 85
Mary, 85
JANNEY, Alice, 54
Ann, 58
Jacob, 58
Martha, 58
Mary, 34
Sarah, 30, 58, 59
Thomas, 30, 34
JARRET, Hannah, 55
JEANS, Joseph, 53
JEMISON, Isaiah, 137, 138
JENKINS, Mary, 100
Sarah, 133, 134
JENKS, Joseph, 34
Mary, 25, 44
Rachel, 69
William, 25, 34
JENNINGS, Thomas, 103, 104

JEWEL, George, 61
Mary, 29
JEWELL, Alice, 64
George, 64
Mary, 64
JOHNSON, Abigail, 130
Ann, 164
Benjamin, 85
David, 4, 85
Debora, 118
Elisabeth, 164, 176
Elisabeth J., 182
Grey, 85
Hannah, 85, 125, 130, 140, 164
Hannah Pickering, 164
Henry, 85
Jane, 85
Jesse, 164
John, 4, 58, 148
John Pickering, 164
Jonathan, 164
Joseph, 4, 24, 50, 52, 57, 60, 71
Lydia, 85
Martha Hutchinson, 164
Mary, 4, 57
Rachael, 4, 24
Rachel, 52, 57, 60, 71
Ruth, 164
Samuel, 4, 57, 164
Sarah, 85
Sarah Ann, 164
Susan F., 85
William, 85, 164
William Hutchinson, 164
JOHNSTON, David, 57
JONES, Aaron W., 165
Amos, 165
Deborah, 44
Elisabeth, 164, 165
Elisabeth Watson, 164
Evan, 112
Ezra, 164
Harriet B., 165
Hiram, 165
Huldah Fenton, 165
Isaiah, 164, 165, 188
Jacob, 38
Jemima D., 165
Jesse, 165
John, 165
Mary Ann, 165
Priscilla M., 165
Rachel, 85
Sarah, 164, 165
Sarah D., 165

-K-

KEARNEY, Hannah, 113
KENNARD, Eli, 127, 136
Hannah, 137
KIMBLE, Sarah, 182
KINMAN, John, 165
Margaret, 165
Nathan, 165
KINNARD, Eli, 131
Elizabeth, 131
Hannah, 131
Joseph, 131
Thomas, 131
William, 131
KINSEY, Abel, 166
Abi, 166
Alice, 166
Aliesta, 166
Ann, 67, 166
Ann Plunket, 166
Asher, 166
Benjamin, 36, 145, 165, 166
David, 165, 166
Deborah, 184
Dorothy, 65
Edmund, 165, 166
Elam, 166
Elisabeth, 166
Esther, 166
Ezra, 128, 132
George, 165
Hannah, 166
Hannah Adeste, 166
Ingham, 165
Isaac, 165, 166
Israel, 166
Jacob, 166
James, 166
Jane, 166
Jemima, 47
Jemimah, 5
John, 63, 165, 166
Jonas, 165
Jonathan, 5, 43, 64, 165, 166
Joseph, 34, 165, 166
Joshua, 166
Lucretia, 165
Martha, 36, 165, 166
Martha White, 165
Mary, 5, 165, 166
Mary Bradshaw, 166
Mary Rice, 166
Nathaniel, 83
Oliver, 166
Phebe, 166
Rachel, 165, 166
Rachell, 42
Robert, 166
Ruth, 166
Samuel, 165, 166
Sarah, 165, 166
Sarah Ingham, 165
Seth, 166
Susanna, 165
Susanna Brown, 165
Tamar, 165
Tamar Fell, 165
Thomas, 47, 69
Ulysses, 165
KIRK, Benjamin, 85, 136
Elizabeth, 11, 85, 131
Hannah, 36, 85,

134
Isaac, 11, 30, 85, 126, 134
Issac, 42
Jane, 42
John, 30
Jonas, 85, 124, 129
Joseph, 64
Margaret, 48
Mary, 11, 47
Phebe, 36, 85, 109
Rachel, 85
Samuel, 53
Sarah, 6, 43, 85
Stephen, 36, 47, 50, 85, 109
Steven, 124
Thomas, 64
KIRKBRIDE, Ann, 167
David, 167
Esther, 167
Hannah, 167
Hannah Bidgood, 167
Latitia, 167
Mahlon, 167
Mary, 167
Robert, 167
Sarah, 167
KITCHEN, Ann, 152, 167
Eleanor, 167
William, 152, 167
KNIGH, Daniel, 48
Thomas, 48
KNIGHT, Ann, 45, 48
Daniel, 45
Thomas, 45
KNITE, Mary, 41
KNOLES, Banner, 15
KNOWLES, Banner, 29, 36
Elizabeth, 29
John, 36, 193
Joseph, 25
Mary, 36, 193
Robert, 193

-L-

LACEY, Abraham, 11
Barbary, 42, 167
Benjamin, 11, 19, 50, 51, 52, 59, 167
Dorithy, 1
Elisabeth Canby, 167
Elizabeth, 49, 51, 66
Esther, 19
Hannah, 1, 60
Isaac, 1, 19
James, 11
Jane, 11, 66
Jemima, 1
Jesse, 34, 167
John, 1, 8, 11, 13, 19, 30, 33, 35
Joseph, 1, 21, 23, 32, 33, 34, 42, 48, 50
Martha, 1, 33
Mary, 1, 32, 39
Rachael, 11, 19
Rachel, 1, 39
Rachell, 1
Sarah, 1, 32, 62
Susanna, 11
Tamar, 167
Thomas, 42, 45, 47, 148, 167
Warner, 19
William, 1, 11, 30, 49, 66, 167
LACY, William, 48
LANCASTER, Aaron, 2, 106
Abigail, 86, 121
Ann, 85
Anne, 86, 125
Benjamin, 2, 85, 86, 99, 103, 109, 111
Elizabeth, 2, 46, 86, 111, 134, 136
Febe, 100, 101, 102
Hannah, 86
Harriet, 86
Isaac, 2, 47, 50, 106
Israel, 86, 138
Jacob, 2, 103, 106
Jesse, 85
Job, 2, 103
John, 2, 86, 102, 103, 126, 127
Jonah, 86
Joseph, 2, 47, 48, 86, 106
Martha, 121
Meraba, 121
Meribah, 115, 132, 133
Morris, 86
Moses, 2, 108, 114, 115, 121, 128, 129, 131
Nathan, 86
Phebe, 2
Rachel, 85, 111, 113, 115, 121, 129, 139
Thomas, 2, 30, 40, 44, 85, 99, 101, 103, 105, 106, 121, 131, 136, 138
William, 86
LARGE, Anne, 167
Ebenezer, 57
Eleneser, 167
Hannah Knowles, 167
Isaiah, 167
Jacob, 167
Joseph, 167
Mary, 167
Samuel, 167
Stephen, 58
William, 167
LARGER, Ebenezer, 54
LAYCOCK, John, 46
Mary, 33
LEE, Ann, 28, 58
Daniel, 15, 26, 52, 59, 64, 71
David, 65
Deborah, 15, 52, 64
Eleanor, 26, 65
Elizabeth, 15,

63
Ellen, 15
Esther, 61
Hannah, 54, 58
John, 15, 26, 42, 45, 58
Margaret, 15, 26, 59
Mary, 15, 24, 31, 58, 65, 67, 71
Meribah, 52
Peter, 90
Rachael, 15, 26
Ralph, 67
Ruth, 15, 26
Samuel, 44, 58
Sarah, 15, 26
Sebilla, 65
Thomas, 44, 48, 50, 58, 62
William, 7, 31, 39, 42, 53, 54, 57, 58, 65
LEEDOM, Benjamin, 56
Jesse, 24, 34, 56, 70
Joseph, 56
Mary, 24, 70
Rachel, 36
Richard, 34, 36, 56, 64
Sarah, 36
Susannah, 72
William, 56
LEES, Elizabeth, 48
Joseph, 32
LENARD, Ann, 53
LESTER, Abel, 87
Albert, 87
Anne, 120
Catherine, 86, 104
Dorothy, 86
Eleanor, 130
Elijah, 86, 120
Elinor, 86
Elizabeth, 130
Ellinor, 110
Hannah, 38, 86, 87, 119, 130
Isaac, 78, 86, 87, 97, 100, 106, 107, 108, 135
Jane, 86, 87, 137
John, 86, 107, 109, 119, 124
Joseph, 86, 104, 122, 127, 140
Katherine, 104
Margaret, 86, 87, 111
Mary, 86, 87, 130, 135, 136, 137
Mary Ann, 87
Morris, 87
Persilla, 105
Peter, 80, 86, 87, 98, 104
Priscilla, 78, 86, 105
Samuel, 86, 87, 117
Sarah, 86, 138
Shipley, 86, 87, 88, 131
Thomas, 82, 86, 87, 136, 137
William, 86, 87, 111
LEWES, Thomas, 42, 44
LEWIS, Abigail, 135
Ann, 87, 105
David, 49
Elizabeth, 87, 98
Ellis, 87, 109
Hannah, 87, 101
James, 87
Jane, 87
Joseph, 87, 136, 138
Lewis, 87, 113, 134, 135, 136
Margaret, 87, 110
Martha, 87
Mary, 87, 109, 119, 120
Sarah, 87
Susanna, 110
Thomas, 46
LINTON, Asa Cary, 192
Daniel, 27
David, 4
Elizabeth, 4, 13, 32
Isaiah, 4, 13, 32, 56, 60, 192
Jacob, 4, 56
James, 13, 56, 60
John, 4, 12, 13, 32, 34, 45, 70
Laura, 13, 25, 56, 60
Martha, 4
Mary, 192
Phebe, 51
Rebekah, 4
Sarah, 13, 29, 56, 60, 62, 65, 66, 68
Silas, 192
Thomas, 13, 56, 60, 192
William, 4, 13, 32, 34, 50, 51, 54, 60, 61
LIVESEY, John, 72
LIVEZEY, Ann, 72
LIVEZLEY, Ann, 25
LOVE, Catharine, 42
James, 64, 66
LOWNES, Mary, 192
Susannah, 27
William, 35, 192
LOWRIGHT, Mary, 121
LOYD, Ann, 108
David, 135
Debora, 108, 115
Evan, 131
Hannah, 111
James, 125
John, 105, 108, 121
Martha, 108, 117
Rachel, 108
Susanna, 123
Thomas, 121
William, 123
LUNDAY, Ebenezer, 54

LUNDY, Ebenezer, 54
Richard, 96
LUPTON, Ann, 167
Jonathan, 167
Joseph, 167
Mary, 167
Mercy, 167

-M-

MCCARTY, Benjamin, 88, 125, 135
David, 134
Elizabeth, 87, 125, 134, 135
Hannah, 88, 125, 135
James, 87, 125, 134
Jane, 87, 135
Jesse, 134
Job, 88, 125, 135
Joel, 87, 125, 134
John, 87, 125, 134
Lydia, 134
Margaret, 134
Martha, 134
Mary, 87, 125, 129, 130
Phebe, 87, 126, 134, 135
Samuel, 87, 125, 134
Sarah, 87, 125, 127
Silas, 87, 125, 134
Thomas, 87, 110, 111, 125, 135
MCCOOL, John, 109
MCCOOLE, Catherine, 113
Elizabeth, 112
Mary, 113
Samuel, 113
Walter, 96, 98, 100, 101
MCCORD, Ann, 136
MCDOWELL, Ann, 167
Eleaser, 167
George, 167
Hannah, 167
Mary, 167
Robert, 167
Sarah, 167
William, 167
MCGRAY, Mary, 57, 59
MAGILL, Agnes Whitson, 168
Charles, 168
David, 168
Jacob, 168
Jane, 168
John, 168
Jonathan P., 168
Mary, 168
Rachel, 168
Rebecca, 168
Rebecca Paxson, 168
Sarah, 155, 168
Susan, 168
William, 155, 168
MALMSBURY, Rebecca, 60
MALONE, Alice, 168
Francis, 168
Hannah, 168
James, 168
John, 168
Levi, 168
Mary, 168
Phebe, 168
Rachel, 168
Rebecca Goode, 168
Rebeckah, 168
Sarah, 168
MANNING, Elizabeth, 54
MANNON, Hannah, 136
MARDON, Sarah, 30
Thomas, 30
MARGAN, Debora, 97
Deborah, 97
MARSHALL, Thomas, 36
MARTINDALE, Amos, 69
John, 41, 62
Jonathan, 72
Joseph, 59
Miles, 64
Rachel, 55
Strickland, 70
William, 62, 64
MARTINDELL, Amos, 72
Joseph, 70
MARTINGILL, Strickland, 28
MASON, Benjamin, 30
Elizabeth, 123
Mary, 44
Richard, 30
MATHER, Bartholomew, 80
MATHERS, Bartholomew, 61
MAYCOCK, Catherine, 99
MERRICK, Amos, 23, 68, 168
David, 168
Elisabeth, 168
Elizabeth, 23, 68
Enos, 70
Jason, 25, 73
John, 23, 60, 61, 68, 168
Sarah, 23, 61, 68, 168
Sarah Armitage, 168
MICHENER, Abraham, 169
Absalom, 169
Arnold, 169
Barah, 168
Cynthia, 169
David, 169, 170
Deborah, 169
Elisabeth, 168, 169, 170
Elisha, 169
Esther, 169
Esther Dyer, 169
Esther Vickers, 169
George, 113, 168, 169, 170
Grace, 169
Hannah, 113, 168, 169, 170

Isaiah, 169, 181
Jacob, 170
James, 170
John, 168, 169, 170
John D., 169
Joseph, 168, 169
Joshua, 170
Josiah, 169
Joyce, 169
Katherine, 169
Mahlon, 169
Margaret, 168
Marmaduke, 169
Mary, 168, 169, 170
Mary Haworth, 169
Mercy, 169
Mesach, 168, 169
Mordecai, 168, 169
Nathan, 169
Rachel, 169
Rebecca, 170
Rebeckah, 169
Robert, 169
Sarah, 168, 169
Sarah Day, 169
Sarah Fisher, 168
Sarah Trego, 169
Thomas, 169
William, 168, 169
MILLER, Mary, 106
Robert, 93
MIRICK, Samuel, 43
Samuell, 43
MITCHEL, Enoch, 54
George, 61
Susanna, 61
MITCHELL, Alice, 41
Elizabeth, 42
George, 32
Richard, 42
William, 32
MITCHENER, Arnold, 54, 58
Mechack, 30
William, 30
MITCHINER, William, 44
MOOR, Mary, 51
MOORE, Andrew, 33
Christianna, 144
James, 33
Joseph, 144
Richard, 81
MORGAN, Ann, 97, 118
James, 97, 99, 102, 103, 115
John, 106, 108, 123
Mary, 115, 119
Sarah, 98
Susanna, 97
MORRICE, Susanna, 101
MORRIS, David, 88
Elizabeth, 18, 36
Elizabeth More, 135
Gainor, 96
Hannah, 18, 36, 58
Isachar, 18, 36, 64
Isacher, 57, 58
Issachar, 35
Joseph, 18
Lydia, 18, 35
Mary, 18
Morris, 88, 110
Rachel, 135
Samuel, 88, 135, 137
Sarah, 18
Susanna, 88, 96, 98, 102, 104
Thomas More, 135
William Henry, 170
MORRISON, Hannah, 115
MURFIN, Barnabas, 96, 98
MURRAY, Lindley, 71

-N-

NAILER, Hannah, 43
NARY, Jane, 170
Margaret, 170
Robert, 170
William, 170
NEAL, James, 43
NEULINGS, Jacob, 33
NEWBORN, Ann, 49
Ashton, 49
David, 5, 47, 48, 49
Dorothy, 5
George, 5, 39, 49
Hannah, 5, 49
Isaac, 49
John, 5, 49
Mary, 5
Solomon, 49
William, 5
NEWBURN, Amy, 55
Ann, 53
David, 29, 52, 62, 67, 73
Dorathy, 73
George, 38, 46, 52, 55
Hannah, 52, 53, 73
Jacob, 73
John, 25, 73
Jonathan, 68
Mary, 61
Rachel, 73
Sarah, 73
Susanna, 25
Tamar, 63
Tamer, 73
William, 25, 49
NEWMAN, Margaret, 88
William, 88, 102
NISSON, William, 96
NIXON, Abel, 88, 140
Abigail, 88
Beulah, 88
Edward Roberts, 88
Hannah, 88, 138
Margaret, 86, 88, 100
Martha, 88
Mary, 88
Samuel, 88, 122
Sarah, 88, 133

Susanna, 88
William, 88, 92, 107, 139
NIXSON, Margaret, 131
Mary, 139
Sarah, 132
Susanna, 139

-O-

OGILBY, Joseph, 105, 109
Patrick, 98, 105
Rachel, 105
Rebecca, 105, 109
OGLEBY, Patrick, 88
OSMOND, Ann, 70
OWEN, David, 97, 98, 124
Margaret, 118, 127
Thomas, 118
OWENS, Mary, 88
Owen, 88

-P-

PAINE, John, 2
PAIST, Alice, 19
George, 19
John, 19
Jolly, 19
Jonathan, 19
Robert, 19
Yuclydus, 20
PALMER, Ann, 36
David, 28, 36
John, 88
Jonathan, 36, 157
Joseph, 48
Obadiah, 88
Sarah V., 88
Tamar, 28
PANCOAST, Hannah, 48
PARKER, Ann, 96
Humphrey, 47, 53
Thomas, 53
PARR, Joseph, 114, 117
PARRY, Benjamin, 171
Charity, 170
Charles, 170
Daniel, 171
David, 48, 52, 170, 175
Elisabeth, 170
Grace, 170
Hannah, 170
Isaac, 88
Jane, 170, 171
Jane Paxson, 171
John, 170, 171
Joyce, 170
Margaret, 171
Martha, 171
Mary, 170
Mary Armitage, 170
Mercy, 170
Philip, 170
Phillip, 170
Rachel, 170
Rachel Fell, 170
Ruth, 171
Samuel, 170
Sarah, 170
Seneca, 170
Susanna, 170
Tacy, 170
Thomas, 170
PARSONS, Ann, 46
Jemima, 61, 64
John, 47, 57
Joshua, 61, 64
Mahlon, 61, 64
Mary, 61, 64
Naomi, 61, 64
Rebecca, 61, 64
Richard, 49, 55, 61, 64
William, 51, 64
PARVIN, ----, 88
PAST, John, 27
PASTE, Alice, 28, 71
Euclideus, 71
Eucloridas, 28
George, 28, 71
John, 28, 71
Jolly, 28, 71
Jonathan, 28, 71
Robert, 71
PAUL, Hannah, 137, 138
Joseph, 80
PAXSON, Aaron, 171, 172, 173
Abigail, 171, 172, 173
Abraham, 171, 172, 173
Alice, 173
Amelia, 173
Amy, 173
Ann, 171, 173
Ann Plumly, 171
Anna, 173
Asher, 173
Benjamin, 49, 172, 173
Betsy, 194
Catherine Rice, 173
Charles, 172, 173
Deborah, 172, 194
Deborah Taylor, 172
Eliada, 172
Elias, 172, 173
Elisabeth, 171, 172, 173
Elisabeth Brown, 172
Elisabeth Lupton, 173
Elizabeth, 32, 61
Emmy, 71
Esther, 194
Ezra, 172
Hannah, 70, 171, 172, 173
Hannameel, 174
Henry, 171, 173
Hester, 173
Isaac, 173
Jacob, 172, 173, 180
James, 26, 47, 48, 59, 60, 171
Jane, 171, 172, 173, 193
Jane Parry, 173
John, 173
Jonas, 171
Jonathan, 168,

172, 173, 174, 193, 194
Joseph, 33, 46, 172, 173
Joshua, 172
Latitia Knowles, 172
Letitia, 194
Lydia Blakey, 172
Mahlon, 170, 173
Margaret, 171
Margery, 171
Mariam, 184
Martha, 171, 172
Mary, 26, 151, 171, 172, 173, 194
Mary Heston, 173
Mary Hodge, 171
Mary Horsman, 171
Mercy, 173
Moses, 151, 171, 173, 174
Oliver, 156, 172, 173
Phineas, 172, 173
Rachel, 168, 172, 173, 174, 193, 194
Rebecca, 171
Rebeckah, 193
Reuben, 173
Robert, 173
Ruth, 156, 172
Ruth Watson, 172
Samuel, 173
Sarah, 57, 59, 167, 171, 172, 173, 174, 193
Sarah Harvey, 171
Thomas, 167, 171, 172, 173, 174
Timothy, 172
William, 171, 172, 173
PEARSON, Ann, 174
Elisabeth, 174
Elisabeth Duer, 174
Enoch, 174
John, 174
Joseph, 174
Lawrence, 174
Margaret, 174
Margaret Smith, 174
Mary, 174
Phebe, 174
Rachel, 174
Samuel, 174
Sarah, 174
Sarah Hall, 174
Thomas, 174
William, 174
_ _ _, 58
PEIRSON, Ann, 89
Betty, 88, 89
George, 88
Hannah, 88
Isabel, 89
Samuel, 88
Tom, 88
PENINGTON, Isaac, 39
Margaret, 133, 134
Martha, 48
Paul, 44, 45
PENNINGTON, Anna, 26, 72
Daniel, 30
Elizabeth, 26
Martha, 26, 72
Thomas, 26, 72
William, 26, 72
PENOCK, George, 27
PENQUITE, Abigail, 11, 174
Abigaile, 6
Agnes, 11
Agness, 47
Esther, 23, 67, 69, 174
Gorshom, 174
Hester, 11, 63
Jane, 6, 41
Johannah, 11
John, 6, 13, 32, 41, 42
Mercy, 6, 43
Nicholas, 11, 38, 174
Rachael, 6
Rachel, 6
Sarah, 6, 32
Thomas, 174
PENROSE, Abel, 80, 89
Abigail, 89
Ann, 90, 139
Benjamin, 89, 90, 112
Clementine, 90
David, 132
Edith, 90
Edward, 89
Eleanor, 116
Elinor, 89
Elizabeth, 89, 90
Enoch, 77, 89, 90
Enos, 90
Evan, 75, 89
Gainor, 89
Hannah, 90, 121, 134
Israel, 89, 129, 130
Jane, 89, 90, 129
Jesse, 89, 117
John, 89, 90, 110, 131
Jonathan, 89, 106, 126, 128
Joseph, 89, 90, 113
Josiah, 135
Lavinia, 90
Lydia, 90
Margaret, 89
Martha, 89, 90, 134, 135
Mary, 89, 109, 116, 117, 119, 125, 126
Morris, 89
Nathan, 89, 90, 133, 134
Rachel, 89, 90, 135
Robert, 89, 96, 97, 99, 109, 110, 125, 126, 133
Samuel, 89, 118, 119

Sarah, 89
Susanna, 89
Tacy, 90
Thomas, 89, 90, 136
Washington, 90
William, 89, 90, 114, 115
PETTIT, Lydia, 181
Martha, 180
William, 181
PHILIPS, Edmund, 107
Mary, 117
Prudence, 62, 68
Sarah, 124
Thomas, 153
William, 117
PHILLIPS, Aaron, 174
Christiana, 90
Edmund, 100, 101
Elisabeth, 174
Elizabeth, 100
Mary, 99, 174
Mary Clauson, 174
Mercy, 175
Moses, 90, 174
Rachel, 175
Rebecca, 174
Robert, 174
Samuel, 175
Sarah, 90
Sarah Eastburn, 174
Thomas, 90, 174
PICKERING, Ann, 172
Ann Watson, 176
Anna, 175
Benjamin, 175, 176
Charles, 176
Elihu, 172, 175
Elisabeth Carey, 176
Esther, 175
George, 176
Grace Stackhouse, 175
Hannah, 164, 175
Hannah Daws, 175
Isaac, 175, 176
Jacob, 175
James, 176
Jesse, 175
John, 164, 175, 176
Jonathan, 175, 176
Joseph, 171, 175, 176
Mahlon, 176
Martha, 175
Mary, 175, 176
Mary Williams, 175
Mercy, 175, 176
Phineas, 175
Rachel, 175
Rachel Duer, 175
Samuel, 175, 176
Sarah, 175
Sarah Lupton, 175
Stacy, 175
Stephen, 176
Thomas, 176
Watson, 176
William, 175
Yeamans, 175
PIERSON, Samuel, 102, 103
PLUMLEY, Edmund, 67
Elizabeth, 67
PLUNKET, Ann, 167
PLUNKETT, Ann, 66
PLUNKITT, Ann, 34
John, 34
POTTS, Elizabeth, 120
POWNAL, Anna, 65
POWNALL, Elizabeth, 65
Levi, 33
Mary, 67
Simeon, 33
PRALL, Thomas, 67
PREESON, William, 147
PRESTON, Amos, 176
Ann, 177
Deborah, 176, 177
Deborah Chessman, 177
Eleanor, 148
Ellinor, 176
Esther, 176
Esther Large, 176
Euphemia, 177
Francis, 177
Hannah Fisher, 176
Henry, 176
Jane, 176
Jane Paxson, 176
John, 44, 176
Jonas, 176
Joseph, 176, 177
Margaret, 177
Margret Good, 177
Martha, 148, 176, 177
Mary, 176, 177
Mary Hough, 176
Naomi, 177
Nathan, 176, 177
Paul, 176, 177
Rachel, 176
Rachel Beeks, 176
Ruth, 177
Samuel, 176
Sarah, 176, 177
Silas, 161, 177
William, 44, 176, 177
PRICE, Elizabeth, 29
Esther, 177
Hannah, 177
James, 177
John, 29
Joseph, 177
Julian, 48
Naomi Preston, 177
Phebe, 177
Samuel, 177
Sarah, 72
Timothy, 40
PRITTER, Jacob, 134
PURSEL, Mahlon, 69

-Q-

QUINBY, Ann, 177

Elisabeth, 177
Isaiah, 23, 34, 177
Jane Fell, 177
John, 177
Joseph, 177
Josiah, 177
Mariam, 23
Moses, 177
Rachel, 177
QUINN, Jane, 125

-R-

RAINS, Mary, 99, 100, 101
RAKESTRAN, Joseph, 105
RAKESTRAW, Joseph, 105
RANDOLPH, Edward, 177
Elizabeth E., 177
Julianna, 177
Richard, 177
RAWLINGS, Ann, 90
Anne, 90
Jane, 90
Joseph, 90, 106, 125
Margaret, 90, 105
Sarah, 105
Thomas, 90, 105, 106
RAY, Elizabeth, 116
Joseph, 98
Moses, 117
Susanna, 115
REA, Letitia, 100
Matthew, 100
Moses, 121, 122
Susanna, 93, 120
REACE, Elizabeth, 83
READER, Ann, 2
Margaret, 2
Mary, 2
Thomas, 2
William, 2, 40, 41
REDDER, Mary, 65
REED, Jerusha, 125
REEDER, Abraham, 17, 63
Charles, 17, 35
David, 35
Elenor, 17
Elizabeth, 17
Hannah, 17
Isaac, 17
John, 17
Joseph, 17
Mary, 24, 70, 72
Prescilla, 26
Priscilla, 58
William, 17, 45
REES, Elizabeth, 83
Sarah, 108
RENOLDS, Mary, 50
RICE, Catherine, 177
James, 177
Joseph, 177
Latitia, 177
Latitia Hartley, 177
Mary, 167
William, 177
RICH, Alexander, 177
John, 177
Joseph, 178
Mary Michener, 177
Rachel, 177
William, 178
RICHARDS, Martha, 119
RICHARDSON, Amos, 89, 90, 132, 134, 135
Anne, 90
Daniel, 30, 47, 64
Elisabeth, 184
Hannah, 43
Jane, 90
John, 90
Keziah, 90
Lydia, 131
Martha, 90
Rebecca, 90
Sarah, 44, 55, 90
William, 19, 184
ROBERTS, Abel, 90, 91, 96, 99, 100, 118, 136
Abigail, 91, 92, 113, 115, 116, 129, 134
Abraham, 91, 92, 104, 119, 124, 129, 131
Alice, 91, 92, 99, 120
Alriah, 91
Amos, 91, 92, 117, 131
Andrew, 92
Ann, 77, 89, 91, 92, 110, 126, 138, 139
Ashton, 92
Catherine, 129, 131, 132
David, 90, 91, 92, 102, 123, 128, 129
Edward, 90, 91, 92, 96, 113, 119, 120, 129
Eldad, 42
Eleanor, 136
Elizabeth, 91, 92, 122, 123
Enoch, 91, 120
Evan, 92, 131, 135, 140
Everard, 90, 92, 108, 135, 136
Gainer, 91
George, 92
Guy, 92
Hannah, 91, 92
Henry, 178
Hugh, 92
Isaac, 91, 122, 125, 132, 133
Isaiah, 134
Israel, 77, 91, 92, 123
James, 92
Jane, 78, 90, 91, 92, 93, 103, 117, 134
John, 47, 90, 91, 92, 102, 114, 115, 118, 125

Joseph, 92
Latitia, 79, 80, 91, 92
Letticia, 130
Levi, 87, 92, 134, 135
Lewis, 92
Lidia, 92
Margaret, 91, 92, 121, 126
Maria, 92
Martha, 90, 91, 92, 116, 123, 129, 136, 139
Mary, 78, 89, 90, 91, 92, 100, 103, 104, 114, 126, 133, 178
Mercy, 178
Mercy Betts, 178
Mordecai, 92
Nathan, 90, 91, 92, 131
Paulina, 92
Peninah, 92
Phebe, 91, 92
Priscilla, 130
Rachel, 91, 102
Rebecca, 92
Rebecka, 127
Richard, 91, 98, 99, 101, 123, 128, 178
Samuel, 91, 92, 93
Sarah, 30, 89, 91, 92, 118, 119, 126
Sidney, 91
Susan, 92
Susanna, 91
Theophilus, 92
Thomas, 80, 91, 92, 98, 99, 100, 102, 104, 115, 116, 122, 132, 137, 140, 178
Thomas J., 79
Uriah, 91
William, 91, 92, 115, 118, 123, 126, 131
ROBINSON, Elisabeth, 178
Elisabeth Brown, 178
Thomas, 39, 41, 178
ROGERS, Abner, 100, 101, 103, 107
ROOK, Hannah, 119
RORK, Hannah, 121
ROSE, Alice, 55
Amos, 178
Ann, 178
Atkinson, 14, 28
Deborah, 14, 28, 178
Hannah, 14
James, 14, 34, 38, 50, 178
John, 14, 34, 51, 52, 64, 178
Jonathan, 15
Mary, 14, 27
Miriam, 178
Phebe, 14
Priscilla, 58
Rebecca, 53, 178
Sarah, 14, 178
Thomas, 14, 53, 178
William, 14
ROSS, Ann, 35, 52
Atkinson, 27
Cephus, 27
Isaiah, 178
James, 57
John, 26, 134, 138, 178
Joseph, 178
Kesia, 178
Kesia Wilkinson, 178
Mary, 43, 178
Mary Duer, 178
Rachel, 178
Rachel Longstreth, 178
Samuel, 28
Sarah, 28, 178
Thomas, 8, 28, 35, 44, 48, 49, 52, 56, 57, 67, 71, 178
William, 28, 30, 35, 73
ROUTLEDGE, John, 46
RUCKMAN, Achsah, 178
Hannah, 178
Isaiah, 178
Jonathan, 178
Joseph, 178
Martha, 178
Mehetable, 178
Sarah, 178
Sarah White, 178
Thomas, 178

-S-

SACHEVERIL, Eleanor, 118
SAMPLE, Ann, 60
SAMUELS, Isaac, 110
Jane, 93
Jesse, 93
Mary, 93
William, 93, 132, 133
SANDERS, Hannah, 42
John, 50
Rebeckah, 44
SANTEE, Sarah, 138
SAVITS, Mary, 131
SCARBOROUGH, Ann Paxson, 179
Anne, 179
Charity, 179
Elisabeth, 178, 179
Henry, 179
Isaac, 179
John, 121, 124, 157, 175, 178, 179
Joseph, 27, 179
Mahlon, 179
Margaret, 179
Mary, 178, 179
Rachael, 24
Rachel, 71, 179
Robert, 178, 179
SCARBROUGH, Charity, 64
Isaac, 64
John, 48, 64, 110, 123

Joseph, 64
Margret, 50
Rachel, 64
Sarah, 41
SCATTERGOOD, Jonathan, 100
Joshua, 98
SCHOLFIELD, Ann, 64, 179
B., 157
Benjamin, 179
David, 179
Edith, 179
Edith Marshall, 179
Elisabeth, 179
Isaac, 179
Jacob, 43
Jane, 179
John, 39, 68, 147, 179
Jonathan, 50, 55, 59, 179
Joseph, 179
Martha Fell, 179
Phebe, 179
Samuel, 179
Sarah, 179
Thomas, 179
SCHOOLFIELD, Ann, 28
John, 23
SCOLFIELD, John, 31
Jonathan, 31
SCOT, Martha, 125
SCOTT, Abraham, 56, 193
Amos, 56
Benjamin, 23
Elizabeth, 56
Esther, 56
Jane, 179
Jesse, 56
John, 24, 71, 179, 193
Martha, 126
Mary, 23, 55, 69
Rachel, 56
Roscester, 56
Samuel, 193
Sarah, 24, 57, 71, 193
Thomas, 56
SEAGLE, Mirriam, 127
SHADEKER, William, 96
SHADOCKER, William, 104
SHALLCROSS, Benjamin, 28, 36
Leonard, 36
Sarah, 28
SHAW, Aaron, 180
Abigail, 93
Abraham, 139
Alexander, 179, 180
Ann, 94
Anna, 180
Anne, 120
Charles, 180, 181
David, 114, 120, 130, 180
Deborah, 93, 133
Elia, 180
Elisabeth, 179, 180
George, 89, 114, 120, 135, 139, 140, 180
Guli, 94
Gulielma, 93
Hannah, 93, 94, 107, 108, 136, 180
Israel, 93, 94, 132
James, 179, 180
Jesse, 180
John, 93, 111, 129, 132, 133, 137, 170, 179, 180, 182
Jonathan, 93, 179
Jonathan Tyson, 180
Joseph, 93, 94, 112, 114, 130, 134, 136, 139, 179, 180
Joseph P., 180
Josiah, 147, 180
Latitia, 93
Lettitia, 137
Margaret, 137, 185
Maria, 180
Mariam, 133
Martha, 181
Martha Brown, 180
Martha Wilson, 180
Mary, 93, 94, 133, 134, 172, 179, 180
Mary Pryor, 180
Mathias, 180
Miriam, 93
Moses, 93, 94, 120, 132, 133
Olivia, 94
Phebe, 93, 111, 133
Rachel, 114, 120, 139
Rebecca, 94, 180
Rebeckah, 180
Robert, 180
Samuel, 80, 93, 107, 108, 120, 132, 137, 139
Sarah, 93, 124, 133, 139, 170, 180
Sarah B., 180
Sarah Brown, 180
Sarah Goode, 179
Sarah Skelton, 180
Stephen, 180
Susanna, 93, 137, 180
Thomas, 93, 137, 180
William, 93, 94, 115, 118, 129, 134, 180
William Nixon, 93
SHEPHERD, Catherine, 181
Cornelius, 59, 181
Jonathan, 181
Joseph, 147, 181
Margaret, 181
Mary, 181

Rachel, 181
Sarah, 147
SHINN, Hannah, 27
Samuel, 27, 35
SHRIVER, Conrod, 53
SIDDAL, Sarah, 55
SIMCOCKS, Elisabeth, 163
SIMMONS, Henry, 46
Mary, 45
SIMONS, Henry, 45
SIMPSON, Agnes, 181
Agnes Wiggins, 181
David, 13, 35, 69, 181
Elinor, 20
Elizabeth, 20
Hannah, 20, 35, 69, 181
Isaac, 20
James, 20, 26, 69, 181
John, 20, 29, 35, 36, 39, 69, 181
Martha, 20
Rachel, 181
Robert, 20
Ruth, 20, 29, 36, 69, 181
Sarah, 181
SIMSON, Amos, 181
Benjamin, 181
James, 181
Joel, 181
John, 40
Martha, 181
Mary Lowther, 181
Samuel, 181
William, 181
SKELTON, Ann, 181
Elisabeth, 179
Ellinor, 182
Jane, 181
Jane Beck, 182
Jason, 182
Jesse, 181
John, 181, 182
Jonathan, 181
Joseph, 182
Margaret, 182
Martha, 182
Mary, 182
Mary Casey, 182
Mary Townsend, 182
Rachel, 181
Rhoda, 182
Robert, 181, 182
Sarah, 181, 182
Susanna, 181
Susanna Beck, 181
William, 181
SLEEPER, Aves, 94
Budell, 94
Ketury, 94
Patience, 94
Rebecca, 94
Samuel, 94
SLOAN, James, 97
SMALLY, Ann, 53
SMITH, Aaron, 18, 22, 183
Abraham, 3, 14, 17, 183
Albert, 184
Alice Hill, 183
Amos, 22, 184
Ann, 3, 20, 31, 32, 59, 62, 66, 68, 183, 184
Ann Williams, 183
Anna, 22, 66
Asenath, 17
Benajmin, 63
Benjamin, 17, 18, 21, 24, 37, 50, 60, 67, 68, 71, 183, 184
Beulah, 22
Bridget, 63
Bridgit, 29
Charles, 16, 146, 184
Cyrus, 29, 183
Daniel, 184
David, 2, 14, 17, 27, 49, 54, 182, 184
Deborah, 67
Deborah Fell, 184
Dorothy, 183
Eber, 16, 27
Edith, 3, 35, 183
Edmund, 36, 67, 182, 184
Edward, 18
Eleanor, 61, 62
Eleanor Blackfan, 184
Eli, 20
Elias H., 183
Elijah, 18
Elisabeth, 182, 183, 184
Elisabeth Ely, 184
Elisabeth Hughes, 183
Elisabeth Kinsey, 182
Elizabeth, 2, 3, 21, 32, 36, 37, 44, 45, 56, 57, 60, 61, 64, 66, 67, 68, 120, 121
Ellen, 16, 182
Ely, 184
Ephraim, 55, 66
Ephriam, 52
Esther, 2, 17, 22, 42, 59, 62, 183
Ezekiel, 183
Ezra, 9, 15, 20, 57
Fanny, 21
George, 183, 184
Hannah, 3, 14, 17, 21, 27, 54, 183, 184
Harvey, 22
Henry, 22, 183
Howard, 17
Hugh, 184
Isaac, 4, 6, 16, 17, 26, 56, 71
Israel, 68
Jacob, 26, 68
Jacob B., 22
James, 14
Jane, 3, 16, 20, 22, 34, 35, 55, 66, 149, 158, 183

Jesse, 21, 67, 184
Job, 18
John, 2, 3, 6, 8, 14, 20, 21, 22, 24, 34, 39, 43, 54, 57, 59, 62, 68, 71, 182, 183, 184
Jonas, 184
Jonathan, 17, 67, 68, 183, 184
Joseph, 2, 6, 8, 15, 16, 20, 24, 31, 35, 40, 42, 43, 49, 57, 59, 68, 69, 71, 182, 183, 184
Joshua, 67, 184
Kezia, 8, 20
Keziah, 57
Leah, 183
Letitia, 16, 18
Mahlon, 3, 183, 184
Margaret, 9, 20, 27, 47, 54, 72
Margery, 20
Marshall, 29
Martha, 16, 21, 59, 62, 182
Mary, 6, 8, 9, 11, 14, 17, 18, 20, 21, 22, 32, 33, 49, 57, 59, 62, 66, 183
Matilda, 17
Mercy, 2, 54
Moses, 18, 57, 58
Nathan, 22
Nehemiah, 183
Oliver, 18
Phebe, 3, 17, 21, 24, 29, 32, 33, 36, 60, 68, 71, 116, 182, 184
Phebe Canby, 182
Pleasant, 69
Prudence, 183
Rachael, 3, 14, 17, 20, 24, 35
Rachel, 52, 54, 66, 68, 69, 71, 183
Rachell, 45
Ralf, 42
Ralph, 2, 20, 41, 43, 49
Randal, 68
Randle, 26
Rebecca, 63, 184
Rebecca Wilson, 5, 182
Rebeccah, 21, 22
Rebeckah, 6, 16, 183
Robert, 3, 10, 14, 17, 32, 33, 34, 44, 63, 148, 182, 183, 184
Ross, 20
Ruth, 21
Samuel, 2, 3, 8, 16, 21, 22, 24, 29, 31, 32, 34, 35, 46, 48, 54, 57, 58, 60, 66, 67, 72, 149, 158, 182, 183, 184
Samuell, 43
Sarah, 6, 14, 16, 17, 18, 21, 22, 33, 34, 50, 58, 62, 63, 66, 155, 182, 183, 184
Sarah Dawson, 184
Sarah Kinsey, 183
Sarah Townsend, 183
Sarah Williams, 17
Septimus, 18
Stephen, 6, 60, 66
Susanna, 9, 20, 57, 70
Tamar, 183
Thomas, 3, 6, 8, 9, 14, 16, 18, 22, 26, 32, 34, 36, 43, 57, 61, 62, 66, 68, 182, 183, 184
Timothy, 24, 31, 68, 71, 182, 183
Watson, 20
William, 2, 3, 5, 6, 7, 11, 12, 16, 22, 45, 46, 54, 58, 63, 65, 66, 68, 182, 184
SPEAKMAN, Catherine, 63, 64
Esther, 64, 135
Hester, 133
John, 133
Joseph, 63, 64, 118, 119, 120, 133
Kesiah, 89
Kezia, 64
Keziah, 63, 133, 140
Lidia, 133
Lydia, 64
Mary, 63, 64, 133
Micajah, 194
Townsend, 63, 64, 133, 135
SPICER, Abraham, 3
Amos, 3
Ann, 3, 34, 61
Elizabeth, 3, 56
Gulielma Maria, 68
Guly Elma Maria, 3
James, 3, 31, 34, 44, 55
Maria, 66
Mary, 3
Rachael, 3
Sarah, 3
Yeaman, 3
STACKHOUSE, Benjamin, 60, 67
Isaac, 11
STALFORD, Thomas, 106, 109, 113
STAPLER, Christianna, 194
Elizabeth, 194
Hannah, 194
John, 148, 194
STEPHENSON, John, 137
STEVENSON, John,

128
Micajah, 128
STOCKDALE, David, 47, 49, 52
Elisabeth, 184
Elisabeth Smith, 184
Elizabeth, 6, 56, 61
Hannah, 6
John, 6, 11, 25, 42, 44, 57, 61, 64, 184
Joseph, 6, 56, 184
Mary, 6, 39, 61, 63, 184
Mercey, 6
Mercy, 27
Rachell, 6
Rebeckah, 6
Sarah, 6, 46, 61, 63, 184
Susannah, 6
Thomas, 58
William, 45
STOKES, Anne, 125
David, 125
Elizabeth, 92
Hannah, 9
James, 4, 9, 35, 37, 49, 54
Jane, 9
John, 87, 96, 99, 114
Joseph, 9, 72
Mary, 8, 9, 37, 86, 136
Phebe, 9
Rebekah, 72
Sarah, 9
Susanna, 9, 24, 35, 62, 69, 87, 114
Susannah, 54, 72
William, 114
STOREY, David, 19
Elizabeth, 17, 19, 36
Hannah, 19
John, 19, 36
Mary, 17, 19
Rachael, 17, 19
Rebecca, 17
Rebeckah, 19
Samuel, 17
Thomas, 17
William, 19
STORY, Amos, 7
David, 7, 184
Elisabeth, 184, 185
Elizabeth, 7
Hannah, 184
John, 7, 15, 42, 52, 66, 68, 184
Mary, 7, 185
Rachel, 69, 184
Samuel, 66
Thomas, 7, 64, 69
STRADLING, Daniel, 4, 41, 185
Daniell, 43
Deborah, 185
Elisabeth, 185
Elizabeth, 4
Hannah, 185
John, 4, 185
Joseph, 185
Katherine, 4
Lidya, 4
Lydia, 185
Martha, 185
Mary, 39
Mehetable, 185
Samuel, 185
Sarah, 4, 49, 185
Sarah Shaw, 185
Thomas, 4, 41, 185
William, 185
STRAHAM, John, 113
STRAHAN, Ann, 119
Daniel, 119
Thomas, 112, 116
STRAHEN, John, 114, 115
Kezia, 115
STRANDLING, Elizabeth, 32
STRAWHEN, Abel, 128
Christiana, 113
Daniel, 113, 137
Enoch, 132
Hannah, 120
Isaiah, 122
Jacob, 113
Job, 134, 137
John, 113
Mary, 113
Thomas, 113, 119, 122, 135, 136
William, 113
STRAWHENT, Jacob, 94
Staunchy, 94
STRAWN, Abel, 94
Daniel, 94
Enoch, 94
Hannah, 94
Jacob, 94
Jerusha, 94
Job, 94
Josiah, 94
Mary, 94
Staunchy, 94
Thomas, 94
William, 94
William L., 81
STRICKLAND, Amos, 38, 50
John, 10, 38
Mary, 10, 41
Miles, 10
Rachel, 45
Sarah, 45
Thomas, 10, 38, 39, 53
STROUD, Charles, 94
Daniel, 94
Eliza D., 94
Elizabeth, 94
Hannah, 118
Jacob D., 94
James Hollinshead, 94
Macdowel, 94
Simpson, 94
Susan, 94
William, 94
STUCHBURY, Deborah, 39
SURNS, Hannah, 133, 138
SWAIN, Abraham, 37
Samuel, 37
Sarah, 37

SWINEY, James, 24
Rebeckah, 24
SWINNEY, Rebekah, 70

-T-

TAYLER, Peter, 12
TAYLOR, Banner, 185
Benjamin, 40, 172
Elisabeth, 185
Elizabeth, 25
Hannah, 23, 70
Joseph, 185
Martha, 185
Mary, 46
Sarah, 44
William, 62
TERRY, Jacob, 67
Jasper, 17, 18, 36, 69
John, 5, 32, 35, 39, 55
Lucy, 17, 70
Martha, 17, 36, 70
Mary, 5
Rachael, 35
Rachell, 5
Sarah, 36
THACKRY, James, 44
THOMAS, Absalom, 94
Alice, 94
Andrew, 94
Ann, 94, 108
Anne, 95, 108, 124, 129, 130
Daniel, 124
David, 139
Edward, 91, 94, 99, 124, 130
Eleanor, 97
Elizabeth, 36, 94, 97, 113
George, 134
Jacob, 36
Jane, 94, 124
John, 39, 98
Katherine, 96
Leonard, 105, 120
Margaret, 74, 78, 94, 95, 96, 117, 123
Martha, 94
Mary, 94
Miriam, 94
Mordecai, 36
Peninnah, 119, 120
Phebe, 33
Robert, 25, 62, 66, 113, 114, 120
Samuel, 74, 94, 95, 101
Sarah, 106
Tamar, 119
Thomas, 95, 124, 130
Widow, 105
William, 78, 94, 107, 118, 139
THOMPSON, Ann, 185
John, 185
Jonah, 185
Jonathan, 185
Mark, 185
Sarah, 185
THOMSON, Gaynor, 140
John, 115, 116
William, 115
THORNTON, Ann W., 185, 191
Beulah, 185
Carey, 185
Elisabeth, 185
John Pearson, 185
Joseph, 185
Margret, 50
Mary, 185
Rutledge, 185
Samuel Carey, 185
William Pearson, 185
TITUS, John, 33
Phebe, 46
TOMBLINSON, Joseph, 40, 43
Sarah, 42
TOMKINS, Benjamin, 111, 123, 124
Hannah, 55
Joseph, 128, 129
Robert, 111
TOMLINSON, Elizabeth, 60
Hannah, 9, 49, 61, 64, 66
Jane, 64, 73
John, 63, 65
Joseph, 9, 63
Lydia, 9
Margaret, 9, 71
Mary, 9, 23, 31, 68
Phebe, 9, 25, 60, 63
Rachael, 9
Richard, 48, 49, 64
Samuel, 9
Sarah, 9, 63
Thomas, 63
William, 23, 68
TOMPKINS, Elizabeth, 110
Robert, 110
TOWNALL, Mary, 27
TOWNSEND, Aaron, 186
Amos, 186
Ann, 186
Anne, 186
Charles, 186
David, 186
Elisabeth, 185, 186
Elisabeth Watson, 185
John, 182, 185, 186
Jonathan, 186
Joseph, 108, 185, 186
Levi, 186
Mahlon, 186
Margaret Paxson, 185
Mary, 185
Mary Hartley, 186
Moses, 186
Rebecca Shaw, 185
Samuel H., 186
Sarah, 6, 43, 185, 186

Senecca P., 186
Stephen, 185, 186
Thomas, 185
William, 185
TREGO, Albert, 21
Charles, 21
Charles B., 16
Cyrus, 22
Edward, 22
Elizabeth, 21
Hannah, 10
Jacob, 4, 10
James, 22
Jesse, 10
John, 10, 18, 30, 31, 38
Joseph, 10, 16
Joseph Briggs, 22
Joyce, 49
Lewis, 21
Mahlon, 10, 21, 22
Mary, 10, 21, 30
Phineas, 21
Rachael, 21
Rebecca, 10
Rebeckah, 10
Robert, 21
Sarah, 31
Thomas, 10
William, 10, 31, 54
TUCKER, David, 27
Elizabeth, 27, 137, 138
Hannah, 27
James, 27, 186
Lydia, 186
Lydia Allen, 186
Mary, 186
Nicholas, 186
Robert, 186
Sarah, 186
TWINING, Abigail, 38
Alice, 21
Amos, 21
Ann, 8, 15, 21
Benjamin, 6, 44, 46
Beulah, 19
David, 6, 15, 19, 22, 34, 53
Eleazer, 1, 15, 16, 19, 21, 35, 49
Elias, 8, 37
Elieazer, 6
Elizabeth, 2, 6, 21, 22, 30, 34, 53, 66
Hannah, 15, 186
Henry M., 22
Isaac, 6, 19
Jacob, 6, 8, 22, 65, 186
John, 2, 3, 6, 8, 19, 22, 31, 40, 186
Joseph, 3, 6, 31, 68, 186
Letitia, 21
Mahlon, 15, 19, 22
Malachi, 186
Margaret, 1
Martha, 19
Mary, 8, 14, 15, 16, 21, 34, 35, 36, 39, 65, 123, 186
Mercy, 2
Nathaniel, 2, 6, 46
Phebe, 19, 186
Phebe Tucker, 186
Priscilla, 186
Rachael, 22, 31, 35
Rachel, 3, 6, 8
Ruth, 21
Samuel, 21, 44
Samuell, 6
Sarah, 3, 6, 8, 14, 22, 33, 122, 186
Silas, 15, 20, 21, 35
Stephen, 1, 2, 7, 8, 14, 30, 31, 35, 36, 37, 59, 65, 123
Susanna, 22
Tamar, 8, 36
Thomas, 6, 19
Watson, 21
William, 6, 19, 22
TWYNING, Stephen, 137
TYSON, Elizabeth, 123, 126
Henry, 38, 39, 45
Mary, 135, 138

-U-

UNTHANK, Joseph, 102, 103

-V-

VAN VLEET, Joseph, 88
Susanna, 88
VANCE, Agnis, 47
Myra, 120
VANHORN, Mary, 28
VANSANT, Joshua, 32, 55, 70
Rachel, 71
VARNAL, Sarah, 65
VARNOW, Sarah, 63
VERITY, Elisabeth Bye, 186
Elisabeth Duckworth, 186
Elizabeth, 7
Jacob, 67, 125, 126, 186
John, 7, 186
Mary, 7
VERREE, Ann, 10
James, 10
Mary, 10
Robert, 10, 48, 58
VERRITY, Jacob, 57
VICKERS, Abraham, 187
Esther, 186
John, 186
Mary, 186
Mercy, 187
Rachel, 187
Rebecca, 186
Rebecca Dillon, 186
Thomas, 186

-W-

WALKER, Amos, 187
Ann, 187
Asenath Beans, 187
Benjamin, 187
David, 187
Diana, 124
Dianna, 139
Elisabeth, 187
Emanuel, 48, 50
Jesse, 187
John, 187
Joseph, 187
Mahlon, 187
Mary, 187
Phineas, 187
Randall, 187
Robert, 187
Sarah, 187
Stacy, 187
WALTON, Abigail, 128, 136
Abraham, 105, 107, 110, 113, 114, 136
Alice, 187
Amos, 187
Ann, 95, 131, 187
Benjamin, 112, 128
Daniel, 95, 119, 127, 128
David, 95, 111, 112, 188
Deborah, 64
Edith, 95
Elisabeth, 187
Elizabeth, 97, 110
Ellis, 95
Ester, 103
Ezekiel, 121
Gabriel, 140
Hannah, 127
Hannah Carey, 187
Isaac, 95, 101, 105, 115, 128, 187
Jacob, 187, 188
James, 95, 110, 128, 131
Jane, 95
Jesse, 187, 188
John, 187, 188
Jonathan, 188
Joseph, 64, 95, 127, 139, 187
Joshua, 187
Lydia, 95
Lydia Gilbert, 187
Margaret, 95, 105
Martha, 95, 115
Mary, 95, 134, 187
Mary Holcomb, 187
Mercy, 105
Moses, 116
Nathan, 110, 112, 124, 125, 136, 187
Rachel, 114, 187
Robert, 114
Samuel, 107, 188
Sarah, 187
Thomas, 119, 187
William, 187
WARDELL, Phebe, 30
WARE, Robert, 32, 61
WARNER, Aaron, 55
Abraham, 2, 54, 56
Agness Croasdale, 2
Agnis, 42
Amos, 3, 23, 36, 55
Asaph, 56, 63, 64, 67
Aseneth, 22
Aseph, 8
Benjamin, 22, 29, 36, 46, 52
Croasdale, 2, 46
Croasdel, 55
Crosdale, 36
Cuthbert, 8, 56
David, 3, 10, 22, 70
Elizabeth, 3, 22, 23
Esther, 42
Ezekiah, 8
Hannah, 23, 55
Hezekiah, 56
Isaac, 2, 58, 59
Isaiah, 3, 23, 34
John, 2, 3, 10, 23, 33, 34, 36, 42, 66, 188
Jonathan, 3, 22, 68
Joseph, 2, 8, 10, 12, 22, 30, 43, 56, 66
Martha, 59
Mary, 2, 3, 10, 39, 43, 55, 59
Mercy, 10, 66
Mordeca, 8
Mordica, 56
Phebe, 10, 66
Rachael, 10, 22, 36
Rachel, 3, 66
Ruth, 2, 8, 56
Sarah, 2, 29, 30, 47, 55
Seneca, 10, 66
Silas, 8, 56
Simeon, 72
Simion, 3
Susanna, 188
Susanna Buckman, 188
Thomas, 2, 52, 56, 60
WARTON, Elizabeth, 28
William, 28
WATSON, Aaron, 189
Abigail, 134
Alice, 12, 66, 188
Alice Mitchell, 188
Ann, 12, 66, 142, 188
Ann Biles, 188
Anne, 188
Anthony Harris, 189
Charles, 189
David, 35
Deborah, 53

Doctor John, 157
Elisa Ann, 189
Elisabeth, 180, 188, 189
Euphemia, 189
Euphemia Aann, 189
Euphemia Ingham, 189
Framces, 188
Frances, 12, 66, 189
Gulielma, 140
Hannah, 24, 71, 72, 189
Isaiah, 189
John, 12, 31, 57, 66, 172, 188, 189
John Emley, 189
John Hampton, 87, 189
Jonathan, 189
Joseph, 12, 31, 35, 41, 188, 189
Mark, 24, 70, 142
Marmaduke, 189
Mary, 12, 66, 188, 189
Mary Hampton, 188
Mary Verree, 188
Rachael, 12, 35
Rachel, 28, 66, 188
Robert, 188
Samuel Ingham, 189
Sarah, 44, 165, 188, 189
Sarah Woolston, 188
Thomas, 165, 188
William, 189
WATTS, John, 22
Mary Smith, 22
WAY, Phebe, 118
WEABER, Rachel, 66, 68
WEATHERALL, John, 63
WEAVER, Robert, 67
WELDING, Ely, 28
Ruth, 21
Watson, 20, 21
WELLS, Catherine, 27
John, 27
WELSH, Rebeckah, 41
WEST, Elizabeth, 62, 64
Enos, 62, 64
Rachel, 136
Stacey, 64
Thomas, 60, 61, 62, 64
WETHERELL, Rebecca, 69
Sarah, 69
William, 69
WETHERILL, William, 21
WEY, Phebe, 60, 61, 123
WHARTON, Amos, 18
Anna, 18
Daniel, 18, 35
Ezra, 18, 35
Hannah, 18
James, 18
Jasper, 18
Joel, 18
Linton, 18
Martha, 18
Mary, 36
Silas, 18
William, 36
WHILSON, Mary, 33
Thomas, 23, 33
WHITE, Amos, 189
Ann, 55
Benjamin, 182, 189
Daniel, 33, 189
Deborah, 189
Hannah, 120, 189
Job, 189
John, 55, 148
Joseph, 182, 189
Latitia, 189
Martha, 189
Martha Skelton, 189
Mary, 55, 61, 189
Mary Skelton, 189
Mercy, 189
Rachel, 189
Sarah, 189
Thomas, 189
WHITEACRE, Jane, 52
WHITSON, Ann, 57
Anne, 66
Benjamin, 57, 63, 66
Burt, 66
David, 63, 67, 181
Deborah, 57, 66
Elizabeth, 57, 66
Henry, 66
John, 57, 66
Joseph, 66, 67
Margaret, 66
Mary, 25, 57, 66, 69, 70, 71, 73
Sarah, 67
Thomas, 50, 54, 55, 57, 66
William, 67
WIDDOWFIELD, Henry, 52
WIDOWFIELD, Henry, 54
WIGGINS, Agnes, 13, 35
Ann, 19
Barzaleel, 19
Bazaleel, 31
Benjamin, 12, 13, 30, 34, 35, 37, 189
Berzaleel, 31
Berzeleel, 30
Bezaleel, 56
Bezeleel, 34
Bezeliell, 38
Bozaleel, 12
Coothbert, 70
Elizabeth, 19, 26, 68
Isaac, 25, 34
Jesse, 19
John, 15
Joseph, 13, 19, 31, 34, 53, 54,

56
Margaret, 189
Martha, 26
Mary, 19, 31
Phebe, 25
Rachael, 12, 19, 35
Sarah, 12, 13, 19, 25, 37, 56, 189
Tracey, 56
Ulyssies, 25
WILBORN, Amos, 14
Anna, 14
Hannah, 14
John, 14
Joseph, 14
Phebe, 14
Rachael, 14
Samuel, 14
Sarah, 14
Stephen, 14
Thomas, 14
WILDING, Elizabeth, 35
Mary, 35
Watson, 35
WILDMAN, Ann, 30
Betsey, 59
Betsy, 61
Enos, 59, 61
James, 43
John, 59, 60
Joseph, 4, 5, 59, 61
Mary, 30, 41, 59, 61
Rachael, 31
Rachel, 59
Rachell, 40
Rebecca, 40
Sarah, 59, 61
WILKENSON, Abraham, 13
Amos, 13
Elias, 13
Jane, 13
John, 13
WILKINSON, Abraham, 35
Amos, 28
Ann, 31
Anna, 60
David, 60
Elisabeth, 190
Elizabeth, 60
Hannah, 55
Henry, 190
Ichabod, 31, 47
Ichobod, 40, 43
John, 8, 31, 32, 35, 39, 51, 53, 54, 60
Jonathan, 60
Joseph, 42, 49, 190
Mary, 31, 70
Plain, 39
Rachel, 190
Ruth, 39
Sarah Paxson, 190
Stephen, 65
Susannah, 38
William, 60
WILLET, Jonathan, 45, 46
WILLIAMS, Abigail, 121
Ann, 45
Catherine, 38
Driscilla, 104
Eleanor, 96
George, 121
Hezekiah, 104
Humphry, 104
Isaac, 38
James, 104
Jeremiah, 119
Judah, 41
Juday, 41
Thomas, 51
William, 104
WILLSON, Abigail, 86
Thomas, 98, 99
WILSON, Abigail, 140
Abraham, 15
Alice, 119, 133
Amos, 14, 190, 191
Amy, 55, 191
Ann, 190
Anne, 14
Benjamin, 190
David, 30, 190
Ebenezer, 58
Elisabeth, 190, 191
Elisabeth Fell, 190
Elizabeth, 15, 43
Ezra, 190
Frances, 43
Grace, 190, 191
Hamton, 7, 14, 33
Hannah, 15, 39, 190, 191
Isaac, 4, 7, 14, 15, 33, 35, 58, 190, 191
Jane, 15, 62, 95
Jesse, 191
Joel, 190
John, 40, 45, 49, 50, 156, 190
Jonathan, 30, 190
Joseph, 29, 43, 62, 137, 190
Maire Croasdale, 190
Margaret, 156, 190
Margaret Bye, 190
Mark, 95
Martha, 180, 191
Mary, 7, 15, 62, 190
Mary Baily, 190
Mercy, 7, 66, 70, 190
Moses, 86, 95, 137
Nancy, 62
Oliver, 190, 191
Phebe, 124, 128
Pleasant, 7
Rachael, 14
Rachel, 62, 190, 191
Rebecca, 157, 190
Rebecca Canby, 190
Rebeckah, 191
Samuel, 33, 51, 62, 157, 190, 191

Sarah, 7, 14, 15, 62, 63, 72, 190
Sarah Blackfan, 191
Shipley, 95
Stephen, 7, 33, 43, 45, 62, 66, 190, 191
Susannah, 15
Thomas, 32, 33, 45, 63, 190
William, 43
WINDER, Amos, 193
Eleanor Buckman, 193
Elizabeth, 193
John, 47, 51, 193
Joseph, 193
Rachel, 193
Ruth, 193
Thomas, 193
WIRTHINGTON, Mary, 167
Richard, 167
WISENER, Rachel, 72
WISNAR, Rachael, 28
WITHERELL, Sarah, 64
WOOD, Aaron, 7, 57
Deborah, 95
Jacob, 64
James, 7, 33, 57
John, 7, 57
Mary, 7, 57, 64
Mary Shaw, 95
Matthew, 7, 62, 64
Moses, 7, 95
Rachel, 57
Rachell, 7
Rebecca, 57
Rebekah, 7
Sarah, 7
Septimus, 7, 57
William, 7, 62
____, 93
WOODS, James, 42
WORRALL, Martha, 125
WORREL, Martha, 123
WORSTAL, James, 55
John, 28
Ruth, 28
WORSTALL, Esther, 35, 193
James, 19, 35, 193
John, 35, 193
Jonathan, 193
Joseph, 193
Rachel, 193
Robert, 193
Ruth, 193
Samuel, 193
WORTH, William, 33
WORTHINGTON, Amasa, 20
Amos, 20
Amy, 72
Aseneth, 20
Benjamin, 20, 35
Cephus, 191
Elizabeth, 20, 67
Esther, 20
Hannah, 72
Jane, 191
Jesse, 20, 56
John, 56, 72
John Carver, 20
Jonathan, 191
Joseph, 191
Mahlon, 20, 33, 63
Maire, 191
Margaret, 20
Martha, 20
Mary, 20, 56, 62, 68
Mary Ann, 20
Mary Child, 191
Richard, 33, 34
Ruth, 20
Sarah, 63
Spencer, 20
Tamer, 34
Thomas, 20, 71
Watson, 20
William, 20, 35, 56, 191
Zenas, 191
WRIGHT, Elizabeth, 109
Isaac, 191
John, 191
Margaret, 105, 106
Mark, 20
Rachel Pickering, 191
Sarah, 191
Sidney, 191
Solomon, 191
Thomas, 80

-Y-

YARDLEY, Acsah, 194
Ann, 54, 194
Charles, 194
Edward, 192
Elizabeth, 192, 194
George, 192
Hannah, 194
Isaac, 193
John, 194
Joseph, 193
Latitia, 193
Mahlon, 194
Mary, 192, 193
Mercy, 192
Robert, 194
Sarah, 148, 193, 194
Sarah B., 192
Susan, 192
Susannah, 193
Susannah Latitia, 192
Thomas, 192
Thomas H., 192
William, 192
YARNAL, Nathan, 54
YEATES, Rachel, 45
YEATS, Joseph, 41
Margret, 44

-Z-

ZELLY (ZELLEY), John, 99

www.ingramcontent.com/pod-product-compliance
Lightning Source LLC
LaVergne TN
LVHW050619100826
845148LV00011B/1657

* 9 7 8 1 6 8 0 3 4 3 4 8 9 *